UNSEEN

UNSEEN
Believing the Truth, Understanding the Lie

3rd Edition
www.TheUnseenBook.com

James E. Campbell, Jr.
James Q. Campbell

UNSEEN
Copyright © 2012, 2016, 2018 by Unseen, LLC

ISBN: 978-1-948282-14-7

Hardcover ISBN: 978-1-947247-16-1

All rights reserved.

No part of this publication may be reproduced, distributed, or transmitted in any form or by any means, including photocopying, recording, or other electronic or mechanical methods, without the prior written permission of the publisher, except in the case of brief quotations embodied in critical reviews and certain other noncommercial uses permitted by copyright law.

For permission requests, write to the publisher at the address below.

Yorkshire Publishing
3207 South Norwood Avenue
Tulsa, Oklahoma 74135
www.YorkshirePublishing.com
918.394.2665

Acknowledgements
For this third addition

The most challenging aspect of writing this book is that we use many words and phrases that have been used by believers for centuries but often with different meanings. Thus, it has taken a unique eye to review our work to make sure that commonly used words and phrases convey our meanings rather than those of current writers and speakers.

Special thanks to Sandra, adored wife and mother who treasures what God believes and who provided content, additional editing support, and the critical review so necessary to make sure that what we have written accurately conveys what we mean to say.

Thanks also to:

Aaron, beloved son to James E. and brother to James Q., who lives this adventure with us and continually confirms and adds to our insights.

Kat Rutz, our content editor who helped immeasurably with plugging gaps in our explanations to render an easier read.

Malcolm Smith, our friend, for his encouragement and who opened my eyes to the love of God, covenant, and *the lie*. Thus, he caused God's words, logic, and reasoning to come alive in the original language of the New Testament.

Brianna Maestas, our photographer who wasn't hindered by the weather and time of year.

Cecilia Gray, our friend and encourager who practices law out of an intimate understanding of grace.

James E. Campbell Jr.
James Q. Campbell

Contents

Preface xi
About Translating xv
Author's Note xix
Prologue xxvii

                Part 1 1

1. Changing versus Being Changed 5
    What Does God See? 5
    There Is So Much More 7
    Chapter One Endnotes 12

2. Being Changed 23
    Using the Right Meanings 24
    Getting Unstuck 26
    Being 30
    Chapter Two Endnotes 36

3. We Think Therefore We Do 43
    Here's a Story 43
    God's Will Is Simple 44
    Our Perceptions Determine Our Responses 46
    What Is Sin, Really? 46
    Worry Doesn't Work 51
    Truth and a Renewed Mind 52
    Whose Fault Is It? 56
    The Blame Game 57
    Chapter Three Endnotes 61

Part 2 65

4. Untwisting Thoughts 71
   Spaghetti Thinking.. 71
   The Process... 79
   Believe What God Believes................................. 82
   Transformed Understanding 84
   A Heart Exposed: A Testimony............................ 85
   Spirit versus Flesh 88
   Let Go and Let God: A Testimony....................... 96
   What We Know Can Hurt Us. 99
   The Performance Mindset.................................. 104
   Is What You Believe about God Really True? ... 106
   The Lie 108
   Evil Genius: The Auto-Loopback 112
   Obedience 114
   The Lie by Another Name................................. 123
   You Live What You Believe 130
   How do I Stop Worrying?................................... 135
   Faith Is a Gift.. 137
   We Know Too Much 141
   Who Is in Control? 144
   The Power of Unknown Beliefs......................... 146
   Your Feelings Can Lie 146
   Removing Obstacles 147
   Chapter Four Endnotes 148

5. Why We Are the Way We Are 173
   We Need to Feel Important 173
   The Holy Spirit and the Mind of Christ 175
   Understanding Yourself 178

6. Longing for Unconditional Love 187
   The Desire to Be Accepted 187
   Human Beings versus Human Doings 192
   Chapter Six Endnotes 195

Part 3 199

7. Whose Responsibility Is It? 201
   False Responsibilities 201
   It Is Time to Question Our Results 206

8. Emotions 215
   What Causes Our Emotions? 215
   Think the *Truth* rather than Feelings 218
   The Importance of Understanding 221
   Self-talk and the *Truth* 223
   Chapter Eight Endnotes 228

9. Good Fuel 231
   Believing Starts Early 232
   Faith: The Foundation of Life 233
   Man's Greatest Need 238
   You Don't Have to Hit a Wall 245
   Chapter Nine Endnotes 248

10. How Believing Works 253
    Trauma 253
    The Source of Every Symptom Is a Belief 255
    Good Beliefs versus Bad Ones 261
    Chapter Ten Endnote 262

11. *Truth* versus Deception 263
    Recognizing Lies 268
    How *Truth* Affects Deception 274
    Are You Willing? 275
    Begin Learning the *Truth* 279
    How Darkness Reacts to Light 281
    The Power of Your Beliefs 285
    Chapter Eleven Endnotes 287

Part 4 291

12. The Last Sin 293
    The Freedom to Be Honest 296
    Something God Doesn't Know 298
    Why Forgiveness 300
    Coming to The Light 301
    Love Casts Out Fear of Rejection 305
    Listen to Yourself 307
    Recognizing Wrong Beliefs 309
    Repentance 310
    The Greatest Change of Mind 316
    Understanding Strongholds 316
    The Experience 320
    Chapter Twelve Endnotes 325

13. Grace 333
    Grace and the Law 333
    Obedience through Grace 345
    Use Your Symptoms to Learn God's Solution 349
    Chapter Thirteen Endnotes 353

14. Only Believe 359
    The Power of God 362
    Chapter Fourteen Endnotes 371

15. God's Power is Safely Hidden, in Plain Sight 383

Epilogue - God's Symphony 391
My Song 395
Appendix – for students of Koine Greek 397
References 409

Preface

> While we look not at the things which are seen, but at the things which are not seen.
> —The Apostle Paul

There are millions of books on this planet, and they seek to explain everything. From mathematics to English, politics to philosophy, and spirituality to faith, writers try to explain their world and everything in it. With so many other books to choose from, why should you bother reading this one?

Next time you're with a group of believers, I want you to perform an experiment. I want you to ask each person in that group to define faith. If your experience is anywhere close to mine, you'll get ten different answers out of ten people. "Faith is trust in God," one person will say. "Faith is doing what God says," will say another. Or they may quote Hebrews 11:1 (KJV): "Now faith is the substance of things hoped for, the evidence of things not seen." These answers bring us to an interesting question. The Apostle Paul spoke about believers coming to the unity of the faith, but how can we do that if we can't even achieve an agreement on its definition? How are we to recognize faith if we don't even know what it is?

It's a funny thing about words; they only work when everyone uses the same definitions. If you have a conversation about faith with several people, who each have their own definition, you'll all be using the same word yet talking about entirely different things. Each person will leave the conversation thinking they understood what happened, while in reality, they had no idea what anyone else just said. And we wonder why this world and the church can be so confusing.

Have you ever really questioned what the church says and how it acts? I mean, really wondered why Christians act the way they do? We proclaim the glory of God and His power, but do you ever have a sense that the church is just a slightly more moral version of the world? Is something wrong? I mean, where are the demonstrations of power and *truth* spoken of throughout the Bible? Have you ever wondered why Christ and the apostles performed miracles with no more effort than it took them to breathe, yet the church today will have huge prayer meetings and get only questionable results? Have you ever wondered about the church cliché in the 1990s, *What would Jesus do?* You'd often see the phrase on those brightly colored rubber bracelets with the letters "WWJD" (what would Jesus do).

We usually take this as a reminder to act in a way Christ would act, and He most often responded with patience, compassion, generosity, and calmness of self and spirit. We often forget that cursing a fig tree to death or freaking out and flipping over tables are also valid responses if we are to be honest about the possible answers to *What Would Jesus Do.* If you think about it, sometimes Jesus's actions didn't make a lot of sense. Let's face it, the guy was unpredictable.

> "Lord, we need money to pay our taxes!" cried the disciples. Jesus responded, "Come on, guys. Who taught you about finances? Obviously, go catch a fish, pull the coin out of its mouth, and use that to pay our taxes."

That doesn't make sense, and if you were standing there when it happened, "I saw that coming" would be the last words out of your mouth. That's the problem with WWJD. It's based on the assumption that we, under our own intellectual powers, can understand, predict, and emulate the thoughts, words, and actions of the Creator, the God of gods, King of kings, and Lord of lords; that through our own efforts, we can love as He loved.

Is it just me, or does that seem a little arrogant? We know we are supposed to act like Christ, so how do we do it without using our heads to figure out what He would do?

There was a Cracked.com article a few years back entitled "Five Superpowers from the Bible that Put Marvel and DC to Shame." In it, the writer quoted, then paraphrased Mark 4:35-41:

A furious squall came up, and the waves broke over the boat, so that it was nearly swamped. Jesus was in the stern, sleeping on a cushion. The disciples woke him and said to him, "Teacher, don't you care if we drown?" He got up, rebuked the wind and said to the waves, "Quiet! Be still!" Then the wind died down and it was completely calm. He said to his disciples, "Why are you so afraid? Do you still have no faith?" They were terrified and asked each other, "Who is this? Even the wind and waves obey him!"

So they're out in the middle of a hurricane, tossed around like the guys on *Deadliest Catch* and Jesus, because he was just hardcore like that, didn't mind the drenching rain and the loud thunder and continued sleeping. His disciples woke him up and started griping with stupid complaints like "The boat is halfway under water!" and "We are going to die!"

Jesus told them they were faithless wusses and the disciples shut up. If that wasn't cool enough, he chewed out the storm, and it shut up, too. That has to be our favorite part, how he's just annoyed by the whole thing, as if being bothered to stop an entire weather system was equivalent to getting woken up by your girlfriend to go kill a spider in the bathroom.

So now we have another issue. Even if you could intellectually determine what Christ would do in any given circumstance, it's unlikely you could do it. Cursing a fig tree to death, raising the dead, healing the sick, loving the unlovable, knowing exactly what to say and when to say it, and turning a few pieces of bread and fish into a meal for five thousand people are not exactly talents with which you're born.

Have you ever wondered about Christians who go to church on Sunday, talking and acting like they're supposed to but spend the rest of the week living like the rest of the world? What causes that? Why is it so hard to be a good Christian? The church tells them to try harder, recommit to God, and maybe rebuke Satan. So, they do those things and then try again. They work even harder this time to be like Jesus, only to exhaust themselves and end up right back where they started and maybe even worse off. How does someone become truly Christ-like, instead of just faking it? This brings us to another question. Is there a difference between *acting* like Christ and *being* like Christ?

If you spend enough time with a person, you'll learn their habits and mannerisms. You'll hear what they think about a variety of topics. You'll learn about their personality and character. If you spend enough time around them, you may be able to learn everything there is to know about them. Then you might be able to *act* like them, but that doesn't mean you'd *be* that person. To act like someone requires conscious effort. It's exhausting, and mistakes will be made. But if you could *be* them, it would be easy to act like them. It would require no effort. I mean, how hard is it for you to be you? Have you ever heard the phrase, *"You are just like your father?"* How much effort did it take to be that way? It happened because you had learned to *be* you from him. In some ways, you learned to think like him, so you sometimes act like him.

If we only *act* like Christ instead of *be*ing like Christ and then try to convince ourselves and others that we are like Christ, we make ourselves frauds and liars; doppelgangers that irritate and annoy the genuine and honest with false facades and what inevitably comes across with holier-than-thou attitudes. Wouldn't it be great if our *selves* were like Christ so that if we just acted like ourselves, we would automatically be like Christ?

The Apostle Paul said there is no condemnation to those who believe, so why do we so often feel condemned? Why do we feel condemnation from the Scriptures when they're supposed to be *good news*? How can we be as moral as Christ and the disciples, but do it as effortlessly as they did? How do we *be* like Christ instead of merely trying to *act* like Him? Is it really possible to be free? If so, from what are we supposed to be free?

Instead of faking it, is it possible to know deep down that we are loved and to experience God working in our lives?

Well, now you know if you should read this book.

—James Q. Campbell — Coauthor

About Translating

I began writing this book about 25 years ago. At the time, I had begun to acquire an attitude of disdain for the King James translators and those who have come since. As God began to unveil His heart and mind to me, I became angry at both Him, the Church, and translators. Why had they hidden such simple and easy knowledge? My family laughed saying God hadn't hidden anything but had been working to cause us to see it. Of course, they hadn't seen what God had begun to show me either, but neither did they feel slighted by Him. They just watched in amazement as my life began to change, usually for good, but occasionally not so good. Yet, even the bad times always turned out to be good. Later, my oldest son joined me in writing *Unseen* and began to undo some of the attitude it conveyed.

In the last few years, my thoughts have changed dramatically. I now stand in awe of all the translators I so disliked. What the KJV translators comprehended as well as many who are alive today is now utterly amazing to me. In *Unseen* we explain many places where they display a misunderstanding of what God said, as well as how and why it was missed, but just because translators have misinterpreted something doesn't mean that their interpretations are not true statements. It is just that often, God's words tell us far more than we have realized. *Unseen* seeks to help believers understand more of what God means while not rejecting any truth they have learned from the interpretations of others. Just because something is a mistranslation does not mean it isn't true. For instance, the phrase by Peter, "Casting all of your cares or anxieties upon Him," is not a translation but an interpretation of the result of what Peter was explaining. This rendering fails to give us important information if we are to experience what Peter was writing about. Embedded in the original Greek is the understanding of why we have anxieties and exactly what we are casting on the Lord, as well as how to do it. How in the world can you cast your feelings on the Lord if you don't know exactly what is causing them? Without greater understanding, it is very difficult to know how to accomplish what Peter is interpreted to be saying.

And so, as you read *Unseen*, if you sense an unfavorable attitude from me, please understand that is an attitude I used to have, but no longer do. The thing is, to rewrite the book sans the vestiges of those wrong attitudes would require another year or two. We believe the primary message in *Unseen* is too important to delay any longer. The world and the Church need it now. We trust the Holy Spirit will enable you to recognize attitudes in this work that the Cross of Christ forever eliminated inside the New Creation. Like you, I am still learning who I am in Christ.

Literal translations of the New Testament are pretty much incomprehensible, so translators seek to convey a reasonable sense to readers. Oftentimes, these extrapolations are true statements, yet because our conclusions jump past the cause, which may be difficult to explain with just a word or two, we are unable to explain what God has actually said. For instance, the Greek word translated *care, worry,* or *anxiety* in 1 Peter 5:7: "casting all your anxiety on Him…" (NASB). If we cast our care upon Him, what are we, in fact, doing? Casting our feelings, our cares, our worries? Are they different? And, how do you do that? Exactly what are you supposed to do? Feelings are so nebulous. A deficient understanding can leave a person perplexed because they don't know how to know if they have done what they were supposed to do.

After a recent email exchange with a friend I realized I had done what many translators do. God had given me understanding of what He said but it was a paradigm I didn't know how to explain. So, I just tried to explain the effects of the words I now understood. In other words, I interpreted my understanding so it would make more sense to my friend. Thus, I failed to give him valuable information.

I think that oftentimes students of Ancient Greek do not realize the importance of what they have uncovered in their studies, thus they move too quickly to what they think it means. A summary is often easier to understand than all the details that went into formulating it.

A literal rendering of that verse reveals that we are causing our own anxiety. Though standard translations of that passage render a truth, it is not the *truth* Peter was conveying, thus valuable information is left hidden in the Greek words. As normally translated, it leaves many with the question, if they suffer feelings of anxiety that won't leave, what are they to do? God's answer was in plain sight of the translators, but they misunderstood how to explain it. This leaves many believers longing for a zap from God because they find no other answers in His Word. They fail to realize God's plan is better than a zap of power from Heaven, and translations often fail to convey the answer God has given us.

The Greek word translated anxiety is *merimna* (μέριμνα). Its literal meaning is *pulled-apartness, distraction, divided attention*. This is what causes the feelings of anxiety and worry. We split our attention while attempting to take control of everything in our lives. This is a dead end because we weren't made with that ability. But, with this additional information, we now have knowledge with which to work.

Whereas I do not know what to do with feelings of anxiety, when I understand that I have been pulling myself apart by thoughts which cause anxiety, now I know what needs to change in my life so that I will have no more anxious feelings. I need to get rid of those thoughts.

This information gives me the opportunity to get control of my mind. But, how? This is something that the Holy Spirit enjoys teaching us. Now certain scriptures can take on new meaning as we learn to attack distractions with the ability that the Holy Spirit supplies by means of our new life in Christ. Now we can begin to make headway.

Unseen pulls back the curtain to reveal in plain language what has blocked our understanding and kept us focused on the wrong things. Once we understand that dying daily means dying to believing things which God says aren't true, we will discover how God has always planned on ridding us of cares and anxieties inherent in the darkness of this world. This is the means by which His life will appear in us, to us, and to a world drowning in fear. No matter what happens, no matter what anyone says or does, you will know that God's love means you are always safe. You will love fearlessly just like Jesus. Welcome to the world of *Unseen*: Believing the *Truth,* Understanding *the Lie.*

Author's Note

I do not represent myself a scholar of biblical Greek or Hebrew. Probably tens of thousands of students know more than I do. I only know that I know Who authored the Scriptures in a way that has not only allowed me to begin seeing the unseen, but has changed me in ways I could have never imagined on my own.

I can say together with the author of Psalm 119 that "I have more understanding than all my teachers: for the things you say about yourself are my continual meditation."[1] The same author also said, "I will never forget your principles (precepts): for with them you have made me alive."[2] The following is my prayer for you. I realize it may sound a little strange. This is because it uses a paradigm common to the New Testament Greek, which was understood by First Century believers and how the Apostle Paul prayed in his letter to the Ephesians. *My prayer for you is thanks to God that, in Christ, He has given you an attitude fixed on believing the wisdom and revelation that freely flows from what He knows so that you will have known that the eyes of your understanding were enlightened, which enabled you to know who you are in Him, because of Who He is in you.*

Mankind's understanding of God has undergone a tremendous change since the First Century. After those who sought to force Christ's believers to live under the Jewish Law came the Gnostics. Their heresy was devious and attempted to redefine Church doctrines. The work of Jesus Christ had eliminated the separation between God and man and had restored mankind to a right relationship with Him by pure grace. This knowledge was changing societies. Seeking to destroy this new

---

[1] Psalm 119:99 (JEC)
[2] Psalm 119:93

manifestation of life, the Gnostics taught that though Jesus was both God and man, as the Head of the New Creation He was a different type of man than others because He is God. John battled against this heresy directly in his first epistle. The goal of Gnosticism was, and still is, to change the Church's understanding of God's relationship with those for whom He died. Part of their strategy was to modify the meanings of various concepts and words; we address some of these changes in this book. Fairly quickly, the Church's understanding of the union of God and man in Christ was lost. Due to a lack of understanding, Gnostic heresies are still very popular today, and many churches accept them as traditional Christian teachings. They are a prime reason for the loss of the Early Church's power. We address some of these teachings later in this book.

Think of how quickly the meanings of words and phrases change today. When I was a child, the word *bad* meant *bad*. Today, it can mean *good* as in "that guy is *bad*." So, which is he? *Bad* as in *bad* or *bad* as in *good*? The word *cool* used to refer to temperature. In the 20th Century, it came to mean "not dorky." It used to be an insult to call someone a geek. Today, it can be cool to be a geek. I doubt if anyone two centuries ago would have called a good-looking woman hot. Fifty years ago, if you told someone to swipe a credit card, you would be encouraging a crime because the word meant to steal. Also, the word *viral* referred to a potentially deadly event. Today, to most people, it refers primarily to information that is circulating fast over the Internet. The meanings of words have changed, and this is not necessarily bad. But, if someone who lived a thousand years ago heard us talking today, would they understand us? These are just a few recent changes. If you think the meanings of a few words have changed in just the last 50 years, can you imagine how many have changed in the last two thousand?

In Genesis 3:1, God said that the serpent was more subtle than all the life on Earth. I realize that most translations use the word "beast" or "wild animal." However, if you look again, since this story is about the relationship between God and mankind, God would not warn Adam about an "animal" that was simply smarter than all the other animals. If God was concerned about an "animal" that was extremely subtle, it had to be because that subtlety was a threat to Adam and Eve, which means that subtle "animal" had to, in some way, be smarter than they were. As I researched the Hebrew word for "beast" I discovered that it could also mean "life" as in the life of a man. So, the serpent wasn't just more subtle than all the other beasts; it was subtler than all the life on Earth, including Adam and Eve. If Satan was smart enough to convince one-third of the angels, while in the presence of God, to turn against Him, it is evident we have an adversary far more cunning than we have realized.

In the story of the Garden of Eden, we see the serpent's subtlety. He didn't begin by calling God a liar. Instead, he led the First Couple through a process of reasoning to conclude that God was not honest and that they were other than who God said they were. "Has God [really] said?" The corruption of their reasoning included causing them to doubt themselves. Once they weren't sure what they knew, Satan could plant alternative ideas in their minds that they had no basis for rejecting. Now questioning what they had heard with their own ears, it was not hard to expand the deception. Before long, the couple's understanding had become so twisted and confused that Satan's logic had become theirs. From that point, the results were inevitable. Without help, the course of humanity could not change.

Throughout the scriptures, in one way or another, God has pleaded with mankind to join Him in exercising reason. In His greatest cry for mankind to listen, He sent His Only Begotten Son Who is His Very Image, Word, Reason, and Logic all wrapped up in one Man, the last Adam, Jesus Christ. The Apostle John called Jesus the logos. The Greek word *logos* means "word, reason, and logic," thus, Jesus was not only the Word of God, but He was also the manifestation of God's reason and logic in human flesh.

It doesn't take much to realize what happened to the message of the Gospel from the First Century until today. The legal perspective of our Western societies came from ancient Rome. After being subject to the Roman legal point of view, interpretations of the original Greek New Testament text came to have a different hue than known by First

Century believers. Those sincere believers, who were alive around the beginning of the Reformation in the Fifteenth Century, did not realize how twisted the understandings they had inherited had become. Over centuries mankind had been programmed to see God from a Roman war-like Western/legal-like perspective. And, just because there was a Reformation doesn't mean Satan gave up. Isn't it obvious that evil doesn't easily quit? Those believers were not suddenly back on track. The door was simply open for them to take back what they had lost and go on from there. God was working to cause them to rediscover His *truth* which was now right in front of their eyes. But, their perspectives of God and history were filters that prevented them from yet comprehending the grace known by the Early Church. Their understandings were filtered through over a thousand years of culture based on law rather than grace. By then, being a Christian was primarily a matter of doing all the right things. They intuitively knew there was more, but their legal interpretation of the Gospel prevented even the reformers from seeing what it was. Grace was there in plain sight, but it would take centuries of God's continuing revelation of Himself to persuade men that there was another way to understand His *truth*. And, that understanding has continued to grow.

For instance, consider Martin Luther. He grew up under the influence of the legalism of the Roman Catholic Church, yet the day came when he realized that God had a different perspective. Luther recognized that faith alone justified him, without the rules. It was an explosion heard around the world. Since then there have been many instances of God revealing more of Himself. In recent years, people around the world have rejoiced over God's grace, a subject hardly understood for centuries. And, each time God moves to teach us more about Himself there is opposition. Many of those who have attained some state of specialness in their age's system of teaching have felt threatened by the change and have tried to stop it. But, God marches on. The Apostle Paul said, "This will continue until we all come to such unity in our faith and knowledge of God's Son that we will be mature in the Lord, measuring up to the full and complete standard of Christ."[3] This verse

---

[3] Ephesians 4:13 (NLT)

says that we are still divided and often opposed to one another because of the differing things we believe and know about God.

It is time to examine ourselves and see if what we believe is what God wants us to believe. We don't have to fear questioning what we believe. In fact, God encourages it, "Examine yourselves, whether ye be in the faith;"[4] Paul didn't say this to condemn anyone. He knew the subtle persuasion of the enemy. Paul was sent to teach the obedience of believing God rather than people. What a great adventure it is to believe God.

The word *makrothumia* (μακροθυμία) that is commonly rendered as *patience* in Paul's description of the fruit of the Spirit in Galatians 5:22 can be more accurately rendered as *enduring passion*, meaning that God's love for His children is never ending (See Chapter One Endnotes #1). He has an unparalleled stick-to-itiveness. He doesn't quit. He doesn't feel one way today and differently tomorrow. Love isn't something God has and gives to those about whom He feels good. His love is constant, because He *is* Love. Because of God's enduring passion, He never stops revealing Himself, and increasingly His children are hearing Him.

Suffice it to say, what emerged in the Reformation in the Fifteenth Century looked nothing like what the First Century Church understood. In the Reformation, many believers assumed they had returned to the original meanings of the scriptures, but alas, the Roman legal perspective, fully supported by the Latin translation from the original Greek, barred a return to the former understanding (if they had even realized there had been a previous understanding). But increasingly, God is getting His message out, again and again and again. Over the last few centuries, we have had wonderful men and women of God who recognized glimpses of God and clung to what they saw with all their might. But, not until recently have we begun to understand, once again, the methods of the serpent and what it means to be in union with God through Christ. That lack of understanding has enabled the Enemy to manipulate what people believe as well as cause them to look in the

---

[4] 2 Corinthians 13:5 (KJV)

wrong direction for answers. This time we're not going backwards again. This time we will see the full manifestation of the sons of God.[5]

What we typically refer to as translations of the Bible are, in fact, interpretations. Most Bible students don't realize that unless they understand Greek, they have never read a translation. Over the years, publishers have been a little sloppy with the word *translation*. An actual translation of the Greek New Testament is tough to understand. Thus, a text is rendered literally and then interpreted so that it will make sense to readers. The problem is that all of us have our own belief systems which act as filters causing us to see the scriptures based on what we think rather than what the writer may have thought.

If you have ever tried to literally translate anything, you understand how difficult, and sometime even impossible, it is without interpreting some or all of what is said. By realizing this, you place yourself on a much safer ground as you study the scriptures. Always remember, the Holy Spirit wants you to understand what He means even if an interpretation says something else. To understand, begin with telling God that you believe He always tells the *truth* even if you don't understand what He meant. He loves that attitude and will lead you to a full and correct understanding.

For my own study, I like to translate literally and then stop there. When my translation doesn't make sense to me, I ask the Holy Spirit what He meant. Sometimes the understanding comes quickly. Other times, I find that I needed to learn something else before whatever the Holy Spirit was saying could be understood. I can't explain how he shows me, but I can tell you what He has shown me. You may then ask Him yourself. He wants a direct, personal relationship with you and not through someone else and their ideas. He'll use other people to teach you but never with the intent that they stand between you and Him. It is sad that so many people don't believe this.

In the following pages, you will read literal translation, maybe for the first time. Sometimes I present the literal, which may not make sense at first glance, followed by my interpretation. Compare them and see what God shows you. Sometimes a literal translation, as well as

---

[5] Romans 8:19 (KJV)

interpretations, cannot completely convey what a passage means in the original language. So, ask the Holy Spirit to teach you what He means. My prayer is that what you have been taught and many things you may not have understood will become clearer. I expect that you will get a better understanding of what God means so that things that have been difficult to comprehend will finally make sense. I honestly believe that some of what follows will seem so straightforward and obvious that you may have trouble understanding it. You may say, "It can't be that simple." But it is.

The stories are about people I have known, but the names have been changed. My translations of New Testament passages are followed by (JEC).

All Greek text comes from the *Stephanus Textus Receptus 1550*. Greek prepositions are critical. You remember the prepositions from elementary school, right? *Of, by, about, in, within, through, toward, under*, and *upon* are just a few of them. In English, we can often interchange them, and though we technically used the wrong one, the other person still understands what we were trying to say because of context.

So why are we going on about prepositions here? The Greek language was incredibly precise. If I said in Greek, "I walked *into* a wall because I wasn't paying attention," then it would mean that I walked up to and was physically inside the wall. Obviously, this idea is absurd in English, but we would know what speaker is trying to say.

So, what does that mean for the Bible? Below, we've repeated a statement but only changed the preposition. We then interpreted how that simple change completely changes the sentence.

I have faith *in* Christ.
I have faith that Christ came, died, and rose again. I believe Christ existed.

I have the faith *of* Christ.
I have the exact same faith as Christ did.

I have faith *by* Christ.
I have faith because of what Christ did. He enabled me to have faith.

I have faith *within* Christ.
Being inside Christ, I have faith.

I have faith *through* Christ.
I have faith using Christ as the conduit to the source of faith.

You can see how different prepositions completely change the meaning of the statement. Occasionally, we write a preposition in italics, and you'll most often see that when talking about faith. When you see that, take a moment and think about why the author used that preposition. You can come back to this page as a quick reference on the prepositions if you need to.

The first two chapters of *Unseen* may seem a little slow and laborious for some readers. If that is your experience, don't skip them but don't spend a lot of time on them either. They contain critical information for understanding much that follows. Just read through them. Beginning with Chapter Three, it will be easier and will make more sense. *Unseen* contains a message that needs to be pondered.

Prologue

Long ago in a world now forgotten, a young couple lived a life we can barely imagine today. They loved and were loved because they were alive. They were important because they had been created in love by *Love* itself. Their understanding was little, but they didn't need much to enjoy life.

They lived in a lovely and fruitful land—a garden, if you will, that yielded abundance for every need as they worked and tended it without breaking a sweat or worrying if there would be enough. The couple was truly loved by the Master Gardener who was with them often.

Gardens back then were different from today. For one thing, they didn't have weeds. Not only did the couple's garden contain the most delicious fruit and vegetables you've ever tasted, but there were flowers too with many more colors than we could even imagine today. And trees—lots of lush, green trees the likes of which we have never seen. The soil was fertile, supporting unlimited growth. Even someone without a green thumb could have grown a garden to surpass any seen today. The couple hadn't been around long enough even to consider the riches hidden inside the Earth. It wasn't necessary. The garden glistened with rocks, minerals, and metals of unspeakable beauty: gold, silver, copper, and others. Oh, and precious gems too, such as diamonds, onyx, emeralds, sapphires, and everything else you could imagine, and some things you couldn't.

The world was full of everything they would ever need. The couple lacked nothing. Together with the Master Gardener, they would learn to work and subdue the whole Earth, including what was outside their garden. But there was plenty of time for that. Their first job was to simply enjoy their lives together because the garden was created for them. What joy, what peace. There was work to do but oh what fun! Living in this beautiful world, they had no fear; for nothing existed that could harm them. And, best of all, the Master Gardener really liked them and being with them. It was a special place to Him as well. Such a world, such a creation was the type of home that no one would ever want to leave. Of course, you might venture out to explore occasionally, but the garden was more than enough. It contained treasures that could not be discovered even in many lifetimes. I could go on, but then we would never get to where we're going.

The couple's dominion extended to everything they could see. It was a world built on *truth*. Everything the couple saw and experienced was real. There were no illusions, and nothing was fake. It was so perfect that even the animals talked. Though nowhere near the splendor of the humans, animals were a lot smarter than they are today. Tending the garden was not difficult because the animals helped.

But then something of great evil entered their world. It seemed innocent enough—just an animal that moved from branch to branch and tree to tree. The animal talked, but that wasn't unusual because many did. But what this one said was different. It spoke of the Master Gardener, and it didn't say nice things. At first, they paid it no attention. What this animal said didn't make any sense, so they initially just ignored it. But it didn't quit, and finally, it got their attention.

The difference between this talking animal and the others was that it could obviously see things no one else could. At least, that is what it told them. This couple began to wonder if the Master Gardener had been telling them the *truth*. Of course, they didn't want to ask Him because this splendid talking serpent obviously knew something the Master Gardener didn't.

At the urging of the serpent, the day came when they stepped out on their own. If they were created to rule the garden, why did they need the Master Gardener? They could do it on their own. Of course, they weren't old enough, just like young people today, to realize they weren't ready to rule their kingdom by themselves. These new people needed a teacher, but since they had embraced a deception, they were unable to use even the simplest of common sense. They were now controlled by something beyond their comprehension. Like youth today, they weren't wise enough to question if what the serpent was telling them was right. Why should they? What the serpent said sounded good. They could be in control and be their own master gardeners. They could make up the rules, and, of course, their friend, the serpent would help.

What they didn't realize was that *the lie* they had believed was going to turn off that unique, mystical light that enabled the couple to see what their physical eyes couldn't. They hadn't yet learned that they had two sets of eyes. They hadn't learned half of what the Master Gardener wanted to teach them. They were only children in a brand-new world that was understood only by the One who created it. The world was going to become a shadow of its splendor; darkness was going to descend. Although they would continue to see with their physical eyes—the incredible penetrating, beautiful eyes that allowed them to see the majesty of their mystical garden—were becoming blind.

In the presence of such indescribable and inexplicable wonder, they did not consider that it had been a gift from their Creator. Rather, they listened to a voice that kept contradicting what they knew was right, and the thought of replacing their Creator became plausible. Being under-gardeners was no longer appealing. They wanted to be in control. Besides, the serpent said they didn't need the Master Gardener anymore. They were wise enough to tend the garden by themselves. He was just going to get in their way. Yes, they were creatures because they had been created. But they were different from the rest of the creation. They had yet to learn the plans of the Master Gardener. They didn't know that He planned on teaching them to rule their garden and the Earth just like Him. It was a kingdom He created for them. It was theirs to do with as they pleased. But now it would be millennia before mankind would once again see what was invisible for thousands of years.

Unfortunately, when these terrible events took place, that beautiful world disappeared from view. However, it is still here and has never changed. But mankind changed and can no longer see what is; they can only see the deteriorating physical remains of what used to be. They had been created human *Beings*, but instead chose to become human *Doings*. Because of deception, their actions and appearances became more important than the fact that they had been created in the image of their Creator. Their value, their self-worth was no longer dependent on who they were, but what they could do.

The effect on all the creation was rapid and catastrophic. It infected the whole universe and was irreversible. How could something that happened in that garden so devastate and corrupt an entire world? The couple never found out. They never learned the awe-inspiring nature of their own existence. They never grasped what it meant to be created in the very image of the Master Gardener and be like Him in every way; they were only children who had just begun to learn who they were. Animals they were not. More like gods without being God. Over time, He would have shown them what that meant.

Because of just one deception, they allowed error into the world. Later, it came to be known as *the lie*. Of course—though foreign to them—deception is common to us today. It quickly established a foothold and rapidly began consuming the rest of creation. Once started, there was no way to stop it. The most terrible of all was that this error had caused that beloved couple to declare independence from their Creator. Stuck now in an endless circle they believed *the lie* as *truth*, and there was no stopping it. The damage was catastrophic because like a contagious disease, *the lie* rapidly mutated and duplicated into uncountable other lies—all founded on the original—that they could and should be in control. Of course, humans make very poor gods, but we keep trying even to this day because we believe that we must.

They wanted to be like the Master Gardener but didn't realize that they already were. Instead of depending on their loving Creator, who planned on teaching them what He knew, they had decided to take control and do something that promised to make them even better. But, it was not possible to become better. They would have come to know over time that they were already the best.

It took just moments to realize that something had gone wrong, but a paradigm shift of tragic proportions prevented them from recognizing what had happened. The couple became trapped in their deception. Because *the lie* they had believed promised to make them like their Creator, they now believed they were. They had been created to *be* but now were programmed to *do*, and there was no bridge back.

As their beautiful playground began to deteriorate, they came to hate their Creator and blame Him. "It was your fault," they told Him. But the Creator never flinched and didn't give up. He set in motion a plan to make everything new again and cause mankind to see once again that which is unseen today. The Master Gardener was the *Love* that had created them, and nothing they could do would change His nature. He is Love, and the world would one day know it again.

Come with me as I show you what mankind lost and how we can become beings who live in two worlds, going from one to the other at will.

Part 1

In the preface, we briefly discussed the need to understand the definitions of words and concepts correctly. The first three chapters will address the core concepts and definitions used throughout the rest of this book. Some of this you may already understand, some of it may be new to you, and some of it may even contradict what you've been taught. These first chapters may seem slow at times, or like they're needlessly harping on a certain point. If it seems like that, please bear with us and read anyway. We promise the book picks up exponentially the further you get into it.

We divided this book into four parts. Because many of the concepts will be new or different, it may be difficult to remember every definition and concept. To that end, the introduction to each part of the book will include a brief list of words, phrases, and concepts with basic definitions and understandings attached to them.

If you disagree with something you read, at least give us a chance to explain our point. Read that whole part and see if our arguments convince you. At the very least, you will learn some scripturally valid perspectives. We are always eager to hear from our readers in hopes that either they can expose any mistake we've made, or we can help them understand our message.

1. *Faith.* Simply put, we define faith as believing the *truth*. We attach to it no actions, emotions, thoughts, or attitudes. Faith simply believes the *truth*.

2. *Believe.* To hold dear, to treasure something you know. We hold onto and will not be talked into giving up things we treasure. This is what God wants us to do with His *truth*.

3. *Belief.* A Middle English word from *be* and *lief* meaning *be treasured*. It refers to knowledge which you cherish or hold dear.

4. *Being and doing.* Man was created to be loved by God. From His love naturally pours the fruits of the Spirit without any conscious effort on our part. However, mankind has put the cart before the horse. We try our best to *do* love and fail to discover what it means to *be* loved.

5. *Be transformed by the renewal of your mind.* Many believers misunderstand this. To be transformed is not something we do; it is something God has already done within us. He has never desired that you change yourself, nor commanded you to renew your mind. He has already accomplished everything He wanted in Christ and made His life your reality. *Now He just wants to make your reality real to you.* You can't make this happen; only the Holy Spirit can. You can only delay your realization and experience of the *truth*.

6. *Understanding.* If there is a simple formula for understanding how people work, it is quite simply this: beliefs produce thoughts, attitudes, and dispositions, which produce emotions and actions. To put it simply, you automatically live consistent with what you truly believe. With this understanding, you will learn that instead of trying to fight wrong thoughts and actions, it is much easier to let the Holy Spirit address your unknown erroneous beliefs that cause those thoughts and actions.

7. *What is sin?* The Church often holds the definition of sin as those actions or thoughts that are contrary to the will of God. While not inaccurate, it's not very useful either. Sin in the original Greek is *error*. Specifically, it refers to an error of belief, which causes the thoughts and actions that today we call sin. If this definition perplexes you, rest assured that we addressed it in detail and especially toward the end of Part 1.

8. *What is death?* You may find it immensely helpful to discover that death is not the cessation of existence but separation from something. For Adam and Eve, death was not the cessation of life in terms of their existence but separation from each other and God. When a loved one dies, it doesn't mean they have ceased to exist but that we have been separated from them. They still exist, but someplace else. The Orthodox Jewish religion presents an excellent picture of what death is. If a child marries outside of the faith, in some families the child is considered dead. The family member doesn't cease to exist, it is just separated from the rest of the family.

9. *Obedience.* The literal meaning of the Greek word is to "submit to hear" with the intention of believing what is heard. It does not mean to hear with the intention of doing. The doing of the Word will be an automatic outcome of continuing to hear and treasuring what is heard.

10. *Love.* The passionate desire and intention of the Lover to give Himself and all that He is and owns to the beloved. It is the giving of what is most important to the Lover no matter what the cost. Love can be grieved but not offended.

11. *Covenant.* An agreement in which the Father swore an oath that He would do all He declared in the Old Testament in exchange for the Son swearing an oath that He would believe Him. If either violated their oath, they would no longer be Who they said they were.

12. *Paradigm*. Pictures in someone's mind formed by their understanding and interpretation of the world around them. These pictures determine what each person considers to be real. This is why a religious person and an atheist can see the same event with one calling it a miracle and the other random chance (Chapter One Endnotes #2).

13. *Paradigm shift*. A new understanding of information that was previously understood differently. It is reflected in the statement, "Oh, now I get it."

14. *Truth*. The reality in which God lives as well as everything that He says and does.

1
Changing Versus Being Changed

What Does God See?

Have you ever wondered what God sees when He looks at the world? Some say He can't look at the world because He can't look at sin. I don't know where they get that, but it isn't from God (Chapter One Endnotes #3).

The unseen world is real, but impossible to see except by gift from Him. What so many don't realize is that the gift is already theirs; they just have to take it (Chapter One Endnotes #4). Because He is love, God will never force any blessing on you. You must take it. How do you do that? By believing the *truth*. God's gifts are already yours; you just need to agree. Your heart already knows the *truth* about what you are going to read in this book. My prayer is that the pure logic of what follows will convince your mind as it stirs your heart.

If we can't perceive the unseen world around us, it's because of a simple problem. This book is about fixing that problem so that we can see clearly. Human *doings* can't see it; only human *beings* can. Seeing is not something you can just decide to do. It doesn't work like that. In the resurrection of Jesus Christ, God made you a brand-new creature; God says you are a new creation.[1] He is dancing in delight as He works to show you the real you. As you come to see what He sees, you will dance with Him. The point of this book is to explain the process that enables you to discover and be the real you in Christ so that your thoughts, feelings, and behaviors will be a revealing of the Christ who

---
[1] 2 Corinthians 5:17

lives in you.² There are human *beings* and human *doings*, and the latter spend most of their time fighting a version of themselves (their old nature) that God says He got rid of two thousand years ago.

Many people want to change. They try very hard to change, whether it is their diet, a bad habit, or a way of thinking. Throughout this book, when I talk about being changed, I am not implying that you must change yourself. Regarding the type of change you desire, you *can't* do it; only the Holy Spirit can.

A rich young ruler once came to Jesus and said he was doing everything that the Scriptures required, which means he was very religious. He wanted to know if there was anything else he needed to do to be acceptable to God. When Jesus told him what He required in his situation, the ruler was so disappointed that he turned and walked away. Jesus's disciples were stunned. If anyone could become acceptable to God, surely this was the guy. But Jesus had commanded him to do the one thing he couldn't. This guy was so self-assured, so confident that He could meet God's standards if he just tried hard enough. But Jesus hit him where he was vulnerable. He told him to give away his money. Why? Because Jesus wants us to give away all our money? Absolutely *not*! Jesus was just trying to show the man that by his efforts alone there was no way he could become acceptable to God. This man was not capable of letting go of what gave him the importance he so desperately needed (i.e., the money) to gain the acceptance that he wanted from God. The young man required a radical change of heart and mind to one of absolute dependence on God. In Jesus, he had met his match. Since Jesus had required something that he couldn't do using his self-righteous willpower, he gave up and walked away. He had wanted to be able to say to God, "Look at what I've done. Now you *have* to accept me."

That isn't what God has ever wanted. He has never sought people who would serve Him as slaves. Remember, He has all the angels He needs. He just desires children who want fellowship with Him as He lives His life in and through us, which is what He was going to teach that young couple in the Garden. Jesus's response to the disciples'

---

² 2 Colossians 1:27

incredulity was: "With men this is impossible; but with God all things are possible."³ In other words, no man or woman will ever be able to do what is necessary to achieve acceptance with God, but God will do it for us. The *truth* is, He already has! He delights to show you what He has done inside you. When you see it, you will be amazed. Right now, much of what we think about ourselves isn't even true, and until people understand things the Early Church took for granted, it would be hard to convince many otherwise.

Humans judge ourselves from perspectives very different from how God thinks about us. Our opinions of ourselves arise from what we see ourselves do, how we feel, the types of thoughts that run through our minds, and what we often believe others think about us, especially God. Bottom line, we judge ourselves and each other on our doings—whether related to our words, appearances, or actions. However, God looks at the *being* part of us—that part from which the doing, feeling, and thinking flows.

God has lost most of His human creatures. Even though he knows where to find them, they don't know where they are or who they are. He is God. He can see them. But their minds are blinded. Within themselves, they are lost and don't even know it, but in Christ they are truly found, and the Gospel is the good news, the great news that in Christ, God has restored us to bold, confident access to Him by His faith, not ours.⁴

There Is So Much More

This book is for those who are tired or have despaired of a life that has crushed their dreams. It is for those who have considered ending their lives because their troubles have been so overwhelming and for so long that they have become unbearable. It is for those who think it is not possible their reality will ever change.

To get where UNSEEN is going, we must start with the basics. Many words used in the Scriptures did not mean what they do today.

---

³ Matthew 19:26 (KJV)
⁴ Ephesians 3:12

As I write, sometimes I explain the biblical use of a word before using it; other times, I use it and explain it later. When you see a word or phrase in brackets [ ], it is an implied or literal meaning by the original language or an alternative translation. If you're the type who wants to see the details of my translations from the original Greek to English, the footnotes and endnotes will often provide more information.

The reason people think that God is so focused on their behavior is that they don't know what sin is. It is just a word that has been used to describe anything that Christians think God hates. The Church's misunderstanding of sin has caused many to miss the will of God and to miss the mark.[5]

This book is not a Do-It-Yourself manual. It is an explanation of how to cooperate with God in His work to cause you to see what He sees. He is the one that enables you to see the unseen— not by your skill or effort, but by gift from Him. References to the *truth* in this book refer directly to or put primary emphasis on God's *truth* as revealed in the Bible. Truth spelled without italics refers primarily to natural truth unless it is in a quote. However, both overlap at times.

So, what is the *unseen*? Though only the Spirit of God can show you, by having an idea of what you are looking for, you are far more likely to recognize it when you see it.

> But as it is written, Eye hath not seen, nor ear heard, neither have entered into the heart of man, the things which God hath prepared for them that love him. But God hath revealed them unto us by his Spirit.[6]

For example, when someone enjoys peace while their life seems to be falling apart. It can't really be explained. A person's life appears to collapse before their eyes as turmoil assaults everything physical, emotional, and financial, yet they're not upset. They have what could only be described as a supernatural calm. Their joy overrides the trouble.

---

[5] Many translate sin as miss the mark. Yes, of course, that is a meaning of the word *sin*. Ironically, the use of that definition can cause people to miss the mark.

[6] 1 Corinthians 2:9-10 (KJV)

That's only a small part of the unseen. You may be thinking, "Okay, so I can't see the unseen by myself, only the Spirit can show me. Regardless, I still want to see it. So, what should I look for?"

Paul addressed that in the Book of Corinthians: "While we look not at the things which are seen, but at the things which are not seen: for the things which are seen are temporal; but the things which are not seen are eternal."[7]

So, the unseen is things that are eternal. Now we need to know what Paul meant by the words *temporal* and *eternal*. In modern parlance, the word *temporal* usually refers to something that is limited by time as opposed to something that is outside of time—that is, eternity. But Paul means something else. He was not referring to the issue of time, but quality. To Paul, anything that is temporal is subject to the corruption resulting from the fall of mankind in the Garden of Eden. It includes everything you can see with your natural eyes. Before the birth of Jesus, everything was infected by the corruption and nothing could escape it. Since His resurrection, humanity's union with Him is the only way out.

Neither the natural eye nor any device man has created can see the eternal. The unseen, which Paul spoke about, is not subject to corruption because it is a different quality and not changeable by time or anything that mankind does. *Eternal* in Bible verses like 2 Corinthians 4:18 refers to *quality* whether of spirit, God's life, His kingdom, His *truth*, or someone's attitude (Chapter One Endnotes #5).

Like God, His *truth* is eternal. It will never change. Its source will always be love because God *is* Love. He doesn't have love; it is not something that He gives as a present. He *is* Love and cannot act or do anything outside of love. Because He loves you, He gives you Himself. Eternal things cannot be explained or understood in natural terms. Paul says they can only be described in words the Holy Spirit teaches.

> In speaking, too, of these gifts, we do not use language suggested by human wisdom, but the Spirit's language, and so we explain spiritual things in spiritual words.[8]

---

[7] 2 Corinthians 4:18 (KJV)
[8] 1 Corinthians 2:13 (TCNT Part 2)

In other words, to someone seeing through the lens of flesh, what God sees doesn't make sense. He expresses what He sees in words, but they are describing things that make no sense from a natural perspective. From a sense point of view, even if we think we understand what God is saying, we probably don't. We are utterly dependent on Him to show us what He sees.

Of course, you may have already asked God to show you, yet you still haven't seen. If so, it is because there is something in the way and blocking your view. This book is about what that is and how God removes it so that we can see the unseen.

Many people think God is the enemy. They learned from somewhere that God *lets* or *causes* terrible things to happen. After they have had enough terrible things happen to them, God looks like a dreadful person. Unfortunately, they have been deceived and convinced that this lie is true. This is truer on the subject of God's love than any other issue. Contrary to what many think about God, He is very generous. In fact, He is never stingy and never gives anything but good, and He doesn't just love you, He likes you. If given a chance, He'll prove it to you. But the world is full of evil. Evil seeks to convince us that God doesn't care. Evil uses false light to cause mankind to believe that God is the source of evil. But that isn't true, and God is working to persuade you otherwise. God is working to cause you to see with His light, rather than that false light.

Unfortunately, humankind—who was created to be the lords of the Earth—became the servant of Satan thus enabling him to direct our authority when we chose to believe what he said, instead of what God said. But in Christ, we are once again able to use our God given authority as He planned. But the ability comes from an unseen world into this one. It cannot go the other direction. To understand who you are, and the amazing abilities God has given you, you must begin seeing that unseen world. That happens because of our union with Christ, not by your efforts to do something.

Faith is what makes it possible to know God's love in a tangible way, and knowing His love for us opens our eyes to see the unseen. The book of Ephesians says that faith leads us to know the love of Christ as real in our hearts (Chapter One Endnotes #6). That is far more than just knowing *about* His love (Chapter One Endnotes #7).

The first forty-plus years of my life I was filled with turmoil. I lived with many bouts of extreme depression and anxiety, numerous bad thought habits, and an overwhelming sense of rejection from those who were most important to me. My mental and emotional pain was immense. Born again at nineteen I began seeking the Lord passionately. After a short respite, life went from bad to worse. I was tormented by fear and frequented with panic attacks.

Late in my twenties, I found business to be a diversion from my fears. I became a workaholic and could go at an unbelievable pace late into every night. No one I knew could keep up with me. Though very proud of my work ethic, I eventually learned that I was just being driven by something that I had never recognized. Years later, financial problems turned my business career from a diversion into a nightmare. My delicate mental and emotional balancing act tipped beyond my ability to recover. I felt trapped, despairing of all hope that I could ever be normal.

However, God had not given up on me. As I was to discover, even during the most terrible times, He was with me working in the bad to cause blessing. Today, I live a new life. The old is gone, never to return. The process that transformed me is also already working in your life, for good and bad. You have no choice about it. You just need to learn to let it work for good. It is easy once you know how.

Our message is simple. God meant life to be simple. Mankind has made it complicated. Yes, you can experience God in your life *now*. You can know God's love and feel Him working in your heart and mind without having to first reach into your pocket to give or struggle to follow a set of rules.

* * *

James E. Campbell, Jr, James Q. Campbell

Chapter One Endnotes

Note 1

Makrothymía, often translated *patience,* is a compound of two Greek words: *makrós* and *thymós* and can be translated several ways regarding both space and time: *Long-passion, enduring passion, far-stretching breath, deep-hearted, long-lasting courage,* and several other positive meanings. However, if one prefers to envision a God who is always on the edge of anger at anyone who crosses Him, then the word can be understood to mean *long-anger* or *long-wrath.* I define the word *enduring passion.*

Liddell & Scott (1875) Greek-English Lexicon defines:

Makrós –"I. of space, *long, far-stretching, deep, far, far distant, large in size, great*; --II. of time, *long, long-lasting.*"

Thymós –"I. in purely physical significance, *the soul, life, breath;* II. *The soul* as shown by the feelings and passions, *the heart* and so –1. Of the feelings of desire, wish, etc. *appetite,* -2. Of any *vehement passion,* esp. *anger, wrath, rage,* and in a good sense *spirit, courage.*"

Bible scholars have a choice to render *makrothymía* from the perspective of a God Who barely tolerates His human creatures or a God who is passionate about saving them and so would send His Son to die on their behalf. Do you believe that God would give His Son for people He can barely tolerate? God is so passionate about us that He would stop at nothing to redeem us. Thus, He sent His Son to die the death that mankind had to die. There was no one dearer to God the Father than His Son, and that is Who He sent. If God secretly detested those for whom His Son died, then He would have continued the Old Testament practice of substituting a goat or oxen.

Under a common opinion about God, He could have done anything; He doesn't necessarily have to do what He says because, as commonly taught, He is sovereign and doesn't have to keep His Word. Some Bible teachers say that God may interpret what He says differently from the way we do and, since He is unknowable and absolute, we must accept that no one can ever be sure of anything, except that we are going to Heaven when we die. But in opposition to such logic, God has told us that He gave the most cherished thing He had, His Son. This fact strongly suggests God has a passion for us that we have yet to comprehend. In Chapter Four, you will learn how mankind developed its terrible perspective on the God Who the Apostle John declares, "...so loved the world that He gave His Only Begotten Son," and "God is love" (John 3:16 & 1 John 4:8).

I find it interesting that patience in Galatians 5:22 is understood to be a fruit of the Spirit that God requires of His children who He supposedly created in His image, yet God must be different than the image in which He created us. To many, He is impatient and barely contains His wrath. Many people seem to think that God looks forward to the day when He no longer must put up with rebellious, ignorant children. Even though the Apostle Paul said that love never fails, apparently God doesn't believe it.[9] Some believe Satan has won and God has lost. Fortunately, God knows differently. When it comes to persuading children who were deceived into believing He is out to get them, and thus running from Him, His love won't quit. Though they may feel otherwise, nothing can separate anyone from God's love.

Many snarl that God gave His Son, so how dare anyone resist His overtures of love? An underlining theme of what they preach is that God expects us to be patient, yet we can't look to Him as the model for what He expects of us, because He is God! If parents had that perspective, we wouldn't teach our children. Like the world perceives God, we would just threaten, beat, and condemn our children into obedience. I find such an idea to be preposterous and I'm sure you do, too. God created man in His image, yet He demands we be better than Him? That we exercise patience while He sits on the edge of His seat ready at any instant to condemn anyone who refuses Him or just doesn't understand? Such logic is, of course, ridiculous when you lay it out like

---

[9] 1 Corinthians 13:8

this. The *truth* is that God loves with enduring passion. He doesn't quit even in the face of obstacles that slap Him in the face. God's passion is real love. And, according to 1 Corinthians 13:8, it is passion that never fails. "Love never fails."

Note 2

God is a Father and wants His children to learn to reason like He does. To reason like God, we must begin with His words. According to the Greek New Testament, Jesus is the logos. The word logos means *word, logic, reason*. Jesus is not only God's Word, He is the revelation of God's logic and how God reasons. If you want to understand God's logic and how He reasons, look at Jesus. God's logic, His reasoning, His words are founded in love, because God doesn't just love people, He is love.

This book is about the unseen. It is not about something that is invisible but that, rather, is just not seen, because we have been programmed, that is, educated, to see something else. We live in a world system that is very real to us, yet many sense there is another reality, one for which we were created, and they long to know it. This is why I talk about paradigms, because it is a word that sums up what each of us sees and on which we base how we live. People's paradigms are learned and are formed by their belief systems and logic. A paradigm can change as a result of additional information because it can require a change in our logic for things to keep making sense.

Our belief systems and logic are what cause us to see a paradigm. In addition, they can prevent us from seeing a paradigm. We have all experienced changing a paradigm in school when we were learning something new. For instance, math. Something may not have made sense, but the teacher kept explaining it and at some point the light went on and we got it. "Oh, now I see it!" Sometimes a single piece of information can cause us to finally understand something. Of course, a belief system or logic based on untrue information can cause us to see what isn't. This can cause areas of our lives to not work the way we would like.

It is God's will that we learn to think with His logic so we can see what He sees, so that we can enjoy His paradigms. It is by seeing with His paradigms that His reality becomes real to us. To do that, we must learn what He knows and believes so that we can look at and ponder what He ponders. What He knows and believes is found in His Word. Pondering (Psalms 1:2 calls it meditating) is not difficult; we all do it incessantly. The issue is, what we ponder. From Moses until today, the Word of God is crystal clear about what we need to ponder. By acquiring His knowledge and increasingly believing what He believes, we will experience a new way of thinking; His logic will emerge as ours. As we increasingly reason using His logic, we will begin to see what He sees. Realities which we have never known will begin to appear real in our experience and replace things you'd rather not experience. You come to realize His reality has always been right in front of you, but because of your belief system and things you know that aren't true, it was impossible to see what He is seeing.

Though we would all like God to change our reality by zapping us, He doesn't work that way. His plan has always been for His life within us to grow us into our fullest potential, because His life is our potential. This involves a process of continual repentance and faith, which causes paradigm shifts. Of course, someone can wait for it to happen, and occasionally it does. But, God wants our active participation in growing up into Christ, and that is when life becomes a great adventure in which you know you are winning. As the unseen becomes visible, there is an exponential effect. The more we think like God the more we think like God. And, the more we see what He sees, the more we see what He sees.

Understanding things like this enables us to better cooperate with God because it gives us a better grasp on what He is seeking to accomplish within us. If I am building an airplane, I need to understand the parts and how they fit together, and I need to have some idea what it is supposed to look like when I am finished. The more I understand what I am trying to do, the better and easier time I will have doing it.

Note 3

In Habakkuk 1:13 (JEC), the prophet says, "You are of purer eyes than to look at evil, and cannot look on iniquity, so why do you look on them that deal treacherously and hold your tongue when the wicked devour the man that is more righteous than he?" Notice that within the same sentence he both accuses God of not being able to look at sin and then admits that He does.

Note 4

People often misunderstand how we get God's blessings because the Greek word *lambano* (λαμβάνω) is frequently mistranslated. In this usage, it means "to take." But, to many, it is inconceivable that anyone would take from God.

So here is a brief lesson for those unfamiliar with Greek. In the New Testament, *lambano* appears in both the active and middle voices and only twice in the passive. The active voice puts emphasis on someone or something doing something. In the case of *lambano*, it means "I take." If used in the middle voice, it says a "third party," either a person or thing, is involved in the action in such a way that you could translate it, "He hands it to me, and I take it from him." To translate the word as "receive," would mean the original language was in the middle or passive voice, which would imply something pushed on or toward you, even if ever so slightly. But God will never force anything on you, because He is Love. Since *lambano*, in Romans 5:17, is in the active voice, the action is on the side of the person getting the gift (i.e., reaching over and taking it.) In the active voice it should be rendered *take*, instead of *receive*.

The following are just a few examples:

1. John 3:11 (KJV): "Verily, verily, I say unto thee, We speak that we do know, and testify that we have seen; and ye receive not our witness." In this case, the word *receive* should be translated as *take*. Jesus offered it to them, but they chose not to reach

over and take it. (λαμβάνετε is a present active indicative of λαμβάνω)

2. John 3:27 is a splendid example. "John answered and said, A man can receive nothing (can take nothing) except it be given him from heaven" (λαμβάνειν is a present active infinitive of λαμβάνω). By the end of this book, it should be clear to you that not only is "to take" a more accurate translation, but it makes much more sense than "to receive." In fact, *take* is the only translation that makes sense because it is an active voice word.

3. Let's look at Romans 5:17: "For if by one man's offense death reigned by one; much more those the abundance of grace and of the gift of righteousness [*taking*] shall reign in life by one, Jesus Christ" (λαμβάνοντες is a present active participle of λαμβάνω). God doesn't force grace and righteousness upon you. He says it is yours for the taking.

This book is about how to take what God gives you.

Note 5

People tend to think of the word *flesh* as regarding bodies. Likewise, the word *spirit* usually refers to invisible entities, i.e. either the Holy Spirit (the Spirit of Christ), an evil spirit, or the spirit within human beings that gives them life. However, the word *spirit* has other meanings. As will be discussed later, it frequently refers to one's attitude.

Eternal refers to the quality which flows from God's nature and character. He is unchangeable Love. The quality of evil spirits is temporal, which means they have changed. They have separated themselves from God. For humans, *eternal* refers to being united to God and inseparable from Him. Things that are eternal are of the same quality as God.

During His temptations in the wilderness, Satan told Jesus he could grant Him power over everything. In Luke 4:6 (KJV), "is delivered unto me" is more accurately translated as "was given over to me."[10]

---

[10] Many believe the fact Jesus didn't correct Satan is evidence that he was speaking the *truth*. However, in John 8:44 Jesus said there is no truth in Satan (which means

The verb *papadedotai* (παραδέδοται) is the perfect passive indicative of *paradidómi* (παραδίδωμι), which means that the delivery was done and is still effective. However, because of the victory by Jesus over all darkness, Satan can no longer control those who don't believe His lies. That is why the Holy Spirit is so intent on teaching us to believe the truth. Jesus accomplished the destruction of Satan's authority, so people now have a choice. They can choose to remain blind or to see. If they want to stay blind, they will continue to be subject to Satan's deceptions and his error, not realizing they are now free. So practically speaking, they are not free, but they could be by accepting the *truth*.

The Apostle John wrote:

> Jesus added: "I came into this world to carry out God's decisions, in order that those that cannot see may see, and that those that can see may become blind." Hearing this, some of the Pharisees who were with him said: "Then are we blind too?" "If you had been blind," Jesus replied, "you would have had no sin to answer for; but as it is, you say, 'We can see'; so your sin remains."[11]

Being able to admit that we are wrong, don't know something, or don't understand is of immense importance in learning the *truth*. If we are so sure that our knowledge is *truth* that we won't thoughtfully listen to Him who is the *truth*, then what we know likely includes error, and we'll never learn otherwise.

This is a critical issue. We need to say yes to the Holy Spirit because He is the only One who can cause us to know His *truth* the way God knows it. Ask the Holy Spirit to make Himself real to you, and He will.

---

the devil is incapable of telling any type of truth). Nothing he says can be trusted. Jesus didn't respond to Satan because what he said was nonsense, and God doesn't respond to nonsense. Instead, He will address another issue. When He does that, it is worthy of attention because He is telling you what is most important at that moment. Adam couldn't give Satan his power. However, as we will discuss later, Satan didn't need it to control humankind and the creation.

[11] John 9:39-41 (TCNT Part 1)

Note 6

By rejecting His *truth*, the First Couple became blind to God's love. The following passage comes from a statement by the Apostle Paul regarding something extremely important that God has done for His human creatures. It begins by explaining why He has done it. Many theologians and Bible teachers treat this as one of Paul's prayers. However, a literal rendering of the Greek leaves no doubt to me that this is primarily a statement of doctrine explaining the absolute marvel of God's love for us. The result of this aspect of God's work in Christ is that His humans will believe and know His love, which will cause us to be as complete as God Himself.

> For this cause I bow my knees unto the Father of our Lord Jesus Christ, Of whom the whole family in heaven and earth is named. That he would grant you according to the riches of his glory, to be strengthened with might by his Spirit in the inner man, That Christ may dwell in your hearts by faith; that ye being rooted and grounded in love, May be able to comprehend with all saints what is the breadth, and length and depth, and height; And to know the love of Christ, which passeth knowledge, that ye might be filled with all the fullness of God.[12]

Paul begins by bowing his knees to God. Why? Because first, he stands in awe of why God has done what He has done. A literal translation of "from whom every family in heaven and on earth is named..." is "out of whom...." God has given every one of His human creatures His name. Our name comes *out of* God (ἔκ), and every human creature capable of putting words together uses His Family name often every day. What was the first name by which God revealed Himself to mankind? "I Am." Mankind, having failed to recognize who he is, continually says, "I am" and then attaches to that name descriptions which God never planned for His creatures. "I am ugly," "I am poor," "I am bad."

---

[12] Ephesians 3:14-19 (KJV)

Why would God give us His name? Because He created us in His image, thus identifying humans as members of the Heavenly Family. As His offspring, he could give us His ability to *be*, not become, strengthened by His Spirit in our most inward parts.

Why do we need to live in a state of *being* strengthened? Because we need the strength of God to believe, just like Jesus said He needed the Holy Spirit. Jesus, who is God, is also a complete man, but He needed the strength of the Holy Spirit to be obedient. And what was His obedience? The obedience of faith; that same obedience which Jesus commanded the Apostle Paul to preach.[13] It means to intentionally hear and then believe what God says (See Chapter Four - Obedience). What happens when we believe? Christ is snuggled down at home in our hearts and more comfortable than we are in the nicest home we could imagine. With Christ firmly established in our hearts, we are rooted and set up inside Love Himself.

Paul goes on to explain "in order that" (ἵνα) "you will have been fully able" (ἐξισχύσητε, an aorist active subjunctive) "to have seized a tight hold on and comprehend" …the love of Christ "in order that" you will be filled with all the fullness of God. (For an explanation of my treatment of the subjunctive mood, see Chapter 14 Endnote #4.) This is why God has named man out of Himself.[14] Man must be of the same quality of being as God for mankind's union with Christ to be possible. When you know Love Himself is snuggled down inside you, you will have understanding that passes your ability to explain what you know. It is a knowing that is so deep and personal that the individual with that knowledge appears as the image of what they know, which is the image of God on Earth.

---

[13] cf. Romans 16:26

[14] Ephesians 3:15. Many scholars render the Greek phrase "ἐξ οὗ" as "Of whom" or "From whom." However, a literal translation of ἐξ is "Out of." When translated thus, the phrase tells us that God has named us out of Himself. He has given us His Family name.

Note 7

We have so many wrong ideas about God and ourselves. When those incorrect ideas fill the minds of people, it affects how they view what God says. My first venture into Koine Greek was at the University of Florida School of Religion. My professor was kind of down on God, but he loved reading the New Testament in its original language. He was an expert in Sanskrit, so his grasp of Ancient Greek was different from many modern Bible scholars. He understood words. I remember him cautioning our class, "The key to understanding Koine Greek is the prepositions. Pay close attention, and beware of how others translate them." At the time, I didn't know enough to understand, but I never forgot it. His comment is with me every time I open the Greek text. I will be forever grateful for that professor.

For instance, consider Romans 5:1: "Therefore being justified by faith, we have peace with God through our Lord Jesus Christ." What a beautiful *truth*! The trouble is that this translation misses the wonder of what the writer was saying. The problem is the preposition *with*. The word in the original language is pros (πρὸς), which, according to Liddell and Scott, Thayer, Dana and Mantley, and others should be translated as "toward." So, substitute *toward* in the place of *with*. "Therefore being justified by faith, we have peace *toward* God through our Lord Jesus Christ."

Paul wasn't suggesting that there has been a problem from God's side and now He has been appeased. Paul knew the problem was from the human side. People project their feelings about themselves onto God, and therefore see a God who thinks about them, and others, the way they do. If someone assumes that God thinks like he does, then they are likely to suspect, at the least, that God is antagonistic toward them. When someone is against us, we tend to resist and fight back. To expand on what Paul was saying in this passage from Romans: "Look folks, God doesn't have a problem with you so you can stop acting like he does. You may not have yet realized it, but since you are one with Christ Jesus and He has peace toward God, so do you. Accept the *truth* and stop fighting your imaginary war. You are at peace with God. Stop listening to lies about God and yourselves."

Paul was saying that Christ—as mankind—brought humans back to a face-to-face (toward) relationship with God. He so wanted restored fellowship with us that He sent His Only Begotten Son to bear His beloved human creatures into death and out through resurrection into His loving arms. Now in union with Christ, mankind is where God has always wanted us.

We are His beloved, yet we rejected God. Mankind hated God. Paul is telling us that the war is over. We may not have yet realized it but, being in Christ, we now have peace toward God. "Lay down your weapons. God is your friend! You no longer have to defend yourself from God."

2
Being Changed

This book is not going to teach you *how* to improve yourself. Rather, it is going to teach you how to *be* changed by the Gospel, the really good news about Jesus Christ, without the frustration and disappointment which so often accompanies Christian teachings. The word *be* used so often in the New Testament is not a verb of action but of *be*ing. A believer is not someone who is *becoming*, but rather someone who *is*. Unfortunately, *be* is more frequently understood as *to become*, rather than simply *being*.

In the English language, words can have many meanings. Look in any dictionary, and you will see words with their various meanings numbered one, two, three, and so forth. This is also true in the original Greek. The New Testament is full of instances where interpreters haven't understood what the writer was saying, so they picked definitions that made the most sense to them but not necessarily the one that was intended by the original authors. To understand what an author was saying in a passage, we must understand the meanings of his words. Thus, we'll tiptoe into that subject in the following section.

As your understanding grows, you will see that the Bible is not calling you to change yourself, but to let God change you from the inside out. This requires a radical untwisting of our understanding because what we've been taught has been—at the very least—slightly wrong. If you lifted off from the Kennedy Space Center heading for the moon and were off course by a smidgen, you would miss it. Paul's reference to "reaching for the high calling of God in Christ Jesus" was not pointing to a goal that might be achieved in the future but one that is attainable in this life. "I press toward the mark for the prize of the high calling of God in Christ Jesus."[1] But if we're going the wrong direction or we're off by even a little bit, we may suffer things we didn't have to suffer. Even if we're off course, God has promised to get us to our goal; but this world is rough enough all by itself. Why add unnecessary problems?

Using the Right Meanings

As you relax in this message, you will be joining us on a journey my family and I have been on for many years. The parts of this trip are all interrelated. Each thing we have learned has built on something we had learned previously. Over and over, God has retaught us what we thought we already knew but in a way that made it seem brand new. God's Word is fresh and alive and always in the present, even when talking about the past. Whatever He shows you is not for another time. The power in His *truth* is always for the moment you get it and He keeps that energy alive for all future moments, even though you may not feel it. If it is true now, it is true forever.

Much of this book is written in the first-person perspective (I) because it is about my personal experience and understanding (James E. Campbell, Jr.). But my family has lived it with me and could, thus, help me write it and confirm what I share with you.

You and I know that the key to intimate fellowship with God is faith, but how many definitions of faith have you heard? "Faith is trust," some say. "Faith is speaking the Word," cry others. "Faith is doing God's Word," said some seminary student. "Faith is a feeling," says someone who doesn't know what he's talking about. The book of Hebrews says: "faith is the substance of things hoped for, the evidence of things not seen."[2] Though each of these may describe some aspect of faith, none of them define it.

From a practical standpoint, a definition should be able to replace a word in a sentence and the sentence still have the same meaning.

---

[1] Philippians 3:14 (KJV)

[2] Hebrews 11:1 (KJV)

So, let's look at an example. Mary has a little lamb. According to Merriam-Webster.com, the word *has* means "to hold or maintain as a possession."[3] Thus, we should be able to substitute that definition for the word *has* and the sentence make the same or better sense. Mary *holds or maintains as a possession* a little lamb. You can use the word *has* or its definition in a sentence and both will make sense and have the same meaning. Let's try using some of the definitions of faith above and see what happens. I'm going to use a phrase from the King James Version of Hebrews 11:6 to illustrate: "But without faith it is impossible to please him." If we define faith as "doing God's Word," then that verse could be read, "Without [doing God's Word] it is impossible to please him." If that is true, it leaves us with an empty feeling. If faith is dependent on doing God's Word and I fail to do it, how do I ever have faith? Most believers will admit that their attempts to do His Word are hit-and-miss at best.

Let's try a more commonplace definition by using Hebrews 11:1. "But, without [the substance of things hoped for and the evidence of things not seen] it is impossible to please God." I don't know about you, but that makes absolutely no sense to me. Yet, we know that Hebrews 11:1 is true. So how come that definition of faith can't replace the word faith in Hebrews 11:6 and still make sense? Because, Hebrews 11:1 is a description of the results of faith, not its definition.

Let's make this simple. Let's see what the Greeks meant when they used the word *pistis* (πίστις), which means "faith." Review of a Greek-English lexicon—a dictionary that gives an English definition for a Greek word—defines faith as follows: Pistis: Trust, Belief, and Faith. As you will recognize throughout this book, *belief* is the best definition if you want to understand God's intent. So, I translate Hebrews 11:6 as: "Without belief it is impossible to please God." But, of course, it can't mean just *any* belief. God would never say that believing lies pleases Him. So, what does God want us to believe?

Obviously, what He says, His Word, His *truth*, to the exclusion of anything that is not *truth* (Chapter Two Endnotes #1). So, the most

---

[3] By permission. From *Merriam-Webster's Collegiate® Dictionary, Eleventh Edition* ©2012 by Merriam-Webster, Incorporated (www.Merriam-Webster.com).

accurate translation would be: "Without believing God's *truth*, it is impossible to please Him." Much more on this as we proceed.

At this point, I think it is important to explain that every person has a belief system and no two are the same. Your beliefs not only include what you believe about God but everything else as well. For instance, you drive your car someplace because you believe you will get there safely. If you didn't, you wouldn't go, but we don't ever think about these types of beliefs. They just automatically govern our lives. You sit in a chair because you believe it will support you. If you thought otherwise, you would sit somewhere else. These belief patterns were developed long ago so you probably never think about them now.

Grace is another important word. We know that intimacy with God requires His grace, but most have no idea what it is and how it works. "It sounds good, even fantastic, but what does it mean in my life?" you may be asking. For some, it means everything that God does for us. That's not a bad understanding, but there is so much more to it. A proper understanding will change your life. A misunderstanding of grace will make many passages in the New Testament harder to understand. So briefly, grace is God's love in action. It is His favor in every situation and area of our lives. Grace is the constant, continual gift by God of Himself and all that He is and has. It is perfect kindness and generosity. It is the almighty power of God working in you to cause you to be triumphant in life. And, it is always unconditional on His part. We are the ones that have placed conditions on His favor, not Him. This is the basis of the word *awesome*. His grace, His love is so magnificent in the lives of those who take it that they stand in awe—an overwhelming speechlessness that can only be experienced, never described (Chapter Two Endnotes #2).

Getting Unstuck

People everywhere believe God's Word is true and yearn to know and experience His reality but don't know how. If only they could touch His heart and have Him reach out and hold them in His arms, then they believe they would find peace. Many would do or give anything to draw closer to God as believers in the Early Church did, yet nothing they do gives what they long for: the experience of lasting fellowship with Him. Nothing they do seems to result in the change of life which the scriptures promise. Many wonder what they must do to be able to please God.

Fortunately, God understands why so many fail in their pursuit of His will. He understands why they are tied in knots, distressed, angry, hateful, greedy, lustful, unkind, or even worse, and does not blame them. Rather, the Father of all His human children joyously looks forward to teaching them how to live like Him. In fact, He gave us His Word not to keep us in the dark, but so we could know and understand Him. We are the ones that have made it difficult, not Him. Jesus came to save us, not condemn us.

I spoke to a man whose life has been transformed by simply believing God's *truth*. He told me that the night before God set him free from a terrible problem, he had cried out, "I give up. I have done everything I can to change and haven't. If You don't do something, I am destined to remain the same." He was obviously at the point of despair. He had no idea God would answer so quickly or that the answer would be so simple.

You have probably heard it said that God has done all the work. "It is finished."[4] But, your reality seems far from it. The *truth* is that God did change your reality. Now He wants to make it real to you. You already know how to enjoy that new reality, but you just don't yet trust what you know. As your faith grows, you are going to find greater peace, joy, and fulfillment than you have ever known. Faith is the only key to understanding God's heart and it is nothing other than believing His *truth*. From Genesis to Revelation the entire Bible is a cry from the heart of God to believe Him. We speak because we want people to believe what we say. So, too, with God. He never utters vain, empty words. All His words have a purpose. First and foremost, He wants us to believe Him. Without believing what He says, we can never live like He wants us to live. The heart of God yearns for humankind to trust

---

[4] John 19:30 (KJV)

Him. But, you can only trust when you believe. The trouble is that our experiences are often more real to us than God's *truth* so sometimes we trust them more than God.

For years, I went to church and did everything that would bring me closer to God. I prayed, fasted, studied the Bible, witnessed, tithed, gave over and above offerings, and on and on. Aside from an occasional emotional/spiritual experience, the worry-free trust in God for which I longed eluded me. The harder I tried, the more I failed, and the further from God I felt. Today my fellowship with God continues to provide more and more confidence in Him. Now when I visit churches and talk with Christians everywhere, my heart aches. So many want more but have no idea how to obtain it. They go to church regularly, pray, and read their Bibles, yet seem no closer to God than when they started. Some have even despaired, convinced that going to church is a waste of time. Even though I received Christ in my late teens, I suffered terrible emotional problems until much later in life. For years, depression and anxiety were constant companions. I craved acceptance; I needed a friend. Those days are now long gone.

One of God's greatest desires is for His children to mature in Christ. To the Apostle Paul, glory was synonymous with Christ living His life in the believer. "To whom God would make known what is the riches of the glory of this mystery among the Gentiles; which is Christ in you, the hope of glory."[5] In Ephesians, the Apostle wrote that God has given apostles, prophets, evangelists, pastors, and teachers to the Church:[6] "Till we all come in the unity of the faith (believing His *truth*), and of the knowledge of the Son of God, unto a perfect man, unto the measure of the stature of the fullness of Christ."[7] This verse says we will come to the place of believing His *truth* the way He believes it instead of our religious ideas and experiences, and we will know what He knows the way He knows it, and not *know* anything in a way He doesn't know

---

[5] Colossians 1:27 (KJV)

[6] The church or house of God does not refer to the building in which believers meet but to the believers themselves. The believers are the church. The church is wherever believers are, not a building where they meet.

[7] Ephesians 4:13 (KJV)

it. Thus, we will have grown into a mature representation of Christ—a whole man or woman (Chapter Two Endnotes #3).

It sounds like Paul was talking about a new reality. Two thousand years after Christ, the church appears nowhere near *the stature of the fullness of Christ*. Why? Because what God accomplished in Paul and his peers was only the beginning. Unfortunately, since the First Century, the Church has gone backward; but this condition is only temporary.

Today, many define obedience as doing what the Bible says. "If you are serious about pleasing God, then find out what he wants to be done and do it. Discover your purpose and pursue it," many churches claim. "If you are serious about being free from sin, then recommit your life and try harder," shout some preachers, as though man and the power of his will can mimic the mind and actions of God. But, is this the *truth*? After centuries of trying to discover and do His will, are we yet ready to admit we have failed? If the modern Church is doing God's will, where are the love and miracles Jesus promised? In Mark 16:17, Jesus said, "These signs shall follow them that believe the *truth*." Are those signs following you? Maybe it's time to examine what you believe.

To think that you will find your purpose by what you do (including for God), means you are misunderstanding the will of God and the marvelous wonder of His plan for your life. In the First Century, despite the persecution of the Church by the Roman government, people were attracted to the Gospel in droves. But today, many run from its mere mention turned off by all the rules and lack of love from those who claim Jesus as Lord. So, what changed? People everywhere know there is more but have no idea how to experience the abundant life about which Jesus spoke.

I know this: His plan is inextricably tied to knowing the *truth*. Unfortunately, to many, it is more important to know *about* the *truth* than to believe it. They're more concerned with following the rules of their religion and arguing about doctrine than knowing what union with Christ means.

The Bible distinguishes two types of truth: natural truth and God's *truth*. Natural truths are things like the sky is blue, things fall because of gravity, we are eating dinner at the kitchen table, I feel good, I feel lousy, my body is sick, my body is healthy, etc. Natural truths describe things as they appear. Many believe that how something appears is its reality; how things look is how they will be. But God's *truth* is the reality behind everything we see—whether natural truth or lies. God's *truth* is: God is Love, God loves you. God wants you to know Him as He knows you. If my body feels sick, God's *truth* says I'm healed. My finances show that I am poor, but God's *truth* says I am rich. It feels like God has abandoned me, but He said He would never leave me to be mauled by my problems. Bottom line: He is with me no matter what it looks or feels like to me. God's *truth* is true, no matter what my circumstances appear to be.

The result of obedience (submitting to hearing) is to treasure God's *truth* in the face of feelings or emotions that say something else is true. For instance, you feel alone yet God says He is with you and in you. When you believe God, you will refuse to agree with thoughts that say He has left you. The Gospel calls people to believe, that is, to treasure God's words. When you treasure something, you will not let go of it. It is the Holy Spirit's job to actualize that faith so that its reality becomes real to each of us.

Being

Contrary to popular opinion, God does not help those who help themselves and change is not a result of self-discipline or behavior modification. Go ahead and change your behavior. It can be a good thing, but you'll still be the same person. However, when you know and believe you are a new person, it will be reflected in an automatic change in your behavior. You say you have been born again and know you are a new creature in Christ, then sit back and relax. God loves to teach you how to let Him live His good life through you, instead of you burning out while trying to live like you think He wants.

The New Testament speaks of change in terms of *being* transformed: "but *be* ye transformed."[8] The Greek word for *be transformed* is in the

---

[8] Romans 12:2 (KJV)

passive voice meaning it is something that happens to you. It is also in the imperative mood, which doesn't mean God is requiring us to figure out how to change but is a revelation to us that God has commanded our inner selves to *be* changed (Chapter Two Endnotes #4).

I don't believe that Christians have—at least in recent times—thought in these terms but have accepted a harsh interpretation of the Gospel, which often leaves mankind subject to a despotic ruler version of God who can never be understood or satisfied and before whom we must ultimately cringe in fear as we await His ultimate and final judgment. The result of the *be transformed* command was instantaneous and exactly what God wanted. But for it to appear as our conscious reality requires a process that was established by God within each human and that controls our lives. However, it isn't a process but a resting into *truth*, which is the idea that instead of straining or working you rest and relax into the *truth* because God is the one doing the work. Instead of human *doings*, we discover that we are human *beings*.

For learning, we are beginning the discussion as though a process is involved. However, this process is not a formula that we can manipulate. It is God working in us. Our "job" is to say, "Amen, so be it." As it says in Hebrews 12:2, Jesus is both the author and finisher of [the process that produces] our faith. It is all a gift, a free present, from Him. It is time that we begin saying yes to that gift. "Yes, He has given it to me." The change God offers is produced by the Holy Spirit inside the believer. We learn to rest in Him and His love for us. In turn, He lives His life in and through us in a way that is unique to each one of us, thus manifesting the life of Christ in our mortal flesh. It is what the Apostle Paul meant when he said: "For we which live are always delivered unto death for Jesus's sake, that the life also of Jesus might be made manifest in our mortal flesh."[9]

Jesus is 100 percent God and 100 percent human. While walking the Earth, He was utterly dependent on His Father and the Holy Spirit

---

[9] 2 Corinthians 4:11 (KJV) The death to which Paul is referring is not physical but the experiences in which a believer is pushed to the limit by circumstances screaming that God's *truth* is a lie. Through these, a believer, again and again, discovers the utter weakness of flesh (σάρξ) and complete dependence on God.

for everything. Jesus planned on us living like Him, by the Life of God in us through the Spirit. "He that believeth on me, the works that I do shall he do also; and greater works than these shall he do; because I go unto my Father"[10] (Chapter Two Endnotes #5). God's plan for bringing this to pass is not difficult. It is simply a function of Christ *in* us. The question is, how do we get out of the way and allow the Christ in us to *be* Who He is?

Many years ago, I was headed east on Interstate 44 in Tulsa, Oklahoma, about to exit when I sensed God speaking to me. He said, "I am the only One who can live My life, and that includes living it in you."

If we want to see the will of God done in our lives, we must allow Him to do it according to His plan. Though God will use our self-willed determination to benefit others, his greatest blessings inside us only occur by spirit. The works that are done using the faith of Jesus Christ within us are the ones that please God. Though we play a part in the work, God does not intend for us to struggle. If you find the Christian life frustrating, you have learned something about God's will that is not true. His plan has always been to live His life inside you, not because of your willpower, but His grace, which trains us to believe what He says. His grace gives us His life to live. As we grow in faith, His life becomes increasingly evident in us.

> But speaking the truth in love, may grow up into him in all things, which is the head, even Christ.[11]

> Brothers, it is our duty to be always thanking God about you. This is but right, considering the wonderful growth of your faith, and because, without exception, your love for one another is continually increasing.[12]

---

[10] John 14:12 (KJV)

[11] Ephesians 4:15 (KJV)

[12] 2 Thessalonians 1:3 (TCNT Testament Part 2)

In these and many other verses, Paul is pointing out the relationship between the *truth* and growing up in Christ. Paul was speaking about how he had grown up in Christ when he said:

> But by the grace of God, I am what I am, and His grace toward me has not been without results. I have actually done more work than all of the others, although strictly it was not I who did it, but God's grace which was with me.[13]

God's grace is love at work. That work is often done through one person toward others. In this verse, Paul was speaking of God working through him and, just as importantly, by him. Though his mind and body were doing the physical work, it was God empowering and living His grace within Paul. Paul was cooperating with God as He lived His life in his body. This is possible only through union with Christ, which is referred to in the New Testament by the phrase "in Christ." This will become clearer as you understand how your heart works.[14]

When living by faith, the character of Christ becomes evident in both our public and private lives. This is good, acceptable, and pleasing to God.

In the next chapters, I use the term *misbelieve*, which means believing something that is not true. The scriptures refer to *misbelief* as "unbelief," which doesn't mean believing nothing, but believing the wrong thing. In contrast to *belief*, which means believing God's *truth*, *unbelief* means believing something that is not God's *truth*.

Jesus said knowing the *truth* will set you free. But free from what? From everything that hinders your ability to enjoy Him and His ability to live through you. God wants us to grow up *into* Christ. Why? Because it is *within* that union in which we find *everything* that the world—and we—need. The world does not need our dedication, determination, and willpower for Jesus; it *needs* Jesus! He wants to give

---

[13] 1 Corinthians 15:10. (Taken from Norlie, Olaf M., Norlie's Simplified New Testament c. 1961)

[14] See Chapter Four sections "The Process" and "Believe What God Believes."

Himself to it through His Body. Only He knows how to live His life in each person.

This is what Paul was referring to when he prayed in Ephesians "that you may know Who is the expectation of His calling."[15] The world and the church are all caught up in trying to discover the how's and what's of life. That's why people seem always to think that Paul was referring to "what is the hope of His calling, what are the riches…what is the exceeding greatness" (Chapter Two Endnotes #6). But to Paul, the issue was not *what*, but *who*. And Who is that expectation? Christ.[16]

God has called us to expect remarkable things—things that will fill us with awe. He does not want us to hope as in *wishful thinking*. He wants us to expect what God expects, to the point of boasting about it.[17] The end of that expectation includes: "And, [God] hath put all things under his feet, and gave him to be the head over all things to the church which is his body, the fulness of him that filleth all in all."[18]

Paul was describing a victorious church and believers who are not weak and helpless. Jesus believes that the Body of Christ (believers) are united with Him in His victory over darkness. With joy, He anticipates our realization of who we are so that we will act like it. God has already made you fit to be a partaker "of the inheritance of the saints in light."[19] He has also written inside your heart the knowledge you need. "'This is the Covenant that I will make with the People of Israel after those days,' says the Lord. 'I will impress my laws on their minds, and will inscribe them on their hearts.'"[20]

The *truth* is that we have missed the simplicity of the Gospel. God intends for us to enjoy the same freedom Jesus had and now has. Don't let your desire for something complex cause you to miss what God has already finished, which is the answer to your needs. God wants you to

---

[15] Ephesians 1:18 (JEC)

[16] Colossians 1:27

[17] See explanation of Romans 5:2 in Chapter Two section, "Using the Right Meanings."

[18] Ephesians 1:22-23 (KJV)

[19] Colossians 1:12 (KJV)

[20] Hebrews 8:10 (TCNT Part 2)

enjoy Jesus's life in you. It doesn't require struggle on your part, only cooperation. You are already learning how easy it is to cooperate with God so that He can work in your life, so you experience the love, joy, peace, and patience—the absolute victory—which are characteristics of Christ's life. It can often take time for our realization to catch up with our reality, but now you are learning about a whole new life, which is already yours and in you. This takes time, but God is not in a hurry. No one knows what this new life looks like in them until God personally shows you. Only God can show you, and He delights to watch you discover the new creature He has made you. This is a radical change of thinking, and "He who began a good work in you will continue it until the day of Jesus Christ." [21]

God has not made His way mysterious, man has. The rebellion in the garden caused a tragic corruption of God's logic and image in man. It has left many wondering who they are and what is their purpose in life. Those questions are often answered by feelings and emotions that become our truth, rather than God's *truth* being our *truth*. In today's world, feelings have become truer than God's *truth*, especially since the reality, which Adam and Eve enjoyed in the beginning, is no longer visible to the natural eye. Most people judge their reality by what they see. Paul pointed us in a different direction: "And all of us, with unveiled faces, seeing the glory of the Lord as though reflected in a mirror, are being transformed into the same image from one degree of glory to another; for this comes from the Lord, the Spirit."[22] Paul wrote about discovering who we are by looking at Jesus, rather than what we see with our natural eyes. Thus, the longer you look at who Jesus is, the more His reality appears in your experience. You don't have to try to *do* or *be*. As you look at Him, your self increasingly realizes who you are and begins acting like who you are…you are Christ in you. No effort required. Christ lives in you. He knows how to be Himself in you.

History proves that when people see and hear something enough, it becomes their reality. As you let the Holy Spirit fill your imagination with the reality of who you are in Christ, He will provide the power to be

---

[21] Philippians 1:6 (TCNT Part 2)

[22] 2 Corinthians 3:18 (NRSV)

who you are. God says we *can* know Him. He yearns for us to understand Him. But we get His understanding only by believing what He says. That may mean no longer believing what someone else has told you about God. If we don't believe Him, there is no way we can understand Him. Once we understand God, then we know that because He loves us, He has already done and given us everything we need for abundant life and godliness (to be like God). "According as his divine power hath given unto us all things that pertain unto life and godliness."[23] Understanding will help you enjoy God's life—a life free from condemnation, wrong behavior, and emotions; a life free from bad habits, free from bondages. He is a better Lord than anyone else could ever be—including you—because He is Love and loves you with complete care and consideration. He loves you far more than any other human can.

This is not about struggling to change. It is about enjoying the rest spoken of in Chapters Three and Four of Hebrews, a rest in which you see and experience what God has done for you. It is in His rest where God becomes everything you need. Your behavior, thoughts, and desires become a reflection of His heart.

* * *

Chapter Two Endnotes

Note 1

When God says believe, he doesn't necessarily mean to believe what the politicians say or that weird guy at work or even your pastor. The Scriptures say that Jesus is the Word of God and that He is the *truth*. God means for you to believe Him. "At the Beginning the Word already was: The Word was with God; And the Word was God."[24] "Jesus saith unto him, I am the way, the truth, and the life: no man cometh unto the Father, but by me."[25]

---

[23] 2 Peter 1:3 (KJV)
[24] John 1:1 (TCNT Part 1)
[25] John 14:6 (KJV)

The *truth* is what God said, how He said it, and how He meant it. The *truth* is not relative; it is absolute.

To believe means to be treasuring the *truth* God has shown you. This means you have decided it is very important to you. And what do you do with treasure? You keep your eye on it and protect it. You don't want anyone to steal it from you. Satan and the world want to steal it from you. The attitude of a believer is, "No one is going to take this away from me."

Note 2

My interpretation of Romans 5:2 is probably very different from any you have ever read, but it so clearly elucidates where grace is heading that I want you to know it before we go any further. The King James Version translates Romans 5:2 as follows: "By whom also we have access by faith into this grace wherein we stand, and rejoice in hope of the glory of God." Can you sink your teeth into that? I can't. The King James Version just makes this sound like wishful thinking, whereas a more literal interpretation gives me reason to shout for joy! I see the original language saying something very different.

> By means of Jesus we had, by His belief, the bringing up to and then into [as if He gently nudged us into] this favor within which we stand immersed and boast upon our expectation of the splendor, the character, nature, and total prosperity of God in our lives.[26]

Paul didn't just mean that we are happy about something we wish for in the future. He meant that we are so confident of the manifestation of God's life in us that we boast about it.

---

[26] The following provides a clarification of how I arrived at this interpretation. Words or phrases in brackets [ ] are my interpretation of what Paul was implying in the Greek text. "By means of whom we had by [Jesus's] belief the bringing [up] to [and then into, as if He nudged us into it] this favor within which we stand [immersed] and boast upon [our] expectation of the splendor [that is, the character, nature, and abundance] of God [in our lives]." (JEC)

Note 3

Believers are the Church. The brick and mortar building you show up to on Sunday isn't. But what makes the Church different from the world? The people of the Church both believe in Jesus and believe what he believes. "…within faith I live, that of the Son of God," said the Apostle Paul.[27] He wasn't talking about believing *in* Jesus, he was talking about having the same beliefs *as* Jesus. We live what we believe, so if we have the beliefs *of* Jesus, we'll live like Jesus.

We can take the point even further than the beliefs of Jesus. Paul also talked about "the knowledge *of* the Son of God."[28] You could understand this as knowing *about* the Son of God, but Paul was referring to living from the same knowledge of *truth* as Jesus had. That is, knowing the same things that Jesus knew.

It is unfortunate that believers know so much that God doesn't know. By that I mean, there are many things Christians are sure are true that aren't. I'm not talking just about doctrine. This applies to all of us and our entire systems of beliefs. Some of our beliefs are wrong. If not, God wouldn't have needed to give us the Scriptures. The trouble is that we don't intentionally know something wrongly. It may be that someone taught it to us or it is a conclusion we arrived at because of an experience we had. We didn't know any better. Nevertheless, we believe something as true when it is not the *truth*. The problem is that we don't know what we know that isn't true. From another perspective, we don't always know what we know. If we learn that something isn't true, we will very quickly make the proper adjustments so that what we knew as true—which was false—is no longer a part of our body of knowledge. However, if something we believe that is true is false, there is no way for us ever to know differently unless the Holy Spirit shows us. He is the Spirit of *truth* and that is His job. "I will ask the Father, and he will give you another Helper, to be with you into the age—[I mean] the Spirit of the *truth*."[29] If we reject His presence in our lives, how can

---

[27] Galatians 2:20 (JEC)
[28] Ephesians 4:13 (KJV)
[29] John 14:16,17 (KJV)

we *take* His help. *The lie*, which the first couple believed, remains in control of our lives because we continue to trust it.

God is *truth*. He knows about all the wrong and false knowledge we have accumulated. He knows it is incorrect. His knowledge of our false knowledge does not change God's being; rather, He uses His knowing about our fake knowledge to lead us into knowing His *truth*. That often involves convincing us that what we think is *the truth* isn't. Heaven rejoices every time a person who believes error changes their mind and decides to believe the *truth* instead. Jesus not only talks about people being born again but he also refers to people who have been believing a lie but have changed their minds to believe the *truth*. "Just so, I tell you, there is joy in the presence of the angels of God over one sinner who repents."[30]

The Scriptures use the word *repent* or *repentance* in numerous ways, making it clear that it is about much more than eternal salvation. Consider St. Paul's use of the word in 2 Corinthians 7:10 in which he was writing to believers: "For godly sorrow worketh repentance to salvation not to be repented of." He was addressing believers. To be a believer, you must have already repented unto salvation. Obviously, this use of repentance was referring to something else. In this case, the apostle was talking about a change of mind regarding other beliefs.

Note 4

In Greek, the imperative mood is usually a command; but when it is in the passive voice, it is commanding it to *be* in you. How? By the power of the Holy Spirit. Your response to God is, "If you command it, then it is so (in my life)," or you could just say, "Amen." This is real faith, and it's simple. God has never expected or required you to figure out how to live His life. His promise has always been that He will live it in you by the ability of the Holy Spirit. So, when He commands you to let something happen to you, you only say Amen and rest in the confidence that it has been done as God commanded. That is the gist of what happened to Abraham and was explained by St. Paul in Galatians 3:14:

---

[30] Luke 15:4-7 (NRSV)

"That the blessing of Abraham might come on the Gentiles through Jesus Christ; that we might receive the promise of the Spirit through faith (believing the *truth*)."

Think back to Genesis, to God's very first recorded command. A literal rendering of that command was, "Light be!" And, what happened? Light was. God's commands to us are not orders we are to carry out, but Love telling our very selves to *be* what the Word said. No word from God is void of the power necessary to bring what it says to pass, just like His command for light to *be* contained the power to cause light to appear. So, what is our response to His commands? "Amen, it is so." So, when we agree with what God has said, is it possible that it could remain unfulfilled? Was it possible for light to refuse to appear? No! So, when we don't see a command's immediate fulfillment, is it possible something is still happening but we just can't see it yet? Of course.

Because God is Love, He will not force His will on His beloved creatures. Rather, He issues commands and waits for our agreement, our *Amen*. It is very much like when the angel told the Virgin Mary that she would bear the Son of God. Mary would not have been impregnated against her will. Rather, He waited for her to say her Amen: "Be it unto me according to thy word."[31]

Note 5

God does not save some so that they can just get along in misery until they go to Heaven. Salvation is union with Christ, union with His victory, His life. Since we have been authorized to declare we are members of God's family, "He gave them authority to be children of God," we are now empowered by the Holy Spirit as we live on this Earth. Not an empowering of our flesh to do what Jesus would do, but an empowering to believe the *truth* and cooperate with the Holy Spirit. In fact, there is one part of the apostle's statement in Ephesians 3:14-19 where he says that it is the Spirit that provides the strength to believe, which enables Jesus to be at home in our hearts. "That He will give you, by means of His Spirit, the ability to be strengthened by your faith, so that Christ can

---

[31] Luke 1:38 (KJV)

snuggle down in your heart to live."[32] The word *give* in this passage is in the subjective mood, which is defined by most scholars as the mood of probability rather than an assertion or statement of possibility. I call it the mood of intention. It was clearly God's intent to do it; thus, translations using the words *would, might,* or *may* are not forceful enough. Thus, I prefer to render it as *will give*.

Note 6

In Ephesians 1:18 and 9, τίς can be rendered who, which, or what. Paul's life was not about a *what* but a *who*—Christ Himself. Up to this point in this chapter, Paul has been exploding with joy and wonder as he describes what God has done for us in Christ. He momentarily levels off. Then in verse sixteen, he explodes in another crescendo of awe as he explains his thanks to God and prayer that the believers will realize who Christ is in them and who they are in Christ. The first *what* in verse eighteen is followed by the word *is* (ἐστιν). The next two *what's* are not followed by the word *is*, but many scholars assume that is what Paul meant, so they insert *is*. I think they are right. However, Paul is not talking about a *what*, but *who*. His thoughts are so big that if the Greeks had used punctuation, Paul would have followed with ellipses (...)—if the Greeks had them. It is as though the Apostle has momentarily run out of words as He is overwhelmed with thoughts about who has redeemed mankind. It does not do Paul justice to say he introduced a dramatic pause, but I don't know how to make my point better than to suggest this. Christians need to drop *what* and look at w*ho*. If you need a what, then look at Jesus. You'll discover you don't need anything else.

---

[32] Ephesians 3:16-17 (JEC paraphrase)

3
We Think Therefore We Do

Your feelings and actions are your responsibility because they are a result of what you think. As our thinking becomes consistent with God's *truth*, we live increasingly happy and productive lives, despite trying circumstances.

If Jesus were in your shoes, He would always think and respond correctly. Would you like to do the same? Since you have the mind of Christ, you can; not by trying harder, but by simply thinking Jesus's thoughts.

Here's a Story

I was heading west on Alligator Alley toward Naples, Florida, at sundown. The sun in my eyes was blinding. As it disappeared over the horizon, the sky became unusually dark. I found it tough to see. The lights on the cars coming toward me were very dim, and though my lights were on, they seemed to make little, if any, difference. I was having great difficulty seeing the road and became scared. Wondering what was happening, I suddenly knew what I needed to do. I reached up and took off my sunglasses.

Have you ever scoured your house in frustration looking for something that turned out to be right in front of your face? Ever spent ten minutes looking for a pencil you just had in your hand only to find it stuck behind your ear? How about looking for your glasses only to find them on your head? In each of these cases, what was the problem? What you were thinking: *My glasses must be someplace else.* Or like me, forgetting that I was wearing extra dark, mirrored sunglasses and thus was looking at life through those lenses. I had no idea something was distorting my vision. I got all worked up because I didn't realize that something was clouding my perspective.

Neither God nor this book is going to teach you something new. All the knowledge you need to live in the fullness of God was in your heart the moment you were saved.[1] And how were you saved? By believing what Jesus believes—the faith *of* Jesus Christ, which is the same faith he has and the same thing he believes.[2] So why doesn't what is written in your heart seem to show up in your life? Why, despite your desire to see the power of God in you, don't you? Why do you feel the same fear, anxiety, or depression, that are oppressing the rest of the world? Because you are fixing your attention on the same things the world is looking at, things which the Apostle Paul said are temporary.

It is time to begin looking at things that are eternal, which cannot be seen with natural vision. Eternal things never change; you can count on them. By continuing to look at the eternal, you are looking in the glass (mirror) spoken of in James 1:23-25. When you finally begin to recognize yourself, you won't forget what you see and will automatically do what Jesus would do. You *can* understand God's logic and cooperate with Him. When you do, you discover He has not placed a burden on you but is carrying the entire burden and just wants your company.

God's Will Is Simple

The will of God is something often talked about in churches and from the pulpit. Preachers and teachers use thousands of words to explain the will of God and how to find it. Unfortunately, thousands of words are spoken yet no answers given. Believers try everything. We pray, meditate, and try to strike bargains with God, yet the answers never seem to come. God's will is simple. A man named Malcolm Smith said it best: "If God is Love, then what is the will of Love? The pleasure of the beloved." So, what is the pleasure of the beloved (the beloved are you and me)? Health, happiness, joy, peace, comfort, unimaginable blessings, and, above all, a relationship. Forget about the specific will

---

[1] Hebrews 8:10
[2] Romans 3:22, Galatians 2:16 (KJV)

of God in your life. Does God want me to take this job? Does God desire me to buy this car? Does God expect me to go on this mission trip?

As your fellowship with Him grows and you learn His *truth*, you won't have to ask these questions. Whatever you do will be His will because He'll be doing it in you and with you. You and Christ are one person. You are one spirit with the Lord. "But he that is joined unto the Lord is one spirit."[3] How amazing, yet without the Holy Spirit, our minds cannot grasp it. God desires for us to experience the simplicity of knowing Him and doing His will. He is not complicated. When we think like children, we find Him easy.

God has put life-changing spiritual tools inside you. Though you may not realize it, as you are reading this, He is teaching you how to use them, and you'll be surprised how simple it is. Some will say, "This is too simple, how could I have missed it?" The *truth* is that life is complicated only because we make it so. Did you know the answers to many of your concerns are right in front of you? God has already put them there. Answers are often hard to find because we are expecting something else.

What would have happened if I had continued driving toward Naples and not realized that the source of my Twilight Zone experience was right in front of my face? I could have had an accident because, since I could not see and was so preoccupied with the problem, I was not concentrating on what was most important—my driving. Why do we expect answers to be hard and complicated to get? I wondered if I was losing my sight. What would I do if I was going blind? I was tired and a little scared. Yet the answer was so simple, and that simple answer fixed my problem and dispelled the fears that went with it.

---

[3] 1 Corinthians 6:17 (KJV)

Our Perceptions Determine Our Responses

What we think about a situation is far more important than the situation itself because what we believe determines how we respond or react to it. Imagine that you're walking into a room full of people who suddenly become quiet. What you think will decide how you feel as well as how you act. If you were home alone just stepping out of the shower when you heard glass break, what would you think? Your thoughts would determine both how you feel as well as what you do.

Someone makes a remark that could—but may not—be construed as derogatory. It doesn't matter what the speaker meant. What people think about that comment will determine how they act. How often do difficult situations become impossible because of an inappropriate response? How many times has someone's misinformed reaction turned a favorable situation into a nightmare or a bad one into a catastrophe?

Our behavior is always a result of what we think. That is why it is important to have our thoughts under control. The Apostle Paul stressed the importance of right thinking in his letter to the Corinthians:

> For though we walk in the flesh, we do not war after the flesh casting down imaginations, and every high thing that exalteth itself against the knowledge of God, and bringing into captivity every thought to the obedience of Christ[4] (Chapter Three Endnotes #1).

Have you ever tried to control your mind and failed? Of course, we all have. But it can be done because Christ lives in us. He is always working in us not to make us robots but actual participants in His life.

What Is Sin, Really?

Surely God hates sin. Yes, He does. The problem is that the definition of sin has changed drastically over the last 2,000 years. The definition of sin used by the Church today makes it impossible for humans to know

---

[4] 2 Corinthians 10:3-5 (KJV)

when they please God. But the First Century understanding of sin made it possible for believers to cooperate with the Holy Spirit and enjoy unusual manifestations of His power in their lives. And, it enabled them to know exactly how to please God.

The word *sin* is understood by most people to mean disobeying God's law; that is, doing, saying, or thinking contrary to God's commands. Though the Greek can include that meaning, the writers of the New Testament usually had something else in mind.

The Greek word translated sin is *hamartia* (ἁμαρτία). Its meanings in the original language include *a failure, a sin, an error,* or *a mistake*. When we think sin, we automatically think of doing something wrong. When we think of it as error, our entire perspective changes. Instead of being something done that is wrong, it now includes beliefs that are not true. By replacing the word *sin* with *error*, we automatically begin to experience a radical change in our understanding of the scriptures.

Most people believe they are right, especially about religion. They all think that what they believe is the *truth* and all other religions are wrong. Since no two people anywhere have the same beliefs, logic tells us that no one person or group is a composite of pure *truth*. Every one of us is wrong about something; we just don't know what. We all believe some things that are not true. The Bible in 1 John 1:8 confirms that "If we say that we have no sin (error), we deceive ourselves, and the *truth* is not in us." Obviously, if you knew what you believed is wrong, you would change those beliefs, right? This is where the Holy Spirit comes in. He is the only one who can show us what things we believe that are not true and where we are wrong. "And when he comes, he will prove[5] the world wrong about sin."[6]

Over the years, as God has revealed to me the love that caused Him to give His Only Begotten Son, I have realized that my expectation of a wrathful God came from a source other than God. I now see a God Who is doing everything He can to persuade us to believe and trust Him. *The God Who is supposedly angry about our wrong beliefs and the resultant*

---

[5] ἐλέγξει means to convince with substantial evidence that is compelling, to expose and prove wrong.

[6] John 16:8 (NRSV)

sinful behavior doesn't hate His human creatures, but loves them and is doing everything within Love's power to persuade them of His truth. Yes, sin separates us from God, but that separation is not from His side. Error, wrong beliefs, causes *us* to separate *ourselves* from Him. All the while, He fixes His eyes on the horizon waiting for us to come home like the father of the prodigal son. Incorrect beliefs cause us to misinterpret what He says and what He wants. Error in what we believe is *truth* causes us to misunderstand what God says.

Rejecting God's *truth* is what caused the separation in the Garden of Eden all those millennia ago. The serpent introduced error. Adam and Eve believed him and then lived their wrong beliefs. Since then, mankind has misinterpreted most everything God has said. For that reason, the Word became flesh so that God could live His will in front of us, face to face. God became flesh so we could see Him and the image in which He created us.

Have you ever wondered about the phrase the Apostle Paul used in Romans 6:6, "that the body of sin might be destroyed?"[7] (Chapter Three Endnotes #2). Since the beginning of the Church, some believers have understood that phrase to mean that our bodies are sinful, full of evil and wickedness. Some talk about *their old man (old self)* as though it is still alive and reigning. When this type of understanding combines with a misunderstanding of the word *flesh*, it is almost impossible for someone ever to know how God's will, or His *truth*, works in their lives. They will always be swatting at gnats. People are created to understand. When they don't get God's understanding, they make up their own. Thus, there has been mass confusion among theologians' interpretations of these types of phrases as they try to make sense of what Paul said. Solomon said, "Trust in the Lord with all your heart, And rely not on your own understanding."[8]

So how do you get His understanding? I started by admitting that most of the time I didn't understand what God means. How God responded to my honesty was amazing. I learned He doesn't expect me to know what He means. Rather, He loves me coming to Him as a

---

[7] KJV
[8] Proverbs 3:5 (AAT)

little child, "Father, Abba, what did you mean when Jesus said this, or Paul said that?" He doesn't expect me to be God and to know what He knows. Instead, He delights to teach me all the knowledge He has put inside me in Christ. Sometimes that involves study, but when it does, He causes me to want to study. I now ask for understanding and leave things alone until He shows me (Chapter Three Endnotes #3).

I'd like to explain how God, once and for all, eliminated my confusion about the phrase *the body of sin* in Romans Chapter Six. The word *body* can refer to the flesh in which we live, but it can also refer to things like a body of water or land or knowledge. One day, I realized Paul wasn't referring to *evil* bodies of flesh. He was writing about a body of knowledge, specifically, the body of knowledge of error that came out of the Garden of Eden[9] (Chapter Three Endnotes #4). By making ineffective, through His death, mankind's erroneous body of knowledge, Jesus rendered us free from it. The veil was torn. We now know that what Satan says is always twisted and we no longer must believe him. Jesus exposed Satan and is now working to persuade us to agree with God rather than the darkness.

How do you stop error from reigning in your mortal body? By no longer believing it! But how do you stop believing wrong things when you don't even know what they are? This book introduces you to God's principles for doing just that. Without understanding those principles, it is hard to cooperate with the Holy Spirit as He teaches us who we are and empowers us to live with Christ's stature. The Apostle Paul knew it was imminently possible to live free from evil desires. Thus, he didn't suggest we do so; he commanded us to do so.[10]

It is error that causes lust in one's thinking. "Let not error reign in your mortal bodies that you should obey it in the lusts thereof."[11] By eliminating the error that causes the lust, the lust ceases to exist. It's not our mortal (fleshly, worldly) bodies that are the problem, but the error. Thus, he goes on to say that "Error shall not have dominion over

---

[9] The "body of sin" is a body of knowledge that is not from God.

[10] For beginning students of Ancient Greek, commands are indicated by words spelled in the imperative mood.

[11] Romans 6:12 (JEC)

you."[12] Why? Because it has been made ineffective by being exposed as incorrect.

How? When light shines on darkness, the darkness disappears. So, when a lie you have been believing is exposed as being a lie, you can no longer believe it is *truth*. Thus, you no longer have to obey it. "Knowing this, that our old man is crucified with him, that the body of sin (error) might be destroyed, that henceforth we should not serve sin."[13]

If we don't realize that Paul was talking about a body of knowledge that was wrong, much of what Paul writes will never make sense. Most translations assume that the body, to which this passage refers, is the one in which we live. That may be because of the phrase *old man*, which many theologians believe is an old nature that was *crucified with Christ* but somehow managed to escape the effects of that crucifixion. Thus, in their minds, the body of which Paul spoke must be the one made of flesh. Since our bodies feel wrong desires so strongly, surely this is what he meant. But, Jesus broke the power of lies and deception by shining the light of truth on the Liar (Satan).[14] That's what the *truth* (Jesus) did in His victory over the power of darkness. "That through death he might destroy him that had the power of death, that is, the devil."[15] In other words, He exposed Satan's lies for what they are. Jesus is the *truth* that exposed *the lie* and revealed *truth* to mankind. "I am the way, *the truth*, and the life: no man cometh unto the Father but by me."[16]

By the way, what is the power of darkness? Simply put, darkness prevents you from seeing what is there. It blinds you to the truth of your reality and it blinds you to God's *truth*. Do you doubt me? Just walk into a room full of furniture with no lights on and walk around for a few minutes. Your shins will provide an education about the power of darkness after they meet your coffee table. When you know the *truth*

---

[12] Romans 6:14 (JEC)

[13] Romans 6:6 (KJV)

[14] John 8:44, Jesus called Satan a liar. The Greek text can be translated "liar he is" or "he is a liar."

[15] Hebrews 2:14 (KJV)

[16] John 14:6 (KJV)

—I don't mean to know *about* it, but *know* it in the same fashion that God knows it, know it as the body of knowledge that fills your heart and mind—then you will automatically live it. As *truth*, instead of error, increasingly becomes your body of knowledge, you will find that you are *being*—that you "have been" changed.

Worry Doesn't Work

Worry is the attempt to think a solution into existence. We are concerned about so many things and feel it is our responsibility to do something and, we believe, doing anything is better than nothing. Most commonly, the *something* we do is to think, think, think, then think some more. A situation may be beyond our ability, yet we still feel responsible. We still feel like there must be some way to get control.

My wife's name is Sandra. Many years ago, her grandmother asked Sandra's mother, Sonja, "Don't you worry when Sandra is out at night?" To which, Sonja replied, "No, why should I worry?" Sandra's grandmother responded, "What do you mean? Don't you care? When you worry it shows you care!" We have been trained to try to think solutions into existence; hence, we worry.

What was so bad about Adam's and Eve's sin (error)? It was the decision *not* to be entirely dependent on God, that we should be able to solve any and every problem by thinking. All we need to do is *think*.

> Jackie has an excellent job but worries constantly. No matter how qualified she is for each assignment, Jackie has a horrible fear she will make a mistake. Long ago, Jackie convinced her boss she could competently handle any task he assigned, but that makes no difference. There are so many things that might go wrong and she has no idea what they are, let alone how she would handle them.

Worry is a prime example of wrong thinking. We imagine dreadful things and even feel the results, yet it is all in our minds. Something triggers the thought of a problem and within moments we are expecting the worst possible result for a situation that is imaginary. The sense of responsibility forces our minds into overdrive to solve problems that only God can fix—and that's assuming there is even something to fix. If we could think like Jesus, we would be so much happier and realize so much more of God working in our lives for good.

Truth and a Renewed Mind

In and out of church, many teach that positive confession and thinking are the ways to achieve success. However, even though proper speaking is involved in changing our thoughts, it alone does not cause that change. Many believe that confessing the Word of God is the way you get things. But confession comes from the Greek word *homologeo* (ὁμολογέω), which is often represented to mean "to say the same thing as another person, to verbally agree with someone, to say the same conclusion, to confess."[17] Based on this meaning I think confession is a good thing. It is always good to agree with God. When you confess the Word of God, you are just saying His words together with Him. You are agreeing with what God says. As a *being* created in God's image, it is your nature to say what He says and not say what He doesn't say. Thus, confession is simply a tool that enables you to reinforce in your heart and mind what God believes by choosing to say what He says. But confession can be based on flesh or spirit. A lot of very influential Christian leaders do not seem to know the difference.

While writing this Third Edition of UNSEEN, I discovered something wonderful which is consistent with the fact that God considers us His children. One of parents' objectives in raising children is to teach them to think correctly. As the Book of Proverbs says, "as a child learns to think, so will the child become."[18] Many scholars agree that the word translated "confession" in the New Testament (*homologeo*) means "to say together with." However, if you look closely, you will notice that the Greek word *homologeo* can be divided into two other Greek words: *homo* and *logeo*. Homo means "the same as" and *logeo* is the verbi-

---

[17] Cf. Liddell & Scott Greek-English Lexicon, Thayer's Greek Lexicon, HELPS Word-studies

[18] Proverbs 23:7 "For as a man thinks within himself, so he is." (JEC)

zation of the Greek word *logos*, which means "word, reason, or logic." Thus, the original meaning of *homologeo* was "to have the same reason or logic" or "to have the same reasoning." So, how did the meaning get changed? Some theologies state that no one can know or understand how God thinks. Maybe that is the reason that some translators added a "*u*" to *homo* and changed *logeo* to *lego*. It is easier to believe God wants us to say what He says than to believe we can ever think like He thinks. By returning to the First Century meaning of *homologeo (to reason the same as)*, we can see what God is seeking to accomplish within us. He is training us to think like He thinks and believe as He believes because we will then act like sons and daughters of God. The entire creation has been waiting for this. "For the creation waits with eager longing for the revealing of the sons of God."[19]

The Apostle Paul frequently uses the word *spirit* in different ways. Often, he is simply referring to an attitude. In Galatians 5:16 (KJV), he uses the word *spirit* to refer to an attitude set on believing (treasuring) God's *truth*: "This I say then, Walk in the Spirit, and ye shall not fulfil the lust of the flesh." Though many interpreters do, Paul did not put the article *the* before spirit and flesh. I wanted to know why he omitted the article. Amazingly, when translating the verse without adding articles, it makes far more sense. "Walk in an attitude set on believing the *truth* and you will not fulfil the lust of flesh" (Chapter Three Endnotes #5).

Have you ever wondered how you are supposed to walk in the Holy Spirit? By translating *spirit* as an attitude intent on treasuring God's *truth*, it makes much more sense, especially when contrasted with the lust that always arises when one treasures sense knowledge instead of God's knowledge. Paul is very clearly telling us that the way to stop fulfilling the lust of flesh is to live with an attitude that is determined to believe God's *truth*, instead of the lies so often told us by Satan as he falsely interprets to us what our senses are telling us. Please understand, confessions inspired by flesh will never produce the fruit of the Spirit spoken of in Galatians 5:22. In fact, they just reinforce wrong beliefs.

---

[19] Romans 8:19 (ESV)

Confession (verbally agreeing with God's *truth*) is important. If you want to see the unseen, the words that come out of your mouths are important for three reasons:

1. They enable you to tell yourself the *truth* (Chapter Eight).

2. They enable you to learn what you believe for real (Chapters Eight and Twelve).

3. They allow you to share with God what is in your heart, i.e., to agree with God (Chapter Twelve).

Seeing the unseen—part of which is seeing the breathtaking magnitude and reality of God's blessing—is wholly dependent upon the fact that your mind has already been renewed (Chapter Four Endnotes 2 and 25). But, if you reject God's *truth* because it doesn't yet seem real, you will not see it until you agree with Him. Without that renewal, it is impossible to realize you are abiding in God's kingdom while simultaneously living here on Earth.[20] These two ideas are contradictory to the mind of flesh.

Mind renewal has given you much more than the ability to harness those thoughts and feelings you dislike and know shouldn't be there. It has enabled you to cooperate with God and *be* transformed. That is, the transformation that became your unseen reality in your union with Christ can become your experience by just believing that God has done what He said He has done.

God is an intimate God Who is always blessing everyone.[21] In this intimacy, you discover answers that have always been within your reach, but you could not see. I was not going blind on my trip across Alligator Alley. All I had to do was take off my sunglasses, yet I spent almost an hour worrying about the symptoms before discovering the truth.

---

[20] In Ephesians 2:6, Paul says that we are seated with Christ in Heaven, even while we are still living on Earth.

[21] Matthew 5:45

Sometimes we seem to be our own worst enemy. Though situations can be bad, our biggest problems are often the results of what we think about them. By imagining the worst, we sometimes create problems that don't even exist. In many cases, our imaginations turn simple challenges into gut-wrenching crises. For example, if you lost your money, would you see the world collapsing on you or an opportunity for something better?

> Someone scammed Peter out of his life's savings. It seemed like such a good deal, and he wanted what the salesman was offering. Of course, he gave the man the benefit of the doubt when he said things that did not seem quite right because he wanted to believe the opportunity was real. Before he knew it, the guy had his money and was gone.

Was this the end of Peter's world? It looked like it, it seemed like it, and it *felt* like it. But was that the *truth*? Though it was bad to lose his savings, Peter's biggest problem was not the fact that someone scammed him, but what he thought about it. It became a critical time in his life, and how he dealt with his thoughts would greatly affect his future. His anger, fear, anxiety, and depression made his loss almost unbearable.

Losing your job or money would not be easy, but it would not be the end of the world. In any circumstance, there is a choice to believe God is turning it for good or that things are as bad as they feel. Our reactions seem to be automatic. For many, losing their life's savings or job would look like the end of the world.

Is there a way to change our negative reactions? If you grew up always seeing the glass half empty, is there a way to begin seeing it half full? Yes, and it is the same thing that dispelled the fear of losing my sight. That single factor is knowing the *truth*! Not just the facts about what happened, but also the *truth* about what those facts mean. How circumstances will ultimately affect us is usually not readily apparent. If we are not looking for the *truth*, our imaginations will give us something else.

Consider that Joseph—the one spoken of in the book of Genesis—was kidnapped by his brothers and sold into slavery. The terror and heartbreak he must have experienced as he was being taken far from home, his dreams suddenly dashed. Yet in his autobiography, he says, "And the Lord was with Joseph."[22] When King David was fleeing for his life because his son, Absalom, was trying to kill him and seize the kingdom, many of his subjects said, "There is no help for him in God."[23] The valley, through which he was walking looked like death. But, because David believed the truth, he expected good rather than evil. "Yea, although I walk through the valley of the shadow of death, I shall fear no harm, because Thou are with me."[24]

Whose Fault Is It?

Consider something that happened to you that was beyond your ability. Even though you had no control over the situation, did that mean you were not responsible for your thoughts? What happens to you and how you react are two different things. We cannot always determine what happens to us, but we can control how we respond.

Your feelings and actions are your response to what happens, and your response is always *your* responsibility. So how do we get dominion over our feelings and actions? By being honest with God about our thoughts and allowing the mind of Christ to *be* in us. Then without trying or thinking about it, our thoughts, emotions, attitudes, dispositions, and actions will be the same that Christ himself would have if he were in our place, in our bodies, under the same circumstances, which He is.

Paul stressed the importance of our thought content:

> Finally, brethren, whatsoever things are true, whatsoever things are honest, whatsoever things are just, whatsoever things are pure, whatsoever things are lovely, whatsoever things are of good report; if there be any virtue, and if there be any praise, think on these things.[25]

---

[22] Genesis 39:2 (KJV)

[23] Psalm 23:2 (KJV)

[24] Psalm 23:4 (A translation of the Old Testament Scriptures from the original Hebrew by Helen Spurrell)

[25] Philippians 4:8 (KJV)

This is the way Jesus thought and it is possible for us to do the same. Is your goal to let the mind of Christ be in you? If not, I believe that will change when you see how. "Let this mind be in you, which was also in Christ Jesus."[26] (By the way, in case you are not aware, in the original language *let this mind be in you* is a command. Do you remember how God's commands work (See Chapter Two Endnote #4)? Like the author of Psalm 119, I love God's commands. When we agree with them, they fulfill themselves.

The Blame Game

Have you ever had a good friend start an ugly rumor about you? How did you react? Were you forced to act that way? If others are responsible for your emotions and behaviors, then your only hope of a better life lies in them. You cannot experience life as God intended but are dependent on someone else. Even if people have wronged us, we are solely responsible for what we think about what they did.

People's refusal to take responsibility for their lives is a destructive societal problem. Many blame others for the way they feel and act. They do not realize that their own wrong thinking is causing their problems. For example, the rioting that has occurred after high-profile courtroom trials where people blamed the riot for their actions or the parent who shakes his baby saying he couldn't help it because the child's crying was driving him crazy. How about those brothers in California who could not help brutally murdering their parents because of the way they had been treated?[27] Remember the story of Adam, who said, "Lord, it was the woman You gave me, it's her fault."[28] Of course, some of these people may have been wronged, but regardless, they still blamed others for their actions when they alone did their deeds.

Have you ever exploded in anger? Who was responsible? Can someone else really make you react violently? No! Your reactions are your decision. Am I saying that someone didn't threaten or hurt you?

---

[26] Philippians 2:5 (KJV)
[27] Menendez brothers, 1989
[28] Genesis 3:12 (JEC)

Of course not. But you are responsible for your reactions. No one determines your responses but you. Have you ever done something wrong? Who was responsible for your action? You! Even in extreme situations where someone appears to react before thinking, the foundation of their thoughts, which caused that reaction, was their responsibility.

The Apostle Paul told us how we should think:

> Summing it all up, friends, I'd say you'll do best by filling your minds and meditating on things true, noble, reputable, authentic, compelling, gracious—the best, not the worst; the beautiful, not the ugly; things to praise, not things to curse.[29]

This is one of the results of growing up in Christ. Unfortunately, attempts to rule our thoughts often lead to frustration. Why? Because our efforts are not by means of spirit but using the will of flesh.

Jesus said anything born out of the flesh is destined for failure. "That which is born of the flesh is flesh; and that which is born of the Spirit is spirit"[30] (Chapter Three Endnotes #6). God has designed a straightforward method for changing our thoughts, and it is not through willpower or behavior modification. The Holy Spirit can enable you to think and respond automatically without struggling. It is possible for peace of mind to guard your heart continually. "And the peace of God, which passeth all understanding, shall keep your hearts and minds through Christ Jesus."[31]

> Connie was in her early twenties, and like most people in their early twenties, money was tight. Her secretarial job barely paid the bills, let alone allowed her any luxury. She desperately wanted out of what appeared to be a dead-end life. Of course, she was still very young. When she found out Karen had a part-time job that paid about $500 a night for just a few hours of work, she joined her. The fact that

---

[29] Philippians 4:8 (msg)
[30] John 3:6 (KJV)
[31] Philippians 4:7 (KJV)

she had to take off her clothes and dance before a room full of people may have violated her well-ingrained moral upbringing, but hey, who would know? She really needed the money. However, she had been raised to believe it was wrong.

One night, the impossible happened, a family acquaintance happened to see her performance. Word got back to her parents. She was humiliated. How could this have happened? Connie was angry. First, she blamed her former employer, who had not paid her enough, then she blamed her parents.

Who was at fault, really? Who took the job and did the dance? All by herself, Connie had decided what she wanted and how to get it. Not liking the consequences of her decision, she denied responsibility for it, she refused to suffer by herself and instead blamed others even though they had nothing to do with her decision.

Connie's biggest problem was not the nude dancing or even the consequences. Rather, it was her denial of being responsible for her actions. To hide her shame, she blamed others for what she did. Her philosophy? *Don't admit you are wrong and you won't have to pay the price.* Far too many live by this rule, and it can have terrible results. If Connie had been honest with herself, she would have admitted wrong thoughts caused her to make bad decisions. One sad thought was that she alone was responsible for improving her financial condition, that she could not depend on God for help. Other wrong ideas allowed her to justify getting nude and dancing in public, and yet others allowed her to deny that the consequences of her actions were her own fault. Connie's wrong thoughts resulted in immoral behavior. The right thoughts would have led to good behavior.

Bill's story was entirely different. For years, he did many things that hurt his family, friends, business associates, and others. He borrowed money from friends and didn't repay them. He got involved in business schemes with no concern whether they were ethical or moral. He did not hesitate to sell something, take the money, and never deliver the product or service. Worst of all, he fully justified cheating on his wife. But Bill was quick to tell people about Jesus Christ and confess Him as Lord.

Like Connie, the day came when Bill's activities caught up with him. He was devastated when his wife kicked him out and filed for divorce. Then Bill woke up and realized that his behavior would never get him what he really wanted—a prosperous and happy life with the woman he loved. Bill quit blaming others and finally admitted that he—and no one else—was responsible for his actions. Bill began to change. This was not another ploy just to get what he wanted. Bill was finally becoming honest with himself.

The greatest change was in Bill's attitude toward God. God was no longer a name to drop in conversations, but to be trusted and believed. His newfound fellowship with God affected every other area of his life, and it gradually became apparent to others that Bill was a changed man. Eventually, his wife saw that the change was authentic and began seeing him on a serious basis. They were ultimately remarried and have never been happier.

What was the difference between Bill and Connie? Bill took responsibility for his actions, whereas Connie didn't. What brought about the change in Bill's life? A fundamental change in his thinking. He became honest with God and admitted that he was the problem. This was the beginning of right-thinking, and it eventually resulted in good feelings and actions.

Taking responsibility for wrong thoughts and actions does not mean that you necessarily know how to stop or even want to. God loves to help everyone. As our hearts become more and more honest, we find it easier and easier to take His help. Try this approach. "God, what I said/did/felt was wrong. I don't know how to change me, but you do. Teach me the *truth* that I don't know. Thank you for loving me without conditions."

If you don't want to change but know you should, be honest with Him about that too. God loves you. He knows why you do what you do, and He doesn't want you to have to wait until the afterlife to enjoy His reality. He wants you to enjoy Heaven on Earth. "Our Heavenly Father… make Your Kingdom appear, Your will *be*—on Earth, as it is in Heaven."[32]

Just because you have been unable to conquer an area of your life doesn't mean it is not possible; it just means you don't yet know how. Once you understand how God works in your life, you will be able to cooperate instead of getting in the way.

*　*　**

Chapter Three Endnotes

Note 1

St. Paul is saying that by means of flesh (believing what we feel and that what our physical senses report is truth), our minds are left subject to and often dominated by imaginations, reasonings, and mental pictures that claim to be real and more accurate than God's *truth*. But the scriptures say: "For the weapons of our warfare are not carnal, but mighty through God to the pulling down of strong holds."[33] Many translations imply the same as the King James Version—that the weapons are mighty through God or in His service. However, since the article and noun are in the dative case, it would be more accurately translated "by God" (τῷ Θεῷ) instead of "through God." In other words, we cooperate with the Holy Spirit and *He* uses the weapons to expose any knowledge that claims to be from God or superior to what He knows, which is not consistent with Christ's obedience—the obedience of always choosing to believe God's *truth* above all other knowledge. When the Holy Spirit shines light into darkness, it destroys it.

---

[32] Matthew 6:10 (JEC)

[33] 2 Corinthians 10:4 (KJV) Since God is using the weapons from inside us, *we* are using the weapons. That's how marvelous is our union with Christ. All we do is believe His *truth*, and He lives the victory of Christ in us. This is the Gospel.

That victory included defeating every stronghold. So, the pressure is off us, but most don't know it. The fear that a stronghold will never be conquered is a lie. But if we listen to that lie long enough, our emotions will join in and agree. Then we can become convinced *the lie* is *truth*.

God is using His weapons in us. Even though we may feel something that completely contradicts the idea of victory, God never misses His target. The victory is already ours, so it is time to thank Him for it, even though we don't feel it. Your mind and feelings will eventually catch up. When you recognize a thought is a lie, say so. "This thought is not a thought that God thinks so it's not my thought either. It's a lie!" Of course, another thought will tell you that since you *feel* that lie is true, it must be. But that thought is a lie, also.

Note 2

By exposing as false the body of knowledge (i.e. the body of erroneous knowledge) that began to accumulate after Adam and Eve accepted *the lie*, Jesus made it incapable of dominating those who no longer believe it is true.

The Greek word often rendered *destroy* or *destroyed* in the New Testament is more accurately understood as "rendered inoperative" or "made idle" or "weakened to the point of an inability to control." This does not mean that what has been "destroyed" is gone but that, through the work of Christ, it has been made unable to dominate people who know and believe that it no longer controls them because of what God did to it. As long as the thing that was "destroyed" is able to persuade a person that it still controls them, they remain under its power.

Note 3

In 2 Peter 3:16 (KJV), Peter mentions those that struggle with understanding God's *truth*: "As also in all his epistles… in which are some things hard to be understood, *which they that are unlearned and unstable wrest*, as they do also the other scriptures, unto their own destruction." He says that the wrestling or struggling is done by those that are unlearned and unstable.

Do you ever *struggle* with understanding the will of God? Do you ever feel stressed because things in the Bible don't make sense or add up? You are troubled and confused because sometimes the Word just doesn't make sense? Then as offensive as this may sound, you are one of the unlearned and unstable regardless of your position in the church or society or others' possible high opinion of you. God doesn't say this to condemn, but to educate you. He is not upset with you. He just wants to grow you up in His knowledge, so you know what He knows. Then you will be learned and stable and enjoy His rest. Believing lies without realizing it has caused all of us to, at times, wrestle with our own knowledge and understanding of the Scriptures. God is the only one that can explain how He thinks and He delights to reason with His creatures that are learning His logic.

"Come now, and let us reason together."[34] We are not capable of understanding God's logic unless He teaches it to us, which He wants to do. But if someone remains convinced that they know, that they see, then they will continue to be blind. "'If you had been blind,' Jesus replied, 'you would have had no sin (error) to answer for; but as it is, you say, 'We can see' so, your sin (error) remains.'"[35]

Note 4

For me, the logic of using the word *body* is simple. It refers to a body of knowledge. As with most words, dictionaries often have multiple definitions for words, usually numbered 1, 2, 3, etc. Included in definitions for *body*, you will find references to a human or animal body, the main section of a thing like the body of a car, a volume or mass of information such as a body of knowledge or beliefs, etc. Surely, you've heard the word used in the context of an ocean or lake, e.g., a body of water. In fact, the word is often used about an artistic creation as in the body of a work of art. A review of various Greek-English lexicons

---

[34] Isaiah 1:18 (KJV)
[35] John 9:41 (JEC)

reveals that σῶμα (body) can mean *a whole* of a thing, as in a body of evidence, information, beliefs, etc., "τὸ σῶμα τῆς πίστεως" (the *body* of the belief).

Simple and reasonable changes in our understanding of what Paul meant by sin and body result in a radical transformation of our understanding of the Bible. The Scriptures begin to make sense in a wonderfully logical way.

Note 5

Sometimes in Scripture it's hard to determine whether the writer is speaking about spirit or the Holy Spirit; but then, that makes sense. Jesus called Him the Spirit of *truth*.[36] His ministry is to teach us the *truth* not as a bunch of facts but the body of knowledge that fuels our hearts. He seeks to manifest inside our hearts and minds the very attitude of God Himself, which is always to treasure the *truth*. So sometimes it doesn't seem to matter whether you translate spirit as the Holy Spirit or an attitude set on believing God's *truth*. Since you could correctly say that just as God is Love, so too He is an attitude that wills to believe *truth*. (Please do not misconstrue my statement and accuse me of claiming the Holy Spirit is some "attitude." He IS God and coequal with the Father and the Son.)

Note 6

Jesus did not say that the flesh is bad. He was saying that whatever originates from *the* flesh remains flesh. Likewise, anything that finds its source in *the* Spirit remains spirit.

---

[36] John 14:17

us that if we can figure out the right things *to do*, we will achieve the results we desire. And of course, it left us feeling like we are under the stern, watchful eye of a God who must be just like us, ready to condemn the slightest mistake. *The lie* said we would be gods, and many take that to the extreme by seeking to be a god over others.

The Bible often refers to faith (belief) as a seed. Seeds grow and become plants, which then bear fruit that produce more of the same. Error produces more error; *truth* produces more *truth*. This understanding is critical if we are to comprehend how *the lie* has multiplied into a plethora of other errors, many of which we believe right now.

The importance of understanding the sections titled *The Lie* and *The Lie by Another Name* in Chapter Four is paramount if we want to understand how to be free from actions and thoughts not consistent with those of Christ Jesus.

Man's core motivation is to be loved and valued. God planned on fulfilling this need through a personal relationship with each of us, but *the lie* twisted man's thinking about how to find that fulfillment. It has caused people to search for value in a myriad of ways all independent of God. There is no limit to the number of ways humankind attempts to realize its value, but every manifestation of *the lie* has a common thread. Each demand that we do certain things or perform in a manner that contradicts the plan of God.

3. *Law*. In Romans 7:12, the Apostle Paul said the Law is good. But, how can that be if those who try to do it are cursed when they fail? God never intended for "The Law" to become a bunch of legal rules. The word *torah* means *instruction, direction, teaching, doctrine*. It was meant to teach the Children of Israel that they were no longer slaves but a free and mighty people. God sought to instill them with a new way of thinking about themselves so that they could be who they now were. But, they refused. They did not think there was anything wrong with the

way they saw God, themselves, and the inhabitants of the land. They knew better than God. When you look at believers today, little seems to have changed.

Beginning in Chapter Four, we occasionally substitute the word *instruction* in the place of *law*. In the New Testament, the word *law* as used by Paul usually reflected the Jews' understanding of the word as a legal issue – do it so you don't get in trouble. But sometimes, the Apostle Paul used *law* with God's meaning, i.e. *instruction*. The Instruction which God delivered to the Jews was designed to take them out of the slavery/victim mentality into the victorious mindset that was supposed to be theirs after seeing all the miracles of their deliverance from Egypt. God wanted them to see themselves as He saw them. That's why Joshua told them to become absorbed in God's words. They were to hear, look at, talk, think about, and consider what God had done and who they were as His People. They were not supposed to forget. His words would instruct their minds and hearts into thinking and believing the *truth*. In UNSEEN, we treat God's Word and "laws" as instruction designed to train His Children to be who we are. Once our thought-life agrees with who God says we are, we will automatically act like who we are and will not need laws to tell us what to do. We will be living from the Kingdom of God. This is the gist of what Paul was saying in Chapter Three of Galatians.

4. *God's love*: The undiminishable, unoffendable, absolute, determined, unwavering, constant, irrevocable desire and intention to give Himself, and everything He possesses, to every one of His children, to protect, help, and educate us, at any cost to Himself, even when we knowingly or unknowingly reject Him... without ever violating our free will. God's love yields to our desires and intentions when we refuse Him, yet remains inside us closely involved seeking to persuade and help without ever attempting to force us to yield. His love is vulnerable to grief and pain yet He is forever passionate and never gives up

hope; He never ceases seeking to convince us that because He IS love, He cannot lie, thus His love will never fail, thus He refuses to quit loving us even when we declare hatred and do everything in our power to hurt Him. His character, His essence, His nature is so able and strong that nothing that happens or that we do, think, say, or feel, nor any effect of the lies we have believed can ever turn Him against His beloved human creatures, every one of whom He created to be and act like Him. God's passion for us to know Who He is and who we are will never end. For God to ever revoke His love would be for God to revoke Himself, because His IS love. This is covenant love. Man's only response to this love is to be immovable in believing it.

The difference between false love and God's love is like laying fool's gold next to the real thing. When a person finally recognizes the difference, they will forever after seek only pure gold.

4
Untwisting Thoughts

Have you ever poured freshly cooked spaghetti into a colander? The noodles are all twisted together, right? Have you noticed that while still hot, you can pull out any strand and it will not break? The whole strand will come out intact. But what happens once the spaghetti cools? It would take skill and a very sharp knife to remove a strand.

Our beliefs are just like a bowl of spaghetti. If you recognize a new misbelief and immediately reject it, it did no harm; but if it cools and becomes embedded in your belief system, then it is an entirely different matter. We all experience thoughts and beliefs—right and wrong—that are twisted together. Of course, if we recognized a belief that wasn't true, we'd stop believing it. The problem is we believe things because we want to believe them. We love our beliefs and sometimes lie to ourselves because the perceived benefit is greater than the concern that it might be a lie. It is time to let the Holy Spirit start untwisting our thoughts.

Spaghetti Thinking

How would you feel if Christ was in your mind doing your thinking for you? Though God will never force His thinking on you, Jesus wants to help you think like He does. Because of your perfect and complete union with Him, He can do it by the ability of His Spirit inside you. Thinking like Him is not something that can be accomplished using willpower or practice. It is a gift which is yours for the taking. But, what you may not have yet realized is that you must learn how to use God's gifts. Just because parents give a child a car on his or her sixteenth birthday does not make the child a seasoned driver. That takes training, practice, and time. So too with the gift of the mind of Christ. Now that we have it, God's plan is to train us how to think. But, if we are convinced we already know how to think like God, the power of that gift waits to be discovered. The Apostle Paul said, "For who hath known the mind of the Lord, that he may instruct him? But we have the mind of Christ."[1] He also wrote: "And be not conformed to this world, but be transformed by the renewal of your mind."[2]

The more you think like Christ, the more you will act like Him. Your feelings and actions will change without even trying. You will begin enjoying the fruit of the Spirit of God living in you. "The fruit of the Spirit is love, joy, peace, patience, gentleness, goodness faith, meekness, temperance."[3] Since you are in union with God and Christ is now your life, when you learn to think like Him the fruit that is present in God becomes automatically present in you.[4]

There are two parts to God's work in us. First is the new birth in which a person's confession agrees with Christ's death, burial, and resurrection. This individual is a new creation, and now shares in all that belongs to Christ.

> He that spared not his own son, but delivered him up for us all, how shall he not with him also *freely give us all things*?[5]
>
> For all things are yours; Whether Paul, or Apollos, or Cephas, or the world, or life or death, or things present, or things to come; all are yours.[6]

---

[1] 1 Corinthians 2:16 (KJV)
[2] Romans 12:2 (JEC)
[3] Galatians 5:22-23 (KJV)
[4] Colossians 3:4 (KJV)
[5] Romans 8:32 (KJV)
[6] 1 Corinthians 3:21-22 (KJV)

Second is to *be* transformed by the renewal of your mind."⁷ The word *be* does not mean to *become* transformed; it means to be in the state of having been transformed. I explained it to myself as "Be already transformed."⁸

When God met Moses in the burning bush in the desert, He said, "I will send thee unto Pharaoh, that thou mayest bring forth my people the children of Israel out of Egypt."⁹ "And Moses said unto God, Behold, when I come unto the children of Israel, and shall say unto them, The God of your fathers hath sent me unto you; and they shall say to me, What is his name? What shall I say unto them?"¹⁰ "And God said unto Moses, I AM THAT I AM. Thus shalt thou say unto the children of Israel, I Am hath sent me unto you."¹¹

God is *being*. He *is* I AM. His identity is not found in what He does, but in who He *is*. That is where we are to find our value, our importance, as well. We find our identity in who He says we are and who He created us to *be*. For instance, God does not have love; He *is* Love. He doesn't have power; He *is* power. He doesn't have peace; He *is* peace. He doesn't have grace; He *is* grace. He created humankind in His image not just to be a picture of Him but His actual presence. He intended that wherever mankind would be, He would be there as well because we would be one with Him. Of course, you could also say that wherever He is, we are, too. In Christ, our being is united to His so that the only difference between us is that He is God and we are His creatures. We were created to be and act like heirs of God. When people look at us, His intention is that they see Him. We are to live our lives in such a union with Christ that people will hardly be able to tell the difference. Are they looking at a human being, or God?

---

[7] Romans 12:2 (JEC)
[8] *Be* is the present imperative active of *is*.
[9] Exodus 3:10 (KJV)
[10] Exodus 3:13 (KJV)
[11] Exodus 3:14 (KJV)

> And when the people saw what Paul had done, they lifted up their voices, saying in the speech of Lycaonia, The gods are come down to us in the likeness of men.[12]

Remember the rich young ruler in Matthew's Gospel? He asked Jesus what he could do to have eternal life. If you think eternal life is just being saved and going to Heaven when you die, then His answer doesn't make sense because the Apostle Paul said in Romans 10:9 that to be saved, you just need to confess Jesus is Lord and believe God raised Him from the dead. So why would Jesus add a greater burden on this young man by telling him to give away all his money? Jesus wasn't adding burden at all. He was talking about something other than just going to Heaven when we die. Eternal life is God's life; it is who He *is*! Jesus was talking about living the same quality of life that is within God that is impossible for a man to achieve through willpower. Only God can accomplish it. We can do all the right things and do what we think Jesus would do. But that is not life, it is religion. For human creatures, eternal life is when God (by the agency of Christ in us) lives His life through us. That is impossible for any human to accomplish; but not for God! For this reason, He said to His disciples. "With man it is impossible, but with God all things are possible."[13]

Try all you want. It is impossible to be who you were created to be unless God does it in you. God has given us His AM-ness (Chapter Four Endnotes #1). Thus, much of the Greek New Testament is written in terms of *being* rather than *becoming*. As John said, "As He is, so are we in this world."[14] Notice John didn't write, "as He is, so we are to become in this world." The power of the Gospel of Christ is not to be found in getting zapped with power by God or having enough faith or doing the right things. It is solely in our union with God through Jesus Christ. The power of the Early Church was because they understood their union with Christ.

---

[12] Act 14:11 (KJV)

[13] Mathew 19:26 (KJV)

[14] 1 John 4:17 (KJV)

Christ had forever eliminated the separation between God and man thus enabling early believers to recognize the ability inherent in their union with God in Christ. But, the Gnostics sought to introduce a doctrine that would destroy the power of that union. Jesus had declared His work completed. "It is finished."[15] The Gnostics taught a different outcome, "It was finished for Christ, but His followers have to wait until they die." The only way they could sell such a doctrine was to fabricate a lie that reintroduced a separation between God and mankind. But to succeed, that doctrine couldn't deny the resurrection of Christ or the fact that He was one hundred percent man. Their doctrine simply stated that there was a slight difference between the manhood of Jesus after the resurrection and the humanity of those He rescued. That difference accounted for why Jesus was righteous yet believers still suffered from sin.

According to Gnosticism, much of what Jesus had done created a *positional reality*, which upon the return of Jesus would become *actual*. This explanation made it possible to be saved yet still want to sin.

When believers don't understand what God accomplished in Christ, but want to live like they know God wants them to, dualism is an easy yet unsatisfying doctrine to swallow. The power of Gnosticism is that it prevents believers from understanding how to take the grace of God and the gift of righteousness.[16]

Because of this erroneous doctrine, many people now believe that complete union with Christ is for some time in the future. But, such a terrible teaching forever negates the idea of union with God through Christ. If believers are not united to Christ now, they never will be. God says our union with Christ is now. One of the most used prepositions in the Greek New Testament is the word *en* which means *within or inside*. It means that we are united to Christ *now* and in the *future*. The power of our relationship with God is not because God empowers us to live life for Him by using an independent gift of His power. It is because the life of Christ within us empowers us as He participates *with* us, *in*

---

[15] John 19:30 (KJV)

[16] Romans 5:17

us. God lives His life *in union with* us which is why Jesus said we can expect to do greater things than He did[17] (Chapter Four Endnotes #2).

Unfortunately, the Gnostic dualism heresy introduced in the First Century has become accepted modern Christian theology. You may have heard it referred to as "the sin nature" or that people have two natures which are at war with each other.[18] Many who teach this believe it is what the Apostles taught. These people are just teaching what they have been taught, which is what their teachers were taught. And since they read the Bible through the lens of what they have been taught, they only see what they *expect* Paul to have meant. The Gnostic heresy became such a threat during the First Century that even the Apostle John spoke against it. In 1 John 4:2, John addressed the foundation of Gnosticism which claimed that Jesus wasn't fully man. Since He was just a little different, His experience was not exactly like the rest of humanity. From this gnostic logic came many heresies we see today. Any teaching that says Jesus had it better or different than the rest of mankind underhandedly strips the Gospel of all power. It renders Christ's life as a human a fake.

That late First Century believers began to accept a doctrine of dualism is understandable. Paul wrote that "anyone who is in Christ is a new creature."[19] All believers want to live godly lives yet there appears to be a conflict between who God says we are and how we feel. Many believers are perplexed why sin still seems to rule them when the Bible says it shouldn't. As time progressed and the realness of Christ's resurrection grew more distant, the Church lost its grasp of what Christ had accomplished. It became necessary to account for the desire to sin and yet enable believers to still be saved, hence, the dual nature theology.

Today, anyone who seeks to return to the Early Church's understanding is often declared a teacher of false doctrine. But as just stated,

---

[17] John 14:12

[18] Coauthor James Q. here, think of it this way. We're part of the body of Christ as much as your fingers are a part of your body. If we have sin, then the body of Christ has sin. If the body of Christ has sin, then it cannot be perfect, and if He's not perfect, the entire story and redemption becomes quite useless.

[19] 2 Corinthians 5:17

even the Apostle John fought against this dualistic teaching of the Gnostics. It is amazing how the darkness has succeeded in deceiving God's children.

The Bible says you *have* the mind of Christ, not that you *will have* it.[20] Believers are one with Christ and since He has only one mind, we have only one mind, too -- His. You can't have two minds if He has only one. The unintended consequence of the logic of much modern theology is that believers can only be partially in Christ because if part of their being has yet to be converted that part cannot be in Him. But, one hundred percent of Christ was raised out of dead, not just part of Him. And, Christ's death was every human's death, which means His resurrection was ours also.[21] Though some may not accept or believe it, His resurrection was for, and as, every human being. The preaching of the Gospel is to get them to believe and accept it. Sadly, many preach that salvation is by grace if unbelievers first get right with God or some other nonsense.

Considering the difference between *being* and *doing*, much misunderstanding of mind renewal comes from the fact that the word is often mistranslated. The word *renewing* is a verb while the Greek word from which it comes is a noun. To the early believers, it was not an act, but a fact (Chapter Four Endnotes #3). How often have you been told you need to renew your mind? According to Paul, you can't because it already is renewed!

But now we face a new problem. We too often fill our minds with thoughts we know Jesus wouldn't think. So, what's going on? If the scriptures say to *be* transformed by a mind that has already been renewed, how do we do it? How do we *be* transformed?

Let's start with the notion that everything that God says is true, and He means every word He says, which means our minds have really been renewed. Let's also assume that Jesus was telling the *truth* when He said, "Without me you can do nothing."[22] Should we conclude that God is wrong and that there is still something wrong with our minds? No.

---

[20] 1 Corinthians 2:16

[21] 2 Corinthians 5:14

[22] John 15:5 (JEC)

But it would be proper to admit that something may be wrong with our thinking. If not for the fact that our minds are already renewed by the work of Christ, the expectation of the splendor or glory of God in our lives, which Paul wrote about in Romans 5:2, would be in vain. "This favor within which…we boast upon our expectation of the splendor of God."[23] Also, Paul said, "Therefore if any man be in Christ, he is a new creature: old things are passed away; behold, all things are become new," which includes our minds.[24] How can we boast with such expectation if our minds have not already been renewed (Chapter Four Endnotes #4)?

Behold is a fascinating word. It is frequently used in the Bible yet often overlooked in Bible teachings. It is always in the imperative mood, which means it is a command. Why would God command us to behold something? Because there is more to it than what appears on the surface. So, you keep looking at it because God wants to show you something that may not be obvious at first glance.

What are the *all* things that Paul wrote about when he said, "…all things are become new"? Is anything not included in the *all*? Our bodies still look the same but they are now the temple of the Holy Spirit, thus they have changed, though not yet the final version. In fact, Paul says it is the Spirit of Christ within a believer that keeps the body alive and healthy[25] (Chapter Four Endnotes #5).

Since God's Word is true, then there must be another way to understand that erroneous concept of *renewing the mind*. It is obvious to me that those who have rendered *renewal* as *renewing* felt forced to so the verse would make sense. I prefer to not do that. I believe we can ask God what He means, and He'll tell us. Our problem is that we don't usually want to wait for His answer, which regarding the Scriptures, may take some time. Why not ask God and then wait until He shows you what He means?

---

[23] Romans 5:2 (JEC)
[24] 2 Corinthians 5:17 (KJV)
[25] According to the ancient Hebrew concept of covenant, what happened to Jesus happened to us.

The Process

There is a *process* working in every human that dominates our lives, for good and bad. Being familiar with this process enables us to cooperate with the Holy Spirit and begin experiencing the *renewal* about which Paul spoke. It was established by God and is how the Holy Spirit causes us to live the life of Christ while in these bodies on Earth. The process to which I refer resides in your heart and is called *believing*. Mind renewal becomes your experience as you cooperate with the Holy Spirit and believe His *truth*.

Man was created to live what he believes. Believing occurs in the heart, out of which the issues of life flow. Our foundational beliefs, many of which we have long ago forgotten, provide the fuel for our thoughts. Our thoughts—many of which we are not even aware—control our behavior. Consider Paul's statement in 2 Corinthians: "I believed and therefore have I spoken; we also believe and therefore speak."[26] This verse is not talking about positive confession. It does *not* refer to confessing the Word of God. It is talking about one of the things that happens automatically when you truly believe something. That belief will show up in your behavior, including your speech. But as you will see, it goes far beyond that.

Consider God's response to the building of the Tower of Babel.[27] "And the Lord said, Behold, the people is one, and they have all one language... and now nothing will be restrained from them, which they have imagined to do"[28] (Chapter Four Endnotes #6). The more you think about something the more real it becomes, even if it is a lie. Experiencing the mind of Christ *being* in us starts by agreeing with the Holy Spirit when He exposes your wrong beliefs to you. Then with His help, you decide to no longer believe those misbeliefs are right and choose to believe God's *truth* instead. You stop believing things that Jesus knows aren't real and start believing what He knows is true. It is that simple (Chapter Two Endnotes #2).

---

[26] 2 Corinthians 4:13 (KJV)
[27] Genesis 11:1-9
[28] Genesis 11:6 (KJV)

How many people do you know that try to please God and always feel like they fall short? The problem isn't that they don't work hard enough or have enough discipline. The problem isn't that they are inherently evil. Their trouble is just a lack of understanding. Some of the things they believe to be true are false, but they don't know it. There was a time when I was more aware of things I felt I did wrong than of God's unconditional love. I wanted to trust and obey but, like the Apostle Paul said, so often I did wrong things. St. Paul addresses this issue in detail in the book of Romans. "For to will is present with me; but how to perform that which is good I find not. For the good that I would I do not: but the evil which I would not, that I do"[29] (Chapter Four Endnotes #7).

Some people teach that God is mysterious, and no one can truly understand Him. They say that since He is sovereign, we can never be sure what He is going to do. I think they are saying that God cannot be trusted. That He doesn't have to keep His Word because it could get in the way of Him dishing out some judgment on someone. However, God is a reasonable person who wants to be understood. In fact, He longs for us to know Him. If He didn't, then why did He give us His Word? Why would He reveal Himself through the Bible if He doesn't want us to know Him? Why didn't He just turn out the lights in the beginning? Sometimes a little logic can take you a long way. Plain and simple, He gave us His Word so we can understand Him. When the disciples asked Jesus to show them the Father, He replied, "Those who have seen me have seen the Father."[30] I don't think He could have made it clearer. The Father wants us to understand Him so much that He sent His Son, who is His exact image. The Father is just like the Son (Chapter Four Endnotes #8)!

We know that Jesus is kind, compassionate, and caring. We know that He is Love. Unfortunately, many see Him as the buffer between them and God the Father, as though God is some big old grouchy Being that enjoys pulling wings off flies and destroying what He created. I think they are afraid of the Father because *they think* He secretly hates

---

[29] Romans 7:18-19 (KJV)

[30] John 14:9 (TCNT Part 1)

people who aren't perfect. What a sad perspective. This is an example of knowing something that God doesn't know. But Jesus said He is the full image of God and when you look at Him you are seeing the Father. This means that our Father is kind, compassionate, and caring. He doesn't want mankind to suffer, so He sent Jesus to reveal that fact. "For God so loved the world, that he gave his only begotten Son."[31] Jesus went about doing good and healing all that were oppressed of the devil.[32]

The desire of our Father's heart is for us to know Him. He sent Jesus as the human representation of Who He is and what He thinks about us. Jesus lived His Father's love and faithfulness to us right before mankind's eyes. In fact, the Apostle John quotes Jesus saying, "Anyone completely seeing me has completely seen the Father."[33]

In His prayer in the upper room, Jesus tells us again how wonderful it is to know the Father. "And this is life eternal, that they might know thee the only true God, and Jesus Christ whom thou hast sent."[34] Eternal life is not the duration of life, but the quality. Knowing God the way Jesus meant changes the quality of our lives. It gives us His quality of life, which is what God *wants* us to have!

Not only does God live in the light and want us to know who He *is*, but He is logical and wants us to share His logic.

Remember God pleading with Israel? "Come now, and let us reason together, saith the Lord."[35]

God is always the same; He never changes. In the same way He wanted to reason and talk with Israel, He wants to reason and talk with you. God doesn't want you to follow a list of rules. He wants fellowship with you, and as it grows, you will increasingly realize His life in you. The type of fellowship God desires is not distant and uncaring. It's real, up close, and personal. He wants you to be His friend. Speaking to Israel (Jacob), He said, "But you, Israel, are my servant. You're Jacob,

---

[31] John 3:16 (KJV)

[32] Acts 10:38

[33] John 14:9 (JEC)

[34] John 17:3 (KJV)

[35] Isaiah 1:18 (KJV)

my first choice, descendants of my good friend Abraham."[36] Abraham is your father too. You're a child of God because of His covenant with Abraham and Jesus. (If all you saw in the preceding verse is the words *my servant*, what do you think might have caused you not to notice *my good friend, Abraham*?)

> This is why righteousness depends upon faith, so that it may be God's gift, and that the fulfillment of the promise may be made sure for all Abraham's descendants—not only for those who have the Law, but also for those who simply have Abraham's faith. For, in the sight of that God in whom Abraham believed, and who gives life to the dead, and speaks of what does not yet exist as if it did, Abraham is the father of us all.[37]

God wants to be friends with you. Read James' statement: "And the scripture was fulfilled which saith, Abraham believed God, and it was imputed unto him for righteousness: and he was called the Friend of God."[38] Put your name in that verse, as in: "God calls me His friend." People watched Jesus with sinners, and He was so engaged they called Him "a friend of publicans and sinners."[39] God likes friends! He's not repulsed by people who do wrong.

Believe What God Believes

For years, I learned that being a good Christian depended on reading the Bible, praying, witnessing, tithing, and serving others, but it never worked for me. No matter how much I did, I always felt like it wasn't enough. I lived under a constant feeling of condemnation. It was an excellent day when I began to know that what I did for God had no bearing on His attitude toward me. What joy to discover that God did not want me to be His slave. Rather, He just wanted to love me. I was

---

[36] Isaiah 41:8 (msg)
[37] Romans 4:16 (msg)
[38] James 2:23 (KJV)
[39] Luke 7:34 (KJV)

created to *be* loved. In fact, John says, "We love because He first loved us."[40] This does not mean that because Jesus loves us, we are to go out and love people. It means that once we realize God's love for us, we will automatically love others. We won't be able to help it.

God's plan is for us to be so caught up in His love that we can't help but love the world like He does. Love will motivate us in every situation because God's natural response is always out of love and we were created in His image. His love is without conditions; so is ours. He loves the beautiful and ugly, the good and bad, and the weak and strong, equally. There is nothing about us that causes Him to love us. He loves us because we exist. He created us out of His love to live in His love. He wants us to know how good and kind He is toward us and will spend forever showing us. "That in the ages to come he might shew the exceeding riches of his grace in his kindness toward us through Christ Jesus."[41]

A meaningful change began when I finally understood how my heart works and how God created me to function. I began to blossom when I learned one of the principles of God—*beliefs create thoughts, actions, and habits*. Life changed dramatically when I realized that God's plan is to conform all my beliefs to His. That's why He sent the Holy Spirit. Why does He want my thinking to be like His? Because, my thoughts and actions will automatically follow suit.

God created inside us a certain process for changing our lives. It is the process by which we are saved and the process that Satan used to bring the corruption into the Garden. Everyone lives their lives by this process. You can't escape it. I will assume that as you read this you have been born again. (But if you haven't been, what I say still applies to you. So just relax and enjoy this. In fact, you might find much of what I write is even easier to accept.) God raised all of mankind from dead when He raised Christ. But, just because that is true doesn't mean all have accepted it, because they haven't. Now, by the power of His Holy Spirit, He is "working in us to cause us to will His will and do it"[42]

---

[40] 1 John 4:19 (KJV)
[41] Ephesians 2:7 (KJV)
[42] Phil 2:13 (JEC)

(Chapter Four Endnotes #9). God is still working on the worst people you can think of.

How are we saved? According to Paul, by believing God raised Jesus from the dead and confessing that He is Lord. "For if *with your lips* you acknowledge the truth of *the Message* that Jesus IS Lord, and believe *in your heart* that God raised him from the dead, you will be saved."[43] Nothing else is needed. If you accept Him as Lord, it is the beginning of a new life. All you need to know is who you now are. That's why He gave us the Bible. You learn who you are by learning who He *is*. Of course, accepting Jesus as Lord, by default, meant you rejected another belief, i.e., that you were lord of your life. Every person experiences this differently but when boiled down to the essentials, Paul's description always fits.

So, once you are born-again, how does God continue the process of transforming you? How do we grow up into Christ? God teaches us the *truth* so that we will know His love. As we agree with God that He loves us like He says, we will increasingly believe, think, and act like Him. He gave us the Bible and the Holy Spirit, who inspired it so that we can know Him.

Your heart already knows God's *truth*. "This is the covenant that I will make with them after those days, saith the Lord, I will put my laws into their hearts, and in their minds will I write them."[44] Cooperation is simply a matter of agreeing with Him. Just believe and say Yes or Amen (it is so). This is not mental assent and has nothing to do with your feelings. We agree with God because we know He is right and can never lie.[45]

Transformed Understanding

One of the keys to cooperating with God's *truth* so that you can *be* transformed is understanding the single most destructive issue in our lives.

---

[43] Romans 10:9 (TCNT Part 2)
[44] Hebrews 10:16 (KJV)
[45] Titus 1:2

> *That damaging problem is...all the things we believe that are not true; things we have believed because we thought they were true and never learned they are not! They include beliefs about self, family, friends, God, life, money, everything. There are unknown untruths throughout our belief system, and God wants us to change our minds about them.*
>
> *Your belief system not only affects your ability to make friends or money, but it also affects every other area of your life and is the sole determiner of your happiness and fulfillment. It is our belief systems, not what we possess, that cause a poor person to be happy and a rich one to be miserable. No one has a belief system exactly like yours. Thus, no one else thinks like you.*

Humans are created to understand and therefore we seek it. If we don't take God's understanding, we will make up our own. That is why King Solomon said, "Wisdom is the principle thing so get wisdom, and with all thy getting, get understanding."[46] Solomon was talking about getting understanding from God, rather than creating our own.

A Heart Exposed: A Testimony

At the height of a personal crisis, I began to understand how people are created to function. I was depressed at an early age—around six or seven. During my junior year of high school, I was in a motorcycle accident that left me unable to function normally for years. A severe skin condition resulted in massive facial scarring, compounding the emotional trauma. My mental and emotional distress grew worse through college as I suffered severe anxiety and increasingly depressed mood swings. I spent thousands of dollars for counseling but to no avail. Diagnosed manic-depressive while in graduate school at Oral Roberts University (ORU), emotional turmoil prevented me from finishing work toward a master's degree. The pressure of my studies as I struggled to stay sane was too much. I left the University and found a job teaching

---

[46] Proverbs 4:7 (KJV)

science and math in a public school. A year later, I went into business, something with which I was very familiar. I was in my mid-twenties.

During my years at home, my Dad had seldom missed an opportunity to tell me how worthless certain people were. The fear that my Dad, in turn, would call me useless or worthless ate at me, though I knew his comments about others really meant he already thought I was. Somewhere along the line I picked up phrases like "Make yourself useful" and began saying them to myself. My fear of failure resulted in frequent panic attacks. I have always been a thinker so, even though I may have appeared passive physically, my thoughts were always raging inwardly. After many years in business, the feverish mental activity and fear caught up with me and I burned out. Burnout can be terrifying. Mine lasted over a year. Except for continual terror, it was a period of emotional numbness. It seemed like my life was over. If not for a top-notch manager, my company was doomed because I could not complete a logical business thought.

The proformas I had created left me scratching my head.[47] Though I had created them, I no longer understood what they meant. I felt dead, and my doctors were of little help. None of the antidepressant medications helped. On the verge of suicide, I admitted myself to a Christian psychiatric hospital. For years, I had done everything I could to enter God's rest but to no avail. My experience in that hospital left me feeling worse than ever. It took only twenty-four hours in that institution to realize that no program or person could give me the thing I needed most—command of my mind. Before I left, God arranged a life-changing experience.

Frank was a former client; one I was glad to see leave. He was not only angry and mean, but several times, had reduced my employees to tears. Then one day, he attacked me with a vengeance. It had been especially painful because I knew he was the head of a respected Christian family institution. Though I *felt* no bitterness, what he had done was never far from memory. Imagine my surprise when I learned he was my counselor. In a very brief encounter, we spoke about his behavior.

---

[47] Pro-formas are spreadsheet profit-and-loss projections that I had created for business plans.

Actually, I talked about it; he denied everything. But finally, he said, "If I've done anything to hurt you, I apologize." Something inside me said that was the best I would get from him and that I should forgive him. Even though I didn't think it was important, I did just that. I said, "I forgive you." Boy, was I surprised and embarrassed when suddenly I broke down crying.

I had been unaware that my little grudge against Frank had been raging bitterness. Forgiving him had opened a reservoir of pain in my heart I did not know existed. The result? I suddenly felt freer and more in control of my life. I had to call my attorney to get them to release me, but I left that hospital. I was free from the bitterness and rage that I held against Frank. On the surface, it seems as if I was set free from that deep depression because I forgave someone who had hurt me. This type of conclusion is an example of how *the lie* has hidden in our belief systems.[48] Because mankind is now performance-oriented (life is all about doing and having), it is easy to conclude that something happened because of what was done. Unless we let the Holy Spirit show us how we have believed *the lie*, we will continue to look for what someone did that caused a result so that we can either do it again and get the same result or avoid certain outcomes.

Is this confusing? Then back up for a moment and consider this. It was not just the act of saying I forgive you that set me free, but what caused me to say it. I had simply changed what I believed about Frank, what he had done, and my responsibility in the situation. I realized I was no longer responsible for making Frank pay for his deeds. He was God's responsibility, and God would have to handle him. The *truth* was that God was in charge of dealing with Frank. *The lie* was that I was God and responsible for dealing with Frank. When I realized this my beliefs changed, and I could truly let go and let God do what He does, which is to change Frank by loving him. Forgiving Frank happened because of a change in my beliefs. I had realized that I was no longer his judge. Forgiving Frank was the natural outcome of releasing him into God's just and loving hands. In fact, the Greek word translated forgive means "to release." You are releasing someone so God can deal with

---

[48] Covered in Chapter Four, Section *"The Lie."*

them. You are releasing your claim as a god who wants to punish the offender to the only God. They are now His business.

After this experience, I realized that the human soul is very deep. There are many layers of experience and beliefs deep within our hearts, of which we are not even aware. Though buried out of sight, some of them still dramatically affect our lives. I see evidence of these beliefs as I respond or react to life, sometimes in ways that leave me perplexed. It's those times when I ask myself, "Why did I do that?"

Spirit versus Flesh

Many Bible teachers struggle to understand the seventh chapter of Romans; however, it becomes straightforward with a little background. The Apostle Paul's uses of the word *sin* primarily referred to error and not wrongdoing. By the word error, he is referring to knowing and believing things that aren't true (Chapter Four Endnotes #10). Wrong beliefs cause havoc in our lives. This is why the ministry of the Holy Spirit is so important. He is the only person who knows the truth about what we believe and can lead us into the *truth* we so desperately need.

(Note: Many translations frequently and incorrectly add the article *the* before instances of the words *spirit* and *flesh* when there is no article in the original text. In addition, Greek scholars often eliminate the article before *spirit* and *flesh*, saying the Greeks only used it for emphasis. That tells me they frequently have no real idea what God is saying. Paul often used the word *spirit* (without the article *the*) to refer to *an* attitude of intention to believe God's *truth* regardless of evidence for or against it. His use of the word *flesh* (without the article *the*) usually refers to *an* attitude of deciding to believe that the experiences of our flesh reveal ultimate *truth*.)

When you cease looking at *sin* as wrong-doing and see it as *error*, and when you stop thinking of *flesh* as an evil body and instead understand it as "beliefs based on experiences while living in a corrupt world," Paul's message begins to make more sense. Remember when Paul cried out, "I've tried everything, and nothing helps. I'm at the end of my rope. Is there no one who can do anything for me?"[49] Paul was obviously referring to his and everyone else's experience.

> I realize that I don't have what it takes. I can will it, but I can't do it. I decide to do good, but I don't really do it; I decide not to do bad, but then I do it anyway. My decisions, such as they are, don't result in actions. Something has gone wrong deep within me and gets the better of me every time. It happens so regularly that it's predictable. The moment I decide to do good, sin is there to trip me up. I truly delight in God's commands, but it's pretty obvious that not all of me joins in that delight. Parts of me covertly rebel, and just when I least expect it, they take charge. I've tried everything and nothing helps. I'm at the end of my rope. Is there no one who can do anything for me? Isn't that the real question?[50]

Paul then answered his own question: "The answer, thank God, is that Jesus Christ can and does. He acted to set things right in this life of contradictions where I want to serve God with all my heart and mind, but am pulled by the influence of sin to do something totally different."[51]

Substituting the word *error* in the place of *sin* causes many verses to make more sense. *Sin* has somewhat of a nebulous meaning, whereas *error* is identifiable. With the help of the Holy Spirit, we can understand the process for getting rid of error. Using the word *error* leaves no room for some indefinable force roaming around inside of us that causes us to act and think in ways contrary to God.

Some places where Paul uses the word *mind*, he is referring to a thinking that is directed by God's *truth* (i.e., spiritually minded). Likewise, sometimes his use of the word *flesh* relates to a thought-life ruled by a person's understanding of their experiences apart from God's

---

[49] Romans 7:24 (msg)
[50] Romans 7:18-24 (msg)
[51] Romans 7:25 (msg)

truth (i.e., carnally minded). "I thank God through Jesus Christ our Lord. So then with the mind I myself serve the law of God; but with the flesh the law of sin."[52]

In Romans, Paul says, "For they that are according to flesh mind the things of the flesh and they that are according to spirit mind the things of the Spirit."[53] When you look at Romans 7:25 in the light of what I have been saying, it should begin to make more sense. Living according to flesh is living by believing what your natural senses are telling you. Your physical senses tell you what they see, hear, feel, etc., and *flesh* means believing that your senses tell you the *truth*. Things are as bad or as good as your feelings say they are. God may say He loves you but that storm that just wiped out everything you own, for example, says He doesn't. Then your insurance company calls the destruction "an act of God" so, apparently, God doesn't care, at best. Flesh may also cause you to have an evil desire to do something you know is wrong. When you believe that wrong desires are just part of living in your body, you will be unable to resist or miserable while you try.

When you stand firm in the belief that God loves you and would never seek your harm, it is an example of spirit. Not the Spirit of God but spirit, an attitude determined to believe God's *truth* is final and absolute and the only *truth*. Though a child of God can live by the minds of flesh and spirit (i.e., contradictory beliefs), they will produce inconsistency, confusion, and condemnation as one moment we find ourselves doing exactly what we should, and the very next moment doing what we shouldn't. This was James' point. "But let him ask in faith, nothing wavering. For he that wavereth is like a wave of the sea driven with the wind and tossed. For let not that man think that he shall receive anything of the Lord. A double minded man is unstable in all his ways."[54] In other words, if your prayers are based on beliefs that are a mixture of God's *truth* and Satan's lies, you will struggle and be less than stable. You are double-minded.

---

[52] Romans 7:25 (KJV)
[53] Romans 8:5 (JEC)
[54] James 1:6-8 (KJV)

Paul's ultimate intent is to clarify the power of *the law of the Spirit of the life in Christ Jesus* versus *the law of the sin (error) and the death*, which he compared in Romans 8:2 and beyond. The article *the*, which in the original text is in front of *sin* and *death*, does not exist in most translations. But, its presence points to a particular error and death, which is explained in Chapter Four, Section *"The Lie"*. *The law of the Spirit of the life in Christ Jesus* makes it possible to live by spirit—that is, by believing God's *truth*. *The law of the sin and the death* causes people to live by flesh, which is basing beliefs on natural evidence. *The law of the Spirit of life* tells us that believing God results in righteousness, which produces life. *The law of the error and the death* says that believing Satan's lies results in evil and spiritual death.[55] *The law of the sin and the death* refer to the original error and the death that followed it.

Believing lies is bad for at least three reasons. It is an act of embracing darkness, it results in a declaration of independence from God, and since we always live what we believe, it results in thoughts and behaviors not consistent with being a new creature in Christ. To *be* who we are in Christ requires believing His *truth*, which is possible only by the work of the Holy Spirit. He alone can expose and deal with the lies that prevent the life of Jesus from being "manifest in our mortal flesh."[56] This is the process to which the Apostle Paul specifically referred in Romans 8:13: "For if ye live after the flesh, ye shall die: but if ye through *the Spirit* do mortify the deeds of the body, ye shall live."[57] Though this statement is true, due to a mistranslation this is not what the original verse says. The original language says, "if you by *spirit* put to death the deeds of the body, you shall live."[58] There is an enormous difference. The word *spirit* refers to an attitude fixed on believing God's *truth*. The word *Spirit* relates to the Holy Spirit, to whom Paul refers

---

[55] Human beings never cease to exist. Thus, the result of refusing to believe God's *truth* is not cessation of existence but separation from God's quality of life, i.e., spiritual death.

[56] 2 Corinthians 4:11 (KJV)

[57] Romans 8:13 (KJV)

[58] Romans 8:13 (JEC)

in the next verse. "For as many as are led by the Spirit of God, they are the sons of God."[59]

Like many Christians, I always thought that this verse was a mysterious reference to the Holy Spirit leading me around to do things that God wanted done. But, Paul tells us exactly what the Spirit is leading us to do in verses thirteen and fifteen. The Spirit is leading us in the process of learning to believe the *truth*. The Spirit is leading us into an attitude (or spirit) by which we believe and live God's *truth*. Remember, Jesus called Him the Spirit of *truth*. It is evident that the Spirit of God is all about *truth*.

I realize that this may be an entirely unusual way of viewing the Bible from what you have been taught; but what we have been taught hasn't worked. It hasn't produced the tremendous fruit and ability about which Jesus and Paul spoke. Jesus said, "If you continue in my word, then are ye my disciples indeed; and ye shall know the truth, and the truth shall make you free."[60] Free from what? Whatever is hindering the life of God from bearing His fruit in you (Chapter Four Endnotes #11). If we stand our ground in His Word regardless of our feelings and experiences, we will *see* our salvation (Chapter Four Endnotes #12). It is not a matter of you doing the right thing. It is knowing and believing that God is working in you to cause you to see the victory He is giving you right now, because He loves you and swore an oath to do so.[61] "But thank God for giving us the victory by means of our Lord Jesus Christ."[62] No matter what happens, no matter what we feel, we stand our ground in that belief knowing that God is working to make it real *to* us. It is already real *in* us. We just may not yet see or feel it. If we are tempted to believe that God is a liar, or we don't have the strength to endure something, we can remind each other of what Paul told the Corinthians: "There hath no temptation taken you but such as is common to man: but God is faithful, who will not suffer you to be tempted

---

[59] Romans 8:14 (KJV)
[60] John 8:31-32 (KJV)
[61] Luke 1:73
[62] 1 Corinthians 15:57 (JEC)

Unseen

above that ye are able; but will with the temptation also make a way to escape, that ye may be able to bear it."[63]

So, you think that you cannot bear the pressure, the trial that you are facing that is flooding your whole being? God says He won't let any trial be so bad that you are unable to bear it. So, you may think you can't stand it, but God says you can. He is with you to ensure it.

In Romans 8:13-15, most translations have it right in that it is God the Spirit who is doing the work. But the question is: what is the Spirit leading them to do and how do they do it? This is a critical issue! We *must* know, or our lives will be hit and miss until we die; we will continually miss the mark.

Remember I talked earlier about inserting the meaning of a word in its place? Let's see what happens when we do that with verse thirteen:

> For if ye live according to (in agreement with) [an attitude of believing what your natural senses tell you], ye shall die: but if ye by [an attitude determined to believe God's *truth*] do mortify the deeds of the body, ye shall live.[64, 65] For as many as are led by the Spirit of God, they are the sons of God.

Living in agreement with flesh is nothing more than basing your understanding of life on worldly experience or on what you see, hear, and feel, or have been taught by someone who doesn't know better. Mortifying the deeds of the body through spirit refers specifically to the change of behavior which comes from changing our minds about the lies we believe and choosing to believe God's *truth*. That change occurs because of what Paul calls the *Law of Faith*, which says that we automatically live what we really believe (Chapter Four Endnotes #13). Very simply, *the law of faith* says that beliefs have as much effect

---

[63] 1 Corinthians 10:13 (KJV)

[64] The preposition *kata* (κατά), which is often translated "against" can also be translated "according to" or "in agreement with" in the accusative case, which makes more sense.

[65] The noun *spirit* (πνεύμαται) is in the dative case and could easily be arguably translated "by spirit."

on behavior as the law of gravity has over an object dropped from a tree. Nothing with mass escapes the pull of gravity. Likewise, believing the *truth* always produces behavior consistent with *it*. Of course, the opposite law is also valid. *The law of unbelief* says that believing a lie always promotes behavior consistent with lies. Hence, if thoughts, behaviors, or emotions in your life are inconsistent with what you think you believe, it is evidence that you may intellectually agree with God's *truth* in an area but are still embracing some lie. The only way to get to the bottom of this is by the ability of the Holy Spirit. His love for you is so great that He yearns to shine His light of *truth* in your heart and forever rid you of the cause of your trouble.

When we change our minds about the lies we believe and choose to believe the *truth*, even in the face of contradictory evidence that may be overwhelming us through our five senses, the Holy Spirit causes our experience to catch up with what we believe. The things that troubled us will eventually cease to do so.

Paul's words in the seventh chapter of Romans express the frustration of a believer who does not understand why it is so difficult to live according to God's standards. The reason becomes apparent in Chapter Eight where Paul says that pleasing God is only possible by being spiritually minded. The mind of flesh results in death (Chapter Four Endnotes #14).

> That the righteousness of the law might be fulfilled in us who walk not after the flesh but after the Spirit. For they that are after the flesh do mind the things of the flesh; but they that are after the Spirit the things of the Spirit. For to be carnally minded is death; but to be spiritually minded is life and peace. Because the carnal mind is enmity against God: for it is not subject to the law of God, neither indeed can be. So then they that are in the flesh cannot please God.[66]

---

[66] Romans 8:4-8 (KJV)

(Note: In the original language, there is no article before the words *flesh* and *spirit* in this passage. Paul is referring to flesh and spirit, not *the flesh* and *the Spirit*.)

God wants us to be free from everything that hinders our ability to believe His Word and do His *truth*. This becomes possible only as we hold fast to the *truth* and, thus, come to know it intimately. Knowing His *truth* makes us free. "And ye shall know the truth, and the truth shall make you free."[67] God loves for us to know His truth, and will show it to anyone who asks. We come to know His *truth* by believing it. "That Christ may dwell in your hearts by faith (believing the *truth*); that ye... May be able to comprehend with all saints... the love of Christ."[68]

Many times, I've felt like the *truth* was elusive, yet once I saw it, I have realized He had been showing it to me for a long time; but I had instead let my thoughts and emotions trap me in mental darkness.

The fact is, we are all suffering from that type of mental entrapment of our lives; but He will not stop working until we have let go of it. God never shows us *truth* and expects us to believe it by willpower; rather, He gifts us with the ability to believe it. With the revelation of a *truth* comes the gift of believing it. However, there are other reasons we may fail to believe His *truth* besides mental entrapment. In Luke, Jesus discusses them. For instance, the Holy Spirit may show someone the *truth*, who seems to embrace it. But before long, they become choked with unbelief or worry and reject the very thing in which they had previously rejoiced. Speaking of how one group of hearers responded to the seeds of His Words, Jesus said, "[by] That which fell among the thorn bushes are meant those who hear the Message, but who as they go on their way, are completely choked by this world's anxieties and wealth and pleasures, and bring nothing to perfection."[69]

---

[67] John 8:32 (KJV)

[68] Ephesians 3:17-19 (This is the knowing where we are aware that we know. It is a supernatural knowledge, a knowing that passes the knowledge acquired from reading a book.)

[69] Luke 8:14 (TCNT Part 1)

The law of the spirit of life says that if you live by spirit (an attitude set on treasuring God's *truth* instead of what your senses tell you), you will automatically live the *truth* you believe and be free from *the sin* and *the death*. "For the law of the Spirit of Life in Christ Jesus hath made me free from the law of sin and death."[70] As you walk in spirit you will learn to recognize lies and will grow out of their devastating effects.

Let Go and Let God: A Testimony

Years ago, I spent some time translating the book of Romans. Not until recently did the impact of my translation of Chapter 5:5 hit me. "Because the love of God has been squandered and continues in that condition inside our hearts by means of the Holy Spirit, Him having been devoted to us"[71] (Chapter Four Endnotes #15). Yes, the Greek word commonly translated "given" can also be rendered "devoted." It implies that it was the decision of the triune God, who loves us with perfect love, to devote the Holy Spirit to loving us from inside us.[72] It was not just a decision by the Holy Spirit to pour out God's love in our hearts, but the joint decision of Father, Son, and Holy Spirit to devote the Spirit's entire attention to loving us. It is a love so massively overflowing within us that the Greek text makes it appear God is wasting it. But He isn't. That's how important we are to Him, the Holy Them.[73] Out of that overflowing love comes the Holy Spirit's primary ministry, which is to train us in the *truth*. Sometimes that is as simple as showing us something we haven't yet seen. But sometimes, it involves first exposing wrong beliefs that get in the way of the *truth* we want to live. This can be a short process but may also require a prolonged period, which can be very painful as we hold on to wrong beliefs with white knuckles because we are so convinced that an erroneous belief is right. In the latter case, the mental and emotional pain can be excruciating.

---

[70] Romans 8:2 (KJV)

[71] Romans 5:5 (JEC)

[72] The word *triune* refers to the Holy Trinity—Father, Son, and Holy Spirit.

[73] Refers to the Triune God, the Holy Trinity.

This is not God's fault but because we often unknowingly hold on to a belief that is contrary to our very nature and, just like a physical sickness, results in a loss of the inner harmony that God created us to enjoy. We were no more made to believe lies than we have been created to be sick or broke. To teach us the *truth*, the Holy Spirit must expose things we believe that are not true because they block our ability to believe His *truth*. As the light of God's *truth* searches your heart and mind to prove wrong beliefs, you will sometimes feel unpleasant—sometimes for quite a while. But that unpleasantness is always a prelude to greater joy and peace. Since the Holy Spirit directs and assists the process of helping you change your beliefs, you are safe, even though you may not feel that way (Chapter Four Endnotes #16).

It is reassuring to understand how God is working in you. His love comforts us in the turmoil that sometimes results when He brings to light the things that must change in our beliefs. It is important to God that you come to know He *is* Love, and what that means, so that during those times of turmoil and internal discomfort you can rest in His promise that He will never abandon you to your troubles, regardless of the source or reason for those problems.

Though the work of Christ on your behalf is complete, He is working in you to make your reality in Christ *real* to you. The heart of man is profound and complex, and we do not know ourselves as well as we think we do. Unfortunately, things we know and have believed are true but which are not the *truth* hinder us from realizing what the Holy Spirit has been telling us, which then prevents us from experiencing the life we were created to live. Many people think they already know what is important and are not interested in learning anything else. It is sad that so many of God's children are content with just a little more of this and a bit more of that and a few adjustments here and a few over there when God has so much more for them. It's called free life! God wants us to experience the abundant life about which Jesus spoke. To do so, there must be a radical readjustment of our goals and understandings of life. No matter what you have achieved, you've barely scratched the surface of Christ's gifts in you. I not only want to provoke you to lift your sights, but to show you how to do it.

James E. Campbell, Jr, James Q. Campbell

It was more than a few years ago that I realized how tired I was of trying to be a good Christian and be different. My behavior had grown more spiritual yet inwardly little had changed. When I admitted that I was just acting religious like so many others, something wonderful happened in my heart and mind. I began learning how to let go and let God. He began showing me how to cooperate with Him, and I experienced Jesus's words:

> Are you tired? Worn out? Burned out on religion? Come to me. Get away with me and you'll recover your life. I'll show you how to take a real rest. Walk with me and work with me—watch how I do it. Learn the unforced rhythms of grace. I won't lay anything heavy or ill-fitting on you. Keep company with me and you'll learn to live freely and lightly.[74]

When I finally realized that it was not my responsibility to be a good Christian and admitted I was incapable of it, God began to take over. In fact, this change in my belief system set me free from the desire for pornography, which had bound me for years.

I was frustrated and under a dense cloud of condemnation. Despairing that I was destined to forever live with that lust, I remember saying to God, "I give up. From this moment on, I will never again try to be a good Christian. If I am confronted with an opportunity to sin that I cannot resist, I won't even bother trying to resist. But this I know, Your word is true, and it is true for me. It is true about me. I don't know how to make myself obey You, so I am no longer going to try. But this one thing I will do. You are God and are good and Your mercy endures forever, so I will worship You." Then I got down on my knees and worshiped God. Within moments, something totally unexpected happened. My despair and frustration ceased, and freedom exploded in my heart. The lust for pornography disappeared.

This was a dramatic experience for me. Experiences like this have happened a few other times but the process that God works in us is quiet

---

[74] Matthew 11:28-30 (msg)

and we don't usually notice the change until later. There are some who would say that a decision like I made would cause a person to start sinning. To the contrary, that decision allowed God to remove my desire for pornography. I had finally let go of my struggle to do God's will and had let God do it within me. Rather than increasing my desire to do wrong, something deep inside had changed. My tendencies toward those desires disappeared. My fear that God would punish me if I did not perform properly ceased.

Please understand, the worship did not set me free. Rather, it was the fact that I finally believed the *truth* about my inability to serve God and was honest about it. It was a gut-wrenching experience, not something I did because somebody else had done it. I was at the point of despair, ready to give up, and let God do with me what He would. If that meant sending me to Hell, then so be it. How did I "let go and let God?" I let go when what I believed changed. It was not an act of willpower. It was God's love. Since He could do nothing else, He let me struggle until I had no energy left to fight my problems. Of course, this wasn't God's preferred set of events to get me to the point where I could change. He just works in conditions as they are. I want to make it very clear that God did not cause or have anything to do with the problems that troubled me. The world provides plenty of problems all by itself. God never desires to add to them. He can't. He is Love. The second I quit struggling, He was there loving me, and I was free.

What We Know Can Hurt Us

The freedom that is in Christ can feel uncertain and frightening and once we are there, it is wonderful. Unfortunately, even though people may dislike rules, regulations, and laws, that is where they tend to be the most comfortable. Freedom can be scary and that is why people cling to rules. Citizens often like it when Congress is busy passing laws because it means they are doing something important and must be taking control. The answer to every problem seems to be some rule or law. Though they may grumble about them, people like laws because they feel safe. By following rules, we, too, feel in control. This is just one example of how *the lie* has manipulated us. Many people set up their own rules, which only they can follow, because that makes them feel superior. That's the way it is with religions. My laws are the right ones. If you don't keep them, then you are wrong. Following my rules make me better than you. Or we think, *I can't follow the laws like I'm supposed to so I'm no good. There is something wrong with me.*

How do you get a baby to grow and become an adult? Is it through discipline? A good beating now and then? Telling them what they're supposed to be like when they grow up and criticizing them when they don't meet expectations? How about a quality education? Of course not. What all parents should do to make their kids grow is nothing! Did you tell your thirteen-year-old boy to have his growth spurt now? Did you teach your teenage girl to be interested in boys? It happens automatically. It is in their genes. Of course, parents have a responsibility to feed and provide a loving environment where children's bodies, hearts, and minds can grow and flourish. But the idea that we need to add to children as though key ingredients necessary for growth and maturation are missing is preposterous. We can do nothing more than watch and cooperate with Mother Nature (and keep buying bigger shoes) as our children do what they were created to do, which is grow. If this is true for children, why would growing in Christ be any different since we too are God's children? Though you may appear to lack the character of Christ does not mean you are missing something or that you are deficient in any way. Rather, you just need to correct the wrong knowledge you have about God that is preventing you from growing up in Christ.

The wonder of being born-again is that God gives you all of Himself and everything that is His. In the covenant that He swore to Abraham and Jesus, everything that is His became ours and everything that is ours became His (Chapter Four Endnotes #17).

Paul says that once you are joined to the Lord, you are one spirit with Him. "But he that is joined unto the Lord is one spirit."[75] God has put inside each of His children everything we need to grow up into the fullness of Christ.[76] "According as his divine power hath given unto us

---

[75] 1 Corinthians 6:17 (KJV)

[76] The Greek word for *into* is *eis* (εἰς)

all things that pertain unto life and godliness, through the knowledge of him that hath called us to glory and virtue."[77]

That is why Paul says, "Work out your own salvation with fear and trembling."[78] Salvation is in you, now work it out. Paul goes on to say God is working in you to cause you to do it (Chapter Four Endnotes #9). Paul understood how thinking affects our lives and stressed the importance of right-thinking or the right thoughts. "Summing it all up, friends, I'd say you'll do best by filling your minds and meditating on things true, noble, reputable, authentic, compelling, gracious—the best, not the worst; the beautiful, not the ugly; things to praise, not things to curse."[79] Because what we think rules our lives, Paul stated God's desire for us in the gift of a command (yes, God's commands are gifts): "Let this mind be in you, which was also in Christ Jesus."[80] God wants His children to think like He does. He is not instructing believers to add another commandment to their list of things to do for Him. God is not telling us to do anything. Rather, that command is the power to *be*—a literal translation of this passage is "This mind *be* within you!"[81] Our response is, "Yes, thank you. If you have commanded it to be, then it is so."

God is not pushy or demanding. His commands are not those of a totalitarian dictator. They contain the power to fulfill themselves in our lives, but they await our agreement, "Yes, be it so in my life." Then God causes it to be, though it may not always appear to us immediately; and it is not our responsibility to make it be. God wants you to believe that He always does what He says.

He is the only one who can live His life within us. In 1 Corinthians, Paul says we have the mind of Christ: "But we have the mind of Christ."[82] This means that God has not only commanded it to be but

---

[77] 2 Peter 1:3 (KJV)
[78] Philippians 2:12 (KJV)
[79] Philippians 4:8 (msg)
[80] Philippians 2:5 (KJV)
[81] The Greek is the imperative mood.
[82] 1 Corinthians 2:16 (KJV)

that, by that command, it is done. We just say thank you as He works to make it real to us.

Little children have a natural curiosity. No one works harder at exploring and understanding their world than children at play. Children don't believe they already know everything, and they are not ashamed to ask questions. Unlike adults, children do not feel responsible for having answers to what they do not know; rather, they are full of questions. "Mommy, why did he do that?" "Daddy, how does that work?" "Mommy, what is that?" "Daddy, what does that word mean?" Adults, however, already know it all (or think they do). If we don't, we usually hide the fact. When someone says something we don't understand, often, we'll try to figure out what they mean and hope they say something that gives us a clue; but admit we don't know? Never! What happened to our childlikeness? Have we lost it? Jesus said, "Believe me, unless a man receives the Kingdom of God like a child, he will not even enter it."[83] So what happened to that childlike, wide-eyed wonderment? Nothing! It is just covered up. By what? By all that we have learned that is not true.

How do you receive the Kingdom of God as a little child? By believing everything that God says is true, regardless of your understanding to the contrary. When a literal reading of His Word doesn't make sense, it is because of a lack of understanding on your part. Like a child, admit it doesn't make sense and ask God to give you understanding. If it doesn't come quickly, it may be that God needs to teach you something else first, so you will understand when He shows you what you really want to know. Like a child, feel free to keep asking questions, and rather than attempting to create an explanation, wait for God to give it to you. When He does, it will be consistent with the rest of His *truth,* and it will be easy to understand. As I said earlier, man was created to understand. We crave understanding. Unfortunately, if we don't wait to get God's, we will imagine our own. Hence, all the old wives' tales, superstitions, religions, and other misinformation in the world.

What is the single most endearing characteristic of babies? Their innocent trust and dependence. Adults can be highly skeptical and find

---

[83] Luke 18:17 (TCNT Part 1)

Unseen

it difficult to trust. Why? Is it programmed into our genes that at a certain age we stop believing? No! It is because of lies that we consider to be true. Experiences based on *the lie* teach us not to trust. Without an understanding of how to cooperate with God's *truth*, we continue to learn things that are not true. The more falsehoods we believe, the more dysfunctional we become. The result is an increasing difficulty believing God and a propensity to deny anything is wrong. God created man to trust. It is what he has learned that prevents him. As I like to say, "People are born brilliant. It is what they learn that makes them stupid." How is that? Because when we learn things that are not true, those lies become barriers that grow and retard God's intelligence and creativity in our lives. (Obviously, something else is at work when a cognitive deficiency is due to a physiological issue.) It isn't what we do *not* know, but what we *do know* that hinders our growing up into Christ. Things we *know* that suppress our God-given inclinations hurt us far worse than all the things we do not know.

When we need something like food, water, or knowledge, we naturally seek it—unless, of course, something is suppressing the desire. For example, when you get sick and lose your appetite, it is not because your body no longer needs food. It is because something is suppressing your appetite. So, what does this have to do with growing up in Him? Jesus said to enter the Kingdom of God, we must become as little children; not full of ourselves and what we already know, but hungry to learn, full of questions and innocent trust.

> Jesus called over a child, whom he stood in the middle of the room, and said, "I'm telling you, once and for all, that unless you return to square one and start over like children, you're not even going to get a look at the kingdom, let alone get in. Whoever becomes simple and elemental again, like this child, will rank high in God's kingdom."[84]

All the knowledge we have embraced, which is not consistent with God's *truth*, suppresses our *natural* course of growing up into

---
[84] Matthew 18:3 (msg)

Christ. The process of growth is automatic if the forces that hinder it are removed.

For centuries, the feet of many Chinese girls were prevented from growing normally by bindings that were placed on them. Their feet would have grown but were bound to distort the growth. Their feet did grow but the bonds resulted in deformity, which made walking normally impossible. One of the primary obstacles to growth in Christ is false knowledge— that is, information that is not based on God's *truth*, but sense knowledge (flesh), which we rely on as though it is from God. This knowledge has the same effect on our spiritual growth that those bindings had on young Chinese girl's feet. It twists and deforms us; but by agreeing with God's *truth*, we can be made whole in this life.

The Performance Mindset

After creating man, God "saw everything that he had made, and, behold, it was very good."[85] So how did humankind acquire this propensity to believe things that are not true? All our problems began in the Garden of Eden when Adam and Eve decided to believe *the lie* that Satan told them, which is that they could be like gods if they ate the fruit; they believed, then ate the fruit. "But the serpent said to the woman, 'You would not die at all; for God knows that the very day you eat of it, your eyes will be opened, and you will be like gods who know good from evil.'"[86] The result of believing *the lie* was that they began living it. Thus, they ate the fruit. The result of that act was death, which is separation; they separated themselves from God. God is the only life; so, refusing to believe and trust Him left only death. Humankind was lost. It had rejected dependence on God and now didn't know where or who it was. That's why Jesus said He came to seek and to save that which was lost. He wanted all of us back. "For the Son of man is come to save that which was lost."[87]

---

[85] Genesis 1:31 (KJV)
[86] Genesis 3:5 (Scripture is taken from The Complete Bible: An American Translation)
[87] Luke 19:10 (KJV)

Adam's and Eve's actions said, "We'll call you when we need you." But when they rejected Him, they rejected the light because God is light. "God is light, and in him is no darkness at all."[88] Thus, the couple became blinded by darkness. They no longer knew where they were. They could no longer recognize God's goodness. Life was suddenly only about finding their way, figuring out what to do, proving they were right, and getting what they wanted. The Earth began filling with lies. Every future human became infected. There is nothing anyone can do to avoid separating themselves from God before believing Him. But in Christ, we are made brand new and one with God forever. Our fellowship with God is restored.

Since the Fall in the Garden, humankind has been convinced that the means of affirming its value is performing correctly, which often takes the form of trying to be superior, stronger, smarter, wealthier, and so on. The human condition resulting from the rebellion in the Garden of Eden left man with three options for dealing with problems: (1) do nothing, (2) try something, and finally, (3) try something else. However, man's primary problem is not that he is doing the wrong thing; rather, his *being* is wrong. Humans became *Doings*.

Adam chose to believe what someone else said was true. Thus, he chose dependence on his own understanding. Since the *correct performance* is now humankind's solution to every problem, and performance no longer flows from union with God, no matter how good the performance, the result will always fall short. Jesus came to restore to us everything we lost in the mutiny in the Garden as well as everything else God had planned for us. As new creatures in union with God, we are now one with Him and capable of living like Him because we now have His faith and live with His life. Remember Paul's statement: "Yet not I, but Christ liveth in me and the life which I now live in the flesh I live by the faith of the Son of God who loved me and gave himself for me."[89] The source of Paul's life was God's Spirit by means of the faith of Jesus Christ, Jesus's beliefs. Many of us have grown up hearing the phrase from Galatians 2:20: *I live by faith in the Son of God.* Mistranslations

---

[88] 1 John 1:5 (KJV)

[89] Galatians 2:20 (KJV)

like this have made understanding the Bible more difficult. The literal Greek says, "within faith I live, that of the Son of the God" (Chapter Four Endnotes #18). Paul was saying, "I live inside the faith of the Son of God and thus His faith is my faith."

We no longer must be locked in a struggle to find significance through performance because Christ already did the work. How arrogant and prideful is the person who thinks he can improve on it? We are now loved with complete love and acceptance, independent of our performance. We are loved by God, the Creator of the universe. You can have no greater significance. It is possible for everyone to live as great a life as Christ did on Earth because, if you are a believer, it is no longer you who live but Christ who lives in you. You are a distinct and unique individual and, at the same time, united with all believers in Christ. You can now trust God to be everything He is to you, in you, for you, and through you.

Is What You Believe about God Really True?

Trust in God can be defined as resting in the confidence that what God says about Himself and what He has done and will do for us is true. Many believe God is able, but His willingness doesn't reach to them. Many think, "Of course, God is able, but there is something about me that makes Him unwilling." This is not a problem with God, but an issue with your belief. Deep down, you believe something that results in you putting up a barrier to God's love. His desire is to expose the lies you believe so that the *truth* can take their place.

If you find it difficult to trust God and if His peace does not seem real inside you, it is because you believe something about Him, yourself, or your situation that is not true. This is simple for the Holy Spirit to fix, we just have to be patient, which may involve a degree of emotional suffering, but that suffering is not from God. Rather, it is a result of having to unlearn things we have learned that are not true. It is what Paul referred to when He said, "I die daily."[90] Flesh may scream that God's *truth* isn't true. That can be painful as we *resist the devil* by "holding fast our confession of faith."[91] This suffering is one of the things Paul was referring to in Colossians: "Strengthened with all might, according to his glorious power, unto all patience and longsuffering with joyfulness."[92] But the longsuffering doesn't mean misery. Paul says it can be with joy, depending on what we believe.

Sometimes the wrong beliefs can cause gut-wrenching pain, but the Holy Spirit feels what we feel and is working to make things right and to cause us to know and feel His *truth*. Remember, it is knowing the *truth* that will set you free, including freedom from every type of pain. I don't mean *about* the *truth*, but knowing the *truth* like God know it. The *truth* is His body of knowledge. He knows the *truth* as reality, not just facts. God wants you to experience His peace—right now! Regardless of what you have done or are doing, He wants you to experience His peace and is working to bring it to pass.

You may vehemently dispute that anything you believe could be wrong. However, your lack of peace and confidence (or any other fruit of the Spirit) is proof otherwise. This is not to say you don't believe God's *truth*, but conflicting beliefs in your heart are preventing you from enjoying the fruit of believing His *truth*. This was the condition of the man who "cried out, and said with tears, Lord, I believe; help thou mine unbelief."[93] His *unbelief* was the things he believed that were not true. Unbelief doesn't mean you don't believe anything, but that what you believe is erroneous. But his unbelief didn't stop God. Jesus still delivered his son.

It is impossible to trust God when you are double-minded. "A double minded man is unstable in all his ways."[94] When the New Testament refers to a double-minded man, it means a person who has conflicting beliefs, which make it impossible to have steadfast confidence in God.

---

[90] 1 Corinthians 15:31
[91] James 4:7 and Hebrews 4:14
[92] Colossian 1:11 (KJV)
[93] Mark 9:24 (KJV)
[94] James 1:8 (KJV)

If your heart's desire is to fully trust God and experience the freedom that is in Christ Jesus, you must allow the Holy Spirit to work with you to eliminate wrong beliefs (unbelief). This work belongs to God and He delights in doing it. Since our thoughts flow out of our beliefs, one way you can cooperate is to be honest and acknowledge wrong thoughts when He makes you aware of them instead of trying to hide them. God knows the secrets of your mind and heart and is the only One capable of untwisting them. You are safe in His hands because He is patient, gentle, and, best of all, He loves you unconditionally. He will never hurt you.

The Lie

To *be* transformed, it is helpful to understand how mankind ended up in its present condition and why humanity continues to walk around in the same circle, over and over. The scenery may seem to change, but there is always something strikingly familiar with each new view.

To understand how man got into this condition, we need to know what happened in the Garden of Eden. The key to understanding the effects of the rebellion in the Garden is not focusing on what Adam and Eve *did*, but on what they *believed*. They chose to believe *the lie* of the serpent (Satan) rather than God. Satan promised that if they would declare independence by eating the forbidden fruit they would "be as gods, knowing good and evil."[95] Translation? They would become gods, *knowing* right from wrong, good from bad, and no longer *be* completely and utterly dependent on God for anything. It would be okay to learn about God and even acknowledge that He is God, but to be dependent on Him? Never again! They wanted to rule their world based on what they thought was right and wrong.

One result of becoming *as gods* was the beginning of the god complex. People began creating their own standards of morality—what is right and what is wrong—not based on God's love, but on whatever suited their whims. That sense of *knowing* was not a result of union with God, but of believing *the lie*. This attitude passed from the first couple

---

[95] Genesis 3:5 (KJV)

Unseen

to all of humanity. When each of us comes to Christ, the Holy Spirit seeks to begin removing the false sense of knowing, which corrupted the minds of men. By *false sense of knowing*, I mean that people *know* many things they treat as *truth* when they aren't. Thus, the knowledge they think they know is false. They have a false sense of knowing.

Understanding how that corruption has affected us helps us relax and consciously cooperate with the Holy Spirit, while He reveals to us who we are as new creatures in Christ. This enables us to see and experience our new selves, which are free of the damage that had been inflicted on our previous self (referred to by many as *the old man*). That previous self is truly gone, though Satan seeks to persuade us that it isn't.

The first time the Holy Spirit came to dwell in a human was when He descended upon Jesus at His baptism by John. "And the Holy Ghost descended in a bodily shape like a dove upon him, and a voice came from heaven, which said, Thou art my beloved Son; in thee I am well pleased."[96] We were all created to look like Jesus did once He was filled with the Holy Spirit. Man was created in the image of God, but Satan's promise sought to twist that *truth*. In fact, Satan's promise was *the lie* to which Paul so often referred (Chapter Four Endnotes #19): "Who changed the *truth* of God into [the] lie…"[97, 98]

The wisdom and knowledge Satan promised took the place of the wisdom, knowledge, and understanding they would have received by knowing God. *The lie* told them they would no longer have to depend on God, they would be independent. That false knowledge, by which man still lives today, has *never* produced the blessings that God intended for man to enjoy. Instead, such knowledge always contains threads of independence and self-sufficiency and creates an illusion that causes man to think he is on the right track when he really isn't. It has resulted in humankind losing awareness of God's unconditional love. A consequence of believing *the lie* was, for the first time, that humans became

---

[96] Luke 3:22 (KJV)

[97] Romans 1:25 (KJV)

[98] Note: In the original language, there is an article before lie, τῷ ψεύδει and τὸ ψεῦδος. Unfortunately, most translations omit it.

conscious of being wrong. Remember they hid from God? "And there came to them the sound of the Lord God walking in the garden in the evening wind: and the man and his wife went to a secret place among the trees of the garden, away from the eyes of the Lord God."[99] Having lost their link to unconditional acceptance, they began using their newly acquired *"wisdom"* to regain it. No longer capable of simply *being* in God's love, they began doing things that corresponded with their new awareness as gods.

Humans were created to live in God's unconditional love. Once separated from it because of rebellion, they began searching for ways to fill the void. One result of losing the sense of God's love was that Adam and Eve lost their sense of unconditional acceptance by God and each other. They became ashamed. Instead of seeing themselves in the light of God's unconditional acceptance, they judged themselves by what they saw—their appearance and performance. The first evidence of this was covering their nakedness with leaves to hide from each other as well as hiding behind trees from God. They expected to become gods, but reality proved otherwise. Suddenly, having rejected their importance to God, they felt empty and void of worth. They hated the feeling of *defectiveness* and tried to correct it because they now believed they were wise enough to do so. Their attempt to solve problems outside of union with God was *not* rebellion. Their descent into living by flesh was the natural outcome of the rebellion of believing *the error*. The mutiny was the deliberate, with full knowledge, choice to believe *the lie* and reject the *truth*, an act they probably did not even remember.

Wrong beliefs can cause traumatic results. Those beliefs can be subsequently forgotten in the confusion or pain of the trauma, nevertheless, they remain in control. The first couple's evil belief caused all humanity to become performance oriented. Thus, future generations would search for and protect their self-worth through performance, appearance, and possessions. The belief in *the lie* resulted in automatically rejecting fellowship with and utter dependence on God because they now believed that He was judging them just as they were judging each other. Neither spouse any longer held the same importance to the

---

[99] Genesis 3:8 (Extracts from the Bible in Basic English)

other. They ceased seeing themselves as united and began distancing themselves from each other. Remember how Adam blamed Eve? They were no longer together. They had become separate, and because they began to devalue each other, they thought God must too.

Adam had quickly blamed Eve. Even though the Scriptures don't mention it, I suspect she had quite a bit to say later. Believing that they were now supposed to be like God yet knowing they weren't, their lives were no longer oriented around each other but became focused on themselves. *Doing* replaced the importance of *being* as they sought to make right whatever they thought was wrong.

Man was now incapable of comprehending God's knowledge—knowledge that can only be acquired by those who believe Him. Wrong beliefs prevent man from acquiring the knowledge and wisdom of God, just like wrong beliefs kept us from believing the Gospel until, by the help of the Holy Spirit, we changed our minds. Every generation has modified their wrong beliefs and passed them on to the next generation. In fact, I believe the word *iniquity* just refers to poor family belief systems that produce behaviors which pass from one generation to the next. "I the Lord thy God am a jealous God, visiting the iniquity of the fathers upon the children unto the third and fourth generation of them that hate me."[100] However, contrary to many theologies, this is not saying that God is out to get you. If you have accepted the wrong beliefs that your parents taught and refused to change your mind about them, the natural outcome is that you will suffer because of it. But while we may be doing evil, God is there (visiting) seeking to get us to change our hearts and minds.

Whether you call it sin, iniquity, or error, wrong beliefs passing from parents to children, or one person to another, results in hatred toward God and rejection of His *truth*. It's not a mystery. Children learn from their parents. They hear their words and see their actions and often learn things that are not founded on the *truth*. It is common for all types of behaviors and thought patterns to pass from a parent to a child. Examples include hatred of certain people or groups, spouse and sexual abuse, unfaithfulness to others, good and bad work habits, and the list

---

[100] Exodus 20:5 (KJV)

goes on. Some Bible teachers blame certain problems on *generational curses* as though someone spoke a witchcraft type of curse against the person or family. A more accurate explanation is that one generation passes its twisted beliefs to the next, which passes them to the next and so on. These wrong beliefs not only produce wrong behavior, they allow sickness and disease to pass from one generation to the next.

The resurrection of Jesus Christ was powerful enough to render the works of Satan and the error totally ineffective. Unfortunately, ignorance and the refusal to believe God's *truth* prevent people from enjoying the union with Christ that is their victory. But thanks to God, the Holy Spirit is working in each one of us to change that (Chapter Four Endnotes # 20).

Evil Genius: The Auto-Loopback

The lie is eviler than it seems, if that is possible. For centuries, the church has taught about Original Sin (Adam and Eve ate the fruit of the tree of the knowledge of good and evil). But as terrible as that was, something even worse happened. Believing *the lie* resulted in humankind detaching themselves from God, thus losing their intimacy with Him. But once the first couple realized that something was wrong, the obvious question would be: Why didn't they apologize to God and ask for forgiveness? Because *the lie* was designed to prevent that from happening. Of course, forgiveness wouldn't have undone *the death*, but it would have restored Adam and Eve to fellowship with God. But the evil genius behind *the lie* made that impossible.

Consider the progress of events in the Garden:

1. The serpent persuaded the couple to believe a lie.

2. They automatically began living what they believed.

3. They ate the fruit.

4. They became aware of good and evil, right and wrong.

5. They realized something was wrong.

6. They became performance oriented.

7. *The Lie* they had believed said if they did the *right* things everything would go right.

8. They tried to solve problems on their own with no confidence that God was with them.

9. Since they were now performance oriented they automatically looked back to see what they had done wrong.

10. Because they believed their performance was the key to success, they could not see that it was not doing the wrong thing but believing the wrong thing that produced such devastating results.

11. Mankind was now in an automatic loopback mode - results from then on would be perceived as a matter of doing the right or wrong thing.

12. Hence, the answer to all needs, desires, and problems would be figuring out the right thing to do, in every aspect of life.

13. Since they had severed their relationship with the source of real knowledge, they could never be sure they knew everything they needed to know.

14. Their belief systems became increasingly twisted.

15. A growing body of wrong beliefs caused them to increasingly conform to the will of Satan.

16. It became impossible for them to discover the actual problem—wrong beliefs.

17. The cause of the trauma that resulted from believing *the lie* was quickly forgotten in the panic to fix what was wrong.

James E. Campbell, Jr, James Q. Campbell

Obedience

When first introduced to Christ in college, I had high hopes of finding peace of mind. I suffered terrible inner turmoil, anxiety, and depression. After a brief period of joy, old thoughts crowded back in and things got worse, for many, many years.

Twenty years later, upon discovering the existence of *the lie* inside my own belief system, I experienced a startling transformation. Many problematic habits disappeared, and I felt like a new person. Some of the change was surprisingly sudden; my emotions became stable. I knew I had finally found the answer. It had always been Jesus.

I had discovered what God wanted from me. He wanted obedience, but not the obedience I had been taught. The Greek word for obedience is *hupakoé*, which is composed of two words: *Hupo*, a preposition which means *under* and *akouo*, a verb which means *hear*. It is usually understood to mean "submission to what is heard," in other words, "submit to *doing* what you hear." Obedience has been known this way for centuries, but, early believers saw it differently. The literal meaning is "under hear," which they understood as "to submit to hearing." That is very different from "submission to what you have heard."

The Law of Moses had taught the Children of Israel that obedience meant to hearken and behold, ponder and meditate on God's words. They were to savor God's words, to eat and digest them. If the Jews had submitted to hearing the way God instructed, they would gradually have learned a new way of thinking. God has a very specific way for us to hear and if they had done it, they would have changed from seeing themselves as slaves and victims to a mighty people who could take the land God was going to give them. But, they refused.

> ...they refused to pay attention, turned a stubborn shoulder, and *stopped their ears* from hearing.[101]

---

[101] Zechariah 7:11 (NASB)

They didn't take the land as God had instructed because they refused to hear Him. In New Testament days, the Jews continued the same type of disobedience.

> But they cried out with a loud voice, and *covered their ears* and rushed at him with one impulse[102] (Italics added for emphasis).

God wanted to train His children to think not with a slave mentality but as the special people which He had declared they were. "For you are a people holy to the LORD your God. The LORD your God has chosen you out of all the peoples on the face of the earth to be his people, his treasured possession."[103] By obeying, they would have exchanged their slavery mindset for a whole new identity. They would have begun thinking and behaving consistent with their new identity. Instead, they defiled themselves by thinking they were no more than grasshoppers, a very ordinary insect they trampled underfoot without thought.

The story of Mary and Martha is a great illustration of obedience and shows what Jesus thought was important. Unfortunately, many have been taught that being like Martha is the way to live. Have you ever heard the phrase, "Go burn out for Jesus"? Jesus would never tell anyone to do that, but *the lie* has convinced the Church that obedience equals *doing*. The more you do - the better. In fact, I have heard preachers say that until we get busy serving God we cannot please Him. Nothing could be further from the *truth*.

> ³⁸Now as they went on their way, Jesus entered a village. And a woman named Martha welcomed him into her house. ³⁹And she had a sister called Mary, who sat at the Lord's feet and listened to his teaching. ⁴⁰But Martha was distracted with much serving. And she went up to him and said, "Lord, do you not care that my sister has left me to serve alone? Tell her then to help me." ⁴¹But the Lord

---

[102] Acts 7:57 (NASB)

[103] Deuteronomy 14:6 (ESV)

answered her, "Martha, Martha, you are anxious and troubled about many things, ⁴²but one thing is necessary. Mary has chosen the good portion, which will not be taken away from her."[104]

Jesus knew that by sitting under His teaching, i.e., by obeying Him, His words would transform Mary's thinking and believing. That would result in doing what He said. In fact, given the way the Early Church understood the word *obedience* you could define it as "hearing with the intention of believing what you hear." Quoting Isaiah in Romans, Paul writes, "But they have not all obeyed the Gospel. For Esaias saith, Lord, who hath believed our report?"[105] The Greek word in this verse rendered *obeyed* is *hupēkousan*, which is the past tense form of *to hear* and means "submitted to hear." Let's read this verse and use the meaning *submitted to hear* for *obeyed*. "But they have not all submitted to hear the Gospel. For Esaias saith, Lord, who hath believed our report?" So, the word that today we translate obey, those Greek speakers heard as "submit to hearing," which is very different from "submission to what is heard." Paul understood that if you hear and keep hearing the *truth*, with the intention of believing it, that is what will happen. You will believe what you have been hearing. It doesn't usually happen overnight if you are already entertaining a mass of erroneous beliefs, which every human has done. As we continue to listen attentively to God, with the will or intention of believing Him, His words gradually wash away wrong beliefs and we find ourselves thinking in agreement with Him and thus doing His Word. The Early Church understood this. They knew proper hearing and believing caused believers to do righteousness without struggling.

"So then faith *cometh* by hearing, and hearing by the word of God."[106] In this passage, Paul correlates believing the *truth* (faith) with "submitting to hearing." My experience of this *truth* is, "faith comes because of *hearing*, and the *hearing* comes because God speaks to you

---

[104] Luke 10: 38-42 (ESV)
[105] Romans 10: 16, 17 (KJV)
[106] Romans 10:17 (KJV)

personally." I'm not talking about a voice from Heaven but something on the inside of you that penetrates your heart. When we hear and keep hearing God's Word (logos), that Word causes us to recognize when God is speaking to us personally. Something happens in a moment of time in which you just know you have heard from God. Satan will immediately try to convince you otherwise, but you know something changed. What you heard agrees with the Word of God, which is your confirmation that it is from God.

The fight of faith is not to do the right thing but to believe God's *truth* when your experience says His *truth* is not true. When we decide to hear God the way He has told us to hear, we will find faith rising in our hearts and ourselves doing what God says, and be amazed at how God has changed us into a person we always wanted to be. There is no magic involved. God created humans to function based on what we believe.

God does not have an expectation that His children will do evil. This is hard to comprehend from a human perspective, but Love always believes and expects good.[107] Jesus rose from dead and defeated evil. From God's viewpoint, within time His children will realize the wonder of His love and what He accomplished by sending His Only Begotten Son. He is working to cause us to realize we are more than conquerors because He made us that way. Once we believe it we will begin to act like it. Because we have heard it over and over and over, it is easy to believe. Of course, many are waiting for God to prove it to them. Then, they think, they will be able to act like it. But, God's passion is so massive that He won't quit until every knee bows and every tongue confesses that Jesus is Lord.[108] This is because of His marvelous love and not His wrath. When you finally believe God, you won't have any trouble *being* more than a conqueror. Of course, this won't happen when people fear a God Who is standing over them with a whip waiting to crush them. Rather, you see it as you increasingly accept and believe God's tender and patient love for you. He isn't telling you that you must first get more right with Him. If that is what you believe, it is coming from someone else. God would never tell you that.

---

[107] 1 Corinthians 13:7

[108] Philippians 2:10

Paul wrote, "Love never fails."[109] Why are so many "believers" convinced this isn't true. How can anyone who says they believe God's Word side with the forces of darkness who claim that evil has won and will continue to win? Why do people insist on believing the worst about God and humans created in His image?

God is passionate about His creatures, not in a bad way but a good one. His passion is so magnificent that He swore an oath to Himself because of His determination to save His children. Read the following passage from the perspective that God is passionately crazy about you, and remember that God made this oath to Abraham while knowing he would keep screwing up. "¹³For when God made the promise to Abraham, since He could swear by no one greater, He swore by Himself, ¹⁴saying, 'I WILL SURELY BLESS YOU AND I WILL SURELY MULTIPLY YOU.'"[110] Our Father is passionate about blessing His children. He pleads with us to believe Him and stop believing what Satan says. You may ask, "Why doesn't He deal with Satan?" Because He already has. But, until we learn to believe the *truth* in the face of lies, our experience will mirror what we believe, and we will not discover who we are.

When we hear God's Word but do not intend on believing it, we end up knowing we are supposed to do something without knowing how. Since we know we are supposed to live what we have heard, we try to do it by willpower and totally miss the power God has provided. Unfortunately, because of *the lie,* many preachers stress *doing* the Word rather than believing it. Some believers know a lot of Bible verses but have never mixed their knowing with treasuring (believing) them. Let's consider what the Bible says about this. Hebrews 4:1-3 is a passage full of wonder. Unfortunately, because many people are predisposed to see God as angry at sinners, verse three is invariably translated to reflect their misunderstandings. Instead of seeing a God Who is compassionate and feels with us in our trials, many tend to see a God Who hates everyone who crosses Him. This perspective of God causes them to have an extreme misunderstanding of the original Greek text. If you doubt me, show this section of the book to any Greek scholar and pay attention to

---

[109] 1 Corinthians 13:8

[110] Hebrews 6:13 (NASB)

what they say. No one can deny the mistranslation, yet because of the filter of their misbeliefs, they have no other way of explaining what it could mean. A literal rendering of verse three would overthrow hundreds of years of "Christian" teaching, so people continue to fall back on century's old interpretations without giving God a chance to show them His heart (Chapter Four Endnote # 21).

Consider the two points following in this passage from Hebrews.

> ¹Therefore, let us fear if, while a promise remains of entering His rest, any one of you may seem to have come short of it. ²For indeed we have had good news preached to us, just as they also; but the word they heard did not profit them, because it was not united by faith in those who heard. ³For we who have believed enter that rest, just as He has said, "AS I SWORE IN MY WRATH, THEY SHALL NOT ENTER MY REST," although His works were finished from the foundation of the world[111]

(1) The Greek word commonly translated as *anger* or *wrath* is orgé (ὀργή). These meanings are often used in the New Testament, but its root meaning is *passion*. God is passionate and sometimes that appears as anger or wrath; not always in the sense of hatred but sometimes as a parent who gets angry at a child behaving in ways that are harmful to them. If you are a parent, have you ever reacted in anger at your child because they ran in front of a car? Were you angry at your child or was it your passion for their welfare bursting forth? Orgé, a noun, is derived from the verb oregó (ὀρέγω) meaning "to reach, stretch, stretch out," and was sometimes used to describe a parent reaching out to a child.[112] Because of the terrible way that man, after the Fall in the Garden, came to see God, it is understandable how a horrific view has been applied to His passion. But, it is time to return to the Early Church's understanding of

---

[111] Hebrews 4:1-3 (NASB)
[112] Liddell and Scott 1875 pg 1044

God's passion. Instead of introducing people to a loving God, the perspective of the modern Church often brings them to a Father Whom they end up fearing or deciding He is too hard to please. But, Jesus said, "He who has seen Me has seen the Father."[113] The Father is like Jesus and not the terrible ogre that so many believe. (Notice the similarity between ogre and orgé.) Many people think of God as a harsh ogre that lives in the sky.

(2) Point #2 may do more to help those who trust modern representations of God. You will seldom find a translation of Hebrews 4:3 that does not say or imply, "They shall *never* enter my rest." So, ask any Greek scholar which word in the original text can be translated *not* or *never*? They can't tell you, because there isn't one. The words *not* or *never* are added because it is the only way to make the passage fit modern theology. The fact is, rather than being a scary verse the author is pouring out comfort. He was saying that from the beginning our Father has planned for His children to enter His rest. The very last phrase of the verse says just that. God had all of this planned from the time the Earth was founded. My literal translation, with some interpretation added for readability is, "For we the believing enter into the rest, just as He said, 'Even as I swore an oath within my passion, *since they will* enter into my rest...'" Of course, if scholars prefer to use the newer, modern rules of Greek grammar instead of the ancient ones, then maybe my translation won't work for them.

As you keep focusing your attention on God's *truth* with the intention of believing that it is true for you, at some point you will find yourself easily doing it. Why? It will have become your way of thinking. "As a man thinks in his heart, so is he."[114] In my experience, this doesn't happen overnight. And, God is not in a hurry and will never

---

[113] John 14:9 (NASB)
[114] Proverbs 23:7

push you. He knows how He created you to work. If you keep looking at His words, you will eventually realize they are as much yours as His. His Word is gently powerful and will keep washing your mind until you are thinking just like Him.

Have you ever noticed that what many preachers say is never accompanied by the power to do what they preach? This leaves the hearers thinking they must muster up the discipline and strength to do it on their own. Though they may disagree with me, these preachers are telling the congregation that the doing of the Word is dependent upon the hearer's willpower thus, if they fail to obey they are disobedient, and possibly condemned.

When you ponder the Word of God, among other things, you are using God's logic to reason with yourself that you are who He says you are. God knows who you are better than you do because He made you. He just wants you to keep agreeing with Him. How sad that so many believers will argue that they know more about themselves than God does. They say they are sinners, and may even get angry if you tell them they aren't. That's because they treasure such terrible beliefs. But God never told them that. He keeps telling them that in Christ they are the righteousness of God, but many refuse to listen because they think they know better than God. When a person declares they are a sinner, they have de facto rejected their union with Christ, albeit in ignorance. Unfortunately, many not only refuse to hear but they stop their ears and may become furious.

As you keep looking at what God says about Himself and you and agree with Him that what He says is the *truth*, His Word cleanses away the filth of the world that seeks to train us in its way of thinking. Many believers say that someone hasn't obeyed God until they have done what He says to do. That's because they have a faulty understanding of obedience. Their opinion is based on *the lie* that they know better than God. And guess what? If they continue to believe they are terrible sinners, they will act like it and live under a cloud of condemnation. They will never feel like they have done enough for God. He will always seem like a hard taskmaster who can never be fully pleased. But, God is not that type of Father.

God created the concept of training because He understands the deception (darkness) inside which the world lies. Our Father realizes that His children live in an environment saturated with deception and since this is where we are, He is going to train us to think properly right here. Our Father has no plans to make things easier for us by using His power to eradicate the evil that confronts us. Rather, He has always planned on training His children to be who we are; that way we will act like who we are in whatever environment we find ourselves. Then we will rise above the darkness and help others still trapped in it. The Apostle John said, "This is the victory that has overcome the world, even our faith."[115] Notice that John didn't say overcoming the world is the victory. Rather, the victory is believing the *truth*. What a triumph it is, when in the face of terrible evidence and pressure screaming that God's Word isn't real, you can rest in peace and joy because you know it is.

Satan doesn't care what you accomplish for God if you do it from compulsion. In other words, Satan doesn't mind you doing *important things for* God so that you distress and burn out while doing it. Satan will even applaud you. He may also have you lauded and held up as a great Christian. Satan wants us to "serve" God by willpower rather than God's power, but Paul said that whatever a person does that is not out of faith is sin. If we are *struggling* to serve God because that is what we think we are supposed to do, that is sin. "Whatever is not from faith is sin."[116] If this describes you, God is not angry with you. He wants to teach you to rest and let His faith inside you do the works. "Jesus says (in a very personal way to you), Have God's faith."[117]

Today we can do what Israel never did. God has made us new creatures in Christ. By obeying, that is, by hearing and fixing our attention on who God says He and we are rather than what people and circumstances tell us, we will discover a whole new way of thinking. Don't expect a sudden massive change in your logic. Once you decide you want to think like Jesus, the Holy Spirit *trains* you to do so. God has a process, customized just for you. As we continue to look at God's Word

---

[115] 1 John 5:4 (KJV)

[116] Romans 14:23 (NASB)

[117] Mark 11:22 (JEC)

the way He has instructed, we learn to think about ourselves as God does. As we learn to think like Jesus, we will act like Him. God says this type of transformation is a result of continuing to ponder and meditate His Word as described in Psalm 1:2, "…and in His instruction does he mediate (ponder and rehearse) day and night. And he (the person meditating) will be like a tree…and everything he does shall prosper." This is because the Word is a mirror that shows us who we are.[118] As we learn to believe we are who God says we are, we automatically act like it. God wants our actions to be a result of knowing who we are, not the result of trying to convince Him that we are good enough.

Every one of us learned to think the way we now think. In a sense, the world trained us to think this way. It didn't happen by magic. It was a learning process. Now God wants to teach us to think like Him. It too is a learning process. The difference is that now we have the mind of Christ.[119] We have been designed with the capacity to think God's thoughts, but only the Holy Spirit can teach us how to do it. It is only difficult when you don't know how. As the Holy Spirit teaches us how it becomes easier and easier.

How difficult is it for you to act like who you are? Not hard, because you automatically behave just like you think. As the Word of God washes your mind from the filthy images that the world, and possibly other believers, have taught you, you will begin to have a new identity and will act like it, automatically.

The Lie by Another Name

The lie has taught mankind that to succeed at life requires doing the right things. Who would argue with that? Obviously, doing the right things is good. However, *the lie* also tells us that we are the determiners of what are the right things. The trouble is, we are never sure if what we are doing is the *correct* right thing. Often, we don't know until it is too late to change courses.

---

[118] James 1:23

[119] 1 Corinthians 2:16

The only One that always knows right from wrong is God, but because mankind believed *the lie*, he no longer trusts God. Oh, sure, we may *say* we trust God, but too many thoughts in our heads tell us we can't be sure. Trusting God doesn't come naturally to the adult mind.

We read God's Word hoping to get answers as well as the faith we need to trust Him. But mostly, the Bible just gives us a lot of knowledge. If only we could know enough, then things would be better, we think. But, in today's world, education of all types is just… so we can know things. If asked, we may be able to spit out the information, but what good is knowing if what you know is not part of your life and experience? Early believers were taught how to make God's Word real in their lives. It is a process founded on two New Testament principals spoken of in Hebrews 6:1: Repentance and faith – changing your mind about what you believe and instead believing God's *truth*.

As my life was changing before my eyes, I began to realize that God just wants me to be honest with Him, and listen to Him. Because He loves me unconditionally, I don't have to fear how He may react to my honesty. Since I didn't have anyone who could teach me how to listen and hear God, it took a while and I'm still learning. I knew I could never do anything to make myself worthy of God's blessing, yet I tried anyway. *The lie* says I *can* make myself worthy by knowing and doing the right things. However, God says I am worthy because He has made me one with Jesus Christ; I am as worthy as Jesus is, albeit by sheer gift – "the gift of righteousness."[120] As well, the New Testament says, "But whoever is united with the Lord is one with him in spirit."[121] If you are one with Jesus and He is righteous, how can you be anything but the same? But, the liar didn't stop. He kept telling me I was not as righteous as Jesus, even though Jesus and I are one. So, I began being honest with God by admitting that I wasn't sure what the *truth* was. I told Him the lousy fruit of my life was proof that I didn't know the *truth*. In fact, I didn't know anyone who was living the life I saw portrayed in the Bible, especially me. And, I needed God to change me because if He didn't, I couldn't and never would. I suspected that

---

[120] Romans 5:17 (KJV)

[121] 1 Corinthians 6:17 (NIV)

the lie had infected all my *beliefs* and deeper than I was aware. Only God could fix me.

I wanted fellowship with believers that could support me in this life changing adventure. Unfortunately, I found none. Everyone I knew was sure that, if given enough time, they could make *the lie* work in their lives. It *had* to work for them, because they couldn't conceive of life any other way. But, no one has escaped its effects. *The lie* has infected all human thought and communication. It is unknowingly taught from almost every pulpit in the country within grand sounding concepts about how to live the Christian life. But long before any of us ever saw a church lectern, we were learning it at home. It influences every human life, no matter the language or culture. Mankind clings to *the lie,* and only the Holy Spirit can enable us to let go of our death grip on it, because by ourselves we can't even identify how we believe it. In fact, as I sought fellowship with other believers, not one could conceive that they, too, believed lies. As far as all were concerned, it was impossible. Except for my wife, I could not find even one believer that would seriously consider the failure of modern Christian teaching to produce Christians who lived like New Creatures. The prevailing opinion was that we just need to wait on God and try harder to obey Him. It seemed that everyone believed God would eventually change us, if we are serious enough, or when Jesus returns. So, I spent many lonely years seeking to know why so many sincere believers refused to believe that their continual failures to live a Spirit-filled life might be because they had some wrong beliefs.

Much modern Christian doctrine is based on scriptures that someone changed in translation. The fact that many translators have deleted the Greek article "the" from *the lie* is crucial. The discovery of that single mistranslation changed my life forever. But, if knowing about *the lie* is essential to experiencing the fruit of the Spirit, why didn't God make a bigger deal of it in the New Testament? It was years before I discovered that *the lie* was mentioned many more times than in just John 8:44 and Romans 1:25. It was as I became more proficient in Greek and referred to it more often that I discovered *the lie* had another name which has been treated the same way. The article "the" has been deleted. The Apostle Paul makes frequent use of this other name. Other writers who used this name include the Apostle John and Luke, in the Book of Acts, as he recounted the death of Stephen. That other name for *the lie* is *the sin,* which is more accurately rendered *the error*. Removing the article, inadvertently changes the meaning of *the sin* to *any* sin. Without the article "the," there is no obvious way, outside of looking at the Greek text, to know there is a difference between sins. One means any sin (or any error) while the other points to a sin (i.e. *the error*). Unfortunately, because of scholars' desires to create more easily readable Bible versions, they have missed a critical Bible concept.

Let's look at some passages and how the elimination of the article "the" changes the meaning. The rules of modern translating say that many of the Greek articles are not necessary to understand what the writers meant, but I believe the fact that Jesus appeared within a culture that spoke Greek was part of the fullness of times. It was important to God that the New Testament be written in Greek. Ancient Greek was the perfect language for recording God's message because of its quantum essence, which has made it seemingly impossible for many to comprehend its grammar. This is a subject for another book, but suffice it to say that the Holy Spirit knew what He was inspiring, and He didn't waste a single word. Every word from God is full of God Himself. Just because we may not understand what certain words mean or that they seem unnecessarily repetitive doesn't give us the right to discard them. Rather, God wants us to agree with Him that all His words are important, and to ask Him what He means. Rather than trying to figure out what He means, or twisting His words to make them make sense, we need to accept our place as creatures utterly dependent on God for the knowledge He wants us to have. He gladly gives it.

In the following passages from Romans, I focus on just one error in translating, which is the removal of articles preceding the nouns of sin, death, and disobedience. But, I have also noted some other nouns for which most translations also remove the article. When the Greek speakers used articles, it wasn't a quirk of their language. It was because the utilization of the article specified that the noun following it was an instance of a specific "person, place, or thing."[122] So, in the following passages, Paul is not writing about just any sin or death. He is referring to a specific sin and death.

When you see [the] before a noun, it signifies an article that has been removed. In every case, the article deleted from the passage was pointing to a specific instance of that term rather than a general reference to it as though Paul was speaking of just any instance of it. [The] sin, which should be translated *the error*, refers both to *the lie* and Adam's choice to believe it. The appearance of *the lie* offered the potential for a cataclysmic event in human history. The First couple's decision to believe it was the cataclysm.

> **Romans Chapter 5 (KJV):** "[12]Wherefore, as by one man [the] sin entered into the world, and [the] death by [the] sin; and so [the] death passed upon all men, for that all have sinned: [13](For until the law sin was in the world: but sin is not imputed when there is no law. [14]Nevertheless [the] death reigned from Adam to Moses, even over them that had not sinned after the similitude of Adam's [the] transgression, who is the figure of him that was to come...")
>
> "[19]For as by one man's [the] disobedience many were made sinners, so by the obedience of one shall many be made righteous. [20]Moreover the law entered, that the offence might abound. But where [the] sin abounded, [the] grace did much more abound: [21]That as [the] sin hath reigned unto [the] death, even so might [the] grace reign through righteousness unto eternal life by Jesus Christ our Lord."
>
> **Romans Chapter 6 (KJV):** "[1]What shall we say then? Shall we continue in [the] sin, that [the] grace may abound? [2]God forbid. How shall we, that are dead to [the] sin, live any longer therein? [3]Know ye not, that so many of us as were baptized into Jesus Christ were baptized into his [the] death? [4]Therefore we are buried with him by

---

[122] The definition of a noun is a word used to identify any class of people, place, or thing.

[the] baptism into [the] death: that like as Christ was raised up from the dead by the glory of the Father, even so we also should walk in newness of life. ⁵For if we have been planted together in the likeness of his [the] death, we shall be also *in the likeness* of *his* [the] resurrection: ⁶Knowing this, that our [the] old man is crucified with *him*, that the body of [the] sin might be destroyed, that henceforth we should not serve [the] sin. ⁷For he that is dead is freed from [the] sin."

If we are to know what God is up to, we must know what happened to mankind. It wasn't just that Adam and Eve did something wrong. They did something wrong because they believed something that is not true. Since the removal of the articles changes the meaning of the sin, death, and disobedience from specific instances to any instance, there is no reason to look deeper.

The lie was error, believing *the lie* was error, and the behavior by Adam and Eve that resulted from doing *the lie* was also error. All three were errors, and throughout his epistles Paul sometimes refers to them separately and other times together. Paul's use of the term *the death* points directly at precisely what happened to Adam and Eve and not the rest of humanity. *The death* was a separation inside them which spread to the entire human race and the creation. This separation initiated the entropy of the creation. *The disobedience* "of the one man" referred specifically to the couple's decision to believe the serpent, as well as the behavior which resulted from that belief, i.e., they ate the fruit. Paul referred to Adam and Eve together as "the one man" because they were united by marriage. That disobedience was a willful decision which resulted in them separating themselves from God. God didn't separate from them; they separated from God. They were no longer of like mind with Him. They had rejected what God knew and believed and had agreed to a different body of knowledge, a body of knowledge that was contrary to what God knew.[123]

---

[123] This is what Paul refers to in 2 Corinthians 10:5, "Casting down imaginations and every high thing that exalts itself against the *knowledge of God*" (that is, God's knowledge).

Because *the lie* became the foundation of all subsequent human thought and communication, it passed to every generation. No person could escape learning it, if they had even realized it existed. Because Adam and Eve had rejected knowing what God knew, they were left with no other choice than to figure out everything by using the only knowledge they accepted as real. There was only one voice to which they were attuned: Satan's. His was the voice that had offered what they had decided they wanted. From then on, the voice of God would always seem foreign, and unfamiliar. The voice of the serpent was now free to establish in human beings a body of knowledge that was not God's. The First Couple's descendants had no way to know about the knowledge their parents had rejected. Thus, the foundation of all future knowledge would be *the lie*.

But God already had a plan. It included giving humankind His Word so His human creatures could learn Who He is. But Satan knew the importance of language and worked to change the meanings of words so that even if people heard God speak, they would misunderstand Him. But, God knew this would happen, and He had a plan for even that.

Many Greek nouns, just like sin and death, have articles preceding them, so by removing the article "the" we lose the opportunity to know what God is saying. Changing the meaning of words is one of the ways that Satan has been able to cause such confusion among people, especially changing the meanings from the First through the Fourth Centuries. God said the serpent was subtler than any other life. Until now, we may not have realized what He meant. Hopefully, now we are beginning to understand. Knowing the continual and incessant deceptions we are facing should alert us to our need for the Holy Spirit. Up to this point, men and women have been like children that are sure we know everything. Unfortunately, the "everything" we think we know was founded on *the lie*. It may have taken 2000 years to understand this, but God said He would never give up on us, and He hasn't. Now that we know our understanding of God's *truth* may be infected by *the lie*, we can finally understand what has prevented us from consistently living the Spirit-filled life.

In summary, *the lie* was also known by another name that is usually translated *sin* rather than *the sin*. It is *the error* that Adam and Eve accepted as the *truth*. The first Christian believers knew about *the lie*.

Knowledge about *the lie* and training to recognize it was a must for the Early Church.

You Live What You Believe

When we are born again, false knowledge, which can result in wrong beliefs, does not automatically cease. That's because we have an enemy who is constantly present and whispering his lies through every medium possible. This includes invisible mediums of which we are not even aware, but that is a subject for another time. Overcoming that false knowledge is accomplished with the help of the Holy Spirit in His continuing work inside believers. That's why Jesus told the disciples to wait in Jerusalem until the Holy Spirit would come to them and they would take His power (Chapter Four Endnotes #22).

> And once, when at a meal with them, he charged them not to leave Jerusalem, but to wait there for that which the Father had promised, "Of which," he said, "you have heard me speak. For John baptized with water, but you shall be baptized in the Holy Spirit before many days have passed."[124]

Their salvation was not complete until He ascended and sent the Holy Spirit to be with and in them.

> I will talk to the Father, and he'll provide you another Friend so that you will always have someone with you. This Friend is the Spirit of Truth. The godless world can't take him in because it doesn't have eyes to see him, doesn't know what to look for. But you know him already because he has been staying with you, and will even be in you![125]

---

[124] Acts 1:4 (TCNT Part 1)
[125] John 14:16-17 (msg)

> At that moment you will know absolutely that I'm in my Father, and you're in me, and I'm in you.[126]
>
> As they met and ate meals together, he told them that they were on no account to leave Jerusalem but 'must wait for what the Father promised: the promise you heard from me. John baptized in water; you will be baptized in the Holy Spirit. And soon.' When they were together for the last time they asked, '"Master, are you going to restore the kingdom to Israel now? Is this the time?' He told them, 'You don't get to know the time. Timing is the Father's business. What you'll get is the Holy Spirit. And when the Holy Spirit comes on you, you will be able to be my witnesses in Jerusalem, all over Judea and Samaria, even to the ends of the world.'[127]

After being born again, we still tend to believe what we have always believed. This means each of us may still see a twisted view of God. We do not yet comprehend Him as He really is. Thus, we may keep performing for Him, only differently than when we were *of the world.*

Though we now live by the faith of Christ, the darkness in the world exerts tremendous pressure as it tries to trick us into accepting old familiar beliefs as truer than what the Gospel proclaims. If we don't guard our hearts and minds but instead keep hearkening to the lies which fill the airwaves, we will once again agree with them. By agreeing with the darkness, we let it dominate us. God gave us His Word so we could learn the *truth* and know what to believe. When we believe His *truth,* the darkness can't control us.

After his encounter with God on the road to Damascus, Paul didn't immediately run around the world preaching the Gospel.[128] Like all of us he was steeped in *the lie.* It took time before he understood and

---

[126] John 14:20 (KJV)

[127] Acts 1:4-9 (msg)

[128] Galatians 1:16

could teach the nations the *Law of Faith* instead of *the works of law*.[129] God has made it ever so possible to experience His fullness and love in this life. The greatest joy of salvation is coming to know God in *truth*, which is possible because of the renewal of our minds that was accomplished by the Holy Spirit.

I want to show you how simple He has made it. We live in a world that screams that God's *truth* is a lie. When our thoughts are under the influence of flesh, the warfare can sometimes feel overwhelming. Man was created to live by faith, not by the will of flesh (from whence comes willpower). Because humans live out of what we believe, it is not necessary to focus on living correctly, but rather on believing God. As you learn the *truth*, you become filled with faith and you automatically and increasingly reflect the character of Christ without struggle. "How can that be?" you ask.

As we have said, what a person believes automatically determines how they live. You may have heard someone say, "I have decided to live what I believe." That is not possible because you were created to automatically live your beliefs. You have no choice about it. You cannot make yourself live what you believe nor make yourself live something you do not believe. I am not talking about changing your behavior. Just because that changes doesn't mean you have been changed. God intends for our hearts and minds to be fixed on His *truth* so that our thoughts and behaviors flow out of Him. But nowhere does He tell us that it is something we must *do*. Rather, it is the life of Christ in us that does the work. When someone asked what he must do to work the works of God, Jesus said, "believe."[130] That has not changed.

The contents of your belief system are critical. There is nothing more important than believing the *truth*. Unless we believe God's *truth*, we may do works *for* God (by flesh), but we will never do the works *of* God (by spirit). By the way, in case you're wondering, the works of God are everything that Jesus did including His every day, non-miracle behavior and manner of living.

---

[129] Galatians 1:18, Romans 3:27, and Galatians 2:16

[130] John 6:29: "Jesus answered and said unto them, This is the work of God, that ye believe on him whom he hath sent." (KJV)

If we want to do God's will, we must simply believe. Believe what? The same thing that Paul believed: "And the life which I now live...I live by the faith of Jesus Christ."[131] In plain English, "I live by believing what Jesus believes." And what does Jesus believe? The *truth*. When this scripture says the faith of Jesus Christ, it means Jesus's faith, just like the car of Bill means Bill's car or the attitude of Kristy means Kristy's attitude. Many translations render this verse *I live by faith in Jesus Christ*, but a more accurate interpretation of the original Greek is, "I live inside the faith of Jesus Christ." It is Jesus's faith and His belief system by which Paul lived. He wasn't trying to act like Jesus, because the *Law of Faith* states that what you believe reflects in your behavior, both good and bad. He didn't have to figure out what Jesus would do because that would come automatically.

Though Adam could do nothing to undo the spiritual death that entered the world, it is conceivable he could have reversed the other effects of that false knowledge. How? By admitting he had erred, that the knowledge he had acquired was a lie, and by choosing instead to believe the *truth*. But he did not. Why? He believed that *the lie* was the *truth* and never questioned why his reality was not consistent with his beliefs. The auto loop-back was in control. Even after Satan's promise proved untrue, Adam refused to change his mind. He continued to believe that he had gained knowledge that made him a god. He was truly on his own, no longer subject to anyone or anything. The deception he had accepted began feeding upon itself and producing even more deception. Adam and Eve moved further and further from God's *truth*. Adam knew he was wrong but could not admit it. After all, now he *knew* the difference between good and evil just as Satan had promised, which meant he was a god. As a god, he could not admit he was wrong.

We are the same today. People hate to admit they believe lies or are wrong. As a result, we refuse to examine our beliefs, especially about spiritual things. But our lack of godliness and spiritual power and our failure to abide in God's love is evidence that something is wrong. Some have been believers long enough that they should display some semblance of maturity. Instead, most are still like children, struggling

---

[131] Galatians 2:20 (KJV)

with the flesh, determined to do their own thing, or convinced that if they try hard enough, God will be pleased. Some become very defensive when certain beliefs are challenged, usually a sign that deep down they know something is wrong. The writer of Hebrews put it this way:

> By this time you ought to be teachers yourselves, yet here I find you need someone to sit down with you and go over the basics on God again, starting from square one—baby's milk, when you should have been on solid food long ago! Milk is for beginners, inexperienced in God's ways; solid food is for the mature, who have some practice in telling right from wrong.[132]

False knowledge, which is a result of knowing things that God doesn't know, causes man to experience other than God's reality. "God is light and in Him is no darkness at all."[133] False knowledge is synonymous with darkness. Historically, all sorts of literature equate light with truth and darkness with deception. It is the same in the Scriptures. In darkness you are blind, you cannot see. You cannot know what you are facing unless someone tells you. And, if they can't be trusted to tell you the *truth*, then they may cause you great harm. But, when the light comes on, you can see where you are and where you are going; you can see reality. In the darkness, you can't see reality. This is when evil can invade your imagination making you unable to determine what is real. Even if someone is in the dark, it is easy for God to find them and His light shows them which way to go. When you head toward His light (Jesus) you find Him. "Jesus spoke to them and said, 'I am the light of the world. He who follows me will never walk in the dark, but will have the light of life.'"[134]

When a person embraces error (believes it), it produces evil deeds in his life. The only way to reverse the effects of wrong beliefs is to allow

---

[132] Hebrews 5:12-14 (msg)

[133] 1 John 1:5 (KJV)

[134] John 8:12 (Taken from the Translators New Testament © British & Foreign Bible Society 1973. Available from http://shop.biblesociety.org.uk/)

the Holy Spirit to expose them. It requires humility of mind to admit you don't know as much as you think you do, that you may be wrong, and thus ask the Holy Spirit to teach you. My prayer is that He will show me what He knows and expose everything I believe is true that isn't.

To suggest that they have wrong beliefs is offensive and repulsive to many people. These refuse to bow their hearts to the Holy Spirit, often preferring to work harder to prove that what they believe is true. Jesus described them perfectly. "For every one that doeth evil hateth the light, neither cometh to the light, lest his deeds should be reproved."[135] I have known people who were terrified of being wrong. Many so fear it they refuse to consider the possibility. They hate the light. The Apostle John was even blunter: "If we say that we have no sin (error), we deceive ourselves, and the truth is not in us."[136]

Adam and Eve embraced darkness. The light was no longer their ally. They could have asked God for help but that would have been the antithesis of *the lie*, which they believed was the *truth*. The future condition of man was set in stone. If not for the love of God, there would be no hope.

How Do I Stop Worrying?

Let's look at a common way *the Lie* affects us. In his first epistle, Peter is commonly translated, "Casting all of your cares (or, anxieties) upon Him because He cares for you."[137] Though there is a profound *truth* in this statement, it is not what the Greek text says (Chapter Four Endnotes #23). Let's focus on the word usually rendered *cares, worries,* or *anxieties*, because by not understanding what is underneath these interpretations we lose critical information about what is causing these symptoms.

Have you ever had a persistent care or anxiety that just wouldn't go, or stay away? Multitudes of people have. Depending on what the care is about, some can ignore it, though for most it remains in the background ready to pounce. Some imaginations can remain unshakeable.

---

[135] John 3:20 (KJV)

[136] 1 John 1:8 (KJV)

[137] 1 Peter 5:7

For many, the only answer is a form of drug whether, endorphins from exercise, alcohol, pharmaceuticals, or a host of other legal or illegal supplements added to their daily intakes.

The only way to get rid of anxiety is to eliminate what is causing it. God does not do magic. His goal is to teach His children to think and reason like Him. To that end, He does not take away our problems but instead teaches us to use His words to reason through issues as Jesus did.

The word in the original text is *merimnan* (μέριμναν), defined by Thayer as "Care, anxiety." Other lexicons agree. Using an interpretation for *merimnan* like *care*, *anxiety*, or *worry* causes us to miss what Peter was telling his readers. The literal definition of *merimnan* is *"the result of being pulled in different directions, dividedness, what's left when something is cut into pieces, distraction."* This is a difficult meaning to insert into the English sentence, and would make it sound strange. (i.e., "Casting all your pulled-apartness or distraction upon God.") So, substituting an interpretation in the passage makes it possible to write a more meaningful sentence. Unfortunately, by doing this we miss important information. As I have said, God wants to teach us His reasoning, so we can go through our trials just like Jesus went through His.

We need to know what is causing us to have those *cares*, *anxieties*, *worries*. From the literal meaning of *merimnan*, we have discovered the cause of our worries and, thus, have something into which to sink our teeth. Rather than casting our feelings and wild thoughts upon the Lord, and hoping He will work magic and get rid of them, we have discovered that we are causing our anguish. Due to the influence of *the lie* we feel we must get control of everything in our lives, at the same time, but humankind was not created for this. As Jesus said, we were created to deal with one thing at a time (a mind's eye that is single, looking at one thing at a time), and always by the ability the Holy Spirit gives us. We believe we must handle all of life because *the lie* tells us we are ultimately responsible for everything. But, by believing *it*, we inadvertently reject God's immediate help. So, we may try to trust God to take our cares and deal with them for us, but He can't! Why? Because we secretly hold onto them as we try to think through every conceivable way to fix them while we wait for God to help us. Without realizing it, we often tell God, "I won't let you touch what is *causing* my feelings until you take the feelings away." But, if we insist on holding onto problems, God will not force His will upon us. Which means He will not compel us to let go of them.

What a quandary. We want God's help, but we won't let Him. We fracture our minds as we attempt to deal with all of life. We feel pulled apart; we have divided attentions as we struggle to be gods in our lives. The result? We are anxious and our minds filled with worries and cares. Throughout the Word of God, He begs and pleads with us to set our attention on Him, "Look at Jesus." He wants us to feel safe and secure. Alas, we refuse to believe Him. We have been convinced that we MUST keep our eyes on the problems until God shows up. Unfortunately, our attitudes hinder Him.

Faith Is a Gift

Being born again does not stop the effects of the world's darkness on our souls. Yes, God makes us alive with Christ, puts His Word in our hearts, and writes it in our minds, but He doesn't stop there. "This is the covenant that I will make with them after those days, saith the Lord, I will put my laws into their hearts, and in their minds will I write them."[138]

Now you must work it out. "So now work out your own salvation with reverence and awe."[139] I recently translated this verse and was surprised by what I learned. The verb usually rendered *work out* means so much more. This is just a rough paraphrase of what I learned: "Drill down to the conclusion of your salvation, which will expand until you see something so utterly awesome that it will cause you to tremble." This is what Paul meant when he said, "That's why we have this Scripture text: No one's ever seen or heard anything like this, Never so much has imagined anything quite like it—What God has arranged

---

[138] Hebrews 10:16 (KJV)

[139] Philippians 2:12 (TCNT Part 2)

for those who love him."[140] Our minds have been renewed. Now it just needs to become real to us (Chapter Four Endnotes # 24).

It matters not who we really are if we believe we are someone else. You can be royalty, but if you think you are a homeless person living on the street, you won't act like royalty and will eventually find yourself homeless and on the street. Likewise, if you believe you are royalty, you will act like it. I'm talking about believing the *truth* about yourself and not what others tell you; believing what God says about you, because His is the only testimony that is True. You are not trying to make yourself change. Rather, you just agree with God Who says you have already been changed. When we agree with Him, He can show us the beautiful real world that we have been in all along. Once we begin to see where we live in Christ rather than what the world wants us to see, our whole perspective changes. We start to realize who we really are and begin bearing the proper fruit.

But, don't get introspective and try to start seeing if you are bearing fruit. That is God's business. Just trust He is faithful to do what He swore to do.

> I entreat you, then, Brothers, by all God's mercies to you, to offer your bodies as a living and holy sacrifice, acceptable to God, which is for you reasonable worship. Do not conform to the fashion of the age; but let your lives be transformed by your new attitude of mind, so that you may discern what God's will is—all that is good, acceptable, and perfect.[141]
>
> This is how we experience the transformation which God has accomplished in us by His Holy Spirit.

So how do you begin the journey God has set before you? By agreeing with the fact that, without Christ, you can do nothing and that His *truth* is right, regardless of what you feel or experience to the contrary.

---

[140] 1 Corinthians 2:9 (msg)

[141] Romans 12:1-2 (TCNT Part 2)

Unseen

Though you may think you're okay, when compared to the standard of Christ, it should be obvious that your thoughts and beliefs are deficient. If you're not sure, read again about the life and character of Jesus and what Paul says it means to be a new creature in Christ.[142] Ask yourself if that is a description of you. In fact, it is! But only the Holy Spirit can make your blood-bought salvation real in your experience so that you and others can see it.

But then, why is it so hard to believe the *truth*? Many will say, "Our experience is so often contrary to what you are saying, James." This is what Paul was referring to when he mentioned the "fight of faith."[143] That is, the intention to believe the *truth* when everything in your life is telling you the *truth* is a lie.

Right about now, I imagine that Satan may be heaping you with big piles of condemnation that you aren't good enough, that you just don't believe right or enough. God says that is not supposed to be your concern, but His. The Apostle Peter said we should cast all cares upon God and let Him take care of them. "Throw all your anxieties upon him, for he makes you his care."[144] Now we know that means throw your pulled-apart thinking upon God. That includes worrying about your beliefs. You can tell the powers of darkness to talk to God about your thinking and believing because you only listen to Him, and He doesn't condemn you for anything. "There is then no condemnation to those in Christ Jesus, who don't walk according to flesh but according to spirit."[145] The scriptures say you live by Jesus's beliefs, whether you feel like it or not. It is His faith that has filled you with His life.

Let me explain my shortcut to having the faith of God. It's so simple that it is may seem hard to grasp. Because you are in union with Christ, His faith lives in you, too. Whether I feel like I have faith or not I tell God, "Ignore me and just look at Jesus's faith, because His faith is my faith." This way it doesn't matter what I feel or think because I have trusted that since Jesus believes the *truth* and He and I are one, His

---

[142] Read the Gospels of Matthew, Mark, Luke, and John, and then 2 Corinthians 5:17
[143] 1 Timothy 6:12 (KJV)
[144] 1 Peter 5:7 (TCNT Part 2)
[145] Roman 8:1 (JEC)

believing the *truth* is my believing the *truth*. And, since Jesus believes all the *truth*, I don't have to be concerned whether He is believing the right *truth*. This is my faith.

Of course, we want to know what we believe in Christ. We don't want to actively believe something He doesn't believe and as we trust His faith, He works to help us with that. It is possible for someone to feel like they have trouble believing something they know is *truth*. That's okay. Their turmoil is a sign that their believing is going in the right direction and they are already in the fight of faith, about which I have just spoken. The fact that you even care about whether you believe the *truth* is a sign that the Holy Spirit is working in your life. This is part of the suffering I spoke of earlier. Take this as an opportunity to rest in God's love and talk to yourself about what it means to be unconditionally and limitlessly loved by God. One thing it means is that He likes you. Period. You can tell yourself that "God likes me" because He does. You can't change that. Give it time, and the confusion will be gone. Our lives are already open to God's eyes. He sees everything, so it is safe to admit that we believe things that are not true, that we are not living like the God in whose image we have been created. It serves no purpose to try and hide. God loves us, which means, we can come boldly to the Throne of Grace. He is eager to help us (Chapter Four Endnotes # 25).

The writer of Hebrews makes it clear that not only can God see our deepest secrets, He understands us and wants to help.

> God's Message is a living and active power, sharper than any two-edged sword, piercing its way till it penetrates soul and spirit—not the joints only but the very marrow—and detecting the inmost thoughts and purposes of the mind. No created thing can hide from the sight of God. Everything is exposed and laid bare before the eyes of him to whom we have to give account.[146]
>
> Now that we know what we have—Jesus, this great High Priest with ready access to God—let's not let it slip through our fingers. We don't have a priest who is out of

---

[146] Hebrews 4:12-13 (TCNT Part 2)

touch with our reality. He's been through weakness and testing, experienced it all—all but the sin. So let's walk right up to him and get what he is so ready to give. Take the mercy, accept the help.[147]

Long before we believed into Jesus, the *lie*'s tentacles had reached into every facet of our lives and seized control. Unfortunately, we still cling to many of those beliefs. *The lie* will often try to manipulate its way into our believing after our salvation. Thank God, He has made it so easy to *be* saved or no one would have a chance. Being translated from the power of darkness into the Kingdom of His Son has made the experience of a complete salvation on Earth imminently probable. "For God has rescued us from the tyranny of Darkness, and has removed us into the Kingdom of his Son."[148] I don't remember who said this, but I like it: "God has taken us out of the darkness; now He is taking the darkness out of us." I'm not talking about whether you will go to Heaven; rather, if you will begin to experience Heaven on Earth.

God's plan from the beginning was to pour Himself into man and then live His life in and through us in a union first revealed in Christ. "Even the mystery which hath been hid from ages and from generations, but now is made manifest to his saints: To whom God would make known what is the riches of the glory of this mystery among the Gentiles; which is Christ in you, the hope of glory."[149] Being born-again brought you into union with God. It is time to allow the mind of Christ to be revealed in you; thereby, producing His likeness in your body.

We Know Too Much

You are a child of God, but where do you go from here? How do you begin enjoying the life and ability of Christ in your mortal body? Invite the Holy Spirit to uncover the lies you believe so He can help you exchange them for the *truth*. It is the things that you think are true that

---

[147] Hebrews 4:14-16 (msg)
[148] Colossians 1:13 (TCNT Part 2)
[149] Colossians 1:26-27 (KJV)

aren't which are inhibiting your life. This process does not begin with trying to figure out what you believe that is wrong. You can't. It is entirely up to the ministry of the Holy Spirit. You *are* entirely dependent on Him. He alone knows the secrets of your heart. Only He can reveal them to you. Any time you discover a mistaken belief in your heart, it is because the Holy Spirit showed it to you, whether you asked Him to or not. Cooperating with this work of the Spirit provides the first means of realizing your intimacy with Him and thus, with God. Maybe you can remember the day you finally said, "Jesus is Lord" and meant it. Even if you didn't realize it, previously you believed *you* were lord and responsible for everything. The weight under which you had lived suddenly lifted because the Holy Spirit had taken your burdens.

Lies create stony ground and thorns in hearts, which hinder the *truth* from becoming real to people. This is what Jesus was talking about in the Parable of the Sower.

> The seed is God's Message. By the seed which fell along the path are meant those who hear the Message; but then the Devil comes and carries away the Message from their minds, to prevent their believing it and so being saved.
>
> By the seed which fell upon the rock are meant those who, as soon as they hear the Message, welcome it joyfully; but they have no root, and only believe it for a time, and when the time of temptation comes, they draw back.
>
> By that which fell among the thorn bushes are meant those who hear the Message, but who, as they go on their way, are completely choked by this world's anxieties and wealth and pleasures, and bring nothing to perfection.[150]

Like deception, *truth* has its own type of leaven.[151] As the number of lies in someone's belief system decrease, the *truth* will grow and produce fruit all by itself. This means there is no struggle to grow up into Christ just as a child does not struggle to become an adult. The

---

[150] Luke 8:11-15 (TCNT Part 1)

[151] Matthew 13:33

Scriptures illustrate *truth* and lies as seeds. Both types of seeds grow, both eventually bear fruit, and that fruit will contain more seeds of like kind. Just as weeds can choke out fruit-bearing plants, so can fruit-bearing plants choke out weeds. The type of harvest you get depends on which plants you care for better. Fruit-bearing plants and weeds don't live together well. Neither do *truth* and lies.

When you received Christ, it was only by childlike faith. For most of us, it happened at a moment during which our adult guards were down, and we momentarily became like little children because we faced problems we could not solve. Remember what the Apostle Paul said? "As ye have received Christ Jesus the Lord, so walk ye in Him."[152] How? By faith, that faith we see in little children. Because of my chance meeting with Frank, who was a former client and the director of that hospital, I was confronted with the fact that I did not know myself as well as I thought. It was an opportunity to be honest about myself with myself. With that honesty, I opened my heart and mind to things God wanted to teach me. My unrecognized arrogance had prevented me from learning things I desperately needed to know. Finally, I could say, "God, I don't know. Please teach me."

The main reason we fail to find answers is not that they do not exist, but because we overlook *solutions that are often right in front of our faces.* We are expecting something else, so we unconsciously dismiss what God is showing us. Once willing to admit we do not know as much as we think, answers to even previously unrecognized problems can become apparent. In other words, the fact that we often act like know-it-all adults causes us to ignore the best and simplest of answers. Alas, we live so far below the glory for which we were created. How could answers be right in front of us? The Bible says God always supplies our needs and that Jesus has been made unto us everything we need, which means the answers we need right now are here.

---

[152] Colossians 2:6 (KJV)

> You can be sure that God will take care of everything you need, his generosity exceeding even yours in the glory that pours from Jesus.[153]
>
> But you, by your union with Christ Jesus, are God's offspring; and Christ, by God's will, became not only our Wisdom but also our righteousness, our Holiness, our Deliverance.[154]
>
> For in him dwelleth all the fullness of the Godhead bodily. And ye are complete in him, which is the head of all principality and power:[155]

Do you have a need? Then God has supplied an answer. Just because we do not see His answer does not mean He hasn't given it. It just means we are missing something. "Having eyes, see ye not?"[156] We are blinded to God's blessings by what we believe that is not true. Wrong beliefs cause us to see things other than what God is showing us.

Who Is in Control?

I spoke earlier of learning that the thing I needed most was help with my mind. I had always hoped that some miracle would change my life, but I was tired of waiting. Of course, things had changed; but they had gone from bad to worse. What was needed for things to change was to exchange my wrong beliefs for right ones. We see examples everywhere of people whose lives are out of control while they wait for something or someone to give them what they need.

Many years ago, my wife told me about standing in line to make a purchase in a store. Behind her, two teenagers were involved in a discussion about video games. She heard one say he wanted to rent a video player and game. His friend said, "Your TV is too old. There is no way to connect it." He responded, "Well, then the president should

---

[153] Philippians 4:19 (msg)
[154] 1 Corinthians 1:30 (TCNT Part 2)
[155] Colossians 2:10 (KJV)
[156] Mark 8:18 (KJV)

get us a new one." My wife was struck by the seriousness of this kid's attitude. From other comments he made, it was obvious he was used to government handouts. Some on welfare blame others for their poverty. To them, their problems are someone else's fault. Some complain they have *never* had an opportunity. But if they understood God's will, their opportunity is right now. God has made it possible for them to rule their lives not by flesh, but by spirit, which means believing God's *truth*. This is the only way to develop their God-given potential. Many wait for someone else to give them what only they can do for themselves.

The terrible damage caused by taking drugs is a prime example of the control issue:

> John's life was out of control and his reality less than desirable. Not knowing how to achieve the order and stability he needed, he took drugs to escape. He used the drugs to distract himself from problems and issues with which he was unable, unwilling, or afraid to deal. The drugs provided John a false sense that he no longer had to deal with his issues, which was really no control at all.

How many times have kids, who were raised to believe in sexual purity, depended on the other person to say no? After giving in and violating their standards, how often do they still refuse responsibility saying, "It was his/her fault" or "I couldn't help myself?" Even people in prison whose lives are under someone else's dominance can still be in control of themselves.

If you are unable to rule your thoughts, it is not because of what someone else does, but because you are believing things that are not true. If this sounds harsh, it is still the *truth*. I learned in that psychiatric hospital that nothing could make me think crazy thoughts except me. No matter what happens, I am the only one that could take back control my mind.

James E. Campbell, Jr, James Q. Campbell

The Power of Unknown Beliefs

My experience in that hospital showed me that I really did not know myself. This led to even more life-changing discoveries. I had been filled with self-hate but would never have admitted it. Once I could admit it, God was able to show me why I believed I was a terrible person. That belief was based solely on my opinion of my performance. Of course, others may have helped me develop that opinion, but I was solely responsible for what I believed.

It was *unknown* wrong beliefs that had prevented me from enjoying the love with which God and others had loved me. This recognition surprised me. Many times throughout life people had said they loved me. Unfortunately, I had learned to believe that my *terribleness* was bigger than all their love. When someone stated that they loved me, it meant nothing, because I knew better. I *knew* I was a terrible person. I believed that if anyone really knew the *truth*, they would not love me. Thus, I hid from people by wearing masks and behaving in ways that kept them from knowing the real me. No one could love me because I wouldn't allow it. Years of not receiving love (because I was unknowingly rejecting it) brought me to the conclusion that I was not lovable. It never occurred to me that I could be causing my sense of rejection.

My thoughts began changing once I realized that my life had been dominated by *the lie*. That single erroneous belief made me feel unworthy and unable to accept love, even though I craved it. With all my heart, I wanted to be accepted by people; but unknowingly, I had put up barriers. I remember the day in 1977 when Jim Buskirk, Dean of the Seminary at ORU, said to me, "James, I don't know what to do with you. You crave love, but no matter how much attention I give you, it is never enough."

Your Feelings Can Lie

Emotions are great at telling you what you feel and bad at telling you the *truth*. Today, I look back and recognize I was lovable because God loved me even then. That I did not *feel* wanted did not change the fact that God wanted me. My bad feelings had no bearing on God's love for me. I now know I cannot make God love me more or cause Him to love me less. His love is based on His unchangeable nature, not on my beliefs, emotions, or behavior. My feelings were lying to me. So how did discovering I believed *the lie* help me? It made room in my heart for the *truth* to grow. Until the Holy Spirit exposed the dark roots of those lies, they were strongholds that dominated my heart and mind, keeping me bound and in pain (Chapter Four Endnotes #26). My trust in *the lie* produced stony ground in my heart. It was my faith in that evil belief that produced the weeds that choked out any love which I craved.

Once I knew the *truth* about God's love and *the lie* I had believed—even though I still did not *feel* His love was true—I shared that with God and then thanked Him that His *truth* is right, regardless of how I continued to feel. Fortunately, by that time I had learned that my feelings could not tell me what was and wasn't true. I had trusted them to be right (I called it my spiritual sense) and had been led further astray by them. This was a milestone. I had finally chosen to believe God's *truth* was true despite feelings to the contrary.

Removing Obstacles

When I believed His *truth*, something deep within me began to change, and later my feelings followed suit. Once I realized that I had been created to *be* loved and that in God's love there was nothing wrong with me, His love began to be real. Understanding that God never has an unkind thought toward me or demands anything from me enabled me to relax. My fear of rejection subsided, and I began seeing myself in a whole new light. I became increasingly open to new discoveries about myself. I began discovering all sorts of lies that I believed both about life, myself, and others. To this day, I continue to exchange lies for the *truth* and my peace and joy continue to grow.

Chapter Three of Hebrews explains that sin, and the consequent failure to enter God's rest, is a result of unbelief. Chapter Four explains that the way to enter God's rest is to believe His *truth* instead of lies.[157]

---

[157] After completing this book, go back and read Chapters Three and Four of the book of Hebrews and, in the light of these comments, you will understand them much better.

Believing God's *truth* is the only way to undo the effects of lies. The more we replace lies with His *truth*, the more we enjoy His rest. The result of exchanging our false knowledge for God's causes the removal of every obstacle preventing us from growing up into Christ. The renewal of our minds, which we now know has already occurred, allows the life of Christ to be manifested in us. We just need to let the Holy Spirit teach us what to believe and how to think.

As the Holy Spirit shows you what you already believe because of Christ's faith within you, your believing will increasingly reflect His and you will realize that He has already transformed you into a vessel that pleases Him, and you will be able to increasingly act like it. You are already who God says you are. As you come to see yourself as God sees you, if you have been distressed, you will experience "the peace that passes understanding" growing in your heart and mind."[158]

* * *

Chapter Four Endnotes

Note 1

How often do you say, "I am..." and then attach some description like "I am a child of God." It is so unfortunate that many people attach a bad description to their am-ness like "I am stupid" or "I am sick" or "I am ugly." God created us with the predilection to talk of ourselves as I am's in order that we would have a continual reminder of who we are. Humans are created in God's class of being. In Christ, God's image has been restored in us. We are as close to being like God as possible without being Him. "Yet You have made him a little lower than God, And You crown him with glory and majesty!"[159]

Though the Bible uses a number of names for God, the most prominent name God ever called Himself is "I AM." I AM is God's family name and the name which He gave His children when He created us.

---

[158] Philippians 4:7 (KJV)

[159] Psalm 8:5 (NASB)

We call ourselves "I am's" all the time. The word "God" is not I AM's name, but it is a description of Him. Thus, when I AM told Moses, "You shall not take the name of the Lord thy God in vain, He wasn't talking about using "God" in a cuss word. He was referring to the same type of *taking* as in a bride taking her new husband's name. He was referring to the misuse of the wonderful name of "I am" like "I am stupid," "I am ugly," "I am poor," "I am a sinner," etc., because, since Jesus arose from dead with us in Him, those are lies, and thus taking the name of the Lord in vain. Because the Children of Israel believed "I am a grasshopper," by taking the name of the Lord in vain, they convinced themselves they couldn't enter the promised land.

Note 2

The Greek word usually translated *renewing* is the dative singular feminine of the noun *anakainwsis* (ἀνακαίνωσις). It is not a verb; it is a noun that means *renewal* or *restoration* and should be understood as an existing reality, instead of something you should do.

Note 3

From the Liddell and Scott 1875 Greek-English Lexicon, I discovered that one of the most glorious prepositions in the Greek New Testament is the word *meta*. The fundamental meaning of *meta* is *with*. However, since there are other Greek prepositions that mean *with*, I wondered if there was something different about *meta*. All more recent lexicons, including versions of Liddell and Scott, have removed an astonishing meaning of this word. It is a meaning that changed my life. When used with the genitive case, the word *meta* contains the sense of, "with, doing as you do." This amazing definition is not used by theologians, yet before 1875 it was considered a valid meaning. It offers tremendous insight into our union with Him. For instance, the last verse of 2 Corinthians says, "The grace of the Lord Jesus Christ and the love of God and the fellowship of the Holy Spirit be with you all."[160] My literal

---

[160] 2 Corinthians 13:14 (ESV)

translation, which includes the Liddle and Scott 1875 meaning of *meta*, reads, "The grace of the Lord Jesus Christ and the love of the God and the fellowship of the Holy Spirit… with all of you doing as you do. Amen." God can never leave us or forsake us because He is with us doing as we do. This is union and the key to living in the victory of Christ.

Note 4

The subject of God's glory in the believer is massive to St. Paul, and especially evident in the book of Romans. Toward the end of Chapter Four, he discusses God's promise to Abraham, which he clarifies in Galatians 3:14 as the gift of the indwelling of the Spirit of God. Jesus sent the Spirit to be the presence of God in believers. He begins Chapter Five discussing the splendor of God's presence in believers and the incredible expectation we have of seeing it manifested in this life on Earth. He says that hope is so firm we can literally boast about it.

Romans 5:2: "καυχώ μεθα ἐπ' ἐλπί δι τῆς δόξης τοῦ Θεοῦ." "We *boast* upon expectation of the glory of the God." The standard definition of *kauxometha* is *rejoice*, yet its primary meaning is *to boast or vaunt oneself.* We are not just rejoicing in what God has promised, but boasting in our expectation of the glory or splendor of God being manifested in our lives here on Earth, not after death but now, within us, while still in this body. He goes on in the rest of Chapters Five to Seven to explain how sin (error) has worked in humankind and how God has overcome it by Christ inside us. In Chapter Eight, Paul describes the relationship of flesh and spirit to our minds. This is the nitty-gritty of how believers experience their union with God and how in our union with Christ He causes us to be more than conquerors.

Unfortunately, due to a failure to understand God's logic and how He defines many words, accompanied by a misunderstanding of the rules of Greek grammatical sentence construction used by the Spirit, the church today fails to understand the absolute simplicity of God's thoughts. God hasn't made Himself difficult to comprehend, *we* have. We need to come to God as little children first believing that what He says is true even when we don't understand it and then asking what He means. But instead we have come to Him like adults demanding to know what He means so that we can then decide if it should be part of our believing. We treat God as though He intentionally obscures His will. How absurd to think that God has revealed Himself through His Word but then refuses to tell us what it means. Could it be that people are demanding that God declare Himself on their terms instead of His? And so, in His quiet gentle way, He waits for those who will humbly say, "Teach me, because I don't know." We are creatures and will never understand or know Him unless He shows us first. The thing is, He has.[161]

Many will never enjoy trusting God until they have the right foundation. Of course, they have probably been taught that their foundation *is* Christ. They have been told that because they believe in Him, their foundation CAN'T be wrong; but we need to go deeper. Just because you have been born again doesn't mean Jesus is your foundation. So, what does a foundation "which is Christ" look like?[162] In the Kingdom of God, foundations are made of knowledge, specifically the knowledge of God. If the body of knowledge out of which you live is not God's, your foundation is not from God. Are you sure what you know is the *truth*? Only God can show you, and He wants to.

Is it outlandish to say that God, who made you His child in Christ, would want you to know what He knows? If you want a solid foundation, you need to know what Jesus knows. How are you going to do that? By learning His *truth*. That's why He sent the Holy Spirit.

Do you confess dependence on God when in fact, before you can trust Him there is something you *have to* do? But, you aren't sure what it is? If you do know, can you ever do it perfectly? You may be one of those who believes that if you try hard enough, or wait long enough, you'll eventually know. All the while, you wonder why God has made it so hard. But, He hasn't, humankind has.

---

[161] John 14: 9
[162] 1 Corinthians 3:11

Note 5

There are numerous beautiful translations of 2 Corinthians 5:17. The following are just a few:

a. "I have learned that man is a new creation. All former views of man now perish. He is a new being, all is new and wonderful" (*St. Paul from the Trenches* by Gerald Warren Cornish).

b. "If, then, any man is in Christ, he is a new creation; the old state of things has gone; wonderful to tell, it has been made over, absolutely new" (*The New Testament* Part 2 by Joseph L. Lilly).

c. "If anyone is in Christ, he is a new creation altogether. The old has passed away and has become altogether new" (Taken from Norlie, Olaf M., Norlie's Simplified New Testament c. 1961).

d. "Therefore, if a man is a Christian he is a brand-new creation. The old guy is gone: look, a new man has appeared" (*The Cotton Patch Version of Paul's Epistles* by Clarence Jordan).

e. "For if a man is in Christ he becomes a new person altogether—the past is finished and gone, everything has become fresh and new" (*The New Testament in Modern English* by J. B. Phillips).

But what about our bodies? Let's look at several translations of Paul's words in Romans 8:11.

f. "Nevertheless, once the Spirit of him who raised Christ Jesus from the dead lives within you he will, by the same Spirit, bring to your whole being new strength and vitality" (*The New Testament in Modern English* by J. B. Phillips).

g. "And if the Spirit of him who raised Jesus from the dead lives within you, he who raised Christ Jesus from the dead will give Life even to your mortal bodies, through his Spirit living with you" (TCNA Part 2).

h. "If the Spirit of him who raised Jesus from the dead lives in you, then he who raised Christ from the dead will make even your mortal bodies live by causing his Spirit to live in you" (*The Translators New Testament* by British and Foreign Bible Society 1973).

When these two verses are considered together, it is evident that God has left this new creation inside of mortal bodies but fully intends that they be filled with life (including health) until it is time for us to discard them.

i. "Therefore, if anyone is within Christ, he/she is a new creation. The old things have passed away, behold, a new [creation] has emerged."[163]

Note 6

The subject of imagination is too big for this book. I will address it in some other work. However, your imagination is in your heart and is ruled by what you think and believe. It can be full of imaginary things (good and bad), or it can be the place where you see God's reality and where His kingdom and presence become so real that you begin living a life you can't even imagine until the Holy Spirit shows you. I believe our imaginations were created as a place where we can play with God, but they are often the playground of Satan.

I have found the book, *Telling Yourself the Truth* by William Backus and Marie Chapian of immense value in understanding self-talk, which fuels our imaginations. The book provides many examples with which it is easy to identify and can help you become aware of beliefs that are creating unproductive or painful thoughts.

Note 7

In Romans 7:1, Paul spoke about people seeking to live by the law, which is the same as living in agreement with flesh instead of faith,

---

[163] 2 Corinthians 5:17 (JEC)

which all of us are continually tempted to do. In fact, you will see in verse twenty-four, even Paul was not immune to such temptations. In verse one he is writing to brothers and sisters in the Lord and not unbelievers. "Surely, Brothers, you know (for I am speaking to men who know what Law means) that Law governs a man only as long as he lives" (TCNT Part 2).

In verse four, he reminds them that they died in relation to the law by means of their union with Christ so that they could have become related to another, that is, the One Who was raised out of dead so that we would bear fruit by God. We realize that most modern translations to not convey such an understanding, but when considered from a literal standpoint as well as the whole message of the Gospel, we are convinced that Paul could not have meant anything else. "Wherefore, my brethren, ye also are become dead to the law by the body of Christ; that ye should be married to another, even to him who is raised from the dead, that we should bring forth fruit unto God." (Rom. 7:4, KJV).

In verse five, he reminds them that at one time their lives had been based totally on what their flesh perceived as reality. They had yet to believe into Christ and couldn't help themselves. They were incapable of keeping the Law. A more literal rendering of what the Apostle was saying is: "For when we were inside the attitude of believing what our flesh told us, the passions [that come from believing] belonging to the errors, the passions [that come through] the law, inside-worked inside the members of us (i.e., of our bodies) into the to have produced the separation" (Rom. 7:5, KJV). (This is easier to understand when you comprehend how the New Testament writers used the article *the*.)

In verse six, he says they have been delivered from the Law, which is now dead, so that they can live in newness of spirit. (Remember, by "newness of spirit" Paul meant newness of living by believing the truth instead of flesh.) "But now we are delivered from the law, that being dead wherein we were held; that we should serve in newness of spirit, and not in the oldness of the letter" (Rom. 7:6, KJV).

In verse seventeen, he blows away the Gnostic teachings that make the risen Christ slightly different from believers. First Century Gnostics taught that Christ was a slightly different type of human being from those for whom He died, and today many believers embrace a variation of that teaching in which they believe Christ was really crucified but the presence of wrong behaviors and desires in us is because of the lingering presence of an old evil being (the old man), which is proof that we have not yet been fully crucified. However, Paul didn't blame an *old man*. Rather, he laid the blame squarely on the error hiding in our hearts. "Now then it is no more I that do it, but sin (error) that dwelleth in me" (Rom. 7:17, KJV). This is a lot easier to fix than an invisible and elusive old man who refused to die with Christ and is still roaming around inside our minds and bodies.

In verse eighteen, he says that flesh—the attitude set on believing what our senses tell us—can't help us. As long as we insist on living by what we feel, we have no way of performing *good* works. "For I know that in me [that is, in my flesh,] dwelleth no good thing: for to will is present with me; but how to perform that which is good I find not" (Rom. 7:18, KJV).

Then in verse twenty, he again says the source of wrong doing is the error we believe: "Now if I do that I would not, it is no more I that do it, but sin (error) that dwelleth in me" (Rom. 7:20, KJV).

In verses twenty-two and twenty-three, he contrasts "the law of God according to his inward man" with a different law affecting his body. The law affecting his members is the law of error that operates by flesh (the attitude of agreeing with what our senses tell us). The senses in our bodies can contend with what we know and believe: "For I delight in the law of God after the inward man: But I see another law in my members, warring against the law of my mind, and bringing me into captivity to the law of sin (error) which is in my members" (Rom. 7:22 and 23, KJV).

In brutal honesty Paul cries out in verse twenty-four as someone who knows how living by flesh affects everyone that loves God. He recognized that when he obeyed flesh he felt trapped, wretched. (Remember, to *obey* flesh means to submit to hearing it. And, *flesh* is the attitude of believing that what you see and feel is more real than God's *truth*.) "O wretched man that I am! Who shall deliver me from the body of this death?" (Rom. 7:24, KJV).

The primary meaning of the word *death* is separation. By *death*, Paul did not mean a cessation of existence but the separation that results from believing things that God doesn't believe. The behavior that results from separating ourselves from God's truth is a wretched feeling for those who love God. It is especially terrible for those who don't know why they are the way they are. When we believe error, knowingly or unknowingly, we automatically reject some of God's truth and live the error instead. The *body of death* about which Paul wrote refers to that body of false knowledge (i.e., of error) which when believed causes the death of separation. It is that body of knowledge which flesh longs to embrace because it is contrary to what God knows and believes. And remember, Paul, too, had to obey the things he was teaching. When he didn't, by default he obeyed error. That is what he was talking about in verses twenty-four and twenty-five. A few sentences later, in verse 8:1, he went on to say that only by living in complete agreement with an attitude set on believing the truth can anyone live free from condemnation and, in verses thirteen and fourteen, Paul tells us that it is the Holy Spirit that leads us into believing the truth.

So, in verse twenty-five Paul said that by means of his renewed mind, he served the Law of God; but when focusing his attention on flesh, he served the law of error. "I thank God through Jesus Christ our Lord. So then with the mind I myself serve the law of God; but with the flesh the law of sin" (Rom. 7:25, KJV). So, what is the law of error? It's like the *Law of Faith*. You live what you believe. If you believe error, you will live it. If you believe the *truth*, you will live it.

God had no intention of creating a discipline called theology for mankind to figure out what He means. Just because people know things about God doesn't mean they know Him. He loves mankind and has no desire to make knowing Him complicated. Knowing Him is simple. It is mankind's embracing of *the lie* that has made it difficult.

Note 8

Jesus was generous, compassionate, and caring, but He could be quite violent to the point of tearing things up when someone turned a temple into a place where access to God had to be bought. But even while turning over tables, He still unconditionally loved those religious people and planned on dying for them. His kindness is eternal; our Father is the same.

As a side note, consider Jesus's comment to the woman at the well in Samaria. Comparing His *truth* to the water that she had come to draw out of the well, He said, "Anyone who drinks the water I give will never thirst—not ever. The water I give will be an artesian spring within, gushing fountains of endless life."[164]

We know from the Apostle John that Jesus is the Word.[165] Paul tells us that the Word is water.[166] Jesus, who is the Word, was speaking of Himself when He told the woman at the well that the water He would give her would flow through and out of her in a quality of life that can only be described as eternal. Jesus was speaking of the unending and unstoppable flow of the water of life.[167] Once in us, it will always prevail. That water, that life, is Love Himself—Jesus.

Note 9

The word *cause* is not in the original language. My logic for this extrapolation is quite simple. In 2 Corinthians 2:14, the Apostle Paul writes that God "always causes us to triumph in Christ." God never forces us against our wills so, if we are going to triumph, it will be because we cooperated with Him as He lives His will in us. God is determined to cause us to triumph. I believe that nothing is over until we triumph. God is the one who defines that, but the definition does not include either failure or error. This means that He works inside us in all situations and circumstances to cause us to will His will and then do it, even though we may not be aware of it.

---

[164] John 4:14 (msg)
[165] John 1:1
[166] Ephesians 5:26
[167] Revelations 22:1

Note 10

A proper definition of sin is critical to understanding the will of God and the New Testament. As previously discussed, the church has long understood sin as something done that is not the will of God. While not completely wrong, this perspective causes us to misunderstand much of the New Testament. Because Greek-English lexicons also define *hamartia* (ἁμαρτία) as "error" then *hamartano* (ἁμαρτάνω) must also mean "to err." Since mankind's problems began with *the lie,* and a lie is an *error*, it is perfectly reasonable to use *error* in the place of *sin.*

When we understand words as God meant them, it is much easier to comprehend what He wants and what He is doing in our lives. Look at language today. The meanings of so many words have changed in just the last one hundred years. It is so common that I don't even need to give examples. The same has happened since the Holy Spirit inspired the Scriptures. Once we know what He meant by certain words, our body of knowledge will more accurately reflect what God knows.

Note 11

I like the King James Version translation of the word ἐλευθερώσει, a future active indicative of ἐλευθερόω (*make free*). A Greek-English lexicon will also translate it as *to set free, deliver,* or *release*. You might ask, from what? From whatever is hindering you from realizing the finished work of Christ in your life. You can take this sentence as far as you can imagine. However, ἐλευθερώσει is the future active indicative form of ἐλευθερόω, which means that the experience or realization of being released from bondage doesn't necessarily take place immediately. It requires patience as you continue to stand your ground, and continue to believe God is Love and is working to make your reality real to you.

The key to standing your ground is God's love. Ask Him every day for more insight into His love for you. Flesh tells us that our troubles are proof that God doesn't love us, but He says He does, and He can't lie. "God is not a man that he should lie; neither the son of man, that he should repent" (i.e., that he should change his mind).[168]

Note 12

The Greek word often rendered *continue* or *abide* in John 8:31 can also means *stand one's ground*. I believe this is to what Jesus was referring; not spending time reading and speaking the scriptures but standing in what you believe. This passage will be better read as "If you stand your ground in my word." Paul was referring to this very thing in his comment about "the fight of faith" (1 Tim. 6:12). Likewise, he wrote: "Wherefore take unto you the whole armour of God, that ye may be able to withstand in the evil day, and having done all, to stand…above all taking the shield of faith."[169] I also understand it to mean "snuggle down comfortably as in nicer than the nicest home you could ever imagine.

Note 13

In Romans 3:27 (KJV), the Apostle Paul introduces the phrase *"law of faith."* "Where is boasting then? It is excluded. By what law? Of works? Nay: but by *the law of faith.*" This law is like the law of gravity. You don't decide to obey it; you automatically do. I have frequently heard Christians say that laws are necessary because Christians will just abuse grace and use it as a license for sin. That's because of a misunderstanding of grace, faith, and law.

Since Paul is very clear regarding the importance of the Law, how do we reconcile law and faith? Because faith (believing God's *truth*) is the only way to fulfill the Law. Paul is so adamant about the issue that he makes an emphatic statement in Romans 4:31. Rather than voiding the Law by faith, it is faith that establishes it. How? Because when we believe the *truth*, we automatically live it. Thus, by means of accepting

---

[168] Numbers 23:19 (KJV)
[169] Ephesians 6:13, 16 (KJV)

the *truth*, the Law becomes established in our lives. "Do we then make void the law through faith? God forbid: yea, we establish the law."[170]

Note 14

Translation after translation misses what Paul is saying in Romans 8:4-8.

> That the righteousness of the law might be fulfilled in us, who walk not after the flesh, but after the Spirit. For they that are after the flesh do mind the things of the flesh; but they that are after the Spirit the things of the Spirit. For to be carnally minded is death; but to be spiritually minded is life and peace. Because the carnal mind is enmity against God: for it is not subject to the law of God, neither indeed can be. So then they that are in the flesh cannot please God (KJV).

What does Paul mean? A paraphrase of the King James Version using some substitution of definitions should make this clearer.

> That the righteousness of the law might be fulfilled in us, who walk not according to what our five senses are telling us our reality is, but because we have a mindset of believing God's *truth*. For they that live according to what their natural senses tell them is their ultimate reality think in line with those senses. But, they that live according to a mindset of believing God's *truth* think in line with the Spirit of *truth*. For if the foundation of your thoughts is based on your flesh senses, it means living separated from what is good (that is, living in death). But, to have thoughts founded on an attitude of believing God's *truth* means real life and peace. Because a thought life which is based on natural senses disagrees and even hates God's *truth*, for it rejects His *truth*. In fact, it cannot do otherwise. So then,

---

[170] Romans 3:31 (KJV)

they that live with a mindset that believes their natural senses are the *truth* cannot please God.[171]

The word *spiritual* gives many readers difficulty because it seems hard to define. Spiritual means having the characteristic of spirit. As you will remember, the word *spirit* can often refer to an attitude set on believing the *truth*. Thus, *spiritual* often means "having the characteristic of an attitude that treasures the *truth*."

Note 15

The word often translated *poured out* or *shed abroad* is the Greek word *ekxew* (ἐκχέω). In Romans 5:5, it is the perfect passive participle. Greek lexicons also put it *squandered*. To me, that more accurately describes the grace of God. It is more than enough. It is overflowing, and since it is in the perfect tense, that means it is complete and will never diminish. That squandering of His love inside our hearts will never go away.

Note 16

It is painful to realize that you believe lies and don't know what they are, yet others can see the results in your behavior. When I realized this, it was embarrassing. I want to believe the *truth* so that it is what people will see me living. But sometimes, our beliefs are so deep and personal that facing them can cause real emotional pain. There is no way around this. But the Holy Spirit is gentle and kind and will not force you to face something you aren't ready to face. However, circumstances may sometimes force you to face misbeliefs. When that happens, the Holy Spirit is there to help you through it. After a while, you come to enjoy finding out where you've been wrong, because when the Holy Spirit reveals a *truth* that replaces the error you hadn't recognized—now you're right. Then you experience more freedom. Jesus said when you know the *truth*, it will make you free. "And ye shall know the truth, and the truth shall make you free."[172]

---

[171] Romans 8:4-8 (JEC paraphrase)
[172] John 8:32 (KJV)

Note 17

The subject of covenant is beyond the scope of this book. However, since God could swear by no name greater than His, He swore to Himself, by His name. This means that He took on the full responsibility of fulfilling His promise. No matter how badly and how many times Abraham might screw up God put His own name on the line. In terms of covenant, God was saying that if He didn't keep His promise, His name would be worthless. Remember that God put Abraham to sleep and stood in his place when the oath was made. God swore to God. Why? Because, mankind was not capable of fulfilling our side of the covenant, so God took our place and swore for us as us. Once God became man in Jesus, it became God's responsibility to keep mankind's side of the covenant. And, He did. God's covenant with mankind was through the Son of God Who became a man. We are not separate beings from Christ who are responsible to keep the covenant. Rather, God has determined that no matter how long it takes, every human being, at some point, will recognize what He has done and His love for them and will then gladly bow their knees. God has made Himself 100% liable to keep Abraham's faith for all of mankind by becoming "the seed" spoken of in Genesis 22:18 and Galatians 3:16.

God kept His Word. He fulfilled His promise to Abraham. Jesus was born and became the complete fulfillment of God's covenant with Abraham and mankind. Through Abraham, every family of mankind has been blessed. The New Testament is the revelation of the fulfillment of that blessing.

The following verses from Romans and 2 Corinthians show what each party in a covenant gives to the other.

> If God didn't hesitate to put everything on the line for us, embracing our condition and exposing himself to the worst by sending his own Son, is there anything else he wouldn't gladly and freely do for us?[173]

---

[173] Romans 8:32 (msg)

God gives us everything that is His. "For he hath made him to be sin for us, who knew no sin; that we might be made the righteousness of God in him."[174]

And in return, He took everything we had, which included all our error. This is a covenant of love.

Note 18

The language *of the Son of God* is in the genitive case and should be put in the possessive, i.e., the faith belonging to Christ. i.e., His faith.

Note 19

English translations usually render τῷ ψεύδει "a lie," however, the literal is *the lie*. τῷ is the article *the*. Paul was pointing back to *the lie* which the first couple believed.

Note 20

Genesis 3:1-7

> The serpent was clever, more clever than any wild animal God had made. He spoke to the Woman: "Do I understand that God told you not to eat from any tree in the garden?"
>
> The Woman said to the serpent, "Not at all. We can eat from the trees in the garden. It's only about the tree in the middle of the garden that God said, 'Don't eat from it; don't even touch it or you'll die.'"
>
> The serpent told the Woman, "You won't die. God knows that the moment you eat from that tree, you'll see what's really going on. You'll be just like God, knowing everything, ranging all the way from good to evil."

---

[174] Corinthians 5:21 (KJV)

> When the Woman saw that the tree looked like good eating and realized what she would get out of it—she'd know everything!—she took and ate the fruit and then gave some to her husband, and he ate.
>
> Immediately the two of them did "see what's really going on"—saw themselves naked! They sewed fig leaves together as makeshift clothes for themselves.[175]

Okay, what just happened here? How did this seemingly tiny and insignificant course of events doom all of mankind?

Because two people didn't follow some simple directions, why are we all stuck in a state of sin and error? This was just the beginning of *the lie*. *The lie* caused what would today be described as a god complex. We made God's responsibilities our responsibilities. The problem is, we can't handle that. Mankind welcomed the responsibility of determining what is right and what is wrong. But, when we determine what is right, then we must enforce it. When we decide something is wrong, we must meet out punishment. As gods, it is our responsibility to fix what is wrong and make it right.

God is never wrong, and believing ourselves to be gods, we cannot be wrong either. Since God cannot be held accountable by a higher power, we disdain authority because it is a constant reminder that we are not gods. God deals out rewards and punishments, so we confirm our godhood by doing the same. When we hear God's *truth, the lie* causes us to believe it is our responsibility to transform ourselves and enact it in our lives. Because we feel ourselves to be gods and capable of anything, many reject the Holy Spirit's work in them. If we admit our need of Him, it would be proof that we cannot do it on our own; but that is not possible, for we are gods. "Just give us a little more time." This *error* causes us to try to act like God, but without His abilities.

You have probably asked: So why, because two people thousands of years ago messed up, are we still paying for it today? *Truth* cannot produce bad fruit; lies cannot produce good fruit. Perfect can only be created by the perfect, and imperfect by the flawed. Adam and Eve,

---

[175] Genesis 3:1-7 (msg)

now imperfect, could not have created perfect children. It is that simple. *The lie* ingrained itself into their very DNA through the corruption they initiated to be passed down through the generations. This is *the lie*: I am God, I must be, which means, He isn't. We can deny we believe this, but the fruit of our lives proves it. No amount of human effort can escape believing error. Only God can and has done it for us in our union with Christ Jesus.

Note 21

Someone who produces a readable version of the New Testament, they must first translate it for themselves. But, what they create for themselves will not make sense to the average reader. Adding to the difficulty is the fact that all of us have our own perspectives through which we interpret life. After translating, to produce something that will make sense to those who only read English, they interpret in a way that will hopefully make sense to readers. Obviously, good translators seek to accurately represent what they believe the original writer had in mind. But, due to complexities inherent in Koine Greek, it is usually not possible to produce an interpretation that fully conveys what is written, so people do the best they can. Unfortunately, because of our loose usage of the word *translation,* I believe a great disservice is done to readers. That's why I like it when Bibles are described as paraphrased versions of the Bible. The *truth* is, every version of the Bible that you can purchase today is a paraphrase; it is an interpretation of what the interpreter believed the original writers meant. Unfortunately, when enough scholars arrive at a similar understanding, it is easier for someone to assume they are actual translations.

Have you ever wondered that the King James Bible is called the Authorized King James *Version*? And, there are names of other Bibles that contain the word *version,* too: the American Standard Version, the Standard American Edition-Revised Version, the English Standard Version, New International Version, and New Century Version. In fact, if you google for a list of Bible *versions* you will find many titles that don't include the word *version*. It's just good to understand that each "translation*"* is someone's interpretation or *version* of the original

Greek, and all *translations* are considered *versions*. Merriam-Webster's online dictionary contains several definitions of the word *version*. One definition of *version* is, "a translation from another language; *especially*: a translation of the Bible or a part of it." However, Webster's primary definition is "an account or description from a particular point of view especially as contrasted with another account..."[176] As you can see, they define a *version* as being the result of someone's *viewpoint*.

So, a question? What happens if a translator's viewpoint is not the same as the author's view point? Can you see how this could present a problem? I contend that a change in viewpoints since the First Century has caused a significant distortion of our perspective of what God has been telling us. If it is possible to have hundreds of versions of a Bible passage, many at least slightly different from the others, all claiming to be real translations, which one is correct? Which one accurately represents what the Holy Spirit was saying? Maybe none of them exactly describes what God said.[177] I'm so glad God has given us His Holy Spirit to instruct us.

Note 22

Lēmpsesthe (λήμψεσθε) is the future indicative middle of lambanó (λαμβάνω). The use of the middle voice signifies action on the part of the giver (The Holy Spirit) and receiver (believers told to expect power, which is all of us). The Holy Spirit does not force ability on His beloved. He offers it and we can take it, or not.

---

[176] By permission. From *Merriam-Webster's Collegiate® Dictionary, Eleventh Edition* ©2017 by Merriam-Webster, Incorporated (www.www.Merriam-Webster.com).

[177] The remarkable thing is that we still have copies of God's original words. Though there are some differences between "original" texts, they are all close enough to each other that we can be certain we have what the Holy Spirit inspired. Now we just need to understand Greek grammar and their definitions of words.

Note 23

Thayer and others say that the word translated anxiety or cares is derived from the verb *merizó*, which means "to be drawn in different directions; to divide; i.e., separate into parts, cut into pieces."[178] HELP Word-studies adds to that, "*mérimna*, 'a *part*, as opposed to the whole' – properly, drawn in opposite directions; 'divided into parts' (A. T. Robertson); (figuratively) 'to go to pieces' because *pulled apart* (in different directions), like the force exerted by sinful *anxiety* (*worry*)." HELPS goes on to say, "an old verb for worry and anxiety – literally, to be *divided*, distracted (*WP*, 2, 156)."[179] As you can see, the root meaning of the word is what causes anxiety, that is, when our minds are being pulled apart as we try to juggle too many things at one time. But, who causes the pulling apart of our minds? We do it because we are believing *the lie*, which tells us we must do more than we can truly handle. We split our attention in several directions when we try to control multiple issues at one time. The result can be feelings of severe anxiety. Man was not created to think of several things at one time, i.e. be double-minded. We were created to be single-minded, that is, focused.

This is exactly what Jesus was talking about in the Sermon on the Mount when He said,

> The light of the body is the eye: if therefore thine eye be single, thy whole body shall be full of light. But if thine eye be evil, thy whole body shall be full of darkness. If therefore the light that is in thee be darkness, how great *is* that darkness![180]

When the eye of your mind is focused on just one issue at a time, your vision is clearer. Your body will be full of light meaning healthy. Surely you are aware that much sickness and disease is the result of

---

[178] Greek-English Lexicon by Joseph Henry Thayer - 1889

[179] HELP Word-studies copyright © 1987, 2011 by Helps Ministries, Inc. For complete text and additional resources visit: TheDiscoveryBible.com

[180] Matthew 6:22, 23 (KJV)

distress that radiates into our bodies from our minds. Notice that in verses 25 through 34 Jesus specifically addresses worries and cares. He hadn't changed subjects. He was still talking about the same thing. How do I know that? Because of His use of the word "evil" in verse 23. The Greek word is *ponéros* (πονηρός). It means, "causing toil or hardship,"[181] "toilsome, bad,"[182] "full of labors, annoyances, hardships; pressed and harassed by labors."[183] Jesus was talking about a mind that is in overdrive trying to solve too many problems at one time. Another name for too much thinking is *worry*. Worry may start with a single issue like, "I need money." But, before long it can mushroom into many images of needs which arise from not having enough money. Before long you are juggling a thousand problems stemming from not having enough money. This is toilsome, laborious, oppressive mental labor, which I would easily call worry. Most interpreters render Jesus saying, "an eye that is evil." But, if we want to deal with the real problem affecting our lives, we need to know it is not the lack of money. We know this because in the very next passage Jesus says God will take care of that. Rather, the real problem is the splitting of our attention into so many fractured pieces that we can no longer control our thoughts. We are oppressed. Unfortunately, many have been in this condition for so long that they have forgotten how they got there, if they ever knew in the first place.

Note 24

Romans 12:2 (JEC) says, "be transformed by the renewal of your mind." The word *renewal* is a noun with the article *the* preceding it. It is speaking of a fact of our *being*. Since we have the mind of Christ, now it is time to be who we are—that is, start thinking and living like a transformed person (1 Cor. 2:16). A transformed person is not one who follows the rules, but one who believes the *truth* and thus, by default, lives it.

---

[181] Liddell & Scott Greek-English Lexicon 1875
[182] Strong's Exhaustive Concordance 1890
[183] Henry Joseph Thayer Greek-English Lexicon 1889

Note 25

Boldly means to be confident that God will never criticize you for what you say. The Greek word means *freedom of speech*. God your Father is a teacher and will guide you in learning how to speak properly just like any good parent. In the meantime, He listens to your heart and knows what you mean to say. If you say something that is out of line, He'll teach you why it was out of line and what you should be saying. No one criticizes a two-year-old for talking like a two-year-old. People love it. For a moment, think of yourself as a two-year-old and just learning how to speak to God. God's not upset at you. Why should you be?

Note 26

The easiest and best way to explain strongholds is to consider the battles waged by the U.S. against the Japanese in the Philippines during World War II. As US troops stormed those beaches, they took devastating fire from Japanese soldiers—but, from where was it coming? In many cases, all our troops saw was mountains and cliffs covered with dense foliage. They were being killed by hidden enemy fire. The fire was coming from strongholds—caves and hiding places in the cliffs and mountains—through which our soldiers could not see the enemy at work. All they saw was the results of the enemy's presence.

Before I break down the language of 2 Corinthians 10:3-5, let's look at several translations of this passage.

   a. For though we walk in the flesh, we do not war after the flesh: (For the weapons of our warfare are not carnal, but mighty through God to the pulling down of strong holds;) Casting down imaginations, and every high thing that exalteth itself against the knowledge of God, and bringing into captivity every thought to the obedience of Christ (KJV).

   b. Human indeed we are, but it is in no human strength that we fight our battles. The weapons we fight with are not human weapons; they are divinely powerful, ready to pull down strongholds. Yes, we can pull down the conceits of men, every barrier of pride which sets itself up against the true knowledge of God (Knox translation 1935).

c. For though we live an earthly life we do not wage an earthly war. Our weapons of war are not earthly ones but, in God's service, are powerful for the overthrow of fortresses. We are engaged in confuting arguments and overthrowing every barrier raised against the knowledge of God (TCNT Part 2).

Paul first says that though we are walking around in bodies of flesh, we are not engaging in warfare that is based on sense knowledge. "For though we walk in the flesh, we do not war after the flesh,"[184] He goes on in verse four to say that the weapons we use are not anything our senses can comprehend. "For the weapons of our warfare are not carnal, but mighty through God to the pulling down of strong holds."[185] But here's where it gets fascinating to me. Most of the translations I have read speak to the fact that the weapons—whatever they are—are of divine nature or, at the least, powerful with God's assistance: "mighty through God." But the Greek says δυνατὰ τῷ Θεῷ, which is in the dative case. Since the root meaning of *dunata* is *able*, which includes the might or power necessary to accomplish something, I think a more usable translation is, "able by God," meaning that God uses the weapons in us. It's not that we must know what to do, but that God knows and is using the weapons within us (by the presence of the Holy Spirit) to unenable the strongholds. We just need to cooperate with Him by believing what He says is *truth*.

What are the strongholds? Lies, which we have become convinced are true, that have created an emotional pull we are unable to question. They can be single lies or multiple lies that are linked together. Strongholds in our own lives often leave us sure the problem is somewhere else and not something we believe. The enemy can use these firmly held beliefs to fire thoughts at us from inside our own minds. These thoughts usually feel like our own thoughts. When we believe they are, it is easy for them to hide from us.

---

[184] 2 Corinthians 10:3 (KJV)

[185] 2 Corinthians 10:4 (KJV)

Verse five makes it clear that the strongholds are firing thoughts, imaginations, reasonings, and anything else that can paint pictures of a *reality* that is other than God's *truth* (God's knowledge). "Casting down imaginations, and every high thing that exalteth itself against the knowledge of God, and bringing into captivity every thought to the obedience of Christ." This is why the protection of our hearts and minds is so important. I believe King David was aware of this when he said: "Search me, O God, and know my heart: try me, and know my thoughts."[186] Likewise, with Solomon, "Keep thy heart with all diligence; for out of it are the issues of life."[187]

---

[186] Psalm 139:23 (KJV)

[187] Proverbs 4:23 (KJV)

5
Why We Are the Way We Are

Humankind has accumulated massive amounts of knowledge. We study far away galaxies, have walked upon the moon, and gone deep into the Earth. We know much about how our world and universe work. Not too long ago, the news media reported that scientists may have found the God Particle. Scientists have found the answers to all types of problems, but about the two things that have the greatest influence on our lives, mankind remains ignorant. This chapter is about both— our beliefs and our thoughts.

We Need to Feel Important

In the last chapter, I spoke about how being honest with God and choosing to believe His *truth* enabled me to experience a new freedom. God's love and acceptance became real and continued growing even more so. If I had been unwilling to admit the *truth* about a lie I believed, I would still be mired in it. As it is, I now enjoy a new reality made possible only by the work of the Holy Spirit.

Mankind has lost its sense of value and, even worse, the Church has too. People search for self-worth in what they and others think about them. We crave to be appreciated, and the fear of rejection can drive us to extremes. Not believing they can ever gain acceptance, some become loners who say that they are too busy or do not like people. Others seek the perfect appearance, hoping to be more desirable. Some try to fill the void with food as though enough of it will somehow satisfy the hunger in their hearts. Others search for fulfillment through owning things. In their minds, enough things or money will make them more valuable and important than those with less. The self-worth of some rises when they are seen with the *right* people or in the *right* places. Many have low self-esteem due to a lack of control. Since they can't control their own lives, they seek to order the lives of others.

Man is created to discover his value through a voice from the outside. That voice was to be God's, telling us He loves us and we're important to Him. But mankind can no longer hear His voice and does whatever it takes to get others to say, "You are important." Because of performance orientation, many cannot conceive of their self-worth apart from what they have or do.

> Al once told me that he had a superior intellect, that his understanding was way above normal. He is hiding behind an attitude of superiority to protect himself from a feeling of worthlessness, which he secretly believes. Of course, Al has never voiced that lie because it is too painful to admit. His fear leaves him paralyzed, unable to consider that the lie *you are worthless* may not be true. He is so afraid that lie is right that he can't even allow himself to consider it. Al's parents abandoned him when he was a small child, so deep inside he feels he must be a terrible person. He must be because the ones who should have loved him didn't.
>
> Al talks a lot about serving God who has *called* him to his current work. Unfortunately, his *service* is just a way of earning God's love. He so wants to hear God say, "Well done, thou good and faithful servant,"[1] because to Al, his performance is all that matters. Little does he know that there is nothing he could do or not do that would cause God to love him. He has never considered that nothing about him can change the nature of God, who is love. God wants Al to enjoy His love, but he can't. He is so terrified that what he believes about himself may be true that he can't afford to be honest for fear it may prove to be so. Thus, that stronghold remains firmly entrenched.

---

[1] Matthew 25:21 (KJV)

The result of Al's denial is that his fellowship with others revolves around his success and the financial, social, or spiritual poverty of the less fortunate—which is everyone else—and what he is doing for them. His superiority *protects* him from others and the truth. It is his defense against the lies, which he fears, but it also insulates his heart from God's love. Al is desperately searching for a sense of value. Because he knows that the value he seeks is love, he pretends to like others in hopes that they will return it. But God's love does not seek anything in return; whereas Al's show of love is his effort to be appreciated and valued. He is so full of trying to love others that there is no room to enjoy God's love for himself.

Al needs to know he is loved and that he is important; but his attitude, created as a defense against rejection, prevents him from finding the love he is so desperate to experience.

There are many like Al who secretly believe that what they do, say, think, wear, drive, etc., proves they are more valuable and more important. Al's "superior" intellect and constant willingness to help the less fortunate prove to him that he is better than others and thus more valuable.

The Holy Spirit and the Mind of Christ

Faced with more information, choices, and responsibilities than ever before, people are overwhelmed by the complexities of life. Since humans long ago rejected absolute dependence on God, who would have gladly given us the wisdom we need, we are left looking somewhere else for a god to trust. Some try to be their own god and so trust in themselves. Others look outside of themselves. They turn to anyone who appears to have answers like politicians who make big promises, the rich who seem to be successful, church leaders who must know because they have been called to their position by God, or a gang leader. Jesus said, "They are only blind leaders of the blind. If one blind man leads another, they will both fall into the ditch."[2] God wants you to realize He is for you and that you can trust Him. He has placed various offices in the Church to help us grow into that understanding, but these personalities, to whom so many look for guidance, are not God. Often, they don't even know God as well as you already do. Many of them are trapped by believing the lies that they are sure have made them successful. For many, accepting God's *truth* could result in undoing what they have achieved, which is often more precious than obeying the *truth* and helping people discover the absolute wonder of being loved by God.

> And he gave some, apostles; and some, prophets; and some, evangelists; and some, pastors and teachers; For the perfecting of the saints, for the work of the ministry, for the edifying of the body of Christ: Till we all come in the unity of the faith, and of the knowledge of the Son of God, unto a perfect man, unto the measure of the stature of the fulness of Christ: That we henceforth be no more children, tossed to and fro, and carried about with every wind of doctrine, by the sleight of men, and cunning craftiness, whereby they lie in wait to deceive; But speaking the truth in love, may grow up into him in all things, which is the head, even Christ.[3]

God never intended for anyone to take His place in your life. He so wants personal fellowship with you that He says you can call Him Abba (Daddy, Papa).[4]

Have you ever noticed how often we make simple issues challenging? Have you ever wondered why? Think of the small wrong that turns

---

[2] Matthew 15:14 (Taken from Norlie, Olaf M., Norlie's Simplified New Testament c. 1961) Jesus was not limiting his comment to just religious leaders. They just happened to be a good example at that moment.

[3] Ephesians 4:11-15 (KJV)

[4] Romans 8:15

into a big one. You lie to a friend and they call you on it. However, instead of just admitting the fact that you made a mistake and asking forgiveness, you pile a lie on top of another lie, on top of justification, on top of a denial, and then add another lie just to be safe. Before you know it, an issue that could have been solved easily has turned into a catastrophic nightmare. Sir Walter Scott put it succinctly in his work "Marmion."

> Oh! What a tangled web we weave
> When first we practice to deceive![5]

We crave a return to a simpler era while unknowingly making our lives increasingly harder. Many are on that proverbial merry-go-round which they want off, if only they knew how. Overwhelmed with problems, we have lost sight of what is important.

Years ago, I began to realize there are two key issues that, when dealt with properly, take care of everything else. In the early nineties, God started giving me understanding of just what makes me tick. He showed me what controls my ability to yield to Him and enjoy the life that Jesus died to give us.

To experience intimate fellowship with God and enjoy all the benefits of knowing Him, we need to think like Jesus. I'm not talking about doing what Jesus does, but thinking what He thinks—that is, the *truth*. "But that's impossible," you say. Not if you do it the way God planned, which is the only way you can do it. Paul said we have the mind of Christ. We just need to *allow* that mind to be in us. "Let this mind be in you, which was also in Christ Jesus."[6] God does not expect you to *make* yourself think like Christ, but rather He expects you to just *allow* His character and nature to dominate your thoughts. How does that happen? By being a *Being* rather than a *Doing*. That is the goal of the Holy Spirit's ministry in you.

---

[5] Sir Walter Scott in "Marmion" (1808). Lies beget more lies which beget even more. The result is a false reality, a life that doesn't work correctly, a life based on a body of knowledge that isn't true.

[6] Philippians 2:5 (KJV)

Do you want to *be* changed? If you have claimed Jesus as your Lord, since the Holy Spirit is in you, so is the mind of Christ. "We, however, have the very mind of Christ"[7] You are already on the way to thinking like Jesus. You don't make it happen, He does. The experience of *realizing* brought about by the Holy Spirit is greatly enhanced once you accept that the Holy Spirit is God and has poured His love into your heart. He knows you in ways you may be afraid to admit to yourself, yet there is nothing about you that can change His love for you. Regardless of what your religion has told you, He *is* love and there is nothing about you that can change that.

As you come to know His love for you, you will begin thinking like Jesus, who is love. As you increasingly think like Jesus, you will more and more reflect God's love. Remember what John said? "We love because he first loved us."[8] As we increasingly open to His love for us, we see His fullness appearing in our lives, without effort on our part. "And to know the love of Christ, which passeth knowledge, that ye might be filled with all the fulness of God."[9]

Understanding Yourself

It is easy to find someone to tell you how to live. Many ministers do it every Sunday. Just look at the self-help section of any bookstore. However, it is not so easy to find someone who can help you understand why you are the way you are and how to *be* changed instead of just trying harder to change. Rather, it seems everyone always has something else you need to do: Find your purpose; Do what Jesus would do.

How about Jesus's offer? "Come to me, all you who are toiling and burdened, and I will give you rest! Take my yoke upon you, and learn from me, because I am gently and lowly-minded, and you will find rest for your souls; for my yoke is easy and my burden is light."[10] I have learned His yoke really is easy. It is sad that I had been taught otherwise.

---

[7] 1 Corinthians 2:16 (TCNT Part 2)
[8] John 4:19 (KJV)
[9] Ephesians 3:19 (KJV)
[10] Matthew 11:28-29 (TCNT Part 1)

Because we are God's children, He will gladly teach us what He knows. Then we will find ourselves relieved of our performance burdens. He truly has provided a means of living with a yoke that is easy and a burden that is light. The Holy Spirit longs to give you understanding and will do it. Do you believe this? Well, it's true. "But the Comforter, the Holy Spirit whom the Father is going to send in My name, will teach you everything and will remind you of everything that I have said to you."[11]

Many want to understand before they are willing to believe; however, that's backward. Many refuse to trust God's Word because something they think should happen hasn't or something they think shouldn't happen has. They demand that God prove Himself by some other means than what He has already said or done. If you want to understand God's *truth*, do this. Even if something in the Word of God is confusing to you, if you believe that God is *truth*, then tell Him you agree with him. Then say you'd like to understand what He means. This even works when you are referring to a passage that is translated incorrectly. Recognize that you are a child and that you can't even tell the difference between genuine and false without His help. Admit that whatever He meant to say in a verse is true, even though you doubt it or don't understand it. Then ask Him to explain it to you.

Oh, does He love that attitude. So, He'll show you. He may have to teach you other things first. If what you read in a translation does not come out of God, He will show you that, too. He doesn't expect you to trust someone else to explain God. Though He may use others in the process, God wants you to know Him personally, and His self-revelation will be accompanied by peace and love.[12] God always welcomes a questioning heart, even a doubting one. Example, "Father, whatever you mean by (such and such) is right, but I don't understand it. Give me Your understanding. Thank you." My son, who wrote this book with me, prays this way: "God, I believe what You say is true. Did you really say what I'm reading? Explain it to me because I'm having a tough time with it."

---

[11] John 14:26 (Taken from Norlie, Olaf M., Norlie's Simplified New Testament c. 1961)
[12] James 3:17

If you aren't sure that what you hear in church is true, then ask the Holy Spirit. Just because someone has the title pastor, reverend, doctor, or priest next to their name does not mean he or she is the voice of God in your life. The Holy Spirit likes it when you ask Him if something you have learned, or heard, is true. God wants that type of personal relationship with you. If you have doubts, it doesn't take a lot of time to ask the Holy Spirit, "What is the *truth*?" He'll show you, and doesn't expect you to act on it until He has persuaded you. You don't have to be in a hurry, because He isn't. If you're feeling hurried, it is not from God. God doesn't panic. He cares so much for you that He doesn't want you to panic either.

Years ago, I realized that, if controlling my thoughts was crucial to experiencing the abundant life, I was in big trouble, because I couldn't do it without superhuman ability. I didn't know that God intends life in Christ to be simple and that it does not require extra special discipline or effort. A critical point in my life was realizing that God does love me and His overtures of love in the scriptures are to me personally. But before that could happen, I had to admit that I didn't believe it. I knew God loved me. Others had told me so. But I had been afraid to admit that I didn't believe it.

God wants more than a family relationship with us. He desires intimate fellowship.[13] As we grow to think like Jesus and to think God's *truth*, we automatically experience intimacy with Him. God is an intellectual *being*. His intellect is greater than all of humankind combined. Fellowship with Him grows into a thought life based in His *truth*. This is the way Christ's mind works, and we have the mind of Christ.[14] The more your thoughts are consistent with His *truth*, the more sense He will make and the more you will realize harmony with His will.

> *Except in the case of physiological disorders or physical reflex actions, the source of every behavior is always what*

---

[13] A family relationship is just being related as in brother-sister, father-son, and husband-wife. Intimate fellowship means sharing one another's secrets, discussing each other's plans, knowing the other's desires, and sharing one another's lives.

[14] 1 Corinthians 2:16

> *we think.*[15] *Everything we do and feel and tell ourselves is a result of what we think, and everything we think is always a consequence of the combination of our beliefs.*

Enjoying God's life is so much easier when you can focus on only one issue rather than struggling with a multitude of confusing thoughts that sometimes flow so fast you do not even know what you are thinking. That's why being focused on the *truth* makes life so much simpler.

Is it possible that there is just one issue responsible for all your thoughts, the understanding of which would enable you to seize control of your mind and unleash the fantastic potential that is hidden inside you? Yes, there is! The key is not in learning the right things to do, but in understanding—specifically, understanding the source of your thoughts and actions. That is, learning what you really believe. Let me explain.

Does this describe how your soul works? Yes! The *truth* is that your beliefs always rule you. They have worked both for and against you since you were born. They work for you when you believe the *truth* and against you when you believe a lie. How do we know believing occurs in our hearts? The Apostle Paul said, "For with the heart man believeth unto righteousness."[16]

I have been a believer for over forty-five years. I have a degree in Religions, went to seminary, studied the Bible, and prayed religiously. I knew God loved me. That is one of the first things I learned. In fact, I had to know that because I was taught that if a person doesn't know that God loves them they are not saved, and I was terrified of not being saved. What a shock when the Holy Spirit showed me that I didn't really believe it. I *knew* He loved me, but I didn't treasure it. It was just something I said I believed so I would go to Heaven. The problem was that there was something in my heart keeping me from treasuring what I knew was true. But the Holy Spirit fixed that in me, and Jesus sent Him to fix it in everyone. No one can fix this but the Holy Spirit. Thank God, He came to squander His love in our hearts.

---

[15] We define behavior as "what we do and feel."

[16] Romans 10:10 (TCNT Part 2)

Consider a couple of scenarios in which a man has lost his job. In scenario one, he believes and feels life is over. In scenario two, he believes it is the end of something, but not life. In which scenario does the man believe the *truth*? In which is he better able to deal with the loss? For the person in scenario one, though it is only the end of his job, his beliefs and thoughts make it the end of his joy, peace, happiness, prosperity, health, and maybe even his life. The man in scenario two will probably have a much easier time.

The quality of our thoughts and lives is dominated by nothing other than what we believe *about everything*. I don't mean just religious beliefs, because they are only a small portion of our beliefs. The vast majority relate to our opinions about other people, our circumstances, the past and future, and ourselves. It is our multilayered beliefs about everything we see, feel, hear, touch, taste, think, and do that determine our thoughts and reactions to every aspect of life.

Consider some of the ways we approach life and deal with needs:

Self-help programs

Group therapy

Support groups

Positive thinking

Behavior modification

Psychotherapy

Religion

Philosophies

Accumulating wealth

Depression

Attitudes like "If I don't try, I can't fail."

Stealing

Codependency

Blaming others

Denial

Overeating

Drinking

Drugs

And on and on

Most of these represent destructive methods for dealing with life when they are based on *the lie*—independence from God and dependence on someone or something else. Why does one person do one and another person another? Each has different beliefs that result in choosing one method over another.

Have you ever wondered why two individuals from the same environment and similar experiences could develop entirely different outlooks on life? One can become a productive member of society while the other a criminal. Some theorize that behavioral problems are genetic in nature or a result of environmental influences. Those who teach such things unintentionally relegate some people to hopelessness. For those who have believed into Jesus Christ, the key to freedom lies within their hearts.

> But the righteousness which results from faith finds expression in these words—'*Do not say* to yourself "*Who will go up into heaven*"'—that means to bring Christ down—'or "*Who will go down into the depths below?* "'—that means to bring Christ up from the dead. No, but what does it say? '*The Message is near thee; it is on thy lips and in thy heart*'— that means *the Message* concerning faith which we are proclaiming. For *with your lips* you acknowledge the truth of *the Message* that Jesus IS Lord, and believe *in your heart* that God raised him from the dead, you will be saved. For with their hearts men believe and so attain to righteousness, and with their lips they make open acknowledgement and so find Salvation.[17]

---

[17] Romans 10:6-10 (TCNT Part 2)

Mike's depression was tough on his family. He was listless, confused, and unable to work. Since his livelihood was selling insurance, he was in big trouble. If he didn't work, he couldn't pay the bills.

Mike's counselor said the primary problem was his thinking. But, a medical doctor had a different opinion. He said the source of Mike's problem was just a chemical imbalance and proper medications would control his emotions and get him back to a productive life. Unfortunately, Mike has not experienced the full freedom that God wants him to enjoy since then. By listening to his counselor, Mike would have confronted his wrong thinking, which is something he preferred not to do. If there were a way around admitting he was wrong, he wanted it. The drugs provided a convenient escape from reality and the truth.

Mike did not understand that the drugs would only relieve his symptoms. That would have been fine if he used the drugs while dealing with his core problem, which was his thinking and believing. Mike preferred to believe his only problem was the symptoms, which means he'll probably take those drugs the rest of his life. He lost the impetus to correct the real problem and doesn't realize he is trapped and may never discover true freedom.

The chemical imbalance is your body's way of telling you something is wrong.[18] Regardless of the problem, God's *truth* restores your wholeness. Consider this: something happens to leave you feeling desperate, alone, angry, fearful or depressed. Those feelings are your mind and body telling you there's a problem that you need to deal with; it does not mean you're mentally ill. We can either seek to eliminate our

---

[18] Dr. Thomas Szasz wrote a book called The Myth of Mental Illness in 1961. His argument was that what we generally call chemical imbalances are problems in belief. He argued there is no such thing as a mental illness, and attributing our problem to such is equivalent to the people of antiquity attributing sickness to witches. His work has become a classic in the field of psychology. It was not a religious work.

symptoms by the easiest means possible or get God's answer. Our problems can be an excellent catalyst for discovering the *truth*.

The greatest cause of sickness, disease, and behavioral problems is what we think. We used to hear a lot about psychosomatic illness; but today, we hear far more about how our problems are chemical in nature or someone else's fault. I am glad I didn't buy that line because it is wonderful to experience the Holy Spirit working in my life, causing me to know His love. It is not possible to overcome distress unless we first acknowledge the factors causing it. Sometimes that can be emotionally painful. It may seem easier just to ignore or deny problems, but that will not solve them.

You already have the tools necessary to lay hold of that peace that is so great, it "passes understanding."[19] Now you are beginning to understand what makes you tick and how to cooperate with God's work in you. Have you ever heard someone say, "Let go and let God?" I want you to see that the door to understanding that statement is right in front of you and encourage you to walk through it.

---

[19] Philippians 4:7

6
Longing for Unconditional Love

We were created to be loved, to experience God's loving kindness forever. "That in the ages to come he might shew the exceeding riches of his grace in his kindness toward us through Christ Jesus."[1] But because of *the lie*, we have imposed conditions upon ourselves and others that resist God's love in our lives. No matter what it looks like, everyone has suffered the infecting power of *the lie*. It's just that our responses to it are as varied as the number of humans who have ever lived.

The Desire to Be Accepted

The sense of *being* that belonged to mankind before the rebellion in the Garden enabled them to experience God as He *is*. They were blessed before they could have done anything to deserve it. No one blesses something they don't value; neither does God. God blessed them because He valued them. Adam and Eve were secure in the knowledge that they mattered to God. Even after the fall, they still mattered. In fact, they were so important to their Creator that He had planned on sending Jesus before He even created the world already knowing what they would do. "And all that dwell upon the earth shall worship him, whose names are not written in the book of life of the *Lamb slain from the foundation of the world.*"[2] Did He hate them because they had turned toward evil? No! Did He give up on them? No! Instead, He cursed the serpent and declared His intent to send a Savior.

---

[1] Ephesians 2:7 (KJV)
[2] Revelation 13:8: "the Lamb slain from the foundation of the world." (KJV)

> And I will put enmity between thee (the serpent) and between the woman, and between thy seed and between her seed, He shall crush thy head and thou shalt crush His Heel.[3]

Unfortunately, because humans are performance-oriented, they are unable to see God's reality, which can only be seen from the perspective of *being*. Humankind is blind and hides from the light. Until God's light shines in our hearts, we have no idea what God has done for us and how to reach out and take it. "Indeed, the same God who said 'Out of darkness light shall shine,' has shone in upon our hearts, so that light may spread from our knowledge of the splendor of God, as seen on the face of Christ."[4] Today, human relationships are largely performance-based. As a result, we are judged and judge ourselves by what we do. We place value on ourselves and others based on what we have and how we look. People's worth is determined by what they do for us and how they *make* us feel. An individual's importance is determined by what we think of them. We need to realize that everyone is of ultimate importance because God loves them. What people do is not the only measure of their performance in society. Even appearance is part of our performance value. Being better looking or smarter can increase someone's value. Being deformed or a bit odd can result in the opposite.

People crave love and acceptance. We often behave in whatever way we think will win it. Since our attitudes toward people are affected by their performance—which includes appearance— we fear being judged the same way. Hence, the man who believes his value is dependent on owning the biggest and best of everything; or the mother who neglects her family to establish a career, not because of financial needs or the love of an occupation, but because she believes a person's value is reflected in one's ability to accumulate wealth or power; or the man who is so afraid of being wrong that everyone else is always mistaken, regardless of the facts. Because sex is equated with love, many find

---

[3] Genesis 3:15 (*A Translation of the Old Testament Scriptures from the Original Hebrew* by Helen Spurrell)

[4] 2 Corinthians 4:6 (TCNT Part 2)

their value by how enjoyable or frequent their sexual experiences are. People find their value and worth in as many ways as there are people.

> Rick had a beautiful family and a devoted wife. His business was successful, and money was no problem. But Rick has a secret; one he hides even from himself—he is afraid of people, afraid to view them as equals. He finds his self-worth through a mask, which makes him look like he is in control and makes him better than others. If Rick has no opinion on a matter, he is more than happy to listen to others. But once he expresses his thoughts on a subject, there is no more discussion because he cannot be wrong. Rick has another fundamental problem. He believes that imitating the loving character of Jesus Christ will cause God and others to like him. Unfortunately, Rick does not know what it means to be loved, and his masked attempts to look like a loving person are phony. He pats people on the back and asks how they are doing, but his attitude lacks an essential ingredient—sincerity. Rick wants people to see him as a caring Christian and good family man. What people think about him is more important than anything else.
>
> Despite an explosive temper and overbearing management style, Rick has a successful business. The real reason for its stable growth is a quality staff that ignores his ranting and ravings. Rick has surrounded himself with skilled people who have one advantage his family does not enjoy. They can go home at night and escape his demeaning, condescending behavior. The home front is a different matter. Linda cannot do anything right. The self-esteem she had before marriage is gone. Rick "tries" to be encouraging and loving in his way but since the only thing of real importance is his opinion of himself, he can't comprehend the needs of others. His wife needs a partner. She is not an object on display for the benefit of his mask, but a real live breathing person who needs to be appreciated and valued just as much as her husband.

Rick considers Linda's needs a reflection of her deficiencies as a human being. His response to her needs is to criticize and demean her. His justification is the fact that he is right. Period. Rick was stunned when Linda filed for divorce. He is such a great husband and father. Why, just look at what he does for others and how he supports his family. No man can do more. As far as he is concerned, his wife's problems go much deeper than he thought. Rick is still waiting for God to change Linda and bring his family back to him. His self-image is so weak that he cannot admit he is wrong.

One of mankind's greatest needs is to be valued. Many spend their entire lives trying to gain a sense of worth. They do not comprehend what it means to be loved by God and that to Him, who they are is more important than what they do. To them, their value is determined solely by what they or others think about their performance.

We identify people by what they do. If you ask a man, "Who are you?" he will usually describe what he does for a living. He sees himself as a *doing*. "I'm a mechanic, an attorney, a broker, etc." Most of us are the same. We are what we do. We rate our worth and importance by what we do for a living, the car we drive, our looks, talent, wealth, or how much power we have over others. But when we see ourselves as *beings*, we have a different perspective. "I'm a child of God, a new creature in Christ, the beloved of God." To God, our value is not determined by what we do, but by the fact that we are alive and of supreme importance to Him. We matter because we *are*, rather than because we *do*. This distinction is of critical importance because it means our self-worth and sense of value is determined either by a loving God or our evaluation of ourselves, which will never be good enough. No matter how hard we try, we will never reach perfection; but we keep trying, or give up.

We hear much today about class warfare. What causes it? It isn't just the fact that one has more than another. People need to be valued. Since what we have or do is indicative of our worth as human beings, if we cannot accumulate or do the things that we think give us value, we will seek to reduce the importance of others. If I cannot be worth more, then others must be made to be worth less. If I am not important, then I am going to make sure you are not either. We *must* get the approval of those who are important to us; we *must* be accepted by significant others. The cry of man's heart is to be loved. You hear it in words to our music. Love is a constant theme because it is the greatest need of the soul. Some will do almost anything to obtain the love, approval, acceptance, and esteem they so desperately need.

If there is one thing we avoid like the plague, it is rejection. Rejection is worse than death. Man's need for love is profound.

> Sylvia has been abused for so long she sometimes seems like a whimpering puppy. Without a word, she just accepts her husband's criticism. Roger must be right. She really could be better. His cutting words in front of friends and strangers alike hurt, but she puts up with it because "he is under such pressure."
>
> Before his new business venture, Roger's life was in high ranking military positions and the ministry. Unaware of God's love for him, Roger's self-worth comes from always being right, superior, and in control. He covets having others dependent on him for their income. He even boasted once to his general manager, "God has made you dependent on me for your livelihood." Roger craves for people to be dependent upon him. Though Roger espouses high religious ideals, only behind his front door would you see the truth. The few times that Sylvia has attempted to stand up to Roger, his martyr's complex brings her back to her knees. He is quick to whine about being betrayed, that he only means good, that people do not understand him, and that they are abandoning him just like his family did. When presented with conflicts that cannot be resolved through his normal tactics, he complains bitterly about being the only one who must change.
>
> When his bookkeeper, Karen, demanded that he stop demeaning her, he refused. He would *not* change because

he was the boss, and if she wanted to keep her job, she would shut up. If she would frown or sigh in frustration or in any way express offense because of his treatment, it was unacceptable, and he would not tolerate it. But Karen's response was very different from that of his wife. Karen refused to accept his abuse. When Roger declined to change his attitude, she began looking for another job, unafraid of his rejection. Karen knew there had to be a better employer somewhere, and she would never find it unless she began looking.

Long ago, Sylvia lost any sense of her self-worth. Her source of personal value is now found in two ways: doing everything possible to keep Roger from being exposed for what he is and helping women in the various support groups to which she belongs. She proudly announces that she is not codependent and is fully qualified to assist those who are. The thought of rejection leaves Sylvia paralyzed with fear. She accepts Roger's abusive treatment because her poor codependent self-esteem leaves her unwilling to risk the loss of the *only* person that could love her.

Human Beings versus Human Doings

So, what is the real problem? Obviously, when people believe they are or should be in control of life, it impacts their expectations of themselves and others.

Adam and Eve thought they were gods. After all, the serpent had told them that all they needed to be like God was to know the difference between good and evil. Man still believes he knows right from wrong. Conclusion? We must be gods. But if we're gods, then we should be different. We think we should know everything, be strong enough to overcome any obstacle, capable of beating any challenge, able to do whatever is required, never be wrong, always be winners, always in control, liked by everyone, and have the perfect appearance. What a shock for Adam and Eve to find out they were not very suitable gods—and neither are we! Because Adam and Eve left the Garden of Eden as gods, mankind developed impossible and even cruel expectations. Instead of enjoying who we are in our union with God, our focus has shifted to doing and becoming other than who we are— creatures loved by our Creator. Being transformed from a *human doing* back into a *human being* is not difficult. Jesus accomplished it for us when He died, rose from dead, ascended into Heaven, and sent the Holy Spirit back to us.

We live in a world system that is bent on ruining every trace of human *beingness* and replacing it with human *doingness*. It is a system into which all of us were absorbed not only spiritually, but also mentally and emotionally. A system so magnetic and corrupt that only the death, burial, and resurrection of Jesus Christ could deliver us from it; deliver not just regarding the promise of a home in Heaven, but the transformation into mature sons and daughters of God here on Earth. By means of renewed minds, the results of error (e.g., lust, greed, and every type of evil) are no longer attractive to us. You died with Christ, and dead people do not desire to do wrong. Dead people don't think wrong thoughts. They're dead. Yet we are very much alive with a new life, a life full of satisfaction, and a life filled with pleasures that are the gift of God's own life. "A dead man is no longer bothered by sin; he is freed."[5] You cannot imagine it. You can only experience it. The Holy Spirit is the one who causes our new life (our new reality) to be real to us.

Even in his later years, the Apostle Paul continued to seek "the excellency of the knowledge of Christ Jesus my Lord."[6] He wanted to know as God knows (Chapter Six Endnotes #1).

Though none of us would claim we have arrived, our attitudes often reflect that we believe we have. Of course, we know we haven't reached the perfection of God, but surely, we are good enough until He comes to take us away. This type of thinking is a great roadblock to truly knowing God and enjoying a supernatural life. Because of *the lie*, we must be gods; so, we are surely good enough. *The lie* heaps condemnation on us because as gods, we are responsible yet never do a good enough job. We must do better, or blame someone else. No wonder so many

---

[5] Romans 6:7 (Taken from *Norlie's Simplified New Testament* by Olaf M. Norlie, © 1961)

[6] Philippians 3:8 (KJV)

die of heart and other stress-related problems. Though we would not likely ever tell someone else "I am a god," yet that belief is manifested in many ways, and it wreaks havoc in our lives. We don't *want* to believe we are gods; we *must* believe we are gods. We must be gods to prevent terrible things from happening. The behaviors resulting from our self-delusions often leave others perplexed about us or, even worse, thinking we are of no importance.

Simply put, reaching an objective requires knowing where you are, where you are going, and how you are going to get there. Understanding makes this possible; it makes the high calling of God in Christ Jesus attainable. It is only ignorance that prevents us. Understanding enables us to *be* who God has created us to be. Without understanding, we will spend a lifetime striving for goals that may be morally right and may even accomplish great objectives, but will seldom hit the mark.

Having given up honest self-examination, many people never realize their lives are a continual repetition of the same types of problems followed by the same attempts to reach a solution. Many spend a lifetime dealing with the same issues over and over, never finding the solutions they seek. I am reminded of Einstein's illustration of insanity. We try to solve a problem by doing the same thing a thousand times without success. At our wit's end, we give it one more try, because this time it will work.

We need to consider more than what we do or don't do in our desire to live godly lives. God has given us a simple and effective way to approach problems, and it does not start with doing the right thing. So many people are like oxen yoked to a water wheel. The concept of a full and abundant life is foreign to them. They live from meal to meal, paycheck to paycheck. If nothing disturbs their comfort level, they are content for things to remain the same, though they never feel content.

The movers and shakers of society have a slightly different view: keep striving to make more and do a better job. They believe they will eventually succeed. Of course, when things don't work out, many feel guilty and try even harder the next time. They never experience contentment. In general, people think the quality of their lives depends on what they do, what they have, and what happens to them. Getting ahead is defined as more of whatever it is they want: a better job, more money, things, time with the family, freedom from problems, having the right friends, being part of a crowd, and so on. To them, obtaining these things is a result of the correct *doing*. Many believe the way to be loved and accepted is to do the right things. This is a primary theme of television commercials: buy the right car, wear the right clothes, or use the right toothpaste and people will be attracted to you. If you are honest with yourself, even though you know what you're seeing isn't true, something inside still believes some of it.

When confronted by too many problems or challenges, it is especially hard to do all the right things, particularly if you don't know what they are. People experience distress even when they know what to do. Not knowing what to do can be worse; the mental and emotional effects can be overwhelming. Consistent with our example of insanity, mankind continues trying to solve its problems by doing the right things or achieving the proper performance. Churches are no different. In fact, many Christians have it even worse. In addition to the sense that they must be gods (responsible for everything), they now have a new law—obey Jesus. No wonder the world looks at people who profess to be Christians and thinks, "I don't want anything to do with Jesus."

* * *

Chapter Six Endnotes

Note 1

Many people will say that it is not possible believers could come to a place where we all believe and know the same thing. From a sense knowledge perspective, that is true. However, St. Paul makes it abundantly clear that God is going to make it happen. As one body, we are going to believe what Jesus believes, and in the way He believes it. The same with what Jesus knows.

Once again, for English translations, the King James Version is fairly accurate. The trouble many have with it is its ancient form of English, which is sometimes difficult to understand without study. "Till we all come in the unity of the faith, and of the knowledge of the Son of God, unto a perfect man, unto the measure of the stature of the fullness of Christ."[7] Faith is the act of believing God's *truth*. The *knowledge of the Son of God* is not knowing *about* Jesus, but knowing what He knows the way He knows it. This means we can know about things that are not true, but we also understand they aren't true. We are not deceived into believing false knowledge is *truth*. That is to say, because the foundation of our knowledge is *truth*, we can recognize false knowledge for what it is, lies. Also, St. Paul did not put an article in front of the word *measure*. That means that each one of us has a different manifestation of Christ's stature.

For some reason, most translations have trouble with Psalms 8:5 and Hebrews 2:7. But the Smith-Goodspeed translation goes to the heart of God's view of mankind. "Yet thou hast made him but a little lower than God."[8] Mankind is *not* God, but we get close. He created us in His image. "Then God said: Let Us make man in Our image, after Our similitude."[9] That means He created us as close as possible to being God without us being God. We will forever be completely dependent on Him and His life, and we will never be ENOUGH by our own wisdom, strength, and ability. We will always be creatures.

Here's how I paraphrase Ephesians 4:13:

> Until we all come to a place of believing God's *truth* together—in other words, no arguing and fighting over silly doctrines and theology, which are meaningless for God's purposes. It is believing God's *truth* which establishes the law of God within our lives, by default causing us to think and behave like Jesus. When we believe God's *truth*

---

[7] Ephesians 4:13 (KJV)
[8] Hebrews 8:5 (Scripture taken from *The Complete Bible: An American Translation*)
[9] Genesis 1:26 (*A Translation of the Old Testament Scriptures from the Original Hebrew* by Helen Spurrell)

and our lives are built on Christ's body of knowledge, we *be* (are) perfect men and women. This *being*, which we now are, is an accurate representation of the fullness of Christ. We will always be creatures who were created to be slightly less than, but in the same class as, God Himself (a measure of the fullness of Christ).

Part 3

Is this starting to make sense? We know it is. Now we've got the basics covered. We live what we believe. We are aware why we were created. We recognize the difference between living by flesh and living by spirit. We're starting to know what the unseen is. We understand—at least, in theory—why we say one thing and do another or desire one thing and strive for the complete opposite. So, you get it. Now, what do you do with it? How is it applicable to life and church?

In Chapters Seven through Eleven, you'll find out. There are three major points to keep in mind for the next five chapters:

1. We've discussed at length that people live what they believe. We've used many examples from the Bible, and the Bible has a description of this process penned by the Apostle Paul in Romans. It is called the *Law of Faith,* or *the law of belief,* which is a law stating you automatically live what you believe regardless what you may really think.

2. Who is responsible for what? You understand by now that God wants to change us from the inside out and that it is not our responsibility to make ourselves new creatures in Christ. However, because God intends to do the work, it doesn't mean we can experience being new creatures by doing nothing more than sitting at our computers and eating bags of Cheetos. So, what exactly are we responsible for?

In short, our job is to be honest or, failing that, to *want* to be honest, or even to tell God we don't want to be honest. He will work with anything we give Him. The following chapters will explain in greater detail where both ours and God's responsibilities start and end and how they intertwine with each other.

7
Whose Responsibility Is It?

Being responsible is good when it is not based on *the lie*. Unfortunately, mankind is saturated in the feeling of responsibility for everything. Outside of a relationship with God, there is no escape. However, even inside a relationship with God, *the lie* can continue its relentless and devastating work when believers don't know they believe it. That *lie* has given all of mankind a false sense of responsibility and, because of it, we have lost sight of what God really wants—if we ever knew it in the first place.

False Responsibilities

Have you ever known someone whose favorite advice for dealing with an offense or problem is to "get over it," or "forget it" as though that will make all the bad things in life go away? That advice seldom helps. Instead, the troubled person may become a walking time bomb that occasionally explodes for no apparent reason. The issues this individual is either unwilling or unable to face continue to boil inside and can erupt in all sorts of unhealthy ways. Regardless of whether you think another person's problems are real or not is irrelevant. If that person believes there is a problem, they will live like it. Telling them to "get over it" or "forget it" will not change their perceptions since those judgments are based on beliefs.

Faith—which is believing God's *truth*—is a gift.[1] He alone enables you to recognize, to know, to believe, and to agree with the *truth*, and He delights to do it. Believing is never a result of your ability; it

---
[1] Ephesians 2:8

is Jesus Himself (by the ability of the Holy Spirit) accepting the *truth* inside you as though He is you. Of course, you can know all *about* the *truth*. Lots of people do. But that is very different from knowing it as the body of knowledge from which you think. I do not mean to lessen the seriousness of our problems; rather, I want to help solve them. To do that, we must approach them from a possibly unfamiliar perspective. Our thoughts have a tremendous bearing on how we handle problems. Uncontrolled thoughts can cause us to react, rather than respond. When our thoughts are motivated by flesh, we tend to *react* or act irrationally. We tend to push back against what is pushing us, or we behave like a rack of billiard balls being hit by a cue ball.[2] When our thoughts are dominated by spirit, we *respond*—that is we behave rationally and act or speak in a way that would produce the best outcome.[3] We automatically do what Jesus would do as He lives in our bodies with us.

When faced with a problem, it is natural for us to try to solve it. Having been steeped in *the lie* since the mutiny in the Garden, humankind assumes responsibility for everything. Even if we trust God, there always seems to be something else we must do. Deep down, many believe that His blessings are always contingent on some aspect of our performance. In at least some areas of our lives, if we suffer a need, we believe God expects us to do something. But often, we have no idea what that is, so we try this and then that and then something else. Every human being suffers from what I call the False Responsibility Syndrome; some suffer more, some less. Even people who are lazy or appear to have no expectations have it. Man expects himself to solve every problem, every need. His biggest hope is a proper performance to get others to love and accept him. However, we feel responsible for other things also. Even though we may say we trust God fully there are often things in our hearts that cause us to expect ourselves or others to do the impossible.

Many issues are important and need attention, but has God really said He expects you to take care of them? This reminds me of a preacher who used to end his pleas for help with "If you don't do it, who will?"

---

[2] React. To move in a hostile manner against or in opposition to a force or influence.

[3] Respond. To go in a thoughtful, non-hostile way about a power or influence.

That statement was based on a lie to get the congregation to act out of guilt and feel responsible.

If your life is caught up with responsibility to the point it is distressful, it is time to ask God if *He* thinks you are responsible. He has a better answer, a better way, for the following:

1. There are so many poor. I'm supposed to help them.

2. There is so much injustice in the world. I must stop it.

3. If kids are going to be safe at school, we should do something. Stop the bullies!

4. Mankind is wrecking the Earth. We must stop global warming.

5. I must do everything possible to prevent abortions.

6. If I don't work harder and smarter, I will run out of money.

7. The world needs Jesus. I must win more souls.

8. My kids are hanging out with the wrong type of people. I have to stop this.

9. I've got to make people understand they are ruining our environment.

10. If I don't do it, who will?

Satan's strategy is to get people so distracted with responsibilities that they lose sight of God's grace, which is the only thing that can change our perspective to one of peace and joy.

Logically, we know we can't do it all, but logic doesn't figure into the expectation that we must try. This is a prime example of how *the lie* has twisted every human. Our tangled expectations of ourselves undermine our ability to simply *be*. The weight of the world is on our shoulders, so we must do something. Of course, the pressure can become so great that we become paralyzed and sit waiting for someone else to save us.

James E. Campbell, Jr, James Q. Campbell

The issue of *being* seldom occurs to us and isn't important if it does, because there is so much that needs to be done. "If I don't do it, it won't get done." Or in a competitive sense, "If I don't get going, someone will beat me to it." "I must win at all costs." Life is about what we do or don't do because we believe the future is utterly dependent on what we do. This concern manifests in numerous ways. Some think that what they want is impossible, so they settle for less or give up. Others feel they must be able to do it all and be the best. They can't be caught not knowing, not achieving their responsibilities. They expect perfection, without which they are convinced they will be discovered failures. Some believe that by doing or saying something or believing hard enough, they'll achieve the success they are looking for. These people all have swallowed *the lie*. Each person is living under a compulsion to perform, pushed by *the lie*—just in diverse ways.

In general, there are two objects of worry: (1) things we can realistically control and (2) things we can't. The first is easy. If you can fix a concern, you do. But, if something is outside of your ability, that is another matter. Many feel guilty when their kids do not turn out the way they hoped, when they have problems, do poorly in school, or have trouble making friends. Some feel responsible for the starving people everywhere. We can even feel guilty when we don't want to give money to the guy sitting in the wheelchair out in the rain. You know, the one wearing a cast on his leg with his arm in a sling, holding a sign saying, "Homeless, will work for food. God bless you." Yeah, that's the one; the one being pushed by a guy on crutches. We feel guilty even when we suspect there is nothing wrong with either one of them.

We think we must know everything and have all the answers for our lives and our kids' lives. Because we don't, it eats at us. You feel untalented because you do not know how to decorate your home as nicely as your friend. You're uncomfortable when people drop by because your home isn't clean. You're embarrassed that you are not driving a new car or wearing the latest fashion; ashamed that you can't provide enough for your family, that your job is beneath your ability, and that you should be wealthy but aren't. You may be one of many who have the nagging sense that you are responsible for something, yet have no idea what it is. Are your expectations reasonable? Are you supposed to be a god?

I have struggled with trusting God many times. "How much can I trust God and how do I do it?" Have you ever felt the same? Even if we are confident that God will carry our burdens, how do we deal with them until He takes their weight? The *truth* is that humanity believes it is our responsibility to figure out the answers for every contingency that could ever happen. How absurd. Many Christians would deny they believe so, but our reality often proves otherwise.

A sense of responsibility overwhelms us with fear that people will see us as failures unable to fulfill the expectations placed upon us. Like the woman mentioned earlier who was afraid of messing up her job assignments, we feel responsible for accomplishing every task correctly. We presume we are obligated to have answers before we even know the questions (See Chapter Three: Worry Doesn't Work). We place demands upon ourselves that are unreasonable. We expect high results and unfeasible outcomes. False expectations cause people to conclude they should be someone they are not. Unable to handle everything we think people expect, we fear somebody may see the truth; that we can't. The result is denial— denial of the problem, of our actions, of our fears, and of anything that could expose our weaknesses and failures.

We have all known people who, when confronted with the facts, ignore or even deny them. If the facts do not fit their purist perceptions, they cannot be true. In the world of psychology, this is called cognitive dissonance. The *truth* is each of us develops our understanding of the world to make sense of it. The examples are endless.

- The wife who makes every excuse for her husband's beatings, even thinking she deserves them.

- The husband who blames his lust on his wife's lack of attention.

- The student who blames poor grades on the teacher or says that he just cannot do it, rather than facing the truth that he doesn't want to.

- The parent who blames his child's misbehavior on friends, the teacher, the school, society, or movies and refuses to consider the child may only need discipline.

- The parents whose child's behavioral problems are because of anything except their failure to give the child sufficient time and attention.

- The person who eats too much yet blames his obesity on genetics.

- How about the bombing in Oklahoma City? People initially blamed the government, radio talk shows, militia groups, conservatives, liberals, and everyone but the individual who did it.

- Then there was 9/11. Some blamed the terrorist attack on America. It was our fault that they attacked us.

It Is Time to Question Our Results

The cry of man's heart is to feel justified and valued. Yet humankind lives with an overwhelming lack of self-worth. Constantly looking for something to assure us of worth, people resort to a multitude of methods to purchase their value and justify their existence. This places an unbearable burden on people, resulting in not only stress but distress. So, what do we do with these types of loads? Often, we deny them. Multitudes live in a state of denial, unable to cope with the sense that they may be wrong. Others experience guilt, feeling they are condemned by just being alive. Some may redirect that internal condemnation onto others, placing blame and guilt onto anyone or anything that isn't them. I could go on, but I'm sure you get the point.

The lie says we are supposed to be gods, and gods cannot be wrong. Even with *the lie* buried out of sight in the depths of a belief system, those who believe it can sense something is not right but don't know what it is. The fear that we are not good enough or that something is wrong with who we are causes great fear and prevents us from enjoying the peace for which we were created. Mankind was created for something wonderful but carries the burden of responsibility that we must find ourselves and figure out how to create a better future. Many never discover that the wonderful life for which they were created is only realized by sheer gift and can never be earned or achieved. It is something cheerfully given by God. People will often do anything to prove they are right because being right is as close as we can get to feeling like we are gods. Many are not even aware that their thinking goes something like: "The more often I am right, the better person I am." Being wrong is the antithesis of being a god; therefore, "I cannot admit to ever being wrong." I once worked with a man who told me he could not bear the idea of being told he was a bad person. He was terrified of the sense that he was wrong. This is why the word *sin* is feared by so many. The awareness of being wrong can be devastating to many; people understand it to mean they have less value. What is it within us that wills us to defend against the image of being incorrect, or not omnipotent? Our beliefs.

Because of the things I have heard preachers say about God, I stand in awe that our Father, who is the standard of right, is very aware of our error (sin) yet doesn't hate us for it. In fact, He isn't even angry about it. Our Father fully understands what has happened to His human creatures and is passionately intent on bringing us into His reality. The Bible says, "For God so loved the world that He gave His Only Begotten Son."[4] He surely wouldn't send His Son on behalf of someone with whom He was angry and utterly hated. Rather, God is passionate about showing us who we are and how much He loves us. He wants us to know His *truth* so that we will be free and satisfied, so we can *be* who we already are. His solution is to teach us to acknowledge when our natural responses are wrong and see them in the light of His *truth*. Unfortunately, many people are self-deceived, and some want to remain thus. The Apostle John addressed this both in his Gospel and first Epistle. "If we say that we have no sin (error), we deceive ourselves, and the truth is not in us."[5]

---

[4] John 3:16
[5] 1 John 1:8 (KJV)

Jesus publicly addressed the real intent of religious people whose agenda He exposed by telling them what was in their hearts:

> You're from your father, the Devil, and all you want to do is please him. He was a killer from the very start. He couldn't stand the truth because there wasn't a shred of truth in him. When the Liar speaks, he makes it up out of his lying nature and fills the world with lies.[6]

God knows we live in a world smothered in error. But by making us righteous, He has guaranteed that we will never be comfortable or satisfied by living in sin. What a marvelous plan. God died as us to release us from sin and recreated us without it: thus, we will never find contentment or comfort in living a life for which we were not created. Except by His power, we cannot escape living a life of error. If we refuse to agree with God, then we are controlled by the wickedness in which this world is drowning.[7] God knows His children are continually assaulted by evil, darkness, and lies. He also knows who He has made us and who we are, and He knows we are stronger than sin because Christ is our life. Thus, He is sending people like me to instruct His children how to walk through the darkness as the victors, and *be* the "more than conquerors" that they are.[8] But we cannot escape the influence of the darkness if we are unwilling to admit it may be affecting us. But to admit that we have error, especially when we don't even know what it is, can be scary. So, if we *are* willing to admit we have error, what can we do about it? This is when we begin to see how utterly dependent we are on the Holy Spirit, the Spirit of *truth*.

Have you ever wondered why God gave you His Word? To teach you the *truth*. Why? Because you didn't know it. If we already knew the *truth*, God wouldn't have needed to give mankind His Word. We've all seen people who consider themselves the authorities about life. They tell the rest of us how to live. You find them in religious and

---

[6] John 8:44 (msg)
[7] 1 John 5:19
[8] Romans 8:37

political bodies, and every other type of group. Unfortunately, much of humankind's body of knowledge is wrong. There is only one body of knowledge of *truth* — it is in Jesus Christ, but *He* has been greatly misunderstood by everyone, Christians included. God wants all of us to *be* right and to live in the state of being righteous. That's what He means by being "the righteousness of God in Christ."[9] The gift of righteousness is the gift of having been made right by God. He doesn't look at us and say, "I declare you are right even though I know you aren't." When God made us new creatures in Christ, His gift was a right nature, which was included when we were made one with His Son. When someone is united to the Lord they are one with Him. Since His nature is right, by default, those who are one with Him also get a right nature. It is a gift which each person gets when they are born again (i.e. born from above). Members of the Body of Christ cannot have a different nature than the Head of that Body. Because God's children are in Christ, their nature is the same as His, that is, right. God didn't make us right because we do the right things. It was a gift. He gave us a right nature so that we are right. That's how we became members of His family. When we take that gift by agreeing with God that it is ours, we give the Holy Spirit permission to begin teaching us how to live like Christ. Righteousness is a present from God. It is something that God gives us for free by giving us Himself. When God comes to live in a heart, He brings all that He is with Him. It is His life in us and the fact that He has made us right that enables us to stop believing the lie and believe God's *truth* instead. Righteousness, the nature of having a right being, is a gift that our Father gives without a thought about how we act. He knows it is a gift that will ultimately cause us to live right even when it seems impossible for us to do so. In fact, it is the realization that God has given us such a gift that brings the changes that cause our thoughts and behavior to become right. So, if you know the *truth* then you know that God has already made you right. Now, He is teaching you to be who you are. Believing this is the essence of having a renewed mind. In time, right thinking and behavior will follow.

---

[9] 2 Corinthians 5:21

Our minds have been renewed; but many don't believe what God has accomplished in Christ because their flesh experiences tell them it can't be true, yet. So, they keep listening to all the voices and thoughts that tell them they are not who God says they are. Those thoughts and voices serve the devil who continually whispers knowledge in our ears that isn't. It is knowledge that exalts itself above what God knows. So, according to God, righteousness is purely a gift.

Here's what Paul had to say about God's free gift of righteousness from the King James translation: "For if by one man's offence death reigned by one; much more they which receive abundance of grace and of the gift of righteousness shall reign in life by one, Jesus Christ."[10] I love the way The Message version puts it: "If death got the upper hand through one man's wrongdoing, can you imagine the breathtaking recovery life makes, sovereign life, in those who grasp with both hands this wildly extravagant life-gift, this grand setting-everything-right, that the one man Jesus Christ provides?"[11]

We are not righteous because we know more than someone else or because of anything we do or don't do, but because God by sheer gift has made us right with Him. The Apostle John said: "For if we take up the attitude 'we have not sinned,' we flatly deny God's diagnosis of our condition and cut ourselves off from what he has to say to us."[12]

If we want to see what we cannot see, we must be willing to admit our error when the Holy Spirit shows it to us. We are so utterly dependent on the Holy Spirit that without His help, we can't even admit we may be wrong. Without His help, it is impossible even to acknowledge that you believe something that is contrary to God. Satan, the father of lies, hates the *truth* and has flooded the world with lies.

Speaking to religious people, Jesus said:

> You belong to your father, that is, the devil, and are eager
> to gratify the appetites which are your father's. He, for the

---

[10] Roman 5:17 (KJV)

[11] Romans 5:17 (msg)

[12] 1 John 1:10 (*The New Testament in Modern English* Translated by J.B. Phillips, Copyright ©1958, The MacMillan Company)

first, was a murderer; and as for truth, he has never taken his stand upon that; there is no truth in him. When he utters falsehood, he is only uttering what is natural to him; he is all false, and it was he who gave falsehood its birth. And, if you do not believe me, it is precisely because I am speaking the truth.[13]

Faith (treasuring the *truth*) is a gift from God.[14] When you admit you have erred, it is the Holy Spirit Who has enabled you. "Howbeit when he, the Spirit of truth, is come, he will guide you into all truth."[15] This includes the *truth* about what you believe that is wrong. The Holy Spirit is the only one Who can cause you to realize what you believe that is not true.

God's instruction to the Church has always been to keep looking into the mirror of His Word because in it you will see Christ. Keep looking at who He says you are until you realize that *IS* who you are. "As he is, so are we in this world."[16] Then you will begin acting like who you are, and it won't be difficult. "Moreover, we have the Word of prophecy, which is a still surer guide, and it is well for you to give attention to it as to a lamp shining in a dark place until the day dawns and the morning star rises in your hearts."[17]

Doctors' offices, both psychiatric and medical, are filled with victims of distress. Our bodies suffer terribly from the condition of our minds. So much distress is just the result of the fear of being wrong; fear of not understanding; fear of someone finding out you're mistaken; fear of failure, loss, or death; and, most significantly, the fear of rejection because we might not be good enough.

Have you ever compared your life with the righteousness and abilities of Jesus Christ and those in the early church? When you read about

---

[13] John 8:44 & 45 (Knox translation, 1935)

[14] Ephesians 2:8

[15] John 16:13 (KJV)

[16] 1 John 4:17 (KJV)

[17] 2 Peter 1:19 (Taken from Norlie, Olaf M., Norlie's Simplified New Testament c. 1961)

the strength of the Holy Spirit available to God's children and the fruit that should be evident in those who have been filled with His life, do you ever wonder if something is wrong with churches today? "But the fruit of the Spirit is love, joy, peace, patience, kindness, goodness, faithfulness, gentleness, self-control."[18] Within this verse, God is telling you who you are. Not only is Christ your life, but the Spirit of Christ is as much yours as He is Christ's because you and Christ are united! "There is one body, and one Spirit."[19] So why don't Christians and why doesn't the Church show the same attitude, character, unity, and power of the First Century Church?

My heart yearns to experience all of God's fullness. I hope yours does too. So why don't we experience more of God? Why is the evidence of our fellowship with God so far below that which the Apostles and Jesus displayed? In the light of such questions, is the way you are handling life working? Are you bearing the fruit that God anticipates? How long must you continue before you get the results that God promised? Have you ever asked yourself if the way you are approaching life and God is working the way He said it would? Or, is it safer to ignore evidence of failure so that you don't have to admit it? Is it possible that there is an error in your thinking, because of a mistake in your believing?

How many times have you given up smoking just to lose your resolve and start again? What about the man or woman you are attracted to, who is not your spouse? How do you get rid of those thoughts and emotions? You wake up at night in a sweat from the same dream that plagues you incessantly. Is there anything you can do while awake that will make you have better dreams? Is there any way to affect change that doesn't require supernatural discipline? We experience a myriad of negative emotions. Are you tired of just trying to cope? Is there any way to, once and for all, rid yourself of feelings of inadequacy, failure, anger, fear, depression, jealousy, lust, lack of control, insecurity, and the compulsion to apologize for everything even when it is not your fault? No matter what your life is like, there is better available from

---

[18] Galatians 5:22 (NASB)

[19] Ephesians 4:4

the heart of God right now! Wisdom cries out constantly, asking you to hear the simple Words of God's Spirit, the only one who can lead you into the *truth* you already know. "Wisdom cries aloud in the streets, She lifts up her voice in the squares."[20] Have you noticed that the way you react to problems sometimes creates more problems? We keep doing the same things over and over unable to admit we are wrong. Often, we can't admit that we have no other answers. We must do something, and something that does not work is better than nothing. Finally, if we can't conceive of anything to do, at least we can worry. It shows that we care.

I want to restate the formula I gave you earlier. "We feel and act because of what we think, and what we think is always a result of what we believe—about everything." This formula explains so simply how we function and how our hearts work. Once we recognize it, everything can change. Our performance orientation causes us to focus on behavior and things that happen. Even if we can admit that our thoughts are often the source of our failures, we will still focus on performance, albeit, mental performance. "My problem is wrong-thinking, so I have to change my thoughts." But struggling to change your mind is *not* the answer. When we suffer, it is common to blame what we or someone else did. When anything bad takes place, it is human nature to try to correct it. Once the symptoms of a condition are eliminated, we generally put it out of mind and go on to deal with something else. We blame circumstances for causing other circumstances.

> Sherry had had a stressful day helping her husband with the business and was looking forward to a few minutes of peace as she arrived home ahead of him. But the job of a mom does not often provide such luxuries exactly when she wants them. She still had to take the boys to karate class. By itself, the task of driving them two miles to the class was not difficult. But Christopher, the oldest, was in one of his disagreeable moods and had no plans on cooperating with anyone, especially with Mom. His unrelenting

---

[20] Proverbs 1:20 (Scripture is taken from The Complete Bible: An American Translation.)

teasing of his younger brother accomplished more than he expected.

As they were nearing a school, Sherry exploded in anger, screaming at Chris to shut up and sit still. Because of her preoccupation, Sherry failed to notice she was going forty-three miles an hour in a 25-mph zone. In the middle of her tirade, the lights of a police car appeared behind her. As he wrote out her ticket, Sherry mused about what she was going to do to Chris when it was over. But once she settled down, Sherry realized that even though Chris' behavior was inexcusable, her speeding wasn't his fault. It was hers.

8
Emotions

God likes emotions. That's why He created us with them. The problem is when we don't understand where they come from and how they are created, they can become our reality, rather than just an experience. The problem? Emotions can become our *truth*. Emotions are great at telling you what you feel and terrible at telling you the *truth*.

What Causes Our Emotions?

Ron and Beth blame each other for the suffering they inflicted on one another. She is greedy, selfish, and controlling. Though he talks tough to others, he is a wimp, unable to stand up for himself. Because Beth failed to hang up her cell phone properly after talking to him, Ron overheard her plotting his death with her boyfriend. Devastated, Ron went to live with a friend. But that was not the end of the story. Ron seldom stands up for himself; this was no exception. When he stopped paying for her extravagant lifestyle, she went on the offensive and accused him of rape, theft, and spouse and child abuse. Beth frequently showed up at the business, which they owned jointly, emptied the cash register into her purse, and left. She obtained a restraining order and then harassed him with telephone calls. With a restraining order in place, she invited him to dinner. When he showed up, she called the police and had him arrested. After the judge had ordered her to not take their child out of the state, Beth did just that. Even more disturbing, Ron accepted her behavior with barely a word to the contrary.

Ron was depressed and contemplating suicide when we had a very honest talk. "How could this have happened?" he asked. Why did it happen? Why would she do such things when all he had ever done for her was good? Ron was angry and bitter at the prospect of having to leave everything he worked for to be free from the mess that was slowly destroying him. He was convinced he could never again be happy.

It was evident to me that Beth was wrong and had hurt Ron terribly. But was the way Ron felt her fault? Had she *made* him feel angry and depressed? Had she *made* him bitter? Was it her fault that Ron felt like committing suicide? Many people would say yes. Even so, is that the *truth*?

Let's look closer to home. Have you ever fallen in love? Remember how it feels? Your expectations are full of hope as you dream about life with him or her. The feelings are wonderful. For some, it is a surreal period in which everything is beautiful and the future brighter than bright. For those who go on to marriage, things usually change. After a while, those pleasant emotions are not so frequent. This is not to say you love your spouse less, but those delightful feelings are no longer constantly present. Have you ever wondered why? In the first blooms of love, your beliefs regarding the love of your life and your future together were based on dreams and imaginations, not reality. As the relationship matured, your beliefs came to mirror your experience, which was not necessarily bad, but not a fairy tale, either. As your thinking began to reflect reality, so did your feelings. It is what you believed and consequently thought in the beginning that produced the biochemicals that resulted in such wonderful emotions. It is what you believed and thought later that caused your feelings to calm down.

Consider another example. You arrive home from work late at night after a day of reorganizing the office. Feeling dirty and grungy, you can't wait to clean up, get into your pajamas, and open a book. Just as you are stepping out of a long, hot shower, you hear glass break. The last time you checked, there was no one else in the house. How would you feel? What would you do? Most of us would feel fear. The adrenalin would flow, our rate of breathing would increase, our hearts would pump a little faster, our bodies would prepare for fight or flight, and we might very well be seized with anxiety. Why? Because you heard glass break? No, the first thing entering your mind was, "someone is in my home to hurt me." You nervously wrap on a robe and tiptoe to the telephone in the kitchen. As you peek around the corner, the cause becomes apparent. Your cat was playing with the flowers you bought and knocked the vase to the floor. You would obviously have a mess on your hands, but not an intruder. As you realized the truth, the fear would subside, and peace would return. When you believed you were in danger, your thoughts and emotions responded in kind. When you realized the truth, you felt peace.

Many have had the following experience more than once. You are sitting at home waiting for a loved one to return when you hear a siren. Anxiety hits as you picture that loved one in a terrible accident. Within minutes, you hear a familiar sound on the porch and know they are okay. The anxiety disappears, and you relax. What caused such terrible feelings? The reality of the situation? How about what you were thinking? Once again, why did your emotions react to each of these circumstances and why did they return to normal? Of course, biochemicals were involved, but what triggers those chemicals? Very simply, what you were thinking; even deeper, what you were believing.

Your romantic feelings were not the result of magic. They were a result of what you were thinking about your loved one and the future. The feelings set off by the breaking glass were a result of what you were thinking. The anxiety from hearing the sirens was a result of the pictures running through your head. In each case, once your thinking changed, so did your emotions.

James E. Campbell, Jr, James Q. Campbell

Think the *Truth* rather than Feelings

Can you see how thinking affects us? Now we need to understand *how* to control our thoughts. It is only by *bringing every thought captive to the obedience of Christ* that you can come to fully enjoy the hope of glory (Christ in you) in this life. "Casting down imaginations, and every high thing that exalteth itself against the knowledge of God, and bringing into captivity every thought to the obedience of Christ."[1] When Paul writes about the knowledge of God he means God's body of knowledge.

Christ's obedience began with hearing and believing what He read in the scriptures as a boy. The Apostle Paul's ministry was to teach the Gentiles the "obedience to the faith" that is, the same obedience which Christ had (the obedience of hearing and believing the *truth*).[2] You now know that you have power over the source of your thoughts. It is so simple. In fact, its very simplicity is often a threat to those who think their success is a result of some superiority on their part. Remember, the source of your thoughts is your beliefs. Your thoughts are formed by what you truly believe about yourself, your parents, your friends, strangers, your circumstances and other events, your country and its leaders, God, and on and on.

Your beliefs form the foundation of your life. Except for God, nothing in you goes deeper. I am not talking about a few beliefs, but *all* of them together. You have beliefs that are true and those that are not. Opposing beliefs often conflict with each other causing all kinds of emotions and behaviors. This explains why you so often know you believe something to be true, but end up acting in opposition to your belief. It is the layers upon layers of beliefs that began forming early in life that determine the quality of our lives, regardless of our circumstances. Together, all your beliefs create your attitudes and views of life.

Some would say that Ron's depression was strictly a result of a chemical imbalance. But if true, then wouldn't it be appropriate to say

---

[1] 2 Corinthians 10:5 (KJV)

[2] Romans 1:5 (KJV) The word translated *faith* is in the genitive case which is the case of possession. "Obedience of faith" can be translated "faith's obedience."

that his anger and bitterness were also the results of a chemical imbalance? And then, wouldn't we have to say that every other emotion Ron suffered was due to the same? And if true of his feelings, then might it be reasonable to apply the same logic to all behaviors and everything we do and feel? So where does it end? At what point, if any, do we become personally responsible for our actions? Was Ron's depression a result of what Beth did or of what he believed about Beth and himself? If his core beliefs had been better, her actions would still have hurt, but he would not have remained devastated. Ron believed he could never be happy without Beth. Was that true? Was it the end of his life or did he just believe it was? Just because he believed it, did that make it right? Because you thought there was an intruder in the house and felt that fear, did that make it true?

I told Ron that though his wife was wrong, *he* was his biggest problem. It was what Ron believed about his circumstances that made him feel hopeless and depressed. In fact, it was problems with his believing and thus his thinking that got him into that mess in the first place. Regardless of what Beth had done, she could not have continued if Ron had not let her. I warned him if he did not use his problems to motivate himself to begin dealing with the errors in his beliefs, he was destined to continue repeating them in one form or another.

How often have you heard someone say, "He makes me mad" or "She makes me happy?" It is common to credit others and situations for the way we feel and act. When something bad happens, we often look for what we or someone else *did*. Though this is a reasonable place to start, it is not necessarily a good place to end. Unless we deal with the source of our perceptions, we are likely to face the same problem again and again as it manifests one way or another.

Our society is far more concerned about appearance than whether something is true. In general, attractive people have more opportunities than those who are not attractive. Some men are often more interested in a woman's body and face than who she is. Too many women are willing to marry a guy because of his looks, status, or money, and are willingly blind to glaring faults which may wreck their lives. We esteem those who have accomplished important things or can do something for us. What people do is of foremost importance; who they are often is of little interest. We judge ourselves the same way. We like ourselves more when we win than when we fail. In the morning, we compare ourselves to others, and that determines how we feel the rest of the day. We judge ourselves far more harshly than anyone else does. In fact, many of us don't need criticism from others because we do a good enough job all by ourselves. Some are ashamed of the fact they cannot pay the bills, especially when others have money to spare. Others are compulsive, expecting themselves to do every task perfectly because they secretly believe they should be perfect. When circumstances reveal their faults or weaknesses, they are ashamed.

How many times have you been upset because you lost your temper or said something stupid? How many people are discouraged and even hate themselves because of their lack of self-control? How many of us do things because of what we feel, rather than because it is wise? I used to think that if I could do everything right my life would be better, but no matter how hard I tried, it wasn't. If we look at problems from the question "what happened?" there can be many answers. This happened because someone did that. The Twin Towers collapsed because terrorists attacked them. "I am broke because he stole my money." But the answer to what happened doesn't usually solve the personal problems resulting from whatever happened. Sure, we can fix things so it doesn't happen again, or we can catch the responsible party, but what about the damage to our minds and emotions? The mental and emotional suffering from problems is always a result of what we believe—specifically, what we believe that is not true. Of course, it is true that something happened and that it caused certain results that may have been worse than terrible; but it happened, and it usually can't be undone. So, what do we do about the pain we are now suffering?

As harsh as this sounds, it is still the *truth*: The reason we are still suffering is because *we believe lies.* "I feel this because such and such happened." "I am depressed because of what he did." "My future is hopeless unless the government helps me." "Since such and such was so terrible, I will never recover. My life is over." "I will never again be happy." There are times when each of us is motivated by what we feel.

longer hated myself. I forgot to see myself as defective. The *truth* was that my inability to feel loved was a result of the lies I had believed. This discovery led to a profound thought, *if believing a lie of which I wasn't even aware could affect my life so drastically, could other problems I had also be the result of lies I believed?* I knew the answer was yes. Suddenly, I knew I was going to find solutions to other problems that had troubled me for years, and those answers were much closer than I had ever dreamed. That realization alone, without any effort, began to change my thinking. I started feeling better. Of course, there was more to come.

Self-talk and the *Truth*

I will never forget the day a friend gave me a book titled *Telling Yourself the Truth* by William Backus and Marie Chapian. It was the first time I heard of misbeliefs or self-talk, but it made perfect sense. I realized it held a major key to the change for which I was looking. To quote Dr. Backus:

> Your beliefs and misbeliefs are the most crucial factors of your mental and emotional life. Misbeliefs are the direct cause of emotional turmoil, maladaptive behavior, and most so-called mental illness. Misbeliefs are the reasons of the destructive behavior in which people persist in engaging even when they are acutely aware that it is harmful to them (such as overeating, smoking, lying, drunkenness, stealing, or adultery).[3] Misbeliefs appear as truth to the person *repeating* them to himself.[4]

My understanding exploded when Dr. Backus addressed self-talk. He said, "Self-talk means the words we tell ourselves in our thoughts. It means the words we tell ourselves about people, self, experiences, life in general, God, the future, the past, the present; it is specifically, all of

---

[3] *Telling Yourself the Truth*, by Marie Chapian and William Backus, Bethany House Publishers, 1980, page 17.

[4] Ibid, page 18

the words you say to yourself all of the time."[5] Throughout his book, Dr. Backus tied together these two issues which enables the reader to discover the cause of and help correct the mental and emotional challenges confronting them. I learned I was saying things to myself about myself that were not true. I was lying to myself. The only way to stop was to recognize the lies and replace them with God's *truth*.

But weren't all the things I said about myself accurate? No! They were not true because God doesn't say them about me. If I am a new creature in Christ, remade in God's image, then what I felt and feared about myself couldn't be true. In God's eyes, who I am is not defined by what I do. I had believed my deficiencies and mistakes were proof I was not a good person. Many people feel the same way about themselves, but God doesn't think that way. All the mistakes I make and stupid things I may do are only a result of ignorance or believing the wrong things. Since God recreated me in Christ, to be transformed into His image just requires the renewal of my mind, which Jesus already accomplished. Change does not occur by trying to act or think a certain way, but by allowing the Holy Spirit to help me stop accepting lies and start agreeing with God's *truth*.

Unfortunately, my experience (flesh) told me I was screwed up and needed to try harder. Sometimes, I thought I was a hopeless case. All along, if I had realized the *truth*, things would have already changed. It may have hurt to admit, but my greatest problem was (and is) the darkness that I sometimes allow to dominate my thinking. Remember, darkness is synonymous with deception. Since believing takes place in our hearts, any darkness (deception) hidden there is not visible to us without the help of the Holy Spirit. Since lies hide in darkness, once we let them in we can't see them, but He can. And He is for us.[6] The Holy Spirit wants us to know what He knows. Hebrews 4:12 -16 is directly addressing God's ability to know and deal with the minutia of our believing. It also says that we can boldly talk to God about anything, and He will help us, because He understands since He has suffered everything that we have.

---

[5] *Ibid*, page 28

[6] Romans 8:31

Fortunately, erroneous beliefs are simple to correct. It just takes patience and time. In fact, the ministry of the Holy Spirit is to lead us into God's *truth*, to shine the light of God's *truth* in our hearts, and expose misbeliefs. He is the only one who knows what is in our hearts, including how we are deceived. His greatest desire is to help us replace our wrong beliefs with His *truth*. God has already placed His Word in our hearts and written it in our minds. That is done. Now He wants to search our hearts and cleanse us from the darkness we are allowing to hide there. King David addressed this in the book of Psalms: "Search me, O God, and know my heart: try me, and know my thoughts: And see if there be any wicked way in me, and lead me in the way everlasting."[7]

Have you ever called yourself an idiot after doing something stupid? How many times have we thought or said things like "I'm ugly," "I don't have any talent," "I'll never succeed," "I'm superior," "I'm hopeless," "I'll never make it," "I'm not good enough?" Unfortunately, we are unaware of most of our self-talk. We have told ourselves some lies for so long that certain circumstances automatically elicit emotions. These lies now seem to skip the self-talk and go directly to our feelings. As soon as we encounter these conditions we no longer have to tell ourselves a lie like, "I'm such an idiot" or "I'm going to crush him" because we automatically feel the results of what we have believed for years.

- Her father would not hold her. Though she could be model material, she feels ugly.

- This cop tells himself, "There are no good guys!" God help anyone he pulls over because in his mind everyone is evil.

- As a child, told himself, "I can't do it." As a grown-up, he becomes anxious when asked to join a church baseball team.

Every emotion you experience is the result of what you are telling yourself about yourself, someone else, or a situation in the past, present, or future. Usually, the source of what you tell yourself is what you

---

[7] Psalm 139:23, 24 (KJV)

believe; though some misbeliefs originate by repeating what someone else says about us, even though we may disagree. In this fallen world, it often seems easier to believe the bad, though if we thought about it, we would realize it is not true.

> *You feel because of what you think. Your emotions are only a reflection of what you are or have been telling yourself. Because we are unaware of the relationship between our thoughts and feelings, we often interpret our feelings as proof that what we are thinking is true. Thus, our feelings take on a life of their own.*

Thoughts, feelings, more thoughts, and more feelings can become a vicious cycle because we do not realize that our emotions always begin with thinking. But, our thoughts can be so quiet that we are not even aware of them. We allow the feelings that *we have created* to prove that something that is not true is. Our emotions react to self-talk whether the self-talk is true or false.

Consider the scene as you were getting out of the shower. When you heard the glass break, you told yourself, "It's an intruder." Then your emotions responded with fear. *Have you ever considered that fear is a result of what you tell yourself about a situation?* What about other emotions like anger or jealousy? Are they an accurate measure of what has happened, or a reaction to what you have told yourself? Back to the shower scenario. When you find out the cat caused the noise and tell yourself you are safe, the fear subsides. What controlled your emotions this time? You believed the truth.

Now that you know your emotions and actions are a result of your self-talk, what do you want to tell yourself? The *truth* or lies? If you tell yourself a lie, your corresponding action will be based on something that is not true. If you tell yourself the *truth*, your actions will come to reflect God's reality. Bottom line? We desperately need to tell ourselves the *truth*. Unfortunately, the power of our emotions, which seem so real and so right, often make it difficult to recognize the *truth, because it* is calm and quiet. When the emotions inside us are raging, *truth* can be hard to hear.

Grandmother was their primary caretaker after their mother's divorce. Because Jill was the firstborn, much more was expected of her than of Kate. Even at an early age, Jill was supposed to act like a little lady; whereas Kate, was pampered by her grandmother. Jill was not allowed excuses for the way she felt or behaved, but Kate was different. Grandmother forgave Kate's temper tantrums and crying with the justification that she was weaker and more sensitive than Jill and could not handle the realities of life as easily.

Years later, as teenagers coming to grips with life, their experiences were entirely different. Jill had common sense and could cooperate with life rather than fight it. Kate, on the other hand, had been told she was very sensitive, so her life revolved around emotions. Kate had learned to live by her feelings regardless of what the *truth* might be. How she felt was more important than the *truth* and was the issue around which her existence centered. In fact, her feelings defined what she believed to be truth. She was never taught the relationship between her feelings and logic. To her, they were one and the same.

Today, Kate does what she feels. Because she lives by what she feels, Kate is ruled by guilt. Like all of us, she desperately wants a reality on which she can depend, but her emotions cannot provide it. In her early twenties, Kate began drinking heavily to counteract extreme emotional swings. Though she finally dealt with her alcohol problem, she has not faced the fact that her emotions are not the *truth*. She has no idea her self-created world is not real nor that the life she was created to enjoy is rapidly slipping by as she gets older and increasingly set in her ways.

Like it or not, when you accept as truth something that is not, you create emotions that agree with that belief. So, the right beliefs result in truthful thoughts, which lead to feelings, actions, and attitudes that are aligned with what God believes. Conversely, untrue beliefs result in incorrect thoughts, which lead to negative emotions, destructive actions, and bad attitudes. It's a shame we didn't know this formula before now; we could have saved ourselves a lot of grief.

* * *

Chapter Eight Endnotes

Note 1

We seldom consider that God is logical. Many think God seems irrational. Some say we can never know what He is going to do because He is sovereign, as though His sovereignty grants Him the right to lie or change His mind. But God says He cannot lie, and He does not change.[8,9]

One of the trials of raising children is getting them to think logically, so their lives are founded on proper logic instead of emotions and desires. We want our kids to be reasonable and live based on the right rules. We want them to do well in school and understand English, science, math, and the other disciplines they are taught. A civilized society requires thought based on a system of logic to which most members agree. Though no longer the case, our laws were originally based on a system of logic that was comprehensible by most of our society.

As children of God and new creatures in Christ, we possess both the mind and beliefs of Christ and are members of the society of the Kingdom of God. "He rescued us from the dominion of darkness (*the sense-ruled world, dominated by the law of performance*) and relocated us into the kingdom where the love of his son rules."[10] This new realm into which we were transferred by our relationship with Christ has a different type of logic than that with which we were raised. It is God's logic. When our relationship with God seems off, it is because we are trying to think with a form of logic He doesn't have. To be functioning members of the Holy Trinity's community and family, we must learn to reason like Jesus does.

---

[8] Titus 1:2
[9] Malachi 3:6
[10] Colossians 1:13 (The Mirror)

Unseen

The Holy Spirit is intent on training us how to think like God. That's why Isaiah (speaking as the voice of God) said, "Come let us reason together."[11] It is impossible to have intimate, trusting fellowship with someone if you don't understand what they are saying.

I have often tried to communicate with others and found myself frustrated as I realized we were using the same words and phrases yet with different meanings. That's why it is so important to have precise definitions of the terms utilized in this book.

Many Christians have used certain words for so long that when employed in a different context or with a different meaning, they cannot grasp the difference. Thus, they misunderstand what they are reading here. They fail to understand that what they are reading is a complete paradigm shift from what they have always thought. This book is describing key components of the Apostle Paul's message, yet few have ever seen them this way. Again, because *the lie* has distorted their ability to reason in a way that was normal for First Century believers.

God is logical and wants us to understand and think with His logic. He will not give up until we have come to the full maturity of Christ as members of the Body of Christ. "Until we all attain unity in faith, and in the knowledge of the Son of God, and reach mature manhood, and that full measure of development found in Christ."[12]

---

[11] Isaiah 1:18 (KJV)

[12] Ephesians 4:13 (Scripture is taken from The Complete Bible: An American Translation.)

9
Good Fuel

Having become *human doings*, it is not the fact that we exist, but what we do or have that gives us importance. The source of our behaviors (actions and emotions) are our thoughts—many of which are just self-talk. We think happy thoughts and tell ourselves that everything will be great; thus, we feel good. Or we talk to ourselves about a potential tragedy and try to figure out how to fix it. This type of thinking is called worry.

As we realize that our solutions don't work, we may become discouraged and depressed. We think about the future with a special someone and our hearts thrill with excitement. But then worry they will dump us, and the next thing we know, albeit only in our minds, the relationship is over. In each case, what we felt was not based on *truth*. Unless we fill our minds with the proper fuel (*truth*), they will hiccup and sputter and sometimes even break down. Many believe that the proper fuel is a quality education. But haven't we tried that and proved though a good education is important, it does not produce the power of a changed life? Education just allows you to live what you believe in a more effective manner. It surely does not make you a more fit vessel of God or guarantee you a happier life.

I once listened to a couple of farmers talking about running out of gas while hunting deep in the Everglades. They were driving a farm truck, and had only a diesel fuel tank used for refueling tractors. Their single hope of getting back to civilization without a very long and dirty walk was finding more gasoline before their engine quit. They did the unthinkable. They revved up the truck's motor and pumped diesel fuel into its tank. These farmers made it out of the glades but the second the engine returned to idle, it stopped. Yes, it *had* run on the wrong fuel but as soon as they reduced the engine's RPM, it quit.

Do you know anyone that fidgets? Are you someone that always needs chaos or some noise around you? Have you ever tried to slow down and take a break, but something wouldn't let you? You promise you will take that well-deserved rest. Unfortunately, it never happens. Like the Energizer Bunny, we just keep going and going and going until we burn out. So, what produces the energy that generates our thoughts? What we believe. If what you believe is not true, it is like using the wrong fuel in your truck engine in the Everglades. The only way to keep it running is hold the pedal to the metal.

Believing Starts Early

Nowadays, a discussion of believing usually pertains to religion or politics. However, very few of our beliefs have anything to do with a deity or government. The most powerful part of your belief system was established long before you had any concept of a God or the government. The following stories illustrate how easily erroneous belief systems are formed and the harm they can cause.

> Don remembers little of his childhood except for a frequent question from his dad, "Son, what's wrong with your mind?" Through the years, he heard the question repeated many times. Eventually, Don decided there must be something wrong with his mind. Now that he is an adult, his dad no longer says such things, but the effects still linger.

> Todd was only one-year-old and did not understand the angry words his father screamed at his mother, but they still had an impact. Just a few years later, the child is hesitant, insecure, and quick to cry about the simplest things. His mother and father are baffled.

> If his dad said it once, he said it a thousand times, "You're worthless and will never amount to anything." At the age of 25, it had come true.

Alex was a sweet kid, loved by everyone—except his father. In his father's eyes, Alex was not manly enough. Of course, Alex was only eight years old. This instilled in him a belief that he could never be good enough for his father to love him. But, Alex needed to have a man in his life who cared about him.

During his teen years, his father's criticism was incessant. The rejection was painful for those who saw it. Observers never doubted the disdain the man had for his son. His mother was the exact opposite: very loving, tender, and kind. But in all his years at home, she never tried to stop the abuse or get his dad to understand what he was doing to his son.

By adulthood, Alex had given up hope that his dad would ever love or accept him. That did not mean his craving for the love of his father ever ceased; it just meant that he had to find an alternative. In his mid-twenties, Alex moved to a city on the West Coast. Within a few years, his mother informed us that Alex had died from pneumonia. His father would not even mention his child's name.

The beliefs Alex acquired in his childhood, that he would never be able to do the right things to be loved by his own parents, left him feeling like everyone else in his life would never love him; because he just wasn't good enough. Of course, this state of never knowing he was loved left Alex feeling alone, isolated, and depressed. It wasn't because of what others thought about him but because of his beliefs, taught to him by his father.

Faith: The Foundation of Life

Behavior should no longer be a mystery to anyone. We always act consistently with what we believe. Though it is possible to change what we think, act, or feel without altering the beliefs that caused it, that error is still in our hearts and will manifest itself in other ways; possibly more socially acceptable, but perhaps unacceptable too. Regardless of whether our behavior is acceptable to those from whom we seek importance, if it is not a result of spirit, then God considers it flesh. Thus, even positive change can be regarded as not good by God because it is not a result of believing the *truth*, but of something else.

Paul said, "Whatsoever is not of faith is sin (error)."[1] That is, whenever behavior does not flow from believing God's *truth*, it is a result of misconception. But any condemnation you might feel from this is *not* from God. He perfectly understands why we do what we do, and He is always for us, seeking to show us another way. There are no exceptions. In Jesus, He came to bring us home. He hasn't given up on anyone. Only the religious believe otherwise.

What God wants is behavior that is a result of spirit because then it will be fruit based on the *Law of Faith*. Jesus said, "That which is born of the flesh is flesh; and that which is born of the Spirit is spirit."[2] There's no way around it. If the Holy Spirit does it in you, it is good. If you do it in you, it is flesh, regardless of what society, your church, or you think about it.

Let's face it. "It is impossible to please God apart from faith. Why? Because anyone who wants to approach God must believe both that he exists and that he cares enough to respond to those who seek him."[3] The wonder is that faith is a gift from God, it's free, and you already have it. The problem isn't you but the lies that fill the Earth and invade our minds while seeking to confuse and convince us that we are not who God says we are and that we don't believe Him. Those lies often hide in strongholds that disguise their real source. Thus, we don't realize how the darkness manipulates us.

The primary emphasis of the Apostle John's epistles is to show us the essence of God, who he says is light and love. He explains how this shapes believers' behavior. Whatever is true about any aspect of God's character as revealed through Jesus applies to believers also. "Because as he is, so are we in this world."[4]

The Apostle John said, "Those who hate their Brothers are in Darkness, and are living in Darkness, and do not know where they are

---

[1] Romans 14:23 (KJV)
[2] John 3:6 (KJV)
[3] Hebrews 11:6 (msg)
[4] 1 John 4:17 (KJV)

going because the Darkness prevents their seeing."[5] The issue to John was light versus darkness, *truth* versus deception. He was writing to believers, not unbelievers. A major theme of His epistles was the effect of lies (darkness) on believers and how our behavior reflects what is in our hearts. That's why he says so much about being honest with God in the first chapter.

Nothing we write is meant to condemn, but to educate believers about who they are. If you are walking in the *truth* (light) as you may claim, then your behavior will reflect it. It is dishonest to say we are walking in the *truth* while our willful actions deny the very essence of God. The real cry of John is to stop deceiving ourselves and to allow the light of God's *truth* to expose any darkness that is obstructing the glory of His image from shining in us. "The one who claims to be living in union with Him must live the same kind of life He lived."[6] John is not saying believers are supposed to go out and act like Jesus. He is saying that if you abide in Him, your behavior will come to reflect it automatically. As is said so many places in the New Testament, the change doesn't start on the outside, but on the inside. It then works its way out. Dear believers, how have we so misunderstood God and turned His *truth* upside down? We've been fooled by *the lie*.

Whether what you believe is right or wrong does not affect God's love for you. He *is* Love. He doesn't just have it to dole out on whom He is pleases. He loves *you* without condition, without limits, and without hesitation. He is pleased with *you*, who you are, and who He made you in Christ, even if He is not satisfied with your behavior or attempts to gain His favor by your performance. God made you an image of wholeness: Jesus Christ. Now He just wants you to know yourself as He knows you. This is some of the knowledge of God He wants you to realize. He's not waiting for you to do anything or to stop doing something. He loves you because of Who He *is*, and there is nothing you can do to change that. You cannot cause God to change who He is!

---

[5] 1 John 2:11 (TCNT Part 2)

[6] 1 John 2:6 (Taken from Norlie, Olaf M., Norlie's Simplified New Testament c. 1961)

When I speak of God being pleased, that does not mean He is unpleased if you are in error (sin). Of course, some will immediately bring up the subject of grieving the Holy Spirit.[7] "And grieve not the Holy Spirit of God." But that grief is out of love. His love for you is infinite. He always wants the best for you. When you willfully believe or do something that is contrary to His love, it grieves Him, but it doesn't cause Him to hate you or be displeased with you. His grief is that you aren't taking what He has already done for you. Understanding this makes it easier for you to take what He has given you. God adores you and wants the best for you. If you think otherwise, those thoughts didn't come from God. No matter who told you—if they said God doesn't like you or is upset with you, it didn't come from Him. It is knowing the goodness of God toward us that leads us to change our minds about what we believe, not His anger or the threat of punishment.[8]

There is nothing dearer to us or more important than what we believe. We love because of what we believe and hate because of the same. We go here or refuse to go there because of what we believe. Even our desires are a direct result of our beliefs. Whether we fear or feel safe, it is because of what we believe. We are aware of only a fraction of our beliefs, yet all combined they control us. The contents of our hearts determine how we respond to life's experiences, and our hearts are as deep as we get. When people challenge our beliefs, in some cases, they might as well attack us because there is not much difference. A challenge to our beliefs can be threatening. This is why people can react so violently when someone rejects what they treasure, especially if it is their religion.

Do you know why you believe what you believe? There is nothing mysterious about it. You are not born with beliefs but acquire them through living. We treasure what we know because we want or choose to. What we know may be very convincing; it may be true. But, if we believe it, it is because we choose to. No one can force us to treasure something.

---

[7] Ephesians 4:30 (KJV)

[8] Romans 2:4

Beliefs, whether true or false, are knowledge which we have learned to hold dear. Often there is no way to prove the validity of knowledge which we treasure. Our decision to believe something is what seals it as *truth* even if it is false. Yes, the decision can be based in ignorance. Regardless, once knowledge is believed, it is *truth* to the one believing it. This is usually not a conscious decision. Maybe people or circumstances have pushed us toward a belief; nevertheless, nothing can force us to treasure something we know.

What people believe becomes their identity. If it is not the identity God has given them, they will never be fully satisfied. They will always be trying to find out who they are. As our belief systems continue to grow, each new belief is influenced by and twisted together with all other convictions. When a mass of *truths* and deceptions are tangled together, they create confusion.

Beliefs can be so powerful that they make even false knowledge seem real to us. Even if no one else can see or believe a person's false reality, it will still seem real to the person living it.

As an infant just out of the womb, you had no editing mechanism. You were incapable of differentiating good from evil. Whatever you experienced became your truth. It had to be because you didn't have the tools to dispute anything that wasn't true. Hopefully, your parents were a good buffer teaching you right from wrong. But because their body of knowledge included some deceptions, there was no way they could protect you from all the lies, even if they could have recognized them, which they couldn't. Until you were old enough to edit your experiences, life was what it was, and from it were formed your opinions and your beliefs. By the time you were old enough to edit what you were learning, a large part of your belief system was already in place. Your body of knowledge had grown exponentially, including good and bad, *truth* and lies. Much of it is buried so deeply in your heart that it is impossible to dig down and discover what you believe. It would never even occur to anyone to attempt such a thing. By the time someone is a teenager, their body of knowledge is massive. Even if they wanted to, they couldn't question everything they believe. During our teenage years, our body of beliefs and knowledge continues to grow all intertwined, layer upon layer. Now only the Holy Spirit knows what's really in our hearts. Only He can enable us to experience wholeness.

Man's Greatest Need

The greatest need of humankind is to be loved and accepted. Growing up, we learn our value by how others treat us. When people treat us well, we like it; when they treat us poorly, we don't.

> Rod was abandoned by his parents at an early age and grew up with low self-esteem. Today, he desperately needs to feel important. As he became an adult, Rod discovered that people responded well to charm, so he learned to use it to his advantage. Also, he eventually found that a combination of wealth and association with famous people gave him the appearance of being important.
>
> Just turn on the TV today and his belief is easily confirmed. Seemingly strong and wealthy people hold an elevated status in our society, regardless of other socially unacceptable behaviors they may exhibit.
>
> Early on, Rod determined to be rich and, if not famous, then closely associated with those that are. But the truth is, Rod is afraid to have a real relationship with anyone because deep down, in his reality, he feels he is not important. How could he be if he was abandoned by those who were supposed to love him? But Rod can't hide his insecurity from everyone. It manages to show up in all sorts of injurious behavior, usually behind closed doors, especially with those who come to know him.
>
> He has an enjoyable demeanor while in the presence of people whose adoration he craves. But when with those he doesn't feel are critical to his public image, he can be brutal and cruel. Some, especially ones with whom he would like to do business, see through his persona. When they want nothing more to do with him, it is always someone's fault, but not his.

Success and fame, within broad limits, are performance goals that often make some feel important. However, if that is the *truth*, if success and fame are what make someone matter, then why do so many who achieve it live in self-destructive ways, such as overdosing on drugs, committing suicide, and intentionally seeking to hurt or demean others?

The reason we cannot escape the feeling that we are judged by our performance is because we *are*. And, that is how we have learned to judge others. Since our performance is a direct result of what we believe, we perceive a challenge to it as a direct assault on our beliefs. That calls into question our worth, the very thing that enables us to be loved. Almost everything we do, say, think, dream, and feel originates in our search for value and the identity we find in being important. But is it true that our performance is a measure of our worth? Are we only worth what we do?

Many who say they believe in God have been deceived. There can be no question that God is concerned about behavior because He *is* righteousness itself. Paul elucidates God's image of right conduct saying, "But the fruit produced by the Spirit is love, joy, peace, forbearance, kindliness, generosity, trustfulness, gentleness, and self-control. Against such things as these there is no law!"[9] But, over and over Paul says that right behavior is not as important to God as what we believe. In fact, he says that good behavior is a curse to those depending on it to make them right with God or get His blessings. He says that believing the *truth* is what causes someone to be right with God. Believing what God says causes us to live the way God intends with no effort required. How? Because the blessing of the Holy Spirit does it in us.[10]

> He who supplies you with his Spirit and endows you with such wonderful powers—does he do this as the result of actions done in obedience to Law? Or as the result of your having listened with faith? It is just as it was with Abraham— 'He believed God, and that was regarded by God as righteousness.' You see then that those whose

---

[9] Galatians 5:22 (TCNT Part 2)
[10] Galatians 3:14

lives are based on faith are the true sons of Abraham. And Scripture, foreseeing the fact that God would bring the heathen into right relations with himself as a consequence of their faith, announced the Good News to Abraham beforehand, in the words— 'Through thee all the heathen shall be blessed.' And so people whose lives are based on faith share the blessings of Abraham and his faith. All who are depending on actions done in obedience to Law are under a curse, for Scripture says—'Cursed is every one who does not abide by all that is written in the Book of the Law and do it.'[11]

Jesus died to redeem mankind from all evil, both in deed and heart.[12] However, it is important to understand what the Greek word (*ponéros*) often translated *evil* means. According to Strong's Concordance it means *toilsome* or *bad*. Thayer defines it as *full of labors, annoyances, hardships*. Liddell and Scott say it means *causing toil* or *hardship*. Many interpret that to mean *bad behavior*, which can surely be a result. But, Jesus was referring to believing lies which result in people distressing over things they weren't created to handle. As discussed earlier, when we distract ourselves, when we split our attention by trying to control all of life, the result is annoyances, heavy burdens, distresses, and hopelessness. As the above lexicons reveal, the evils from which Jesus came to set us free are the toilsome, laborious, hardships that cause people to bend down under heavy burdens. A picture of Jesus's understanding of evil was a person who spends their life walking through a desert of deep and high sand dunes with no end in sight. It is the picture we get from His words in Matthew 11:28, "Come unto me all you who labor and are heavy laden." This is the evil which Adam and Eve encountered after believing the lie. Their labors turned into laborious, sweaty, hopeless work. Out of the hopelessness caused by believing *the lie* come all sorts of bad behaviors. Though Jesus didn't use our term *evil*, He would certainly find it appropriate today.

---

[11] Colossians 3:5-10 (TCNT Part 2)

[12] As explained in Chapter Four, the heart is where believing occurs. Thus, it is the repository of any error that results in incorrect behavior.

As I have said so many times in so many ways, our behavior is a result of what we believe. Thus, our beliefs, which reflect the body of knowledge within our hearts, is the real target of the Holy Spirit's ministry. Once beliefs are corrected, behavior changes automatically. If our behavior doesn't change, it is because we still believe something that is causing that behavior. Often, more than one belief can be causing a behavior. Only the Holy Spirit can untwist our beliefs.

Satan understands how humans work. Unfortunately, most humans don't. Though he wants us to do bad things, that is not his target. He's after our beliefs. He knows that if he can manipulate them, our behavior will automatically follow suit.

The salvation that mankind seeks through laborious, burdensome work and self-discipline, or by any other means, is impossible. There is no law that any person can obey that will result in setting their hearts free except the *Law of Faith*, which Paul said he was called to teach the Gentiles. "By whom we have received grace and apostleship, for obedience to the faith among all nations, for his name."[13] There is no way any man or woman can see into their own hearts and uncover wrong beliefs, even if they want to. But Jesus said, "With God, all things are possible."[14] God can and has completed the work necessary for our release from all evil, and Jesus sent the Holy Spirit to make our new reality in Him real to us. It is the will of God that every human being knows Him personally and who He has made us be in Christ. "Whose wish is that everyone should be saved, and attain to a thorough knowledge of the Truth."[15] But only He can cause that to happen. No human being is God. We are creatures created to be utterly dependent on the only God for everything.[16] Either He lives His life in us or we don't live it at all. As John said, if God's life is in someone, they have life. If they reject that life, they are living in death. "So, whoever has the Son,

---

[13] Romans 1:5 (KJV)

[14] Matthew 19:26 (KJV)

[15] 1 Timothy 2:4 (TCNT Part 2)

[16] Paul usually includes the word *the* before the name God, which I believe, is to emphasize He is the only God.

has life; whoever rejects the Son, rejects life."[17] Since believers are new creatures in Christ, the renewal of our minds is a fact, not an anticipated or wished-for event that isn't yet finished (Chapter Four Endnotes #24). It is done. Complete. To God, the issue is not renewing our minds or changing our behavior but persuading His children to *take* His gifts.

After receiving the Spirit and being born again, He begins the work of training us to *be* who He made us. As His *truth* grows in our hearts, our behavior takes care of itself. The *Law of Faith* guarantees to establish the requirements of God's commands inside the believer. "Do we then make void the law through faith? God forbid: yea, we establish the law."[18] His commands are neither hard nor burdensome. "For this is the love of God, that we keep his commandments: and his commandments are not grievous."[19] How can they not be grievous? Because his commands always include the fulfillment of what is commanded.

John, recounting in His Gospel what Jesus said in Chapters Thirteen through Sixteen, boiled down several commandments to focus on a single objective— loving one another. This was the passion of Jesus because it was the devotion of His Father. What is His greatest command? To abide in Him[20] (Chapter Nine Endnotes #1). For God to command us to abide in Him is beyond marvelous.

Over and over, Jesus says we should or can love one another. He is persistent in His encouragement. However, if we are going to love, it is because we are abiding in His love for us.

What are his commands?

1. Don't be troubled

2. Believe the *truth*

3. Arise

4. Abide in Him.

---

[17] 1 John 5:12 (msg): It is only a matter of time before that reality becomes real to the unbeliever.

[18] Romans 3:27-31 (KJV)

[19] 1 John 5:3 (KJV)

[20] 20 John 15:4

The command to arise can be taken two ways. I believe it is meant to cause our hearts to arise in the strength of God, though Jesus was also telling them to get up and follow Him someplace. The love that Jesus is speaking about is not the world's kind of love, but God's unconditional love. The New Testament calls it *agape*. *Agape* is only possible when we live by the faith of Jesus who is living in us. Not being troubled, believing (trusting), and abiding in His Father's love are hallmarks of the life of Jesus. He not only commanded us not to fear but to believe and abide, and His commands give us the power to do what they say. They tell us what He has commanded to *be* in our lives. What joy!

God created His human creatures in His image and likeness. That means He created us to be like Him and act like Him. The *Law of Faith* fulfills this. As we believe what Christ believes, Jesus becomes manifest in our mortal flesh. Any believer can learn to treasure what Jesus treasures. "I have been crucified with Christ. So it is no longer I that live, but it is Christ that lives in me; and as for my present earthly life, I am living it by faith in the Son of God, who loved me and gave himself for me."[21]

Our social behavior develops from the sense of value that comes from being loved and accepted. We will do anything to be loved because it is that feeling of love alone that gives life value. Love is what gives life to our hearts and minds. Consider the Islamic extremist who straps on a bomb and walks into a crowded airport. What motivates him to do it? Is there any doubt that he is acting on his beliefs? But what could those beliefs be? We don't have to know because God does. The answer to helping people repent (change their minds about what they believe) is for believers to cooperate with the Holy Spirit. He is the one intent on bringing all of us into the unity of the faith so that we not only arrive at *a stature of the fullness of Christ* but so His love can reach those who are afraid of Him in a way that they will take it.

So how do you cooperate with Him? By simply agreeing with Him when He exposes error in your beliefs. You agree that His *truth* is true and that there may be error in your beliefs, of which you are unaware. Choose to believe He does love you and is working for you instead of

---

[21] Galatians 2:20 (TCNT Part 2)

against you, even though your circumstances and stronghold-based thoughts may say your problems are all God's fault. Instead of trying to do something for God, just sit down and rest in His love. Believe He is loving you without you doing anything in return. You have permission from God to believe that He *is* loving you, even if you can't feel it and even if your entire world seems to be falling apart. When you first believe this, it can be uncomfortable because we usually feel like we should be doing something. Instead, tell God that you agree He is loving you, because He IS Love, and He can never be or do otherwise. Acknowledge that God is Love and His love for you is active on your behalf, even though your experience may say it isn't and that you don't deserve it. Thank God that He is who He says He is and not who the world and your experiences say He is. Talk to God like everything He says He has done is really for you and everything about His love is real for you—because it is (Chapter Nine Endnotes #2)!

Like human parents watching their children grow, He delights as you take those deliberate faltering steps into His arms. Do it even while sinning. He will be gently working to bring you into the full light of His *truth* and will *not* condemn you along the way. God still loved Adam and Eve even after they rebelled. He has not changed. He is not a different God to you. Jesus said the universe lies in darkness. Any place you can go in the world is smothered, choking, drowning in darkness. As you begin to see the unseen, you will understand the darkness. It's horrifying. "Leave them to themselves; they are but blind guides; and if one blind man guides another, both will fall into a ditch." [22] By understanding how believing the *truth* enables you to see God's reality, you can come fearlessly to the light because you realize it won't harm you. It is by living in His light that you can see things the world has no idea even exist. "But now are ye light in the Lord: walk as children of light."[23] "In thy light shall we see light."[24]

We need to know that others value us; we will do whatever it takes to get it. Man was created to learn his value from a voice on the outside.

---

[22] Matthew 15:14 (TCNT Part 1)

[23] Ephesians 5:8 (TCNT Part 2)

[24] Psalm 36:9 (KJV)

God intends that voice to be His. Those who don't hear His continual song of unconditional love within their hearts will seek it from others through performance. A self-righteous attitude is evidence of a person trying to find value by being better than others. They may be listening to a voice telling them they are superior because they follow the "right" rules.

Out-of-wedlock pregnancy is a terrible problem. It's a problem even when it does end in marriage. It usually comes in two forms:

1. A person seeking love, acceptance, and pleasure through sexual relations.

2. A person so craving importance and love that she is willing to create another human being to love her.

In the first case, premarital sex is not only a response to hormones but an even deeper craving for love. In the second instance, she thinks, "If I have a baby, I will be loved and needed by this child." The helpless dependence of a child can produce a powerful sense of worth.

Continuing this thought, consider the many government programs that lock people into dependency.[25] Is it really because the politicians care, or could it be because they are getting something in return? They legally steal what is not theirs to give to others without asking if they want to give it away. Could it be that they find value in their sense of power and the fact that so many people are dependent on them for life? It's a thought worth considering.

You Don't Have to Hit a Wall

The transformation from a *doing* to a *being* is a radical change. Often, this type of change does not occur until our backs are against a wall. It is then that we may be willing to admit that what we have been doing is not working. Fortunately, many are in that position now. Their backs

---

[25] Not all programs do this and not all people find themselves locked in. We're not against programs to help people as a rule, only when they produce dependency instead of helping people get back on their feet.

are against a wall. If something does not change, they will not make it. Dreams will never be realized.

I say it is fortunate because I know from much personal experience that God works inside the trials of our lives to refine us. I do *not* suggest that God sends those trials. It is in the furnace of the trials of life that the impurities in our faith rise to the top where they are skimmed off by the Holy Spirit as we recognize our misbeliefs and change them (Chapter Nine Endnotes #3).

However, no law says we must hit a wall before we can change. Why not listen to wisdom and hear God now? God does not want you to suffer. That is why He gives us the wisdom to enjoy His life in us and avoid all types of problems. Obedience is hearing God's Word with the intention of believing it so that you will be able to *do it*. Those under the Law aren't trying to do it because they treasure it like Jesus does but because if they can succeed God will have to accept them on their terms. Paul was not told to go teach the obedience of *doing* God's Word but to teach them to *believe* it. His actual words were to teach "into obedience of faith," which means the obedience of hearing and believing God's *truth*. Paul was to take his message to the world. "By whom we have received grace and apostleship, for obedience to the faith among all nations, for his name."[26] This type of obedience automatically fulfills Gods instructions (the Law) because it enables Christ to freely live His life in you. As we focus on hearing God's words so we can believe them, in God's timing we will find ourselves living them.

In no way do I mean to imply that believing God's *truth* will keep you from problems. However, it will allow you to experience Paul's promise: "Thanks be to God Who always causes us to triumph in Christ."[27] But, how can He *cause* us to triumph? First, we need to believe that God doesn't lie. He keeps His Word.

> God is not a man, that he should lie; neither the son of man, that he should repent (change His mind): hath he said,

---

[26] Romans 1:5 (KJV)

[27] 2 Corinthians 2:14 (KJV)

> and shall he not do it? Or hath he spoken, and shall he not make it good?[28]

> God is not a man, that He should deceive; Neither the son of man, that He should change. Hath He spoken, and will He not perform? Or hath He said, and will He not establish it?[29]

If He says He causes us to triumph, then He does.[30] (I love to agree with Him about this.) But, unless we allow the Holy Spirit to teach us, we will never know the glory that this promise brings. It was His sovereign decision to make that commitment. To violate His promise and oath would cause Him to cease to be God (Chapter Four Endnotes #17). He *is* Love. He *cannot* lie. He has sworn to finish His work in us, so He will.

Second, since it is His will that we triumph, He is working His will within us. Paul said, "for it is God Who is working in you to cause you to will His will and to cause you to do it."[31] What is Paul talking about here? Two things: (1) God persuades you to will. God knows it works this way. It is a law which He established, which causes everything else He has said to become ingrained in our lives.

> Where is boasting then? It is excluded. By what law? of works? Nay: but by the law of faith. Therefore we conclude that a man is justified by faith without the deeds of the law. Is he the God of the Jews only? Is he not also of the Gentiles? Yes, of the Gentiles also: Seeing it is one God, which shall justify the circumcision by faith, and uncircumcision through faith. Do we then make void the law through faith? God forbid: yea, we establish the law.[32]

---

[28] Numbers 23:19 (KJV)

[29] Number 23:19 (*A Translation of the Old Testament Scriptures from the Original Hebrew* by Helen Spurrell)

[30] 2 Corinthians 2:14 (KJV)

[31] Philippians 2:13

[32] Romans 3:27-31 (KJV)

His will is that we believe Him, believe His Word, believe His Son, and His *truth*. But He doesn't stop at giving us faith. As we believe, (2) He is also working in us to *do* His will, which means to live what we believe. Believing and doing go together; you can't have one without the other. If He works into you the believing, then He also works into you the doing of the belief. This is how the victory of Christ becomes our experience. "Thanks be to God Who gives us the victory by means of our Lord Jesus Christ."[33] We believe into (εἰς) Jesus, which means we are God's children.[34]

The Apostle John says that those who are born of God overcome the world. "Who is he that overcometh the world, but he that believeth that Jesus is the Son of God?"[35] What causes us to overcome the world? Believing God's truth over every other source of knowledge.

"For all that has been begotten of God gets the victory over the world; and this is the victory which has gotten the victory over the world, our faith."[36]

* * *

Chapter Nine Endnotes

Note 1

In a literal translation of John 13:34, Jesus said, "A new commandment I give you *in order that* (ἵνα) you *will* love one another." There is no use of the imperative mood (the mood of command) in this statement. Rather, He uses the subjunctive mood (the New Testament mood of the probability of God's intention). In other words, because of certain commands, Jesus fully intends that the disciples *will* want to love one another but, in this passage, He isn't telling them they *must*. He was

---

[33] 1 Corinthians 15:57 (JEC)

[34] εἰς (eis) Can be translated as motion towards something and eventually being in it. Like walking, literally, into a wall, so that you're *in* the wall. This can, more accurately, be translated "into" in the same sense of being *in*.

[35] 1 John 5:5 (KJV)

[36] 1 John 5:4 (Darby Bible Translation)

giving those commands so that they would want to love each other. These commandments were going to make *will love one another* a probability because it is God's intention, and "love never fails" (cf. 1 Corinthians 13:8).

After Jesus' statement in John 13:34, the first actual command issued by Jesus is found in John 14:1: "Don't let your heart be troubled. You believe in God, believe in me!" Jesus's next commands are in John 14:11. Then in verse twenty-one, Jesus speaks of commandments in the plural. "He that fixes his attention on my commandments." We cannot love one another with God's love until we first know His love for us. Jesus knows that by accepting the commands He has just issued, as well as the one He is about to reveal, we will be inside a love relationship with God. However, He is not telling us we must. Jesus believes that these commands will result in our ability and desire to love each other because their fulfillment will result in a love relationship with God first. But He has yet to get to the big commandment, one that has never been issued before by God. It is in John 15:4 where Jesus finally gets to His point: "Abide in me." Abide is in the imperative mood; it is a command. He is commanding them into the very heart of love from which love for others will flow. This is the fulfillment of John's statement, "We love because He first loved us." He is speaking about settling down in the source of love and becoming comfortable in the Father's love, as well as in Jesus's love. "Observe these commandments 'in order that you can love one another.'" That is only possible by—and is automatically the fruit of—abiding in Him. But for this command to become our reality, we must say yes.

Though Jesus issued several commandments in this passage, it is this one to which He referred in the singular—commandment. So why the previous commands? Because those make it possible to abide. If you are troubled or unbelieving, you don't abide. So, what does abide mean? It means to snuggle down, be at home, and comfortable where you are residing. It is impossible to feel comfortable in Christ if you are fearful, troubled, or unbelieving. How do you abide? Not by feeling like it, that's for sure. You abide by faith.

Note 2

I hesitate to write this because there has been so much bad teaching using James 3:4, however, if you get this the way I mean it, you will find it a big door into understanding faith.

> Or take ships as an example. Although they are so large and are driven by strong winds, they are steered by a very small rudder wherever the pilot wants to go.[37]

I have written much about self-talk, some of which is just our thinking to ourselves. However, some of it comes out in speech. Regardless, God has made it a wonderful tool to aid our faith because it reveals our faith to us.

> But what does it say? "The word is near you, in your mouth and in your heart" (that is, the word of faith that we proclaim).[38]

Paul was saying that what you believe comes out of your mouth, all the time. What you believe is always coming out of your mouth. This is why it is so important to listen to yourself. If you do, you may find that you don't like a lot of what you say, but because your tongue is like the rudder of a ship, it will take you in the direction of the reality where it is pointed. So, if your tongue is pointed toward what is false, then an illusion will become increasingly real to you. Like it or not, you won't be living God's reality. Though others may be able to see what is going on, you won't because you are believing lies. I am not suggesting that you attempt to get things from God by confession. In fact, it is possible for positive confession to work in the realm of witchcraft in which someone is trying to manipulate God. (Don't worry. If you have done so, God hasn't been upset by your behavior. He just wants to get you on track.) The way some teach positive confession is that you can create the substance you want by your confession. That is a

---

[37] James 3:4 (NIV)
[38] Romans 10:8 (ESV)

gross misunderstanding of faith. I am telling you point blank that you already have far more from God than you have imagined. The Kingdom belongs to you right now. But, as long as the faith coming out of your mouth is pointing you in a direction away from what God says, you will keep eating what you are saying. God's reality is the *truth*. I could rephrase Paul's "fight of faith" as the fight to agree with what God says when you don't feel like it and don't want to. As you continue to look at what God says, you are setting your attention on His reality. As your eyes become accustomed to His light, what He says is real will become real to you too. This is not an, "I'll try it" type of proposition. It is a permanent intention in which you decide you will keep agreeing with God for the rest of your life, come hell or high water. So, tell God that you agree He is loving you, because He IS Love and He can never be or do otherwise. Thank God that He is who He says He is and not who the world and your experiences say He is. Talk to God like He has done everything He says and His love for you is real, because it is! Repeat back to God what you learn about His reality. Tell Him His reality is yours even though it may not seem like it. The Apostle Paul was quite clear that we live in two worlds at one time. Even though you may not yet be able to see God's Kingdom, you already live there. Agree with God what is *truth*, not because you feel it but because He says it is. "(As much as we were co-included in his death,) we were co-included in his resurrection. We were also elevated in his ascension to be equally present in the throne room of the heavenly realm where we are co-seated with him in his executive authority. We are full represented in Christ Jesus."[39]

Note 3

Proverbs 17:3: "The refining pot is for silver, and the furnace for gold: but the Lord trieth the hearts." Our beliefs reside in our hearts. Trials heat things up and force wrong beliefs to the top. Pressures, problems, and trials can prove to us that something we believe about God or ourselves is not true. I'm not talking about believing for a new car or for

---

[39] Ephesians 2:6 (The Mirror)

healing. The type of believing that focuses on getting things has little to do with God's faith. His faith is focused on our union with Him. Thus, ours is too. Out of His faith comes the type of abundance and satisfaction that could never be yours if you had all the money and health in the world. With His faith, you don't have any cares. The Holy Spirit is training you to live this type of carefree life.

Trials provide a wonderful opportunity to be honest with God by confessing the error that the trial exposes, which could be simply that you are feeling terror or desiring to do something you know is wrong. Though God does not cause evil, he will work in it so that you discover you are more than you think because you were created in His image. Trials are a wonderful opportunity to face the *truth* about what we really believe and allow the Holy Spirit to lead us to repent and believe His *truth*. This can feel temporarily unpleasant, but the result is wonderful joy and peace.

10
How Believing Works

Regardless whether a physical or behavioral symptom is good or bad, its existence is due to beliefs that started in the Garden of Eden. Understanding how symptoms are caused by what we believe helps us more easily cooperate with God. The Holy Spirit works to rid us of wrong beliefs so we can see the magnificent things He has accomplished in us that are like Christ. God is the only one who can make this happen. All we can do is cooperate, and even that is only possible by the quiet, gentle force of the Holy Spirit. The work of God inside us is real. Some get occasional glimpses of it in their imaginations; but to most, it seems to remain unseen.

God wants us to see what He has done for us. He eagerly anticipates our enjoyment of what He has given us. He looks forward to watching our jaw-dropping, wide-eyed awe as the veil falls away and we finally take in the splendor of His love, kindness, and dazzling gifts. His ability is free to any who will just believe it. While the powers of darkness continually inundate our minds with evil interpretations of what our senses are telling us, we can continue to declare God's *truth* is our correct reality, and rest in His love.

Trauma

We know that all evil in the world began with believing *the lie*. Along with knowing how our hearts work and that all sinful behavior is rooted in lies, this knowledge enables us to move ever increasingly toward the light, so we can see and enjoy the reality of God's Kingdom here on Earth.

Though the emphasis of this book has been good behavior versus bad behavior and right beliefs versus wrong ones, things such as health versus sickness and abundance versus lack are affected by the same laws that apply to conduct and beliefs. But what about genetic disorders, illnesses, and diseases that start before birth? That's a good point. When Adam and Eve decided to believe *the lie* and turn away from God, the corruption that consumed them instantaneously overtook all the creation. The resulting process of deterioration invaded the entire universe. After God had created the Earth, He said it was good. "And God looked at all that He had made, and behold, it was very good."[1] But the corruption changed that. The mutiny of the first couple initiated destruction down to the very genetics of all living things as well as the subatomic structure of the entire universe. The corruption was a plague that consumed everything. Nothing escaped; nothing retained its original glory.

The trauma resulting from the fall in the Garden led to all sickness, disease, and poverty, and even caused the deformities and other issues that occur before a child is born. It was the cause of the disharmony in the entire creation, which now appears in things like weather and other forces that wreak havoc within the Earth such as volcanoes and earthquakes. Mankind does not seem to grasp the all-encompassing effect of lies and the darkness that accompanies them.

Not only do people live the lies they believe—beginning with the most basic one, which is *the lie*—but the darkness created by those lies leaves them blind and unable to rescue themselves or the rest of creation. Because people can see with natural eyes, they fail to realize they also have other eyes, which are blind. They are not whole, yet think they are. *The lie* has convinced people that what they see with physical eyes is all there is.

But, God has put a "knowing" in us that there is more. Deep inside, we know there is another reality, but natural reality is so powerful that without the Holy Spirit, no one sees what God has done. Those who see a spirit world outside of union with Christ are being deceived. Yes,

---

[1] 1 Genesis 1:31 (*A Translation of the Old Testament Scriptures from the Original Hebrew* by Helen Spurrell)

they see something, but it is not what they think. Paul refers to this very thing when he says, "For Satan himself is transformed into an angel of light."[2] If not for God's great love for His human creatures, mankind would have no hope. Remember what Jesus said about the man who was born blind?

> Now as Jesus was passing by, he saw a man who had been blind from birth. His disciples asked him, "Rabbi, who committed the sin that caused him to be born blind, this man or his parents?" Jesus answered, "Neither this man nor his parents sinned, but he was born blind so that the acts of God may be revealed through what happens to him.[3]

Terrible things can happen to a fetus in the womb, but God's attitude is that His children are to fix it once the child is born. So, Jesus did the same thing He delights to see His brethren (that's you) do. He healed the man.

The Source of Every Symptom Is a Belief

God has never desired that mankind live under a weight of trying to do right. His has always planned for the Holy Spirit to work in our hearts to automatically produce a life that is *truth*. The life He gives us is the complete answer to every result of *the lie*. God left nothing out. When Jesus said, "It is finished," He meant it. "After he took the wine, Jesus said, "It's done…complete." Bowing his head, he offered up his spirit."[4]

Hopefully, you have a new understanding of the importance of things you have long known but may not have understood how to use. Don't let anyone persuade you that God is most concerned about what you do because He isn't. His desire is for us to know what He has already done for every one of us so that our hearts will feel the freedom

---

[2] 2 Corinthians 11:14 (KJV)
[3] John 9:1-3 (New English Translation)
[4] John 19:30 (msg)

He has given us. Then He will be able to reveal inside us the glorious life that is now ours. It was this freedom which Paul was addressing in Galatians. He was concerned about believers being persuaded to follow obedience to rules rather than the *truth* to achieve rightness. To Paul, *truth* was not the right set of standards and laws, but the correct body of knowledge. Having God's body of knowledge, which is only available from the Spirit of God by believing the *truth*, enables us to expect the manifestation of Christ in our daily experience. When we depend on adherence to any set of rules instead of simply doing what He asked (that is, to keep listening to His truth until it becomes as much a part of us as it is of Him) to give us favor with God, we are rejecting His favor. Such beliefs oppose the very nature of God.

> This is the freedom with which Christ has freed us. So stand firm in it, and do not get under a yoke of slavery again. Why, I, Paul, tell you that if you let yourselves be circumcised, Christ can do nothing for you. I insist again to any man who lets himself be circumcised, that he is under obligation to obey the whole Law. You people who propose to be made upright by law have finished with Christ; you have lost your hold upon God's favor. But we, by the Spirit, through faith wait for the uprightness we hope for. For in union with Christ Jesus, neither circumcision nor the want of it counts for anything, but only faith acting through love. You were making such progress! Who has stopped your obeying the truth? That kind of persuasion never came from him who called you! A little yeast will make all the dough rise.[5]

Paul was addressing circumcision because that is what the legalists were pushing on the Galatians. But you can substitute any work or rule for the word *circumcision*, and the passage is still true. There is only one law for a child of God, and that is *the law of the Spirit of [the] life within Christ Jesus*. "For the law of the Spirit of life in Christ Jesus

---

[5] Galatians 5:1-9 (Scripture is taken from *The Complete Bible: an American Translation*.)

hath made me free from the law of sin and death."[6] And what is the Spirit's law? The *Law of Faith*. "Where is boasting then? It is excluded. By what law? Of works? Nay: but by the law of faith."[7] This is the law that causes the character, nature, deeds, and love of God to appear in our lives. "Do we then make void the law through faith? God forbid: yea, we establish the law"[8] (Chapter ten Endnotes # 1).

Paul states that believing the *truth* establishes the Law of God in us. It causes us to live love. It isn't something you accomplish by your superior willpower; it is a gift to anyone that says yes. A literal translation of Galatians 2:16 is: "Knowing that a man is not justified out of works belonging to a law but by means of Jesus Christ's belief, we also into Christ Jesus believed." Paul is writing about the *Law of Faith*. It is Christ's faith, His beliefs; it is the same beliefs of the same *truth* that Jesus trusted. It is the result of union with Him who is the *truth*. You don't have to understand to believe; but once accepted, you will come to know.

Now let's move toward comprehending *how* to experience metamorphosis (transformation). We have spent a lot of time discussing the mechanics of believing. We have yet to address how to identify wrong beliefs, how to determine the truth, how to change those false beliefs, and how to use unpleasant experiences to your advantage. There are two types of beliefs: those that bless and those that curse. Your spirit, soul, and body are created to work in harmony as one. God does not look at you and see parts. He sees *you* as a whole *being*. When our beliefs are not consistent with God's beliefs, there will always be symptoms. Remember that the symptoms are not the real problems; rather, they are just the evidence that we have misbeliefs. Symptoms just tell us there is a problem and may give us clues to what it is. Only the Holy Spirit can enable us to identify our wrong beliefs. Based on improper actions, thoughts, words, or emotions, we may suspect that something in our belief system is wrong, but only the light of the Holy Spirit can enable us to see the specifics.

---

[6] Romans 8:2 (KJV)

[7] Romans 3:27 (KJV)

[8] Romans 3:31 (KJV)

How about this illustration to explain the interrelationship of beliefs? Because of an injury to your leg, you begin carrying your weight differently. Because of the limp, you get a blister on your foot, which gets infected. The infected area becomes full of puss and especially painful. Of course, the infection is a problem but not the primary source of your discomfort. You can get rid of the infection yet still have the problem that caused it. The same cause-effect types of relationships impact our mental and emotional lives.

Years ago, I had problems with a few clients. I had advertised high-quality service for which businesses paid a premium. As far as a few people were concerned, high quality meant perfect, and when it wasn't, they were angry. Of course, I often wondered why they didn't quit and go to one of my competitors, but they didn't. The way these few customers treated my staff, and me, affected me for years. As time passed, the prospect of talking to customers provoked increasing levels of anxiety. It made no difference why they called. Whenever my secretary told me a customer wanted to talk, I would become extremely anxious. I heard far more praise than criticism but still became more apprehensive every time the phone rang. The day arrived when, seemingly for no reason, I was terrified to talk to customers. Then I had a remarkable experience. I had gone to a conference on self-worth conducted by Malcolm Smith. In the last session, he spoke about why we need to forgive those who have hurt us. It was not because of anything it would do for the offender, but because of what it would do for the forgiver. Reverend Smith recommended a short exercise for dealing with people who have hurt us, which I found very beneficial. Understanding came several days after I believed what he said. At the time, I was only aware of being tired and hurting. I wanted to know who I was and if my life had a purpose. The pain in my heart and mind was immense. I wanted a change; I wanted to feel good.

I learned two *truths* in that seminar, which very quickly replaced some lies that I believed and changed my life forever. First, I found out that all mankind has believed *the lie, which* causes us to base our value on our performance. Suddenly, I knew why I felt so badly about myself: I was not able to do anything well enough to satisfy the demands that my imagination said were required of me. The moment I learned about *the lie*, I recognized that I had believed it and it was wrong. My value as a person had depended on how well I succeeded, but I had never felt like I accomplished enough, *so the lie further convinced* me that I was no good and never would be. Because of recognizing the *truth* and replacing one lie, I felt something in me change. Then the speaker talked about the unconditional love of God. After over twenty years of being a believer, I had never heard anyone explain it. God's *unconditional* love had always had conditions: give enough, read the Bible enough, pray enough, witness enough, love others enough, and so on. I learned that God's love was limitless, spontaneous, and without conditions of any kind. He even loves me when I believe lies and act on them. I learned that God really is Love. Love isn't something He has or gives; it is what He *is*. He doesn't place any demand whatsoever upon anyone to earn His love and kindness. He loves us because of Who He is, not because of anything about us.

Suddenly I realized that my self-hate and insecurity had been a result of not believing God loved me, even though, until that moment, I would never have admitted it. My religion had taught me that if I didn't believe God loved me I wasn't saved, so I had to believe it. But deep down, I knew it couldn't be true. I *knew* I wasn't good enough. Immediately after learning about *the lie* and admitting I had believed it, the *truth* about God's Love suddenly became real to me. I had never felt loved because I had never felt like I was good enough to be loved. But, God loves me whether I believe I am good enough or not. What I and others thought didn't matter to Him because He *is* Love. He can't *be* anything else. Nothing I can do or not do can change Him. Since then, I have never been the same. Those revelations to my heart from God's heart enabled me to write this book.

Reverend Smith didn't stop there. He spoke of what forgiveness is and what it does. I discovered that a lifetime of "faith" had been wrong. What I had been taught about faith had not been true. In that seminar, I experienced such a radical, overwhelming, instantaneous, and incredible change that I was game for whatever else he said. Please remember, I still had none of the understanding that God began to give me later, which is the subject of this book. At the speaker's suggestion, that night I made a list of everyone I could remember who had ever hurt me in any way. In the list, I included what they had done. Once completed, I read it out loud—including what they had done to me and how it hurt—and then I deliberately forgave each person. In other words, I released them into God's hands. I decided I would no longer try to be a god. Now they were His to do with as He pleased. I did this because I was tired of holding such pain within my heart. I did not expect something to happen—though I hoped it would. The next two days were striking because of what *did not* occur. Six times in those two days, I took calls from customers; the type of calls that I had so feared. Each time, my reaction surprised me. Taking those six calls felt no different than taking calls from friends. Since then, I have felt total peace answering calls even from angry people. What happened inside me that caused such a remarkable change? I have no idea. I just changed what I believed about how God loved me and how I was no longer the judge of the people I had forgiven. As a result, I experienced a dramatic change in a seemingly unrelated area. I did not know when I forgave all those people that it would have any effect on my reaction to customers. I was thrilled to discover the ramifications that changing just one belief could have. I since have had many similar experiences.

Sometimes the beliefs that cause troublesome symptoms are so much a part of our identity that we deny there could be a connection between them and the symptom. We would rather suffer than admit certain dear, cherished beliefs are wrong. But like the right beliefs, untrue beliefs have the power of reproduction. Our beliefs are like seeds. They grow and reproduce. Jesus also compared the things we believe to leaven, which causes flour to expand. "God's kingdom is like yeast that a woman works into the dough for dozens of loaves of barley bread—and waits while the dough rises."[9] And Jesus gave them this warning: "Take care to be on the watch against the leaven of the Pharisees and the leaven of Herod."[10] "A little leaven leaveneth the whole lump."[11]

Our beliefs are not static. Wrong beliefs produce more of the same, which produce even more mistaken beliefs. Unless we are willing to

---

[9] Matthew 13:33 (msg)
[10] Mark 8:15 (TCNT Part 2)
[11] Galatians 5:8-9 (KJV)

change our mind about our wrong beliefs, we will suffer increasingly adverse effects as we grow older.

Good Beliefs versus Bad Ones

For most people, changing beliefs—whether for good or bad—is often unintentional. People often acquire the right beliefs not because they are intentionally looking for the *truth*, but happen to stumble upon it. People confronted with the *truth* at a time when they are receptive may change their beliefs. Unfortunately, too many would rather change what they feel or do than what they believe. We love what we believe. We just don't always like the effects they have on us. We seldom examine beliefs, so we have little chance of seeing how absurd some are. Intentionally, or unintentionally, we have chosen our beliefs— most of which now hide out of sight. No building is stable if it has a weak foundation; so, it is time to let the Holy Spirit re-establish our foundations.

Beliefs can curse or bless. Beliefs that curse do so because they are inconsistent with the *truth*. They result in recurring unsound thoughts and dysfunctional emotions and actions as well as physical sickness. Yes, of course, what you eat and how you treat your body affects your health. But why does one person treat their body one way and someone else another? Because of what they believe! Don't our emotions contribute to our health? Doesn't distress cause sickness? If we could eliminate or reduce it, wouldn't that have a significant impact on disease? Why do people suffer from mental and emotional illness? Could it be because they believe lies? Distress is a result of wrong beliefs—very often the belief that the person is responsible for things they cannot control but think they should. That's pretty stressful.

It seems the medical community has decided that almost every physical, mental, and emotional problem is a disease or a chemical imbalance. Unfortunately, rather than treat the whole person, they see symptoms as the real problems. They think if you can get rid of symptoms the problems will be fixed. But that isn't the way things work. The darkness prevails because while in it we are blinded to the *truth*.

Yes, of course, diseases are real and chemical imbalances can cause all sorts of problems. Yes, we need to deal with them. But without addressing the actual cause of the disease, we just leave the door open for new and different symptoms. Believing *the lie* and its offspring is the absolute source of every evil that afflicts mankind.

Beliefs that bless are right ones. They are consistent with the *truth* and enable us to deal with every issue of life effectively. Trust based on God's *truth* promotes thoughts, emotions, and actions that result in healthy, happy, and contented lives, even in disagreeable circumstances. The right beliefs enable us to experience the love and value we crave. Remember Jesus's response to the woman with the issue of blood? "Daughter, be of good comfort, thy faith hath made thee whole."[12] Jesus said that because she believed the *truth* her body had been made whole.

* * *

Chapter Ten Endnotes

Note 1

Throughout the New Testament, you will find references to commandments. Sometimes the reference is clearly to love one another. Other times, it seems to be speaking about other commandments. The Bible verse 1 John 3:23-24 is an example. Jesus had more than one command, and it is true that all of them related to love. Paul wrote, "For all the law is fulfilled in one word, even in this; Thou shalt love thy neighbor as thyself."

So how do *you* make yourself love with God's love? You can't. It's impossible. But, God can and will do it in and through you.

The *Law of Faith* - what an astonishing law, and it is so simple. It is the key to dwelling or abiding (snuggling down) inside Christ. Cooperation with the *Law of Faith* enables you to fearlessly abide in God's love and be a vessel of that love.

---

[12] Matthew 9:22 (KJV)

11
Truth versus Deception

> All the darkness in the world cannot
> extinguish the light of a single candle.
> —Saint Francis of Assisi (1181-1226)

In Part 1 we defined faith as believing God's *truth*. Adam's and Eve's embrace of *the li*e created a stronghold of false knowledge representing itself as God's knowledge. *The lie* has infected man's perception of all knowledge to the extent that now, without help from the Holy Spirit, it is impossible to be certain the knowledge we are considering, or already believe, is true. According to God, the greatest need of mankind is to know the *truth*.[1]

In Chapter Eleven, we will apply the principle of believing God's *truth* found in Paul's *Law of Faith* to believing any knowledge, whether true or false. We call this the *law of faith* (no caps), which is how all believing, regardless of what is believed, works.

What is *truth* and why does it matter? God's *truth* is His reality and forms the body of knowledge out of which He lives, that is, the knowledge of God. Though God knows the lies we believe, He doesn't believe them with us. He believes what He knows, and His faith is His reality.[2] Likewise since God created mankind in His image, man's faith causes his perception of reality. Until we know God's *truth*, what we are aware of as *truth* is at best a mixture of true and false knowledge. God's *truth* is of the same quality as God. In other words, it is eternal. Human knowledge learned from experiencing the creation is temporal.

---

[1] Hosea 4:6, John 8:31 and 32
[2] God's faith underlies and supports all reality; cf. Hebrews 11:1

The Apostle Paul said this temporal knowledge will pass away.[3] The knowledge that will remain is God's knowledge.[4]

Within the creation are several types of knowledge. Natural knowledge is the facts of the creation which cause its mechanics to work; this is temporal knowledge. Basic math is the purest example of temporal or natural knowledge. Then there is false knowledge which contradicts the facts of the creation and is none-the-less often believed to be true. When false knowledge is believed, the substance that it forms can seem so real that it becomes a person's reality though it is a deception. The other type of knowledge is what God knows. God's knowledge, which is synonymous with *truth*, is the fuel which causes the mechanics of the creation to work. False knowledge is a void within which there are no real facts. Everything believed in a false knowledge vacuum is an illusion. The only way to get rid of such fantasies is by introducing true facts, which must be believed. When we eliminate facts from knowledge, then it becomes false. Though a basis for reality may seem to exist, it is just an imagination exalting itself above what God knows. Since God's *truth* is the underlying reality of the creation, when man tries to replace them with false facts, something always goes wrong.

Because what people believe is true to them, their "faith" creates a type of substance which can also seem real, yet be an illusion. You've seen delusional psychotics, if not personally at least on TV. They see and hear things that normal people don't. If asked, they will say that what they see and hear is the *truth,* and if you disagree they may react very badly. This principle applies to all of us. No matter whether the knowledge we believe is true or false, it forms the basis for what each of us thinks is real and, thus, meaningful. The *law of faith* says that when false knowledge is believed, it will create for that believer an illusion of *truth* which in turn will create feelings and emotions that will be perceived as confirming the false belief. Some scientists say people create their own realities. What you believe to be true will take on its realism inside your mind. If people choose to believe false knowledge, it will take on a realness in their minds that they will treat as reality.

---

[3] 1 Corinthians 13:8, 9
[4] 1 Corinthians 13:12

But, at best, the reality we can experience by believing temporal or false knowledge is only temporary. You can never trust it to continue. It will always eventually collide with God's reality, which is eternal and unchangeable.

The authors have written UNSEEN to help readers learn to use the *Law of Faith* as God intended so that you can go from living solely within a temporal reality to God's reality. As you increasingly see and understand God's *truth*, your reality will conform to His. It is all a function of whose *truth* you choose to believe. To know how to choose God's *truth*, it is necessary to understand what happened to mankind in the Garden of Eden and how that affects us today. This was common knowledge to many First Century believers.

Every word of God's *truth* describes reality in the Kingdom of God. Through UNSEEN, we seek to remove the barriers preventing you from seeing that reality. As the obstacles fall (the obstacles being the fake expectations and substance which appear when believing false knowledge) and we continue to look at and think about His *truth*, His reality becomes increasingly real to us. Similarly, if we choose to keep looking at and thinking about evil, it will become increasingly true to us. The fact that what we keep looking at becomes more and more true to us is a critical issue and the reason that God says those whose attention is single-mindedly fixed on His *truth* are blessed (Chapter Eleven Endnote #1).

Jesus said, "I myself am the Way, the Truth, and the Life; no one ever comes to the Father except through me."[5] Knowing His *truth* is knowing Jesus Christ Himself. The more our thoughts are consistent with God's *truth*, the more our minds will reflect Christ's and the more we will realize He is with us and in us all the time. When God's *truth* is the foundation of our belief system, it makes us experience the love, peace, and rest that our hearts crave. Believing the *truth* results in behavior that is consistent with our own and others' well-being. Though the Bible is a perfect standard for all *truth*, much can be discovered through common sense. For instance, if someone who is important to you doesn't like you, does that determine your value as a human being?

---

[5] John 14:6 (TCNT Part 1)

If you believe it does, you will never be free to enjoy who you are. You will live with the impossible and miserable task of pleasing someone else to be liked.

In the last few decades, we have seen a severe erosion of society's standards—much of which has been a mixed blessing. Laws and attitudes based on outright lies have been torn down, and many more people now possess the legal right to be all they can be. But in the process, many truths have also been rejected. Much of our society has not only challenged the concept of absolute *truth*, but they have also discarded it. The result? Those that reject absolute *truth* create their own standards, which result in a society where people become victims and depend on someone else to make their lives better. Or they may become tyrants seeking to manipulate and run others' lives because they see themselves as gods who know what is best for everyone. We have all been victimized by something outside of our control that happened to us, which we didn't like or want. Many have been victims of our own stupidity or foolishness. But some people take it farther and believe someone else owes them for their inconvenience or loss. They demand someone else must pay. Believing *the lie* can cause someone who has been treated badly to feel like a victim. Of course, it may just be in their mind. But what if they were treated poorly? *The lie* says they should get even. Believing lies causes people to imagine things that aren't even close to reality.

Unfortunately, believing *the lie* often causes people who have suffered hurt to hold bitterness in their hearts. It is a terrible barrier to taking the blessings inherent in God's love and keeps them bound to their perceived problem. They become enslaved to it and fail to experience the freedom from that pain that comes from Christ. They indeed are being treated terribly—by themselves. They are a worse enemy to themselves than anyone else possibly could be. Unfortunately, enablers take advantage and seek to capitalize on those people's belief in *the lie,* so they can become saviors (gods). That is what gods do. They strive to control. They find their importance from creatures rather than The God. Victim mentality is everywhere, and it is wrong. If you become a victim, you give the power of your life to someone else. Regardless of what happened to you, God says your life is brand new. Everything related to your old life is gone; you have become new. "So, if anyone is in union with Christ, he is a new being! His *old* life has passed away, and a *new* life has *begun!*"⁶ You no longer must be a victim.

God has not said you have to do anything to *become* new, because He has done it for you. You already are new. It is things we believe God has said, which He hasn't, that cause us to be afraid and not see what God has done for us. It is not time to *become* changed; it is time to *be* changed. God says you are not a victim of anybody or anything. God says He has released whoever hurt you, and it's time for you to do the same. It's time to release them into God's hands. This doesn't mean you have to ever get near that person, because you don't. And, it doesn't mean God is going to let them get away with doing something wrong, either. Either they will take the forgiveness that Jesus bought with His own blood and *be* new creations inside whom God will work just like He is working in you or they will pay their debts with their suffering. For someone to insist on remaining a victim means that they have not yet recognized God's love. He's been ready to open their eyes for a long time. The question is, are they? Victimhood is common in our legal system where some people are always blaming and suing others for damages. Commercials by some attorneys encourage people to be victims. Let's face it. No one likes to be wrong. So, if we are not willing to take responsibility for something, it is likely that we will lay the blame elsewhere.

Of course, there are situations where something happens that was not your fault and over which you had no control, which can affect your life forever. Consider the parents whose child is killed by a drunk driver. When the parents lack a standard that includes forgiveness, they become bitter, angry, unable to be content with the judgment of law, and unable to release anyone. How many times has this type of tragedy resulted in the destruction of a family? The driver was wrong, but it is only the parents' inability to forgive the driver or themselves that can ultimately destroy their family. How often have we seen people who suffered terrible tragedies become victims? Now they hate themselves

---

⁶ 2 Corinthians 5:17 (TCNT Part 2)

and the world. Someone else owes them; everyone they meet is going to pay. They have lost control of their own lives. Only knowing the *truth* like God knows it will set them free. *Truth* ultimately builds up. It enables people to live abundant lives even after such a tragedy. Disasters happen, and they are horrible, but lies that are treasured tear down and make tragedies even worse.

Recognizing Lies

We need practical ways to identify untruths and how to stop their effects. There are many ways. Let's just start where we are right now. Ask God to open your eyes to know His *truth*. He is safe. Yes, He becomes angry about evil hurting His creatures but, unlike humans, He distinguishes between His human creatures who He loves unconditionally and what they did that may have been wrong. He can separate the two. He sometimes doesn't stop evil because mankind insists on it, and God will never force good on anyone. He waits passionately for openings in our hearts, so He can show us His love. He despises the lies and seeks to teach us His *truth*. God knows our real problem is the lies we believe. That's why He sent Jesus who is the *truth*.

> But God's angry displeasure erupts as acts of human mistrust and wrongdoing and lying accumulate, as people try to put a shroud over truth. But the basic reality of God is plain enough. Open your eyes and there it is! By taking a long and thoughtful look at what God has created, people have always been able to see what their eyes as such can't see: eternal power, for instance, and the mystery of his divine being. So, nobody has a good excuse. What happened was this: People knew God perfectly well, but when they didn't treat him like God, refusing to worship him, they trivialized themselves into silliness and confusion so that there was neither sense nor direction left in their lives. They pretended to know it all but were illiterate regarding life. They traded the glory of God who holds the world in his hands for cheap figurines you can buy at any roadside

stand. So God said, in effect, 'If that's what you want, that's what you get.' It wasn't long before they were living in a pigpen, smeared with filth, filthy inside and out. And all this because they traded the true God for a fake god, and worshiped the god they made instead of the God who created them—the God we bless, the God who blesses us. Oh, yes![7]

God has given us the *truth*. Unfortunately, we have spent a lifetime rejecting much of it. It is time to find out what we have denied and start believing all of God's *truth*. Here is where we learn the value of the Holy Spirit's ministry. He alone knows what is blocking our hearts and how to cause us to see His *truth*.

Those of us who desire to overcome problems by the ability of God need a way to discover which beliefs are gumming up the works. We *can* learn to recognize the fruit that comes from lies, how to uncover lies, and how to correct the assumptions based on the lies. God has made it simple. It is a primary ministry of the Holy Spirit. The hardest part is the patience that the process requires, but the Holy Spirit helps with this also.

Remember that believing things that are not true produces symptoms. How you react to the circumstances in your life via thoughts, emotions, and actions provides a clear signal that you believe the *truth* or a lie. Just because you feel good does not mean what you believe is the *truth*. Just because you feel bad does not say that you believe a lie. The following examples are clear signals that you need to make some changes:

- If you feel good about something that you know is wrong.

- If you have frequent or consistent bad feelings about something that is good.

- If you act contrary to God's *truth*.

---

[7] Romans 1:18-25 (msg)

- If you struggle with bad thoughts.
- If you fear what people may think about you.
- If you have compulsive behaviors.
- If you are frequently sick.
- If you are seriously troubled by long-term financial problems.
- If you have trouble making or keeping friends.
- If you are confused.
- If you believe *truth* is relative.
- If you believe God loves everyone unconditionally except you.
- If you think God causes tragedies.
- If you think God is not with you in every moment of your life.
- If you think God wants you to suffer.
- If you think someone else owes you and should meet your needs.

I hope you get my point.

A useful aid in the search for misbeliefs is found in the book, *Telling Yourself the Truth* by William Backus and Marie Chapian. They discuss common emotions and attitudes that signal problems with our beliefs, like depression, prolonged anger, anxiety, self-hate, lack of self-control, fear of change, refusal to ever take risks, etc. Many other things signal misbeliefs that are contrary to God, like unhealthy habits, attitudes that harm our bodies or make it difficult to get along with people, and actions, thoughts, and feelings consistent with the works of flesh spoken of in Galatians 5. Misbeliefs, not genetic deficiencies, are responsible for crime and every conceivable perversion. The book by Dr. Backus provides excellent examples of self-talk filled with misbeliefs.

I was amazed by what I read. It provided an uncomplicated way to identify many of the wrong things I have said to myself. Your self-talk is a symptom, which, if recognized early, can enable you to *be* transformed. It is possible to stop the symptoms of misbeliefs. For instance, if someone grows up with his father saying, "You'll never amount to anything," at some point, after making enough mistakes, he begins to tell himself, "Look at what I just did. I'll never amount to anything." From there, the self-talk lies compound. Sooner or later, this young man is feeling depressed because it seems like nothing he can do is right or good enough. He sees life through the lens of being wrong. So even when he does well and excels, he can't recognize it or take it to heart because he believes he is no good and will never amount to anything. By learning to identify the lies he tells himself, he can begin to bring his beliefs in line with God's *truth*. The result is a transformed person.

Regardless whether beliefs are true or false, they are still the basis for our thoughts, emotions, and actions. If the basis of our thinking and behaviors is wrong, then the thoughts and actions will also be. It is important to recognize a type of chatter that comes from the powers of darkness. It tries to convince us that we are the source of wrong thoughts in our minds, because when we believe that, it can make us feel even worse. I have so often heard terrible thoughts running around in my head. It was a wonderful day when I realized they weren't my thoughts. One of Satan's strategies is to bombard people with terrible speculations and then convince them this kind of thinking is their own. If you believe a thought is yours, you are much more likely to act like it than if you know it is coming from someone else. When you hear terrible, negative, anxious, or depressing thoughts, realize they are a trick of the powers of darkness which can't do anything but lie incessantly. Just recognize and admit they are lies and not yours, because you have the mind of Christ. Sometimes they may persist for a while. But, once the liars know you won't buy their lies, they'll quit them. Of course, they will try again later, so this requires continual vigilance. "Above all else, guard your heart, for everything you do flows from it."[8]

---

[8] Proverb 4:23 (NIV)

Eventually, they'll try something else. But, as you keep holding fast to believing the *truth* you will find the attacks become fewer and farther in between. In the meantime, just remember to acknowledge that the self-talk in your mind is lies and not your thoughts, even if it feels like it. The chatter is just the voices of darkness trying to dominate your mind and get you to agree with them. Jesus said to stand your ground in His *truth*. The chatter, and thoughts it creates, can't hurt you; it can't bring itself to pass. Just because we may feel the result of that chatter in our emotions doesn't mean it has become our reality because it hasn't. Jesus said the world is covered in darkness and we are in a real war. The Liar is out to crush us and everything God has created. He is the father of lies and uses tricks to deceive us that we can't even imagine. The Holy Spirit is with us always seeking to teach us how to *be* overcomers.

Another key to discovering what we believe is the fruit in our lives. The amount of wealth we accumulate is not a fruit listed by Paul in his letter to the Galatians. But, how about the quality of our family life and relationships with friends? What about our relationships with neighbors? How about this as a description of a whole and fulfilled life? "But the fruit of the Spirit is love, joy, peace, longsuffering, kindness, goodness, faith, meekness, and self-control."[9] This is exactly the opposite of what many people experience. This list of fruit is just a partial description of the fruit of God's life in a believer. Other symptoms of right and wrong beliefs are found in a person's attitude toward God and themselves. Someone intent on harming their mind, body, or emotions does so because they believe a lie. Those full of self-hate will begin loving themselves as they exchange wrong beliefs for what Jesus thinks about them. As they realize how much God loves them, they will increasingly like themselves.

If we reject the *truth* about God and our relationship with Him, we will unconsciously work against the enjoyment of knowing Him and receiving His blessings. But that doesn't stop God. He continues loving us and doing good to us. Unpleasant symptoms are proof that lies are twisting your believing or pounding on your mind to get in. No matter what you experience, stand your ground. You have chosen God's *truth*.

---

[9] Galatians 5:22-23 (KJV)

You are abiding in His love as He works to establish and settle you in His *truth*.

> Humble yourselves, therefore, under the mighty hand of God, so that he may exalt you in his good time. Throw all your anxieties upon him for he makes you his care. Exercise self-control, and be watchful. Your opponent, the Devil, like a roaring lion, is prowling about eager to devour you. Stand firm against him, strong in your faith; knowing as you do, that the very same sufferings as you are undergoing are being laid upon the worldwide Christian Brotherhood. God from whom all help comes, and who called you, by your union with Christ, into his enduring glory, will, when you have suffered for a little while, himself perfect, establish, and strengthen you.[10]

God's *truth* about every human on Earth is wonderous if they just knew it. God knows who He made each one of us to be in Christ, and He knows that when He can get us to agree with Him our feelings, thoughts, and behaviors will begin to conform to those beliefs. When we refuse to accept His *truth* about ourselves, we will behave in ways that harm rather than help us. Have you ever heard the expression, he shot himself in the foot? We have all done it, and it is usually because we did not believe the *truth*.

The subject of suffering is for another book, but suffice it to say that God does not want you to suffer. It is just part of being in this corrupted world. But in Christ, we can grow through the suffering—that is, from the beginning of it through to the other side—until we get to the place where we are established and strengthened. We get bigger than our sufferings and discover we are no longer suffering. Maybe it is finally gone, or maybe we have grown so resilient that it no longer bothers us.

---

[10] 1 Peter 5:6-10 (TCNT Part 2)

James E. Campbell, Jr, James Q. Campbell

How *Truth* Affects Deception

So how do we get rid of lousy beliefs and exchange them for the *truth*? It is easier if we understand how *truth* and lies interact with each other. The Bible, as well as much modern literature, describes hatred, lying, deceiving, and other wrong behaviors as *darkness*. Likewise, love, *truth*, honesty, and proper behavior are called *light*. Works of darkness are most commonly done under cover of darkness or hidden where they can't be seen. The Bible calls deception darkness because it is the absence of the light of God's *truth*, but it is also like physical darkness in that we cannot see things that can hurt us. Deception is an act done in such a way as to prevent others from knowing about it. On the other hand, good is described as light and is usually done in the open. Works of light are not necessarily done to be seen but are unconcerned if they are.

When you walk into a room that is dark, how do you get rid of the darkness? By turning on the light. Where does the darkness go? Nowhere. Rather, it ceases to exist. How do you get more darkness? By turning off the lights. Is it possible for the darkness to overcome the light and put it out? No! The only way to produce darkness is to turn off the light. You may be asking, "What does this have to do with believing?" *Truth* has the same effect on lies that light has on darkness. When a lie is exposed by the *truth*, it can no longer be represented as true unless we hate the *truth*. Then, of course, we will call a lie the truth. A person's hatred of the *truth* doesn't stop the Holy Spirit. Once His light exposes a person's lie, the Holy Spirit doesn't abandon them, because He loves them. We cannot recognize a lie until we see it in relation to the *truth*; but when the light of *truth* shines on a lie, the ability of that lie to control you is broken. How does it work? Once you recognize that something you have believed is *truth* isn't, you can no longer think it is the *truth*. The reason a lie has power is because we believe it is the *truth*. That is how lies, Paul called them errors, get control. The powers of darkness convince you they are true. But by agreeing with God that a lie is a lie and the *truth* is true, that lie can no longer deceive you. How can it if you no longer believe it is true? Of course, Satan often bundles lies, but the Holy Spirit will help you work through that. It may not initially feel like a lie's influence is gone, but given a little time, your feelings will automatically change.

Darkness seeks to extinguish the light, but it can't. It can only lie and try to convince people it is the *truth*. But Jesus, who is the light of the world, won that war. As His light continues to shine in believers' hearts, we increasingly realize the victory is already ours. The light in us continues to expose darkness until it no longer dominates us. I like the Darby Bible Translation of 1 John 5:4: "For all that has been begotten of God gets the victory over the world; and this is the victory which has gotten the victory over the world, our faith." When do we get the victory? The moment we are born-again. What gets it for us? Our faith! We don't have to do anything to get the victory. The faith and the victory are free gifts from God. They come with being made a new kind of creature in Christ. "For by grace are ye saved through faith; and that not of yourselves: *it is* the gift of God."[11] In the early nineties, many members of Congress came under investigation for what was called the Congressional Post Office scandal. Investigations revealed that numerous lawmakers were involved in certain criminal activities. One congressman was convicted and served time in prison. There was a massive cover-up that went on for years. It was an excellent example of how people can get away with inappropriate behavior for a long time; but when the light of *truth* finally shines on it (and it will), the perpetrators will be exposed for what they are and what they have done.

The power of darkness is not some mysterious force. It simply keeps us from knowing the *truth*. In contrast, the power of light enables us to know the *truth* and see what we may have missed.

Are You Willing?

In the presence of *truth*, lies become evident. Without *truth*, we cannot recognize the lies that control us. It is a simple matter to get rid of a lie once it has been exposed but impossible if we do not even know it is there. We must be willing to admit our errors, that areas of our lives

---

[11] Ephesians 2:8 (KJV)

need change. Unfortunately, many are afraid to admit they are wrong and will not experience the *truth* they need until they do. For those, it may help to remember a simple bit of logic. If you desire to be right about everything, you must admit you could very well be wrong about some things. If you are wrong about something, only by admitting it can you then be made right. If you're unwilling to admit you could be wrong, you will never be right. Often, changes we want are dependent on first addressing a lie with which we don't want to deal. It becomes easier and easier to face your misbeliefs when you accept that God's love for you is not affected by what you believe or do. He loves you unconditionally. He cannot do otherwise because He IS Love. If you realize that you have been resisting the *truth*, admit it to God. "Father, I need your *truth* but have been resisting it. Help me to love Your *truth*." All who love God's *truth* will experience the freedom that is in Christ.

How does someone love God's *truth*? By believing it, by deciding it is worth treasuring and focusing your attention on it. The truth is, we are all ponderers. We all meditate and think about stuff, much of it not in agreement with God's *truth*. Unfortunately, most of us have grown unaware of our meditating. Many thoughts have become so normal for us we don't even consider that they are not true. We have been looking at some things for so long that we do not question them. They have become truth to us. We agree with them. We have grown to treasure them. That is, we have grown to love them. But now, we want to *take* the gift of faith because we want to love God's *truth* instead. We do so by thanking God for His gift, even though we cannot see it. He says it is ours, so it must be. If you'd like, ask the Holy Spirit to give you *truth* that you can ponder. Tell Him you want something in which you can discover treasure; I call it loot. Sometimes I consider and ponder just a sentence or two for days. I know there are marvels hidden in every word of God and I keep looking at it until I see something wonderful. Once I have seen something, it is mine forever, even if it feels like I later forget it. At the right time, the Holy Spirit brings it back to my memory, so I can use it.

Agree that you are a new creature in Christ and it is no longer you that live, but Christ who lives in you. "Therefore if any man be in

Christ, he is a new creature: old things are passed away; behold, all things are become new."[12]

> So if anyone is in union with Christ, he is a new being! His old life has passed away, and a new life has begun![13]

> I have been crucified with Christ and I no longer live, but Christ lives in me. The life I now live in the body, I live by faith in the Son of God, who loved me and gave himself for me.[14]

Eventually, your thoughts, emotions, and actions will catch up with what you believe. The fight of faith is to continue agreeing with God when something in your life says that what God says is wrong. The Church is in the mop-up phase of a fight between light and darkness, *truth* and lies, which Jesus already won. But, He is still seeking to convince us to finish what He started.

It also includes some serious emotional wrestling too. The emotional fight is a result of lying thoughts that seek to make you *feel* like the *truth* is a lie.

Believing the *truth* in the face of an onslaught of contrary emotions can be trying, but Jesus has already triumphed over your feelings. As the Holy Spirit trains you how to live in His *truth*, your present victory will become real to you. His victory really is our victory right now, even though darkness may be blinding our eyes to it. God says if we don't see the victory we can be assured it is ours because He says it is. It is through the process of learning to believe the *truth* that we come to see and know it through experience. As the light in our hearts dispels the darkness, we begin to see what we previously couldn't.

Any time something in your life or mind says that you aren't a new creature and that you aren't the righteousness of God in Christ, you have the right to say it is a lie. "I am who God says I am." Two steps

---

[12] 2 Corinthians 5:17 (KJV)

[13] 2 Corinthians 5:17 (TCNT Part II)

[14] Galatians 2:20 (msg)

may help you: (1) Tell God you want to believe His *truth* and (2) Ask Him to help you believe.

> The father cried, "Then I believe. Help me with my doubts!"[15]

> The father of the boy cried out, with tears, "Lord, I do believe! Help my unbelief!"[16]

Thoughts may be screaming in your head (*"you aren't who God says you are"*), but those aren't yours. They're words and pictures from the principalities and powers of darkness. They aren't the *truth*; they're lies. They may say they have won but they haven't. Jesus did. It's finished. You no longer must agree with those evil thoughts. Thank God that thinking isn't yours even though it may feel like it. Thank Him that Jesus Christ, the real *truth,* lives in you, which means you are already victorious. Stand your ground. "And in nothing terrified by your adversaries: which is to them an evident token of perdition, but to you of salvation, and that of God."[17] Eventually, they'll quit. Until then, they can't hurt you even though they may say they can and it may feel like they can. Remember, the powers of darkness are only lies. You don't have to be afraid of their darkness. The only thing they can do is lie. They can't touch you. "We know that no one who is born of God sins; but He who was born of God keeps him, and the evil one does not touch him."[18]

However, maybe you're reading this and realize you don't feel like you want to believe. In that case, just be honest with God and tell Him how you feel. He can handle it; He appreciates honesty. He'll gently and kindly lead you into believing. He won't force you, but He will help

---

[15] Mark 9:24 (msg)

[16] Mark 9:24 (Taken from Norlie, Olaf M., Norlie's Simplified New Testament c. 1961)

[17] Philippians 1:28 (KJV)

[18] 1 John 5:18 (NASB)

you. The *truth* is you do want to believe; it's only lies that are telling you that you don't. You have just been feeling the effects of those lies.

Begin Learning the *Truth*

A great starting place for learning the *truth* is the Scriptures. However, if you are like many people, the Bible is an immediate source of guilt and condemnation. Why? Because we read it from the perspective of *the lie*, which declares that we are responsible and God is out to "get" us. What a miserable deception in which to live. But now you know about *the lie* and that it has twisted everyone's minds—each in unique ways. You can't do anything about what other people believe and think, but you can do something about yourself. Ask the Holy Spirit to show you your misbeliefs and teach you His *truth*. He will do it.

Every time you read the Bible, remind yourself that God is Love and everything He says is because of His love for you. In fact, every Word of God is saturated in and potent with His love. God cannot act outside of love; so, remind yourself that everything you read in the Bible must be seen through the lens of love. Love is always the motivation for all of God's actions and decisions. If you have trouble seeing His love in the Scriptures, then ask the Holy Spirit to open the eyes of your heart to make it real to you and to understand the Bible through the eyes of His love. Remember that He has squandered God's love inside your heart, and He wants you to know it.

Something else that may help you: any time you read a verse of scripture like John 3:16, "For God so loved the world" Substitute the word *me* for *world* because the world includes you! "For God so loved *me*." When you encounter a passage that causes you to feel condemned, fearful, anxious or any other thing like it, just realize you are misunderstanding something that God means for good. And, likely, you may be reading a poor translation. Just because a translation is popular doesn't mean it is right. When you encounter a passage in the Bible that sounds like God is upset at you, it is probably a mistranslation, because God wants you to know how much He loves you. But remember, interpreters can only translate through the filter of what they already believe. If they think God is angry, that is how they will see what God says, and how they will make Him sound.

Paul says, "There is then no condemnation to those in Christ Jesus, who don't walk according to flesh but according to spirit."[19] What he means is that regardless of what you do, God's loving attitude toward you never diminishes. He loves you and does not condemn you. That doesn't mean He is pleased with what you may have done, but He has already taken care of your behavior which was in Christ on the Cross and is now looking forward to teaching you the *truth* about that. However, just because God doesn't condemn you, doesn't mean you won't feel condemnation. In that same verse, Paul goes on to say that the condemnation will not be able to oppress those who walk according to spirit. So, you have a choice. You can walk according to flesh, which relies on your sense knowledge, bad experiences, and thoughts, or you can walk according to spirit, which has an attitude that chooses to believe that what God says is true even when circumstances, thoughts, and feelings say otherwise. If you walk by flesh, you will feel condemnation. If you live by spirit, you will increasingly enjoy peace. This conflict is the fight about which Paul wrote. If you're unable to make the conscious decision to walk by spirit instead of flesh, then ask God to work in you to make it so. It is a fact of Scripture that He is already working within you to make it real to you. Remember, your feelings come from your thoughts. Feelings never confirm or deny *truth*; they are just feelings. We get into trouble when we believe our physical senses convey God's *truth*. Satan's ability to manipulate our feelings by planting thoughts in our minds and people's insistence that those feelings represent *truth* has given Satan a devious way to control the world.

By the way, the word *condemnation* refers to more than feelings of guilt. It includes things like feeling you are condemned to a particular type of life or condition, whether it be emotional, physical, social, or financial. According to God, as you live by spirit, you will discover your life is not subject to any condemnation. Earlier when Paul says, "Therefore being justified by faith," he is plainly saying that God doesn't condemn you for anything, because you have believed Jesus

---

[19] Romans 8:1 (JEC)

was raised from dead and confessed Him as Lord. Because of deceptions embedded in your belief system, (of which you are unaware), your thoughts are being twisted to cause you to see something that isn't there and not see what God is saying. When that happens, talk to the Lord about your real thoughts and feelings. Be honest with Him. He can take it. Ask Him to show you what He really means and then, throughout the day, ponder it. He won't disappoint you. You aren't responsible for figuring it out. In His time, He will make it clear to you. Until then, He doesn't harbor a single negative thought toward you, because He is Love and loves you. The next time you read that passage may be the perfect time for God to show you what He means.

How Darkness Reacts to Light

Behavior that comes from a lie may seem to be unchangeable or impossible to stop. But once *the lie* that causes it is exposed and replaced with the *truth*, it will stop automatically. If it doesn't stop quickly, it is because there is more than one lie causing that behavior. It's no big deal. Just keep cooperating with God and, eventually, He'll get to other lies in that tangled mess of unbeliefs creating problems. Then your experience will change. It's guaranteed. He is "the starter and finisher of our faith (beliefs)."[20] He *will* complete the work He has started in you; much of it in this life, the rest later. But God has no intention of sitting there and refusing to help while he watches you suffer. Love can't do that. It's impossible.

Even though you may think otherwise, you *can* bear what's happening to you. God said you can. "He will not let you suffer beyond what you are able, but will with the temptation (to believe something other than His *truth*) provide a way of escape that you may be able to bear it."[21] God made you able to withstand what is happening, and He provided a way of escape. As you increasingly believe the *truth*, you will see it.

---

[20] Hebrews 12:2 (JEC)
[21] 1 Corinthians 10:13 (KJV)

The first time I understood this verse I was going through a tough experience and felt overwhelmed. Previously, my reaction would have been, "I can't bear this." But, I remembered that God said I *could* withstand it. If He would not let me be tried beyond what I was able to bear, then as much as I did not want to, I could take it. If I really couldn't withstand it, He would have stopped it. This was one of my first decisions to believe what God said rather than what flesh was telling me.

Inside the evil that men and nature cause, God is always working to cause good to be the ultimate result. "And we know that all things work together for good to them that love God, to them who are the called according to his purpose."[22] God illustrated His passion for turning evil into good in the Book of Genesis when Joseph was sold into slavery by his brothers.

After Joseph becomes second in charge of Egypt, during a famine his brothers appear before him in search of food. Until suddenly elevated to this dominant position, he lived as a slave. But, God had engineered Joseph's ascent to such power, in part, because He wanted to feed multitudes during that famine. When his brothers discovered Joseph was ruler of the world, they became afraid and expected him to take revenge. But, Joseph told them: "For though you devised evil against me, God planned on turning it into blessing."[23] While his brothers were engaged in evil against him, God was carrying out a plan to turn things into a spectacular blessing for Joseph and the entire world. And, throughout the horror and terror of his ordeal, Joseph believed God was with him.[24]

You say, "It can't be that easy." But, God said it *is* easy. "My yoke is easy and my burden is light."[25] So, when we find it difficult to trust God, it is because there is a lie someplace in our thinking that we have yet to recognize. The tricky thing about taking God's yoke is how easy it is. The *truth* is that God doesn't make our lives difficult, we do,

---

[22] Romans 8:28 (KJV)
[23] Genesis 50:20 (*A Translation of the Old Testament Scriptures from the Original Hebrew* by Helen Spurrell)
[24] Genesis 39:2
[25] Matthew 11:30 (JEC)

because *the lie* has infected humanity's thinking. How? By persuading us to believe things that are not true.

As you increasingly believe the *truth*, you will see yourself doing *truth*. Yet, the Word says it is Christ doing it in you. So, which is it? What's the *truth*? In this case, both are God's *truth*. By an act of God (which is a mystery), you are one with Christ and He is one with you. You are in union together, which means it is Him-you and you-Him doing everything together. Don't try to figure it out. Accept it as a mystery of godliness. "And without controversy great is the mystery of godliness," that is, the mystery of being like God."[26] You are one with Him. That's what God says. Paul said, "I live yet not I but Christ lives in me."[27] Again, it's a mystery as well as the *truth*. Hence, Paul's prayer in Ephesians Chapter One.

> And that is why we, from the very day that we heard this, have never given up praying for you, and asking that you may be filled with spiritual wisdom and intelligence, and so reach a perfect understanding of God's will.[28] I have prayed the all-glorious Father, the God of Jesus Christ our Lord, to inspire you with wisdom and true insight through a fuller knowledge of himself. I have prayed that your mental vision may be made so clear that you may know how great a hope is given by God's Call, what a wealth of glory there is in store for Christ's People, and how surpassingly great is the power which he is able to exercise for us who believe in him.[29]

God wants you to understand this. It is only the beliefs and the false knowledge you are holding on to with all your might that can prevent it. If what you are reading right now is logical to you or if you realize that there are probably some misbeliefs in your belief system, tell God. He

---

[26] 1 Timothy 3:16 (KJV)
[27] Galatians 2:20 (KJV)
[28] Colossians 1:1:9-10 (TCNT Part 2)
[29] Ephesians 1:17-19 (KJV)

already knows it anyway. He is eager to help you, but He won't force His *truth* on you.

Many justify wrong beliefs until God's light shines on them. Why not skip the pain and struggle and ask for light now; He will be happy to give it. In fact, even if you don't want the light, He is still shining it on you anyway. You've just not yet realized it. His light is brighter than any darkness seeking to invade our hearts.

In time, you will realize the darkness you are suffering and will be free to embrace the *truth* you might not yet clearly see. Many don't want the light of *truth* exposing the evil in their lives. That's why they love darkness. "Men loved darkness rather than light, because their deeds were evil."[30] The thought of having beliefs and behaviors proved wrong can be a threat to fake self-worth and to the false sense of security and comfort that many enjoy. Thus, they prefer darkness (lying, deception, manipulation) over light (*truth*, honesty, openness). People often continue to embrace lies even in the face of the failures they cause. That's because darkness hates challenge. Unlike *truth*, it despises godly reasoning—that is, reasoning that is like God's.

Our reactions to having beliefs challenged or rejected can vary.

- Anger: "Go to Hell."

- Denial: "There is nothing wrong with me. He/she is the one that needs to change."

- Justification: "I can't help it, this is the way I am" or "I was born with this temper" or "I'm just very emotional" or "I was raised this way."

- Condescension: Saying "I know that" when you don't.

- Repentance: "Oh, good. Now I know what my real problem is so I can *be* changed."

---

[30] John 3:19 (KJV)

- No response: This person is in a fog, which often shows up in an arrogance of such superiority that they are flippant about any evidence contrary to what they believe.

They must be challenged—but challenged in love. "But speaking the truth in love."[31] This is a prime reason for believers to get together. Paul dreamed of believers telling one another the *truth* about who they and God really are. As we continue to hear these *truths*, we begin to see them and eventually act like who we are.

The Power of Your Beliefs

When believed, *truth* is always accompanied by behavior that reflects it. In other words, believing the *truth* is not only the source of the right thoughts and behaviors, *it produces the energy and willingness necessary to create them.* There is no struggle involved. Your behavior changes naturally and automatically. Just like believing the *truth* provides the energy required to live it, believing a lie produces the type of energy that causes someone to sin (err). Have you ever met a successful person who believes they cannot win? Those who believe *I can* usually do, and those who believe *I can't* usually don't.

Beliefs are extremely powerful. Matthew 17:14-21 is the story of a demon-possessed boy who was suffering terribly and kept falling into the fire but whom the disciples were unable to help.

> At the bottom of the mountain, they met a crowd of waiting people. As they approached, a man came out of the crowd and fell to his knees begging, "Master, have mercy on my son. He goes out of his mind and suffers terribly, falling into seizures. Frequently he is pitched into the fire, other times into the river. I brought him to your disciples, but they could do nothing for him." Jesus said, "What a generation! No sense of God! No focus to your lives! How many times do I have to go over these things? How much longer do I have to put up with this? Bring the boy here."

---

[31] Ephesians 4:15 (KJV)

He ordered the afflicting demon out—and it was out, gone. From that moment on the boy was well. When the disciples had Jesus off to themselves, they asked, "Why couldn't we throw it out?" "Because you're not yet taking God seriously," said Jesus. "The simple truth is that if you had a mere kernel of faith, a poppy seed, say, you would tell this mountain, 'Move!' and it would move. There is nothing you wouldn't be able to tackle."[32]

When they asked Jesus why they could not cast out that devil, he said, "Because of your unbelief {Because you believe the wrong things}: for verily I say unto you, If ye have faith as a grain of mustard seed, ye shall say unto this mountain, Remove hence to yonder place; and it shall remove; and nothing shall be impossible unto you[33] (Chapter Eleven Endnotes #2).

This is not some sort of new-age "mind over matter" exercise. Jesus was talking about the result of true faith and true belief. When your actions or emotions contradict what you say you believe, it is proof that your belief system contains error, or the darkness is seeking to deceive you. If you believe something but your life has the opposite fruit, it is because you do not fully believe it. For instance, a deacon teaches the gospel of Jesus's love in Sunday school yet disdains people who do not live up to his expectations, or the businessman who gives to the church but commits crime to get the money to do it. It may be a little uncomfortable to admit your behavior is not consistent with what you believe, but the results can be marvelous. It can be the beginning of a quick end to inconsistencies, but until you admit you have been believing a lie, it continues working against what should be controlling your life, which is the *truth*. You will remain forever inconsistent in that area. Once you recognize that the source of inconsistency is an erroneous belief hidden in your belief system, you can discover what it is and change it.

Man's greatest need is not to figure out the right thing to do, but to believe the *truth*. The ultimate result of correct beliefs always is proper thoughts, feelings, and actions. You *can't* do this on your own, though

---

[32] Matthew 17:14-21 (msg)
[33] Matthew 17:20 (KJV)

the lie will push you to try. The Holy Spirit is here for you. He works gently to cause it to happen. Tell Him that's what you want.

* * *

Chapter Eleven Endnotes

Note 1

Psalm 1:1-3: "Blessed *is* the man that walketh not in the counsel of the ungodly, nor standeth in the way of sinners, nor sitteth in the seat of the scornful. But his delight *is* in the law of the LORD; and in his law doth he meditate day and night. And he shall be like a tree planted by the rivers of water, that bringeth forth his fruit in his season; his leaf also shall not wither; and whatsoever he doeth shall prosper."

Many people think that Psalm 1 is telling them what they should and shouldn't do. *Don't* walk in the counsel of the ungodly, *don't* get near sinners and *don't* sit around with people that scorn God. *Do* meditate in God's law both day and night. Then one day I realized that my interpretation was based on *the lie*. Consequently, though Psalm 1 contained a phenomenal promise, all I could see was the "thou shoulds and should nots." But, as I began to look at it from my new perspective, something struck me. There wasn't a single command in it. It was simply stating a fact, and I knew it was the *truth*. If someone could spend their entire life only following God's advice, only doing what good people do, and never scorning anyone or anything, or being cynical, critical, or sarcastic, that person would be really blessed. I pondered that. I realized the Psalmist was comparing someone not doing those things with someone who delighted in doing them. Then I thought of all the people I have known who seemed to enjoy being negative, critical and cynical. I had been one of them. Amazingly, now that I no longer did those things I felt so good. I realized the Psalmist was saying that the person who delights in God's instruction and meditates in His Word continually is blessed. I knew then that I wanted to spend the rest of my life pondering God's Word and allowing it to be my constant meditation. But, how could I do that? My mind was still so full of stuff, some good but much of it still *laborious and toilsome*. I knew that what I spend my time looking at is what becomes most real to me. I had been a news junkie, and as you know, news reports are seldom good. I was tired of seeing life from such negative perspectives. So, I asked God to show me how to spend more of my time considering His *truth*. It didn't happen overnight, but He did. And, this is how my understanding of God's Word has grown so much and become so real in my life. I will never go back to that old type of thinking and behavior. And then I realized... Jesus was a good Jew and had completely fulfilled God's law and instructions. "Do not think that I have come to abolish the Law or the Prophets; I have not come to abolish them but to fulfill them."[34] Jesus had read and pondered these same scriptures and had delighted in God's Word. Jesus had embraced the Word of God as His own, which, in fact, it was. But, now that I am in union with Christ and one with Him, His word is as much mine as it is His. When He gave me His Word, He gave me Himself. So, I told God that I wanted to think the Word of God like Jesus thinks it. And, each day I do more and more.

Note 2

Matthew 17:20 illustrates an important failure in translation. The original Greek is "διὰ τὴν ἀπιστίαν ὑμῶν" "because of your unbelief." The King James Version translates ἀπιστίαν as "unbelief," which is correct. Every other translation I reviewed rendered it as "little faith," or "not enough faith," etc. The difference between *unbelief* and *little faith* is a vast chasm. They mean two different things. The Greek could also be mean "not-belief."

Unbelief means a mistaken belief or believing the wrong thing. It has nothing to do with having enough faith. You can have plenty of faith (believe plenty of *truth*), yet one erroneous belief can reduce the effectiveness of your faith. Therefore, fellowship with the Holy Spirit and believers who know how to speak the *truth* in love is so important. The Holy Spirit is the only one that can expose to us what we believe that is not true. With all His heart, He wants to do it. He loves to do

---

[34] Matthew 5:17 (KJV)

it believer to believer. He is Love, so He will never demand that you submit to Him, and He will never embarrass you. Rather, He will wait patiently until your life circumstances cause you to want help. We need the Holy Spirit more than we realize. Without His help, we can be so close to seeing blessings that are already ours, yet miss them because of wrong beliefs.

    I'm sorry if this sounds harsh. It is part of God's plan that we were created to live by believing the *truth, because He lives by believing the truth*. Mankind decided to believe something else, and every human has inherited the results of that *lie*. Because human perceptions are filtered through *the lie*, though the unseen is right in front of them, the error prevents them from seeing it. The infection of *the lie* could only be stopped by the death, burial, and resurrection of Christ. He took us and it to death and rose again with a new life, which was no longer subject to its effects. Neither are you. "Sin can't tell you how to live. After all, you're not living under that old tyranny any longer. You're living in the freedom of God."[35] If we refuse to cooperate with the Holy Spirit, He will keep trying to sway our thinking. Until we repent (change our minds about what we believe), we will be unable to see the real target and continue to "miss the mark." There, now that definition of sin fits.

---

[35] Romans 6:14 (msg)

Part 4

So why are we the way we are? Because of our beliefs and the thoughts they generate. We have all learned things that are true and things that are false. The problem is, regardless which they were (true or false), we didn't know the difference. Since then, we have learned even more, layer upon layer. Over time, our beliefs and knowledge have become twisted together. Since *truth* and lies contradict each other, we become conflicted and confused. We see our actions, hear our words, and are perplexed by the contradictions. We say we believe one thing yet act the opposite.

The last four chapters have three major themes: repentance, grace, and a place where God's power is waiting for us, in plain sight.

1. If you've sat in a church pew for more than five minutes, you're probably familiar with the word *repent*. It's usually used in conjunction with coming to Christ and begging or pleading for forgiveness from some sin. Some places it includes feeling sorry. It focuses on wrong actions, thoughts, or emotions. While not completely inaccurate, its use in churches today misses the original meaning of repentance.

    Put simply, the Early Church understood *repent* to mean nothing more than changing your mind about what you believe. Technically, the word covers more than just religion. If you met someone who you didn't like because they were boring, and later realized they were a lot of fun and started liking them, you would have repented from your old belief (they're boring) and adopted the new one (they're fun). You repent when you realize a food you hated as a child is suddenly delicious. When we discuss repentance in the following chapters, we're not thinking about attending an alter call or going in front of hundreds (or thousands, if you're in a megachurch) of strangers and begging God for forgiveness for some sin about which you've been made to feel bad. *Repent* doesn't even mean responding to an alter call where you may confess Jesus is your Lord. In the New Testament, it means to change your mind about false knowledge you have treasured as true. Repentance is easy. What may seem hard is how easy it is. Letting go of wrong beliefs we have long cherished as important feels like death.

2. The idea of the grace of God is thrown around quite often these days, but it seems nebulous at best. So, we must ask the question, "What is it?" Simply put, the grace of God is nothing less than God having given Himself and everything that is important to Him to each of His children, and this includes His goodness in all its actions. In the years before the Early Church, grace could mean *birthday gift*.

3. The Apostle Paul wrote about "a demonstration of spirit and power." Where is it? It has been waiting for us, hidden safely in plain sight.

12
The Last Sin

So how do we begin this life-changing adventure? *Living in God's will is just allowing the truth to work from our inside to our outside.* That's all God wants. "Therefore, my dear friends, as you have always been obedient in the past, so now work out your own Salvation with reverence and awe, and that not only when I am with you, but all the more now that I am away."[1] God has put His Law in our hearts and written it in our minds. "This is the Covenant that I will make with the People of Israel after those days," says the Lord. "I will impress my laws on their minds, and will inscribe them on their hearts; and they will take me as their God, and I will take them as my People."[2]

A believer is a new creature in Christ. "Therefore if any man be in Christ, he is a new creature: old things are passed away; behold, all things are become new."[3] The believer is not only in Christ, but Christ is in the believer. "To whom God would make known what is the riches of the glory of this mystery among the Gentiles; which is Christ in you, the hope of glory."[4]

The single greatest key to allowing the *truth* (Jesus) to reign in our lives is being honest with ourselves and God. Unfortunately, as you're probably aware, it is sometimes not easy to be truthful, especially with ourselves. And we get a lot of help from sources that are not from God. But the more we come to think like Christ, the more we quit trying to hide from the way we have perceived ourselves. We are no longer afraid

---
[1] Philippians 2:12 (TCNT Part 2)
[2] Hebrews 8:10 (KJV)
[3] 2 Corinthians 5:17 (KJV)
[4] Colossians 1:27 (KJV)

of being uncovered. We are truly free because we finally know that the love—the complete, unequivocal acceptance we have been seeking—is now ours.

I have no desire to offend you. I just want you to know the *truth*. There is no one who does not lie, including you and me. Do you know to whom we lie the most? Ourselves. Why? Because the corruption of the creation began with a lie, which convinced us that we are as gods. Since real gods have all the answers and are always in control, we expect ourselves to have answers to every problem with the perfect response in every situation. *The lie* hides so skillfully that even though we may be born-again, we can't see it without the help of the Holy Spirit. It continues to exercise dominance in ways that sometimes leave us dumbfounded.

As a side note, just because you may have no problem admitting you are wrong doesn't mean you're unaffected by *the lie*. It just means it's affecting you in other ways. Without the work of the Holy Spirit in our hearts, none will ever recognize all the garbage they are believing. We may be new creatures in Christ, but we still have opportunities to believe lies. By the help of the Holy Spirit, we can admit it and He will open our eyes to see what we currently don't see. However, if we can't admit that we can't see, Jesus said we remain blind.

> Hereupon Jesus said, I have come into this world so that a sentence may fall upon it, that those who are blind should see, and those who see should become blind. Some of the Pharisees heard this, such as were in his company, and they asked him, Are we blind too? If you were blind, Jesus told them, you would not be guilty. It is because you protest, We can see clearly, that you cannot be rid of your guilt.[5]

The Message Bible puts it this way:

> "I came into the world to bring everything into the clear light of day, making all the distinctions clear, so that those

---

[5] John 9:39-41 (Knox Translation, 1935)

> who have never seen will see, and those who have made a great pretense of seeing will be exposed as blind." Some Pharisees overheard him and said, "Does that mean you're calling us blind?" Jesus said, "If you were really blind, you would be blameless, but since you claim to see everything so well, you're accountable for every fault and failure."[6]

Lying activated the law of *the error* and *the death* (you'll often see it translated "the law of sin and death," but the original Greek says *the* sin and *the* death—because it's referring to a particular sin and death, not just sin and death in general).[7] It is the most prominent characteristic of Satan, who was at one time a father figure to us.

> As for you, you are children of your father the Devil, and you are determined to do what your father loves to do. He was a murderer from the first, and has no place in the truth, because there is no truth in him. Whenever he lies, he is doing what is natural to him; because he is a liar, and the father of lying.[8]

We learned it from him and it governs the world. When a soul is alive to God, the undoing of its influence was accomplished by the renewal of the mind, which, again, God declares is a fact and not an act to be performed by man.[9] Only the Holy Spirit can make it real in your life. The last error from which anyone experiences freedom is believing lies, for all other sins stem from that.

Lying has infected the world and is the most damaging habit remaining after we are made alive in Christ. The powers of darkness seek to permeate our souls and belief systems with lies. Believing *lies* results in every type of sin, including our efforts to be gods in this life, even

---

[6] John 9:39-41 (msg)
[7] Romans 8:2 (KJV)
[8] John 8:44 (TCNT Part 1)
[9] The Greek word often translated as "renewing" is a noun, not a verb. The proper translation is "renewal." Thus, the apostle was using it to explain something that is already a reality and not something you need to do.

after we have believed into Jesus. Before the new birth, we are saturated in deception. The new birth provides the way of escape because it is at that moment that the Holy Spirit snuggles up inside the believer. He is the one who works the *truth* into you. His work is to cause your will to mirror His will and then do it. First and foremost, His will is for us to believe His *truth*. Thus, He wants you to believe Him.[10] Your life in Christ Jesus flows out of that.

The corruption of our thinking from *the lie* is not always apparent, so error based behaviors may not be obvious. For instance, worry, gossip, lies, lust, and dishonesty are all results of *the lie*. Without the help of the Holy Spirit, it is impossible ever to remove *the lie* and its effects from our hearts. We not only believe things that are not true, but we would also often rather die than admit we are wrong.

The Freedom to Be Honest

So, how do we change? First, we must understand that deceiving ourselves is a means of protecting our treasuring of *the lie, that we must be in control*. By not admitting that we made an error, we avoid the trauma of being exposed. Since *the lie* has taught us that we are right, the possibility of being wrong implies being defective, which is terrifying. This is not to say that we never admit we're wrong. It just means that we have trouble doing it about the beliefs we treasure most. Only the Holy Spirit knows what issues are closest to our hearts. Self-deception protects us from having to admit we are wrong.

The only way to overcome self-deception is to know that God loves you unconditionally and that His love for you is generous, thoughtful, kind, and powerful. No matter how much you know that He loves you, you don't yet know it like God wants you to. In fact, stop right now. Take a moment and ponder this: "God loves me, period. He loves me

---

[10] In Romans 1:5 (KJV) Paul writes "By whom we have received grace and apostleship, for obedience to the faith among all nations, for his name." Paul concludes his epistle by saying (Romans 16:26) that, by the commandment of God, His knowledge is being made known "to all nations for the obedience of faith." In both cases, the "obedience to/of the faith" means "...obedience of hearing and believing the *truth*...."

no matter what I do or haven't done and whatever I believe or don't believe. He delights in me because He says He does, even though I don't understand how that is possible." As you sit there, tell God this is the *truth* even though you may not feel it. Do this for five or ten minutes each day. As that realization grows in you, you will experience change.

People often claim to know something when, in fact, they only know facts about it. Above all things, we don't need to know *about* God's love. We need to know in the deepest part of our beings that His love is *for* us. This was the point of Paul's statement in Ephesians 3:17-19, "Being rooted and founded in love through the belief [of the *truth*] in your hearts, that ye may be fully able to seize for yourself, with all the saints, what is the breadth and length and depth and height and to know the love of Christ that surpasses knowledge that you may be filled to all the fullness of God."

The love God has for you is in you. It is time to *be* filled. How? By agreeing it is true. Just agree that the Spirit of God has filled you and is working to make His reality, which is also now your reality, real to you. The world will eventually see it in you. Your thoughts and feelings do not have to agree with what you say. In fact, they probably won't. It is what you say in agreement with God that will become real to you. If you wait for it to feel real before you say it, it won't happen. You do not have to be worthy to be loved by God. You do not have to become worthy to take God's love. God loves you because of who He *is*, independent of anything you do. Nothing you can do or not do ever affects God's love for you. He created you because He wants to love you. You cannot stop the love He has for you. As you say yes, you will come to know it in experience. And, no matter how much you believe God loves you, you probably haven't scratched the surface. Ask Him to help you believe and understand and know His love for you. There is no end to it. Everything you are flows out of His love. "We love because he first loved us."[11] As you increase in the knowledge of God's love for you, you will grow in honesty with God and yourself. Knowing that God loves us without requiring us to do or be anything in return means we

---

[11] 1 John 4:19 (KJV)

don't have to fear to be honest with ourselves. Next, be willing to admit when you feel hurt, desire to do wrong, or have done wrong.

Have you ever been offended by someone who immediately apologized, and you responded "that's ok" or "forget it, it was nothing" when it really wasn't? Do you realize that was a lie? It was *not* okay, and you do not want them to forget it. What they did hurt but unless you admit it—especially to yourself—you will have accepted one more seemingly insignificant lie. You may say something this small doesn't matter. In and of itself, a single act of self-deception may lack serious repercussions. But if you have done it once, your life has probably been filled with many similar experiences. It's a bigger deal than you may think. If it was the first time, it will not be the last, unless you deal with it now. Willingly exposing error to the light nullifies its power. It is good to admit when you have lied to yourself, or when circumstances permit, tell an offending person you have not been honest with them either. "You did hurt me, but I have accepted your apology and forgiven you." Of course, it would be better to be honest in the first place and only respond to a person's apology with "I forgive you." This way, you admit that you do not like what they did but do not hold a grudge.

The same applies to inappropriate behavior. If you refuse to admit you have done wrong, its source (some false belief) remains hidden in your heart, doing only God knows what damage.

Something God Doesn't Know

Do you know you have learned things that God doesn't know? It's true! The All-Knowing God doesn't know many things that you know. "That's crazy," you say. "You're a lunatic." Before you write me off, remember I said earlier that God knows what's in our hearts. He knows what we believe and all about what we have learned, but it is not part of the body of the knowledge from which He lives. Some of what we "know" is wrong; God knows that it is wrong, but it is not part of His body of knowledge.

Mistaken knowledge can control our lives, just as the *truth* that we believe does. In other words, our misbeliefs have become part of our body of knowledge, our body of error, and because we believe them, we automatically live them. God knows what we know, and He knows what of our beliefs are false and what of our beliefs are true. Thus, our false knowledge is not part of the body of knowledge which governs His *being*. He knows intimately about our error; He does not know it as *truth* but as deception. God does not know what we know in the same way we know what we know. Thus, I say that we know things that God doesn't know.

Maybe the following is a better explanation. Many times, I have told the Lord that I want to know what He knows the way He knows it and not know anything that He doesn't know. Likewise, I want to believe what Jesus believes and not believe anything He doesn't believe. Make sense now?

Every aspect of your life is already visible to God, so you do not have to be afraid to admit to yourself and God that something you do or believe is wrong. Admitting our errors allows God to fix them. In fact, a more understandable rendering of 1 John 1:9 is: "If we confess our errors (sin), He is faithful and just to forgive us our errors, and to cleanse us from all unrighteousness (the sinful acts resulting from wrong beliefs)."[12] This is an important way of inviting the Holy Spirit to work in your life since He will never force Himself on you. When we admit to erring, we are giving Him consent to help us, even though we may not know how to ask Him. We are telling Him to "help me to quit being wrong."

Personally, I want to know when I am wrong. If I don't find out where I am wrong, the error will remain. In some cases, I may be the only one who doesn't know I am wrong. That is embarrassing. As a practical example, everyone has walked out of a restroom or seen someone else walk out with toilet paper hanging out of their pants. I'd rather know about that before someone sees me.

---

[12] 1 John 1:9 (JEC)

James E. Campbell, Jr, James Q. Campbell

Why Forgiveness

Forgiveness can be painful because of what it represents. Forgiving someone means giving up responsibility for making them pay for what they did. Remember the False Responsibility Syndrome? Responsibility is not forced upon us; we often welcome it. Unfortunately, we gravitate toward the wrong type. We quickly take responsibility for things we are not capable of handling. When it comes to offenses and hurts, we definitely can't handle them.

Vengeance and anger may seem to provide relief, but they cannot. Unforgiveness is a cancer that hides in our hearts and produces sickness and confusion.

> Phyllis' mother-in-law, Martha, was critical and merciless. No matter what Phyllis did, no matter how hard she tried, it wasn't good enough. In fact, it was wrong. She raised three well-behaved boys. Everyone that knew them loved them, but not Martha. It seemed like she had nothing but criticism for everything related to Phyllis, even to her own son, who was Phyllis' husband. Her mother-in-law was very wealthy and blamed Phyllis for the fact that her son was having such severe financial problems. It was all Phyllis' fault. She knew she had been a good mother and wife but even so, according to Martha, everything was still her fault.
>
> Martha seldom let up and the pain in Phyllis' heart grew. She hoped that some failure would happen to Martha's other children or grandchildren so she wouldn't be Martha's only in-law with problems. Phyllis felt her bitterness was justified. Over the years, the hurt continued to build, and because Phyllis has never faced the pain, she is not only bitter now, but also sick.

There are other reasons people have trouble forgiving. Forgiveness is an admission that we are leaving the person in God's hands to do with as He pleases. Since He is merciful, it is possible He may forgive them, which means they might get away with what they did. Since as gods we believe we have the right to deal out vengeance, we don't like that possibility. Sadly, *the lie* tells us we *must* believe that we are gods. It has been crammed down our throats. With man, it is impossible to fix. But with God, all things are possible."[13]

To some, forgiveness appears weak. They would rather spend a lifetime filled with bitterness than enjoy freedom. Regardless of what you think, no one escapes the damage caused by the unwillingness to forgive. It always comes back to bite the non-forgiver. When we fear the repercussions of letting go of a mistaken belief like, "I can't forgive him because then he'll get away with what he did," the ultimate damage to our hearts and minds is far worse than anything anyone has ever done to us. The person who hurt you will likely never know how successful they were, because they never get to see the result of what you do to yourself in your efforts to cause them pain. Unforgiveness causes far more pain to the person unwilling to release the one that hurt them. But, the act of forgiving strengthens our hearts to direct more energy toward freedom and fulfillment.

Many people misunderstand forgiveness. They fear becoming a doormat, which is not what forgiveness does (Chapter Twelve Endnotes #1). Forgiveness does not mean you have to ever again associate with the person; it is not an act of reconciliation.

Coming to The Light

Being honest with ourselves about what we think and feel and the real motives for our actions is called coming to the light.

> Everyone who makes a practice of doing evil, addicted to denial and illusion, hates God-light and won't come near it, fearing a painful exposure. But anyone working and living in truth and reality welcomes God-light so others can

---

[13] Matthew 19:26 (KJV)

see the God-work it is.[14] This act always brings healing to the soul.

My search for sanity and fulfillment spanned many years. I tried every Bible strategy I heard preached. I could never do everything I was supposed to. I could not muster the depth of discipline required. Years of seeking perfection left me frustrated and robbed of all joy and peace. There was not enough time in the day to do everything I had been taught about having a prosperous family, business, social life, and relationship with God. I saw people who seemed well off in one area of life, but almost always with trouble in another area. For example, the very successful businessman who can't seem to have a good marriage. But, I believed there had to be a key to abundant life, and I wanted to know it. I believed that if God did not want us to know Him, He would not have given us His Word. The fact that we have the Bible is the evidence I needed to believe God wanted me to understand. The key to abundant life had to be plain; I just couldn't see it. There had to be a way other than the frustration I was experiencing. My heart cried out for it. My dissatisfaction with religion turned out to be a good thing. For you, the dissatisfaction may be something else. What it is makes no difference; the fact you are dissatisfied and want change is the important thing.

The process of believing God's *truth* is infectious. Regardless of where it starts, it will spread to other areas. Jesus said wrong beliefs are like leaven (yeast): "Take heed and beware of the leaven of the Pharisees and of the Sadducees."[15] So, too, are our right beliefs. "The kingdom of heaven is like unto leaven, which a woman took and hid in three measures of meal, till the whole was leavened."[16] Regardless of what you believe—right or wrong, *truth* or lies— its influence will spread and bear more of its fruit. "Are you not aware that even a little leaven leavens all the dough?"[17] Believing the *truth* naturally produces

---

[14] John 3:20-21 (msg)

[15] Matthew 16:6 (KJV)

[16] Matthew 13:33 (KJV)

[17] 1 Corinthians 5:6 (TCNT Part 2)

fruit; so, too, when believing lies. "Ye shall know them by their fruits. Do men gather grapes of thorns, or figs of thistles? Even so every good tree bringeth forth good fruit; but a corrupt tree bringeth forth evil fruit?"[18]

There is only one key to experiencing a renewed mind and growing up into the fullness of Christ—that is, believing God's *truth* instead of any other. Our beliefs enable us to cooperate with God as He works in our lives for good, or they make us resist His love, which prevents us from recognizing His gifts. Our beliefs affect our responses and subsequent results in every one of life's challenges. The issue of what we believe is critical; in it can be found the answer to every one of life's challenges. The importance of God's love and trusting it should be emphasized, often to the deliberate exclusion of every other factor that influences our lives.

As our bodies naturally heal themselves, so do our hearts and minds. Our hearts and minds are powerful spiritual organs that will produce remarkable results if given proper care. We cannot force them. It is *not* God's will for you to struggle. Just cooperate with your inner being by rejecting lies. The Holy Spirit is the one who teaches you how to do that. This was Paul's whole point when he said, "For as many as are led by the Spirit of God, they are the sons of God."[19] He was not referring to hearing and obeying some voice; rather, he was talking about putting to death the deeds of the body. Those that are led by the Spirit to mortify (put to death) the deeds of the flesh (the wrong responses of our senses) are the sons of God. "For if ye live after the flesh, ye shall die: but if ye through the Spirit do mortify the deeds of the body, ye shall live. For as many as are led by the Spirit of God, they are the sons of God."[20]

Many versions translate the first instance of the word in the passage as though it means the Spirit of God. However, unlike the second sentence, there is no article in the first sentence. A more accurate translation is: "For if ye live after flesh, ye shall die: but if ye through

---

[18] Matthew 7:16-17 (KJV)
[19] Romans 8:14 (KJV)
[20] Romans 8:13-14 (KJV)

spirit do mortify the deeds of the body, ye shall live."[21] Though that is not enough to prove it doesn't refer to the Holy Spirit, when taken in context with a proper understanding of Paul's use of the word *spirit*, it is clear he is referring to an attitude that chooses to believe the *truth*, which automatically kills evil deeds. When you believe God's *truth*, you are living the faith of Jesus Christ. When you believe the same as Jesus, when you allow His mind to be in you, then you think like He does which automatically mortifies the deeds of the flesh. Only the Holy Spirit can show you how to do this. No one can accomplish it by willpower. If you are struggling, it is because you believe a lie.

    The way to begin cooperating is by being honest. Complete honesty is achieved over time and can only occur as we grow in the knowledge of God's love for us. When we know that we are loved, we find the strength and courage to be fully honest with others and ourselves. Your first act of honesty with God may be admitting that you do not really believe He loves you. Go ahead. Talk to Him about what you believe—good and bad, true and false. When you realize you think something about Him that is not true, tell Him. That realization itself is from God. In fact, ask God to show you what you believe about Him that is not true. He'll be glad to do it. This process takes time, but God loves you the whole way. For instance, some believe God is going to hate them or punish them if they make a mistake. If that applies to you, admit it. Admit what you feel. Then remind the Lord of His *truth* that He loves you unconditionally and can't lie about it. You're reminding Him of His *truth* for your benefit, not because He needs to be told. As we become comfortable talking to God honestly, we become even more comfortable doing it. Did you know that is all a prayer is? It's just talking to God about anything. If you do not *feel* His *truth* is true, admit it and then tell Him that it is true because He says so. "The *fact* is, Father, that you do love me unconditionally, even though I don't feel it and don't feel like I believe it."

    Of course, if you're saying it to try to fool God, don't bother. He knows what's in your heart. Maybe you don't think you believe God's *truth but want to*. That is good enough. Tell Him it is true *because He*

---

[21] Romans 8:13 (JEC)

says so. He'll joyfully take care of the rest. Remember, faith (believing) is a gift of God. "For by grace are ye saved through faith; and that not of yourselves: it is the gift of God." [22] God has never been stingy even though flesh screams that He is, but there can be things delaying the seeing of gifts. The problem is not on God's side, but ours. So, we need help getting out of the way. He is not withholding any good thing for which you ask; "how much more shall your Father which is in heaven give good things to them that ask him?"[23]

Love Casts Out Fear of Rejection

Family is the one group of people from whom we especially need to find unconditional acceptance. If people do not have a family from which they can get unconditional love and acceptance, they will seek it elsewhere. Therefore, it is critical for people to learn the *truth* about the Holy Trinity Family's love. If we do not know the right meaning of God's love for us, we will look for it in some deception. It is the knowledge of God's love for us that truly protects us from being deceived. God loves us without hesitation or conditions. Nothing outside of His self causes Him to love us. He loves us because of who He is. What you do or have done has no effect on His love for you. His care for you is unlimited. There is nothing you have done or can do in this world that will ever prevent Him from loving you. He accepts you just as you are, faults and all. It is God's intention that you be filled with Himself, and only He can make you realize that you were simply created to *be*. You cannot make it happen. He does not need or desire your help, only your agreement.

Some people are attracted to the type of acceptance that depends on following the rules. If the love you are receiving is dependent upon your behavior or accomplishments, it is not love. Unconditional love is never contingent upon someone living according to another's dictates. This is not to say that wrong behavior should be overlooked or

---

[22] Ephesians 2:8 (KJV)

[23] Matthew 7:11"How much more shall your Father which is in heaven give good things to them that ask him?"

accepted, because it often shouldn't. Only God can show you how to deal with it in His love. Knowing we are loved purges fear from our hearts. It is only by knowing God's love that our hearts can release the truth about what we really believe to us.

How do I know believing occurs in our hearts? Paul said, "If thou... shalt believe in thine heart."[24] King David said, "He fashioneth their hearts alike."[25] In other words, because humans are created to live what we believe and because believing occurs in the heart, God has made all human hearts alike. All our hearts work the same. The issue of faith applies equally to everyone. Solomon said to protect your heart because out of it flow the issues of life. "With all watchfulness guard thine heart; For out of it *flow* the actions of life.[26] The bottom line is, since we live what we believe, our lives flow out of what is in our hearts. Without the confidence that you are unconditionally accepted, your inner-self resists giving up its secrets. Thus, you never discover the whole truth about what you believe that is wrong. The threats are too big. Without unconditional acceptance, the thought of someone exposing our misbeliefs causes our hearts to cringe in fear.

We desperately need to know that if those most important to us ever find out the whole truth, they will still love and accept us. Fortunately, God already knows the whole truth about each one of us, and accepts us with open arms. When He becomes your source of love, the fear of being exposed ceases. The day is coming when the family of God will overflow with love for each other and the world. While we are waiting, God is working to remove the obstacles hindering our realization of it. As we grow in the confidence of God's love for us, we can boldly confront misbeliefs without fear of rejection. This type of honesty is not the end; it is only the beginning of real life.

---

[24] Romans 10:9 (KJV)
[25] Psalms 33:15 (KJV)
[26] Proverbs 4:23 (*A Translation of the Old Testament Scriptures from the Original Hebrew* by Helen Spurrell)

Listen to Yourself

Personally, my goal is to exchange all the misbeliefs I have embraced with beliefs based on the *truth*. To that end, I use a tool to help me work through the maze of thoughts that sometimes overwhelm me. Occasionally, I sit down with a journal and write what I am telling myself and what I am thinking. This is how I see, in black and white, what I am telling myself, which helps me to know what I am believing. I just write what I am saying to myself in my thoughts.

Over the years, I have been surprised at how ridiculous some of the things I have believed are. In fact, there have been times when I was shocked to learn some of the things I believed because I was convinced I thought the exact opposite. No kidding!

There have been a few times when I found that something I was telling myself was so terrible or embarrassing that after presenting it to God, I burned the paper. The way I start my journal is to "listen" to my thoughts when I am agitated, paying attention to what I am telling myself. For me, it is not enough to just be aware of what I am thinking. To get the most benefit, I must write it. Seeing my thoughts in writing sometimes makes it easier for me to cooperate with the Holy Spirit as He exposes my misbeliefs and enables me to repent. *Telling Yourself the Truth* by Dr. Backus, who we talked about in chapter 11, explains journaling.

If you take the time to work through your self-talk with a journal, you will undoubtedly discover things you believe that will make you laugh, cry, or sometimes want to hide from yourself. All you do is write what you are thinking. Unfortunately, in this world where there are thought police, after you have dealt with something you may not want others to know, it is probably best to burn that part of your journal. The purpose of this type of exercise is to help you face the truth, both about what you believe is true that is wrong and the *truth* that should replace it. Your journal is not for others to find out what you have been thinking.

James E. Campbell, Jr, James Q. Campbell

The following story is one of the many instances God has used to show me how changing a belief in a lie can set someone free. In this case, I never even had to write it down.

> During the terrible experience of burnout that I mentioned earlier, my secretary (who I will call Tricia) and I grew very close. It was a rough period—one in which my wife and I had no answers. Tricia had been through something similar and was a great comfort to me. As you can imagine, I developed unyielding feelings for her. In fact, I became concerned that I might behave wrongly under certain circumstances. I loved my wife and did not want those feelings for my secretary. My business was very technical and because of my mental condition, it could not have survived without her so terminating her employment was not an option. I was desperate to rid myself of the feelings for Tricia and turned to my wife for help. Sandra has an amazing outlook on things, so I knew she would understand. God calls our spouses *a help*. "Also JEHOVAH God said, It is not good that the man be alone; I will make him a help to be a companion for him."[27]
>
> Though talking to Sandra was good and helped, I still struggled with thoughts and desires for my secretary. Then one day as I was driving across town listening to the radio, I heard two guys having a conversation about men who need more than one woman to be satisfied. Suddenly, I heard myself say, "That's what I believe." For the first time in my life, I was aware that I *believed* I needed more than one woman to be satisfied. *I also knew it was a lie!* The Holy Spirit had worked in the tormenting lust for my secretary and that radio conversation to bring the *truth* about *the lie* I believed to the surface. Only then could it be eliminated.

---

[27] Genesis 2:18 (*A Translation of the Old Testament Scriptures from the Original Hebrew* by Helen Spurrell)

That was a critical moment in my life. I could have reacted as some Christians would, by denying I believed something so horrible. If I had followed one Christian teaching, I would have said, "I rebuke you, Satan."

Fortunately, I recognized that the Holy Spirit had revealed it to me and that He had known about it long before. I intuitively knew it was an opportunity for a new type of honesty with God and I took it. Sure, I may have *felt* I needed more than one woman, but the *truth* was that God had created me to be satisfied by my wife alone.

I remember saying out loud, "Until this moment, if someone had told me I believed I needed more than one woman, I would have told them they were crazy. But the *truth* is, I have believed this, and it is a lie. *Your truth* is, I only need one woman, the woman I married, Sandra." Within seconds, something unexpected happened. I felt and heard something like a *pop*. The desire for my secretary disappeared and never returned. Since then I have discovered many lies in my belief system and experienced many surprising instances of new freedom, but have never again experienced that *pop*.

Recognizing Wrong Beliefs

I know others can often see the results of what I believe better than I can. That is why it is good to fellowship with those who hunger for God's *truth*. "But speaking the *truth* [to one another] in love."[28] In fact, when you fellowship with people who hunger for God's *truth* more than life itself, you will see miracles.

If I refuse to see and acknowledge wrong beliefs, they will continue to control me. Though the thought of uncovering a misbelief may frighten or embarrass me, my awareness of the problems that misbeliefs

---

[28] One of the primary reasons for fellowship with other believers is the sharing of *truth* (Ephesians 4:15). The point wasn't to go to church and get talked at by the guy on stage for an hour or two but to engage and fellowship with one another to offer correction and replace misbeliefs with *the truth*.

cause motivates me to be honest. I have *never not* been excited to have the Holy Spirit show me an incorrect belief and fix it. However, I have learned that is His work, and I cannot hurry Him. This is part of the process of coming to know Him and His unconditional love. The process of exposing the lies you believe is between you and God. No one else knows what is happening in your heart. Others will only see the evidence of a changed life.

Repentance

Repentance is an important word in the New Testament, yet few seem to understand what it means. To most, it has a negative connotation so if you think you understand repentance, hold on to your seat.

First, remember what Jesus said. "If ye continue in my word, then are ye my disciples indeed; and ye shall know [the same way God knows] the truth and the truth shall make you free."[29] Once you understand God's definition of repentance, you will be able to begin moving into the abundance of freedom to which Jesus was referring.

By the way, to continue in God's Word does not mean just to read or study the Bible. The Greek word usually translated *continue* or *abide* has other meanings like "to stand by one's opinion."[30,31] It also means "to snuggle down into." It means to hold fast to the *truth* you have believed from His Word, to stand by your belief in the *truth* and not be moved by experiences to the contrary. It means to be so comfortable with what God says that it feels like home. It is synonymous with Paul's understanding of the "fight of faith" (the fight to believe the *truth* when our experience is telling us it isn't true).[32]

---

[29] John 8:31-32 (KJV) words in brackets ( ) are my explanations, notes, or comments.

[30] Greek: μένω "to abide or stand by one's opinion"

[31] (a) opinion. a personal view, attitude, or appraisal. (Modern Language Association (MLA): "opinion." *Collins English Dictionary—Complete & Unabridged 10th Edition*. HarperCollins Publishers. 23 Nov. 2012. Dictionary.com http://dictionary.reference.com/browse/opinion.) (b) Beliefs or opinions as spoken of in the Scriptures are based on the absolute certainty of the New Covenant and faith as explained in Hebrews 11:1.

[32] 1 Timothy 6:12

Most people are familiar with the word *repent*. It repels many because it is so often used in a legalistic and condemning manner. But, repentance is a tremendous word and is fundamental to a relationship with God. In a religious context, you will commonly hear *repent* defined as "to decide you are wrong and turn around and go the other direction" or "to feel sorry for your sin and choose to stop." But neither definition even gets close to the original meaning. This incorrect understanding is a result of *the lie* and has led to legalism that has caused many people to push away from God. People know intuitively they cannot stop doing wrong things, even though they may want to. The translation of the Greek word for *repenting* means nothing other than "to change your mind upon reflection."[33] Based on this definition, you may recognize that we all repent daily. In fact, you cannot keep track of how many times you change your mind (or repent) each day. The subject is important because Hebrews 6:1 says that an understanding of faith and repentance is fundamental for growing up in Christ. "Therefore leaving the principles of the doctrine of Christ, let us go on unto perfection; not laying again the foundation of repentance from dead works, and of faith toward God."[34] If what you believe about *repentance* from dead works or faith is incorrect, your experience of God will be shaky at best.

Of course, a thoughtful reader of the New Testament would ask himself, "Change your mind about what?" Though this is a proper and legitimate question, our belief of *the lie* usually leads people to the wrong conclusion. Remember how we have discussed man's search for value and meaning through his performance? This is not just a superficial condition; it also goes to the very depths of our believing. Because our performance determines our value, which affects our perspective on life, it is easier to judge the quality of our lives by what we do and possess than by who we are.

---

[33] μετανοία (*metanoia*) "to change your mind upon reflection."

[34] Hebrews 6:1 is talking about specific principles that must be established in a believer's heart before they can move on to perfection. If the principles are not established, there is no moving on to maturity. The principles are the foundation. They're basic. Our lives in Christ do not go deeper. There is no such thing as a *deeper* life.

Doing the right things has become more important than the quality of a person's life. In fact, quality of life is defined by *doing* or *possessing*, rather than *being*. Rather than focusing on the results of union with Christ, we compare ourselves with others. We compare what we do and have with what they do and have or our position in society against theirs. When our understanding is founded on lies, it creates a never-ending spiral of misunderstanding as we evaluate each new experience or piece of knowledge based on prior beliefs that were also influenced by lies. By becoming established in the fundamental *truths* of love, faith, and repentance and building from there, we correct a myriad of misbeliefs in our hearts.[35] Just by correcting one belief sometimes a mass of other ones will change automatically. I call it the domino effect. Too many people assume they already know *the principles of the doctrine of Christ* and thus seek to *go on unto perfection*. Not only have they never laid the foundation this Scripture speaks about, but they miss ever laying it. It is important to note that the Greek text usually translated "repentance from dead works" is more accurately rendered "repentance away from dead works."[36] Changing our minds about wrong beliefs leads us away from the dead works. Why do so few ever discover intimacy with God? Could it be because they don't know the principles of Jesus's teachings?

Before I explain how the New Testament uses the word *repent*, I would like to clarify the confusion regarding faith. Since repentance is all about believing, understanding faith will also make repentance easier to grasp. *Faith* is a noun that means belief or trust. In this book, I have used the definition "belief" because that is the primary emphasis in the New Testament. As you learn to believe God's *truth* and what He says, trust comes with it. It is because you believe that you can say to God, "I trust You." It is because you believe that when you say to God, "I trust You, Lord," you mean it. You can't trust someone who you don't believe.

Why do you think Paul said in Ephesians 6:13, "Having done all to stand, then stand!" He wasn't saying that if you stand the problem will

---

[35] Hebrews 6:1

[36] Greek preposition, ἀπό (*apo*) "away from"

go away, because it *may not* go away. Many believers are waiting for God to take away their problems. God says, "No. In this dilemma, you are going to learn how to stand by believing the *truth* rather than sense knowledge (flesh), and the result will be that you HAVE overcome." In some cases, the freedom you will experience may leave you not knowing if the problem was fixed or you just got bigger than the problem so that it no longer affects you. But, who cares? You will be living the victory of faith, believing the *truth*. God wants us to learn to stand and keep believing that what He says is our reality, regardless of our circumstances. As we stand, continuing to focus our attention on His *truth* rather than problems, we become so caught up in the wonder of our Father's love and our Lord's grace that we eventually forget about the problem. In fact, the third time Paul uses the word "stand" in that passage it is a command. This is serious business. After the command to stand, he describes ways that God's *truth* makes it real to you.

The key to understanding the New Testament is not searching it to learn the right things to do, but to learn God's *truth* and how He believes and thinks. The Holy Spirit gave us His Word so that we could know Him, who He *is*, and what He has done or will do. The Scriptures are a revelation of the God who *is* Love. The Holy Spirit uses those words to teach us about His love. That's why Satan works so hard to make people think that the corruption in the Earth is from God. Satan can't afford to have believers know God's love because the victory that Jesus won for us would then become apparent and God's reality would be real to us. Satan would be finished.[37] Satan doesn't want human beings to learn that Jesus proved he is a liar and they can now refuse to believe him. But God is intent on making sure we know. "And this is the victory, the [victory] having overcome the world, our faith."[38] This verse says that believing the *truth* is the win. Why? Because the goal of the powers of darkness is to cause us to think lies are the *truth*. When we refuse to agree with the darkness, God says we have won.

---

[37] Hebrews 2:14 (KJV): "That through death he might destroy him that had the power of death, that is, the devil."

[38] 1 John 5:4 (JEC) "καὶ αὕτη ἐστὶν ἡ νίκη ἡ νικήσασα (aorist active participle) τὸν κόσμον ἡ πίστις ἡμῶν"

The victory is not getting rid of a problem but believing the *truth* in the face of Satan's lies. We aren't waiting for the circumstances to change before we believe. We believe what God tells us is the *truth* even if conditions say things will never change. We stand by our announcement to ourselves that we will never reject what God says is the *truth*. That's victory! Paul's fight of faith was not to get rid of problems but to stand immovable as problems assaulted him, and to stand in his belief while God worked to deliver him, and then to continue believing after the problem was gone. The victory is the fact that we determine to think the *truth* even though all sense knowledge, including our emotions, is screaming that God's *truth* is not true. We have victory, even though we may feel otherwise.

It doesn't usually feel good to disagree with the powers of darkness. Though they cannot touch us, they know how to manipulate our emotions, which can cause us to want to think contrary to the *truth*. God sees your faith. To Him, that is the victory. So, if God thinks you have the victory simply because you believe His *truth* is the only *truth*, then you have it. And, as you continue to stand, you will see it. But, don't put a time frame on God. He will not stop working until you see your reality in Christ, in this life. If there is a delay, it is not because of God. It is because of us. But, God is working until our eyes are open to see what He has already done for us and inside us.

The battle is between *truth* and lies. Our beliefs automatically produce their fruit. To put it another way, God is *not* result-oriented, but belief-oriented. If we believe His *truth*, He automatically gets the result He wants. So, don't worry about your results. They are God's business. In writing about his and Apollos' ministries, Paul wrote, "I have planted, Apollos watered; but God gave the increase." If you can apply this to the winning of souls, it applies to everything else. In the case of this discussion, we believe, and God produces the results. If you don't see results in your time frame, that doesn't change the *truth*. Just believe; the results and the timing are according to God's plan. Though "the whole world lieth in wickedness," God wants us to live in the light.[39] "But if we walk in the light, as he is in the light, we have fellowship

---

[39] 1 John 5:19 (KJV)

one with another, and the blood of Jesus Christ his Son cleanseth us from all sin."[40] Very simply, if we live an open and honest life with God, we don't have to hide our true selves from others because the blood of Jesus cleanses us from all error and sinful behavior. Satan wants us to live in darkness, being controlled by anything but the *truth*. He is the one who introduced darkness into the world. The obedience of faith is the obedience of believing God's *truth*.[41] The fight of faith is the determination to trust that God's *truth* is true even in the face of evidence that denies it. "Fight the good fight of faith."[42]

God is more concerned with what you believe than what you do. He created us to live by faith; however, we can choose to live by unbelief. Unbelief is not believing in nothing but believing the wrong things. If you live by believing error, your life will be consistent with your unbelief. Likewise, if you live by faith (believing God's *truth*), your life will be consistent with your belief.

I do not think any born-again child of God would dispute that one of the central themes of the Bible is faith. Once you understand that faith is the act of believing God's *truth*, you can appreciate true repentance, which is simply the act of changing your mind. It's not about what you do, but about what you believe. The simple act of changing your mind about what you believe will always result in changing what you think, feel, and do. That is how you were born again—you repented. Repentance was not intended to end there. It is a lifelong process and the primary objective of the Holy Spirit in our lives. Sometimes it is necessary to change a few beliefs before you see dramatic results in your life. The result of being honest and willing to recognize and correct wrong beliefs is powerful. It is how the Holy Spirit causes you to realize your transformed life. It is how you were saved.

---

[40] 1 John 1:7 (KJV)
[41] Romans 1:5
[42] 1 Timothy 6:12 (KJV)

The Greatest Change of Mind

The greatest act of repentance results in being born-again.

> That if thou shalt confess with thy mouth the Lord Jesus, and shalt believe in thine heart that God hath raised him from the dead, thou shalt be saved. For with the heart man believeth unto righteousness; and with the mouth confession is made unto salvation. For the scripture saith, Whosoever believeth on him shall not be ashamed.[43]

Why does someone not yet claim to be saved? Because, he or she doesn't yet believe that Jesus was raised from the dead and is Lord. If you believe Jesus is your Lord, you will say it. If you don't, you won't. Of course, because of the way the *Law of Faith* works, you can intentionally keep speaking in agreement with God even though your thoughts don't agree, and you will find faith will appear inside your heart and mind.

In the previous scripture, Paul points out the two events that resulted in your salvation: (1) you decided you were no longer Lord of your life, Jesus is, and (2) you believed God raised Jesus from the dead. There was a time when you didn't care if Jesus was resurrected and had no interest in His lordship. You didn't want to be saved and you didn't care if you weren't. The fact that you changed your mind was the work of the Holy Spirit. The natural outcome was confessing it. If you do not believe God's *truth* but then change your mind and believe, you have repented. Repentance, or changing your mind about what you believe, is a lifelong process. The Holy Spirit leads you through it.

Understanding Strongholds

It can take a long time to uncover and change some beliefs. They hide in strongholds, which requires patience as the Holy Spirit works while you primarily wait. I have experienced this many times after becoming

---

[43] Roman 10:9-11 (KJV)

aware of an inconsistency in my life, the source of which was not apparent.

Paul deals with strongholds very clearly in 2 Corinthians:

> For though we walk in the flesh, we do not war after the flesh: (For the weapons of our warfare are not carnal, but mighty through God to the pulling down of strong holds;) Casting down imaginations, and every high thing that exaltheth itself against the knowledge of God, and bringing into captivity every thought to the obedience of Christ; [44]

To begin with, Paul is not referring to *flesh* as in bodies but to the attitude of believing what our senses, or flesh, tell us. He is adamant that we don't base warfare on what our senses say. He reiterates that in the next verse by saying that we have weapons with which to fight, and we don't control them by our feelings.

Whatever the weapons are, they eliminate strongholds. So, what are the nonphysical arms to which Paul is referring? He doesn't say in this verse; but he does tell us something far more important. Many translations say that the weapons are mighty through God or to God. I guess that's okay, but that interpretation doesn't help me at all. So, the weapons are powerful *to* God. Hurray! Now I feel truly helpless. God thinks they are superb, but how? It's pretty much the same if we consider the verse from the perspective of the weapons being mighty *through* God except, if they are coming through God, then how do we get them? However, a very literal translation could also be "by God."[45]

"The weapons of our warfare are mighty by God." In other words, the weapons of our warfare are powerful when used by God. Wow! This does not say we must figure out how to use the weapons; it says they are mighty by God! Suddenly, the pressure is off. It's not your responsibility to make the weapons work (yet *the lie* will tell you that it is). The work belongs to God. Since we know that the Holy Spirit's primary reason for giving us His Word is so we can learn and believe

---

[44] 2 Corinthians 10:3-5 (KJV)

[45] τῷ Θεῷ is in the dative case

His *truth*, is it possible that these weapons work by faith, by just believing the *truth*? Yes. This means the weapons are mighty by God by His initiation. I am just a willing vessel. It is His power that destroys the strongholds. Now the remainder of this passage begins to make a lot more sense. "Casting down imaginations and every high thing that exalts itself about the knowledge of God." The term *casting down* means "pulling down to destruction." Or as I like to say, "to destruction of strongholds." So, God is the dominance inside His weapons, which expose and make strongholds powerless.

So, what are strongholds? They are very firm beliefs that hide in our hearts. Strongholds are found in imaginations that exalt themselves above what God knows to be *truth* as well as every bit of knowledge, wisdom, belief, or any other type of thought that claims superiority to God's *truth*. Therefore we need to know the *truth*. Otherwise, how do we recognize wrong beliefs and strongholds when God shows them to us? Without knowing God's *truth*, we may end up temporarily convinced that a *truth* is a lie, or a lie is *truth*.

Paul says, "demolishing imaginations (reasonings), and every piece of knowledge, wisdom, belief or any other thought that exalts itself above what God knows."[46] He goes on to say that these thoughts are being brought into the obedience of Christ. What was the obedience of Christ? The obedience of hearing and believing only God's *truth* (Chapter Twelve Endnotes #2). One type of stronghold is the self-protecting lie. You might even call it a feedback lie. Think of it as a lie that protects another lie.

Consider this possible scenario of one lie protecting another lie. A person believes they're saved because they have done all the right things. He or she believed that God raised Jesus from the dead and confessed Him as Lord. But in truth, they just did it because someone told them they wouldn't go to Hell. Unfortunately, all they did was say words that meant nothing more than a free trip to Heaven. This means they have yet to realize salvation. Jesus hasn't become their Lord.

---

[46] 2 Corinthians 10:5 (JEC)

> Not everyone who says to me, Lord, Lord, will go into the kingdom of heaven; but he who does the pleasure of my Father in heaven. A great number will say to me on that day. Lord, Lord, were we not prophets in your name, and did we not by your name send out evil spirits, and by your name do works of power? And then will I say to them, I never had knowledge of you: go from me, you works of evil.[47]

So, they have said, "Christ came and rose again, and He is Lord." They believe they are now saved from Hell. At least, that's what they were told. But in this example, they don't believe that He is their Lord; they just know they said the right things.

The first lie tells them that if they *do* the right thing, they will be saved. The second lie says, "I made the right choice so now I'm saved." Then some Christian tell them that *is* all they had to do. Once saved, always saved. The supposedly newly born-again person goes on their way. If the subject ever comes up, they express with certainty that they are saved because they did the right things. The person may refuse to address any of these lies because being wrong can be so destructive to their self-image. So, they remain lost. One lie protects another. Fortunately, their false beliefs won't stop God from working to change their minds.

If what you have just read concerns you, then talk to God about it. The relationship is between you and Him, and He will never deny you access to Him. Maybe you are one of those who did the right thing to get saved and now you realize you faked it. Go ahead and tell Jesus what you did, but now for real you are declaring God raised Him from the dead and He is your Lord. It's that simple. You don't have to understand it. You just must mean it. You are now declaring Jesus to be your Lord. The powers of darkness will probably be screaming in your head: "You don't mean it, you don't feel it." Just ignore them and tell God to listen to the words of your mouth.

In case you want to argue that the Bible says a person must *confess* with their mouth, the original Greek doesn't say that. The word

---

[47] Matthew 7:21-23 (Extracts from The Bible in Basic English)

often translated *confess* means *to reason the same as* God, which will ultimately cause a person to say what God says. But, it is possible to say what God says while denying any reasoning that might lead you to think like God (Chapter twelve Endnotes #3).

The concept of lordship has nothing to do with how you act, but everything to do with relationship. It is in an attitude of heart and mind where you know that your salvation is utterly dependent on His love and work for you. You depend on Him for the very faith necessary to be saved. These are not things you necessarily know or understand the instant you are saved. The Holy Spirit teaches them to you. Nonetheless, He is your Lord, and He wants to open the eyes of your heart, so you understand these things. His love for you is the one thing you base your trust upon, as little of that as you may seem to have. Strongholds can leave you feeling like something beyond your power is controlling you. As you rest in God's love, you can be confident He is at work. Just continue to communicate honestly with Him, believe that He loves you, and remember that He understands your predicament. At the right time, the Holy Spirit will bring misbeliefs to the light, and He will show you the *truths* that should replace them.

The Experience

You may ask how discovering your misbeliefs and changing them is going to help you. First, it will bring a new harmony to your life. At this very moment, the fuel that powers your soul is made up of both *truth* and lies. The effect is something like trying to operate a gas engine on gasoline mixed with a little water. Even if it runs, it will sputter and stall. You may be able to move but, eventually, your engine is going to fail. Every time you exchange an erroneous belief for a right one, your soul will work a little better. At first, it may not be particularly noticeable; but before long, you will sense a difference.

You can only get rid of the darkness in your life when the light of *truth* exposes it. Once you have seen the darkness that has been hiding in your heart, you can eliminate it by just exchanging your wrong beliefs for the *truth* (repentance). When the darkness, which is just an untruth you have been accepting, no longer occupies a place in your heart because you have replaced it with the *truth*, the habits, actions, thoughts, and feelings that resulted from it will leave. Why? Because you are no longer living by flesh, but by spirit. For example, step into a dark room and shut the door behind you. What can you see? Nothing. If you try walking around, you are very likely to get hurt if you collide or trip over something. The darkness isn't hurting you; it is just keeping you from seeing what is there so whatever you do may end up causing you pain. In the darkness, you have no way of determining reality. You're subject to whatever you strike. In the darkness, you cannot protect yourself. However, you will be able to see and avoid injury if someone turns on the lights. *Truth* and lies kind of work the same way. When you believe lies, you are living in darkness. So, whatever you see is just what your flesh perceives. This results in distress because you can never be sure of anything. However, if your heart is full of *truth* (light), then you begin to see the unseen. The light of God Himself is in you and enlightening your mind. As you follow His light (*truth*), you can be sure of what you see. When light shines on darkness, the darkness ceases to exist. Of course, it is possible to reject the revelation of God's *truth* and insist on continuing to believe that a lie is true. We've all done it, and the Holy Spirit just keeps working to persuade us until we change our minds. This may sound complicated because you have never thought in these terms, but you're already living what you believe and have been doing so your whole life! Now it is time to believe only the *truth*.

The changes caused by believing the *truth* show up in many ways. It could be that only one belief is responsible for an individual behavior. Then again, it could be several. In the latter case, the Holy Spirit may work on them one by one. This can take time. There have been a few times in which I have had a dominoes-type experience when the Holy Spirit has shined His light on one error and within seconds, a whole chain of wrong beliefs is demolished. The sensation is marvelous. Suddenly, I have a new perspective on a whole arena of thoughts. I don't know how else to describe it. It is a paradigm shift and after it occurs, at some point in time, you'll realize it.

How do you exchange an erroneous belief for a correct one? First, acknowledge a lie for what it is—a lie. Then, say the *truth* that is replacing *the lie* you believed. It is that simple. Once you believe something is a lie, it is not possible for you to continue believing it as true. Often, not knowing right from wrong, we have all chosen to believe something that wasn't God's *truth*. The fruit has always ended up bad. Of course, if someone has enough wrong beliefs it can cause a logic failure in which evil becomes good and good becomes evil.

> Woe unto them who say of evil, it is right; and of good, it is evil; Who place darkness for light, and light for darkness; Who put bitter for sweet, and sweet for bitter. Woe unto them who are wise in their own eyes, And prudent in their own estimation...Who justify the guilty for the sake of a reward, And take away the righteousness of the righteous from him.[48]

In this case, since rotten fruit now appears good, the wrong beliefs become a person's truth. The world is full of people like this.

To say it another way, after confessing a lie you have believed, state the *truth* with which you are replacing it. This way, you make sure that you are not leaving a void into which another lie can slip.

I always repeat the *truth* out loud and tell myself that it is, in fact, *truth* and what I have believed before that moment is a lie. A journal has been a great tool in this regard. I write my *A* and *B* statements. Statement *A* is what I have been telling myself that isn't true. *B* is the *truth* that replaces it. Of the multitudes of lies that Christians believe, let's look at a religious one. For some people, the thought of having to go witnessing is terrifying. If this is a fear you suffer, then the only way to handle it is by being honest with yourself and God. Example: (A) "God, up to this moment, I have believed that I have to go witnessing or You are not pleased. (B) I now know that is a lie and You are pleased with me, even when I don't share Christ with anyone. I am now free to

---

[48] Isaiah 5:20-23 (*A Translation of the Old Testament Scriptures from the Original Hebrew* by Helen Spurrell)

share Christ when I want to not because I must. If I don't want to witness to someone about Jesus, that's okay with You." At some point in time, you may find yourself talking about Jesus and wondering how it happened. It will be a thrilling experience. I have heard preachers say, "If you don't witness to someone, their blood is on your hands." That statement comes from the heart of *the lie*.

The book, *Telling Yourself the Truth* by Backus provides many very personal examples. I don't think it is possible to read it and not see a description of something you are feeling, *the lie* you are telling yourself that is causing that feeling, and how to correct it.

How long does it take this process to produce change? The answer has two parts. First, this is a lifelong process, and it becomes more and more exciting. Second, though the length varies depending on many factors, the Holy Spirit will make sure you see results once you start. Your cooperation in this process is one of His greatest joys. You do not have much influence over the course of coming to God's light. By that I mean you cannot pick and choose the beliefs with which to deal. If you want to experience the wholeness and prosperity of soul for which God created you, the Holy Spirit alone will direct the process. Your job is to be honest when He reveals a lie you believe. Just be willing to admit you are wrong. The second you do, you are no longer wrong.

Like separating strands of hot spaghetti, you can quickly change your mind about a new belief. But once it has twisted with others and cooled, it requires time and patience as the Holy Spirit works to deal with it at the right moments. When a wrong belief has settled in your heart, at some point the Holy Spirit will prompt you to talk to Him about it. But the Bible encourages us to guard our minds with all diligence, before mistaken beliefs get into our hearts.[49] It is easier to keep an erroneous belief out of your mind than to get it out of your heart once it is there.

Often, to deal with the beliefs producing unwanted symptoms, it is necessary to address other beliefs that are linked to or covering them. The Holy Spirit determines the beliefs you need to deal with and in what order. Sometimes beliefs have many parts, so just because you

---

[49] Proverb 4:23 – JPS Hebrew-English Tanakh, 1999.

have dealt with one part does not mean you are finished. Over time, your heart and experiences will naturally bring you face-to-face with beliefs that are interfering with your life. You can never predict what they will be or when they will surface. There is no greater adventure! This process will open your eyes and let you see what the world and many believers can't see—God's reality. Just as your body heals itself, the Spirit of Christ in you (which is now your spirit), also heals your entire person. You just need to cooperate with the process. God is devoted to causing that to happen. You are not on your own in this matter, or any other.

To succeed in this endeavor, you must become honest with yourself. When you find an area of beliefs that is too painful or uncomfortable to deal with, that is okay. God understands, and remember, He places no conditions on the love He has for you. He gives it freely. But by being honest about that issue itself, "Lord, this is too hard to deal with right now," the Lord will bring you to the point where you can handle it. The Spirit deals with things when it is the proper time, not before. However, if you do not want to deal with an issue, tell the Lord. He'll work with you, because He loves you.

You may be wondering if there is another way. No. Your belief system is not static. You either walk toward the *truth* or away from it. If you are not moving toward the light, then by default you are moving toward the darkness. The power of what you choose to believe automatically carries you toward the fruit of that belief. *Trying* to believe the *truth* is not enough and will not work. Take an honest look at yourself. If you have difficulty living something you believe, it is because deep inside your belief is a lie that is messing up the works. You'll never figure out what it is by yourself. When Jesus said, "without me, you can do nothing,"[50] He meant it.

If you are unaware of inconsistencies in your life, compare yourself with how Jesus lived. It will not take long to find areas where your thoughts and behavior are deficient. But, since you now have His nature, everything that is true about Jesus is now true about you, except for the fact that you are *not* God. God wants your life to *be* transformed.

---

[50] John 15:5 (JEC)

His goal is for you to live like Jesus, manifesting His nature and character in the world. Lies in your belief system can prevent you from fully believing the *truth* you embrace. This is the cause of double-mindedness. This is the reason we so often do what we should not and do not do what we ought to do. Therefore, we so often mishear the voice of God. Changing our minds (repenting) of our misbeliefs makes it possible for the things we want to believe to become real to us and in us. If you want to *be* changed and see the unseen, then allow the Holy Spirit to expose the lies that are hindering you, so you can exchange them for the *truth*. When you are ready to begin this adventure, tell Him. He is the one whose ministry it is to lead you. It is His pleasure and one of His greatest desires. He is faithful, and He will do it.

* * *

Chapter Twelve Endnotes

Note 1

After decades of mental and emotional turmoil, I began to experience the healing of my mind and emotions during a seminar by Malcolm Smith called the "Search for Self-Worth." I had been an earnest Christian and church member for over twenty years and knew much about the Bible yet had never heard many of the things he taught. Near the end of that seminar in 1992, it seemed like my life had finally been turned right side up. It was then that Malcolm began speaking about forgiveness. With permission, the following is taken from the workbook that supplemented his teaching.[51]

> Let all bitterness and wrath and anger and clamor and slander be put away from you, along with all malice. And be kind to one another, tender-hearted, forgiving each other, just as God in Christ also has forgiven you (Eph. 4:17-32).
> In the Greek, the tense for "put away" indicates a decisive and effective choice...Do it! Now, make it happen!

---

[51] *The Search for Self-Worth* workbook Chapter Five, www. MalcolmSmith.org

> It is a commitment. It is not saying, 'I'll try, let me pray about it!'
>
> That which is to be put away is the bitterness of heart over some word or act that deeply hurt us at some time in the past.
>
> Bitterness is a state of spirit caused by brooding over the wrong done to us. It is that sourness of spirit that comes from returning to the injustice and replaying it. It is licking old wounds to keep them bleeding...
>
> There is an insanity to this way of thinking; we choose to be hurt repeatedly by the original hurt. The fact is, I can never do anything to the abuser that will heal me; but, as I try to punish the person who hurt me, I continue to be hurt. Hence, Paul says, we are to put it away from us at once.
>
> *The fact that Paul is telling believers to put bitterness out of their lives shows that we bring in, from the past, a lot of unfinished business that can only be dealt with after we have exited the lie and Christ has been owned as Lord* (Emphasis added).

The book goes on to ask, Why do we cling to the hurts of the past? Then Smith answers with:

> This is rooted in the twisted thinking of the lie...that we are God. The unforgiving person takes the position of God, as the one who is in control of the punishment of the abuser.
>
> Our hurt selves cry out within us: 'When you hurt me, I was powerless; but now I have power to bind you in chains to what you have done, and I will make you hurt as you hurt me.'
>
> Even though there is nothing we can do physically to punish them, we feel that we have delivered the ultimate judgment by locking them out of our lives and the lives of as many others as we can influence. In our minds, we have banned them from humanity.

Unseen

But the only way we can do this is to mentally and emotionally return to the scene of the crime and relive its horror.

It is common, among those who see themselves as victims rather than as victimized, to remember the hurt as a means of excusing their present life and behavior.

'No one can blame me for my wretched life. If you had parents like mine, you would be in the same place.'

Many are afraid of forgiving their abusers, seeing it as letting the abusers finally win. To these people, forgiveness is surrendering to the enemy, as letting evil win.

They despise people who forgive for allowing themselves to become doormats.

Others perceive forgiveness as admitting that somehow the other person is right after all. It would be saying: 'Let's forget it. I over-reacted. I am making a mountain out of a molehill.'

The abused person violently reacts to any forgiveness that might seem to condone what was done to them. It would be a betrayal of their inmost self. An enraged sense of justice is demanding that the abuser pays in full.

Remember the story of Joseph in the book of Genesis? He was the favorite son of his father, Jacob, who had given him "a coat of many colours."[52] Because of jealousy, his brothers had kidnapped and sold him to a caravan of slave traders. Many years later, Joseph's family traveled to Egypt in search of food due to a serious famine. There they discovered that Joseph had been sold to a high official and had eventually prospered to become the prime minister of the nation. It's a gut-wrenching story with a wonderful ending. After the death of their father (Jacob), Joseph's brothers—who had betrayed and sold him into slavery—became afraid. Since their father was gone, they were sure their brother would retaliate for the evil they had done.[53] So they sent a messenger to him saying, "'Forgive your brothers' sin—all that wrong-

---

[52] Genesis 37:3 (KJV)

[53] Genesis Chapter Thirty-Seven through Fifty

doing. They did treat you very badly.' Will you do it? Will you forgive the sins of the servants of your father's God?"[54]

Joseph, as second in command of all Egypt, could have acted like a god over his brothers and treated them any way he wanted.

Yet he tells them, "Don't be afraid. Do I act for God? Don't you see, you planned evil against me but God used those same plans for my good."[55] Joseph could have held bitterness in his heart; instead, he had released his brothers to God and forgiven them. They were now God's to do with as He pleased. Yes, his brothers lived in ease for many years while Joseph lived as a slave. But all that time, he carried no grudge in his heart toward anyone.

Because of that, God could work for, in, and through Joseph to achieve a life for him that was better than anyone could have ever imagined.

Note 2

For those concerned about the statement in Hebrews, "yet learned he (Jesus) obedience by the things which he suffered,"[56] this suffering refers to what Paul said in 1 Corinthians 15:31, "I die daily." Paul was talking about the pain that occurred while his senses screamed that whatever bad he was experiencing was ultimate reality. They shrieked that God didn't love him because if He did, terrible things wouldn't happen. Jesus suffered the same way. He didn't have a comfortable ride, though many think He did.

Every day many of Paul's circumstances exalted themselves above God's knowledge.[57] Paul had a choice to believe what his senses told him or what God had said to him. Were those circumstances greater than God? Every day he had the choice to believe God's *truth* or his feelings. That's why he wrote in Romans 6:11 (KJV): "reckon yourselves to be dead to sin." The Greek word for *reckon* means to reason in

---

[54] Genesis 50:17 (msg)
[55] Genesis 50:19-20 (msg)
[56] Hebrews 5:8 (KJV)
[57] 2 Corinthians 10:5

Unseen

yourself that you are dead to sin. It is in the present tense. That means to keep doing it every day. Keep reasoning to yourself that you are dead to error. It is not a one-time event but the fight of faith. You keep reasoning until you realize that God's reasoning is your reasoning. You are who He says you are. You have the mind of Christ, and God is training you to think like Him.

In Chapters Four and Five of his first epistle, Peter wrote about the sufferings of Christ and His believers. He was referring to Christ suffering because of what His flesh senses had told Him. "Forasmuch then as Christ has suffered for us in flesh, arm yourselves with the same thinking."[58] By *flesh*, Peter was not referring to Jesus's body, but to reasonings that arise from the senses. What happens in our minds determines how we perceive what is going on in our bodies. That's why he says to arm ourselves with the same thoughts as Christ. This whole passage is about living by spirit rather than flesh.

Jesus is God, the *truth* Himself, and fully man. While on Earth, He was tempted just as we are.[59] The scriptures show that He suffered the same types of trials that young boys and teenagers face. In His 20s, He faced business and family problems just like others. Then, after being filled with the Holy Spirit and hearing His Father publicly confirm what Jesus had learned from the scriptures, He experienced such an adrenalin rush that it took forty days of fasting to make Him as weak as the weakest of humans so that He could face Satan in the wilderness and still overcome him. Can you imagine the pressure? Jesus has recently heard His Father say that He is God and then Satan appears like he did to Adam and says, "Do you really believe that? If it is true, then things wouldn't be so hard right now. If it is true, then make bread out of those rocks." Just like with us, at His weakest point, Satan sought to convince Him to believe something other than God's *truth*. Jesus suffered throughout His ministry as He saw what *the lie* had done to His creation. He suffered at the end when he was made to be its sin (2 Corinthians 5:21, KJV), and bore "our griefs, and carried

---

[58] 1 Peter 4:1 (JEC)

[59] Hebrews 4:15: "who has in every way been tempted, exactly as we have been, without ever sinning (erring)." (TCNT Part 2)

our sorrows."[60] Jesus was fully man and suffered just as we do when life doesn't look and feel like we think it should. The wrong that He saw, heard, and felt tempted Him to believe other than God's love and *truth*. He was *truth* itself, yet His suffering became so great that the distress caused Him to sweat blood in the Garden of Gethsemane. Oh, blessed Savior! Oh, how He suffered with us and for us.

Paul experienced the death of Christ daily. There is no greater suffering than the fight of faith when you thank God that He is Love, that He loves you, and that He will never abandon you to your problems, even while those issues and your flesh scream it is hopeless and God has failed you. When Paul spoke about the fight of faith, he meant both those times when our senses deny the *truth* we believe as well as those when the Holy Spirit exposes our misbeliefs and we have the choice of believing or rejecting His *truth*. Repenting (changing your mind) about error and false knowledge is a very real death. The passage in Ephesians Chapter Six in which Paul tells us to "having done all to stand, stand" involves death. It is the death to wrong beliefs which have left us vulnerable to effects of darkness. These are times when you discover your weakness as a creature, and that you can do nothing but fall helplessly on God and His *truth*. These can be periods of high anxiety, fear, and tremendous emotional and physical pain. Either you accept you are a created *being* and rest into His love and willingness to meet your needs or you live as though His love is conditional and your success is dependent on you.

Jesus's temptations in the wilderness were to get Him to declare independence from God. Though our trials take different forms, they always urge us the same direction. Either you depend on God or you don't rely on Him.

Note 3

Why was Paul the primary writer of New Testament documents? Because of his training in reasoning through the scriptures. He was not an orator. He was a reasoner. Paul's intention was to educate people, to

---

[60] Isaiah 53:4 (KJV)

provoke them to think and reason. This is IMPORTANT!!!! Throughout the New Testament, the word *homologeó* (ὁμολογέω) is translated *reckon, account, admit, acknowledge, confess, give thanks, confessed,* and more. However, a literal translation of the word is *"to reason the same as"* rather than *"to say together with"* as many teachers render it.

Though there are Greek words exactly matching the two components of that compound word, many translators have inadvertently changed *homo* (same as) to *homou* (together) and *logeo* (to reason) to *lego* (to say). However, this word is not a *doing* issue but rather a *being* issue. We *do* with our tongues, we *be* with our minds. Paul uses this word because he is talking about reasoning.

There is another word related to *homologeo* that clearly means to confess. In fact, its very existence tells me *homologeo* did not mean *to confess*. That related word is *exomologeó* (ἐξομολογέω) used in verses like Philippians 2:11 – "and that every tongue will confess that Jesus Christ is Lord, to the glory of God the Father." It is the same word (*homologeo*) only with the prefix *ek* (spelled ἐξ before a vowel). The passage could be rendered "every tongue out of the same reason(ing)."

Ek – out of
Homo – the same as
Logeo – reason

The battle is for our minds. Human reason has been attacked on a massive scale ever since the Garden of Eden (addressed in Chapter Fifteen). Paul sought to provoke people to think, and he gave them the tools to do so.

You can see evidence of Satan's continued efforts to destroy people's motivation to reason. Just look at every big move by governments to control their citizens. A key component is always shutting down people's reasoning and forcing everyone to think in line with those seeking power. The examples are endless. Not only have people ceased considering the logic of their thoughts, beliefs, and behaviors, not only are they afraid to reason, but in many arenas today they feel threatened if they do so.

James E. Campbell, Jr, James Q. Campbell

Reasoning begins with you and God. We share our thoughts with Him and allow Him to reason with and instruct us. This is a critical process which is intimately involved in learning who we are. We are like God, with the capacity of Jesus Christ to think like Him.

13
Grace

*It takes an adult mind to explain it, yet only
children can see and understand grace.*

God's grace is the gift to you of Himself and His love in action. During our worst problems—regardless of the source even if it is us—God's love for us is not diminished. In the years before Jesus was crucified, the word *grace* included all types of gifts, including birthday gifts. It meant a gift freely given, simply because someone was alive. Since God's grace was yours the day you were born, I like calling it a birthday gift.

Grace and the Law

You've seen how believing *the lie* has corrupted every generation of humanity. You also know that *faith* is synonymous with the faith of the Son of God (Jesus's beliefs). It is how God manifests His life in believers (Chapter Thirteen Endnotes #1). So, what about good works and the Law? We know they are important, but how do they fit into God's plan?

God's grace makes good works easy because they are an automatic result of believing the *truth*. The King James version of Ephesians 2:8 & 9 is, "For by grace are ye saved through faith; and that not of yourselves: it is the gift of God: Not of works, lest any man should boast." My more literal but, thus, harder to understand translation is, "For by the grace you are having been completely saved by means of believing the *truth*, and this is not out of yourselves; of God is the gift, not out of works, in order that not anyone will have boasted." This is one of those literal passages that you must ponder until you see what Paul was saying (Chapter Thirteen Endnotes #2). Because of God's grace, everyone can be made whole by simply believing His *truth*.

The writer of the book of Hebrews said, "Without faith it is impossible to please Him (God)."[1] In other words, unless you believe God's *truth* your works cannot please Him. But now, we need to take a moment and address James 2:20 regarding the fact that faith without works is dead. This scripture is absolute *truth*. However, it is very easy to misunderstand what the writer is saying because *the lie* is so ingrained in our belief systems that any reading of this passage is filtered through that lens.

> [17]Even so faith, if it has no works, is dead, *being* by itself. [18]But someone may *well* say, "You have faith and I have works; show me your faith without the works, and I will show you my faith by my works." [19]You believe that God is one. You do well; the demons also believe, and shudder. [20]But are you willing to recognize, you foolish fellow, that faith without works is useless? [21]Was not Abraham our father justified by works when he offered up Isaac his son on the altar? [22]You see that faith was working with his works, and as a result of the works, faith was perfected; [23]and the Scripture was fulfilled which says, "AND ABRAHAM BELIEVED GOD, AND IT WAS RECKONED TO HIM AS RIGHTEOUSNESS," and he was called the friend of God. [24]You see that a man is justified by works and not by faith alone. [25]In the same way, was not Rahab the harlot also justified by works when she received the messengers and sent them out by another way? [26]For just as the body without *the* spirit is dead, so also faith without works is dead.[2]

In the light of everything we've covered up to this point, this verse can now be understood from the perspective of God's grace. The

---

[1] Hebrews 11:6 (KJV)
[2] James 2:17-26 (KJV)

teaching of the modern Church needs a simple yet radical change. Faith is taught as mental assent. It is not explained as treasuring in the heart and mind, but believing in the head. It's explained as knowing about God as opposed to cherishing the same body of knowledge which He has, which then makes your beliefs the same as His.

So, when James says that faith without works is dead, he is saying if believing the *truth* doesn't result in a change of behavior, it means that the espoused faith is not real faith (i.e., believing the *truth* as God believes it), it is dead, that is, nonfunctioning; it is separated from God's reality. Even if you try harder, your faith will be just as dead. When we believe God's *truth* in our hearts—in other words, when it replaces *the lie* that opposes it—the corresponding works will no longer be an issue. They will be automatic. *This is a reason to rejoice!* In this verse, God is explaining why you aren't living the way you ought to. He is not condemning you. He loves you and is with you to make things right in your life. That's what judgment is: making wrong things right. The modern church equates judgment with condemnation. Nothing could be further from the *truth*.

God does not hand out condemnation. Period. He took care of that in Christ, and it is finished. He loves you and wants to spend all of eternity showing you His kindness. "That in the ages to come he might shew the exceeding riches of his grace in his kindness toward us through Christ Jesus."[3] But remember, the process of repentance (changing your mind about what you believe in order to believe God's *truth*) is a lifelong process, and as you continue to walk in spirit, since God is not condemning you, you are not condemned.[4] My rendering of Romans 8:1 is: "Therefore there is now no condemnation to those inside Christ Jesus who are not living in agreement with an attitude set on believing what flesh tells them but in agreement with an attitude set on believing only the truth."[5] To believers such as this, condemnation cannot find a foothold. You don't have to accept condemnation from the "accuser

---

[3] Ephesians 2:7 (KJV)
[4] Walk in spirit, an attitude of willingness to believe God's *truth* instead of what flesh tells you.
[5] Roman 8:1 (JEC)

of the brethren" (Satan) either. "And I heard a loud voice saying in heaven, Now is come salvation, and strength, and the Kingdom of our God, and the power of his Christ: for *the accuser of our brethren* is cast down, which accused them before our God day and night."[6]

You are free and really are immersed in God's love and favor. "It is through him that, by means of our faith, we have obtained admission to the place in God's favour in which we now stand."[7] He's determined to help you to believe what Jesus believes and know what He knows. God intends for your body of knowledge and beliefs to be the same as the beliefs of Jesus.

"Till we all come in the unity of the faith, and of the knowledge of the Son of God."[8] "With men this is impossible; but with God all things are possible."[9]

When you believe what He believes, He will live the obedience of Christ in you. But His love for you is not dependent on that. His grace (birthday gift) is responsible for allowing faith to be the means of pleasing Him. "For by grace, you have been saved by means of believing the *truth*."[10] If not for God's grace, the means of salvation would still be doing everything in the Law, which is still impossible. The source of God's grace is His love. Love is not something God *does*; it is what He *is*. "God *is* love."[11] There can be no diminishing of God's love any more than there can be a diminishing of God. Likewise, nothing can diminish His grace. However, if we reject it and insist on including works or doing the Law as a component for pleasing Him, we are denying that the death of Christ was sufficient in that area. Thus, we are rejecting God's grace. "I do not frustrate the grace of God: for if righteousness come by the law, then Christ is dead in vain."[12] "Christ is become of

---

[6] Revelations 12:10 (msg)

[7] Romans 5:2 (TCNT Part 2)

[8] Ephesians 4:13 (KJV) The only real faith is Jesus's. Paul is speaking here about the entire church coming to believe what Jesus believes and know what He knows.

[9] Matthew 19:26 (KJV)

[10] Ephesians 2:8 (JEC)

[11] 1 John 4:8 (KJV)

[12] Galatians 2:21 (KJV)

no effect unto you, whosoever of you are justified by the law; ye are fallen from grace."[13] God still expects works and obedience, but they must be a result of spirit, which comes from our union with Christ, not willpower (flesh). But, God is not a harsh taskmaster. Rather, He will lovingly train you to hear and do. He is enduring passion. He won't quit until you get it. The obedience God expects does not justify anyone. He joyfully expects obedience because we are members of Christ. Since Jesus listens to God's instruction, how can we not do the same since we are one with Jesus? Since He is the head of the Body, then by shear default, when He listens to God, we do too. And, remember, obedience is submitting to hearing, which results in faith (that is, believing the *truth*), which results in automatically doing what you believe. You don't try to do anything I have just written. You simply say, "Yes, God, I believe this. Thank you for working it in me," and refuse to believe He isn't, no matter what you hear, think, or see.

Many frequently teach that if you believe something, then the next step is to prove it by doing it. Nothing can be farther from the *truth.* When you believe *truth* in your heart, you will *automatically* do it. You won't be able to help it.[14] If you are not living a *truth* that you profess to believe in your heart, it is because you don't yet really believe it. Something is getting in the way of treasuring it in your heart. Don't be discouraged by this. It is wonderful to discover the reason God's Word is not as real in our lives as we would like. Up until now, you have probably been perplexed about deficiencies in your walk with God. Those days are over. You are on the verge of being established in the principles of the doctrine of Christ out of which the realities of the Kingdom of God grow within you.[15] Now we can cooperate with God as He works to make His Kingdom real to us.

Not once have the authors of UNSEEN told you to have faith. Rather, we have taught you what it is and how it works as well as what

---

[13] Galatians 5:4 (KJV)

[14] James 2:19: "Thou believest that there is one God; thou doest well: the devils also believe, and tremble." They don't try to tremble, they automatically do! The very thought of One God terrifies them.

[15] Hebrews 6:1

has hindered yours. Because of His grace, God has given you all the faith you ever need. Now you are learning how to let the Holy Spirit train you in its use. As you learn to change your mind about wrong beliefs and believe God's *truth* instead, you will increasingly enjoy the fruit that faith automatically produces. In the meantime, God wants you to reject any condemnation that comes your way, because it is not from Him.

The reason you have not believed some aspect of God's *truth* is either because you didn't know it or, before agreeing that a *truth* is true, a lie that appeared valid became rooted in the soil of your heart and established itself there. Long-forgotten wrong beliefs can control our thoughts and behaviors and prevent the *truth* (which we now embrace) from taking root and growing in our hearts. When you realize this, just be assured that the Holy Spirit is excited to teach you. He is not concerned about you making a mistake before you finally get it. That is what training is all about. And, He *is* training you. We can trust God with our lives and the doing of His Word. He promised to make it happen.

So, what can you do? You want God's *truth* to reign in your life yet, sometimes something else seems to be in control. This is part of the salvation Jesus spoke about when He said: "With men this is impossible; but with God all things are possible."[16] Have you yet realized your utter dependence on God? You were created to be filled with God. You can't alter that. He is sharing His life and freedom with you. Freely. Right now. But it can take much longer to experience if you are resisting Him or trying to figure it out, rather than being honest and admitting you need His help. It is not because God is opposing us that we may feel bound to something we don't want. It is because we are struggling to fix our faith rather than trusting He will do it for us. We often think He expects something we don't know how to give Him. The filter of *the lie* is what prevents us from understanding the overwhelming, unconditional love God has for us and how far He is willing to go to help us.

I hope my very literal translation of Roman 5:1 will help you. The KJV translates it thus: "Therefore being justified by faith, we have

---

[16] Matthew 19:26 (KJV)

peace with God through our Lord Jesus Christ."[17] I render Romans 5:1 as follows: "Therefore having been made right [by God] out of [Jesus's] belief, we have peace *toward* God by means of the Lord Jesus."[18] But why would this seemingly nonsensical translation be better? Paul's real emphasis is not that God, after being angry with us is now appeased, but that we are no longer at enmity with Him. The *truth* is that He was never mad at us. We hated Him; He didn't hate us. But because we are now one with Christ, we have Jesus's peace toward Him, though many still think there is a conflict. "Because the carnal mind is enmity against God: for it is not subject to the law of God, neither indeed can be. So then they that are in flesh (*the* is not in the original) cannot please God."[19]

Because God has made us right, there is no longer any reason to hide from Him or be angry at Him. Paul is telling us that we have peace toward God right now. You may think you are mad at Him, but you aren't because you are one with Christ who is not angry at God. This is the way faith works. What God says is the *truth* about you; what you see, feel, or other voices say is not the *truth*. If you feel angry at God, something other than God is telling you that you feel that way, that your problems are His fault. Why do you believe this? According to God, you have peace toward Him. God put peace toward Himself inside you by making you one with Christ, so you have Jesus' peace toward God. Regardless what you think or feel, you have peace toward God because Jesus does. If you think otherwise, those thoughts are coming to you from the darkness and are not yours. Until this moment, you may not have known that! Don't believe your feelings. Trust what God is telling you! He made you a new creature. All that previous stuff is gone no matter what you see or feel or think. This is what Jesus believes.

The problem is people haven't yet discovered the *truth* about God's peace within them. Just like the *renewed* mind, which already belongs to us by means of the work of Christ, people have not realized they are not at war with God anymore. You may have heard a preacher say

---

[17] Romans 5:2 (KJV)
[18] Romans 5:2 (JEC)
[19] Romans 8:8 (KJV)

something like: "God can't look on sin." But God doesn't think like this about us and never has. That's why He had no problem approaching Adam and Eve in the Garden after they had joined league with Satan. He knew they had been deceived and immediately announced His plan to rescue them. "And I will put enmity between thee (the serpent) and between the woman, and between thy seed and between her seed, He shall crush thy head and thou shalt crush His Heel."[20] God was there speaking to the serpent (Satan), telling him that a Savior was going to fix everything and deal with him who had "the power of death, that is, the devil."[21]

Some imply that grace gives us the ability to obey the Law as though somehow it gives us extra strength to do it. But any message like that is wrong. Obedience to God's commandments is always the automatic—though not necessarily immediate—outcome of trusting God's grace. Teaching a message of pure grace will encourage people toward the obedience of faith, which means that Christ's obedience becomes ours automatically. Real grace is the only way to complete obedience and victory. "Those receiving the abundance of the grace and the gift of righteousness shall reign in life through the one Jesus Christ."[22] Reigning in life is *much more* than just winning. It is *much more* than conquering. "In all these things we are more than conquerors through him that loved us."[23]

Over and over, in diverse ways, Paul teaches both grace and the gift of righteousness cause us to see the victory of Jesus over *the lie* that so wrecked mankind. In Romans 5:17, Paul told us that taking the knowing of this grace and rightness causes us to reign in life. No matter what happens, we can rest in the victory of Jesus Christ. We reign inside His reigning. Christ living His *truth* in the believer enables us to live as Jesus lived. We realize we have self-control. Jesus was the most prosperous man who ever lived. Since we are one with Him, we are

---

[20] Genesis 3:15 (*A Translation of the Old Testament Scriptures from the Original Hebrew* by Helen Spurrell)
[21] Hebrews 2:14 (KJV)
[22] Romans 5:17 (KJV)
[23] Romans 8:37 (KJV)

too. Only the Holy Spirit can show us what that looks like. Suddenly, this world's prosperity looks dull. Real grace promotes right living while trying to do law increases error. "A little leaven leavens all the dough."[24] The Apostle Paul said it this way: "The strength of error is the law."[25]

In his Gospel account, the Apostle John explains what it means to be one with Jesus. "And of his fullness have all we received, and grace for grace."[26] In the original language, the word translated *for* means *upon*. Some translations render the passage, "grace upon grace." It leaves one with the sense that John was talking about something too big for words. I can see the Apostle as He wrote—thoughts flowing from his pen as the Holy Spirit spoke in words and pictures. Suddenly, John pauses. The Holy Spirit has just given John a picture of the grace with which God loves us and he is without the words to accurately describe it, so he says, "grace piled upon grace." John saw grace that never ends. However much you take, there is *always* more; it is inexhaustible. To say there could be an end to His grace is to say there is an end to God's love or an end to God!

Mankind believes *the lie* and tries to overcome sin by not doing things that are considered sin. But our efforts to prove we are not sinners by doing good works are, by definition, sin (error). It's a vicious cycle, but Jesus ended it (Chapter Thirteen Endnotes #3). It requires a new paradigm: obedience by hearing and believing the *truth*, which is possible because of God's grace. Such a mindset is righteous because it allows God and His *truth* to live righteousness in us. Paul's phrase, "the abundance of grace" describes a quality and quantity so abundant that no words can describe it. Paul uses the best description possible in a human language, yet it still doesn't justly describe the wonder of what God has accomplished for us. The superfluidity or abundance—the excessively excessive gift—is so great that Paul practically gives up and just says it enables the believer to reign in life. What else is he going to say? Only the Spirit of God can reveal this to someone and He does it

---

[24] Galatians 5:9 (TCNT Part 2)
[25] 1 Corinthians 15:56 (KJV)
[26] John 1:16 (KJV)

in ways that are impossible for us to foresee. This is bigger and more terrific than anything any flesh can imagine.

The destruction which resulted from believing *the lie* in the Garden of Eden was so devastatingly terrible that just one man decimated all of humanity by just that one act of disobedience. No escape was possible by means of anything that any human could do. Entropy had begun and would never cease. "For if by one man's offence death reigned by one; much more they which receive abundance of grace and of the gift of righteousness shall reign in life by one, Jesus Christ."[27]

> So, also, no one comprehends the inner life of God, except the Spirit of God. And in our own case, it is not the Spirit of the World that we have received, but the Spirit that comes from God, that we may realize the blessings given to us by God. In speaking, too, of these gift, we do not use language suggested by human wisdom, but language suggested by the Spirit, and so we explain spiritual things in spiritual words. An unspiritual man rejects the teaching of the Spirit of God. To him it is mere folly; he cannot grasp it, because it is only to be understood by spiritual insight. But a spiritual man is able to understand everything, although he himself is not understood by any one. For who has comprehended the mind of the Lord, and is able to instruct him? We, however, have the very mind of Christ.[28]

Paul saw grace that was surrounded by grace and then covered with grace and all of it set in more grace covered and surrounded by even more grace. This large mass of grace was then submerged in a vessel of unlimited grace (Chapter Thirteen Endnotes #4).

John was pointing to a similar thought when he described Jesus as "full of grace and truth."[29] Think about it. An unlimited, infinite container Who is filled to the full with grace. You can withdraw an

---

[27] Romans 5:17 (KJV)
[28] 1 Corinthians 2:11-16 (TCNT Part 2)
[29] John 1:14 (KJV)

unlimited amount of grace from Him and yet He, the Container, will never have less grace nor does He need to be refilled.

First and foremost, God's grace tells us that, if we believe God, we have been saved. "For by grace you have been saved by means of believing the Truth."[30] It declares that we are justified by believing His *truth*. "Therefore being justified by faith, we have peace with God through our Lord Jesus Christ." [31] Then His grace blesses us with all spiritual blessings in heavenly places in Christ and everything we need for life and godliness.

> Grace be to you, and peace, from God our Father, and from the Lord Jesus Christ. Blessed be the God and Father of our Lord Jesus Christ, who hath blessed us with all spiritual blessings in heavenly places in Christ: [32] His divine power has given us everything we need for our physical and spiritual life. This has come to us through our getting to know Him who has called us to share His glory and virtue.[33]

These promises are for your life now and every day not just after you die. Jesus said He came so we could have life more abundantly, not separation more abundantly. "The thief only comes to steal, and kill, and destroy; I have come that they may have Life, and may have it in abundance."[34]

It is because of God's grace that we are assured He will meet every need. Though Satan means evil, God will always be working within that evil for good. "But as for you, ye thought evil against me; but God meant it unto good."[35] "And we know that all things work together for

---

[30] Ephesians 2:8 (JEC)

[31] Romans 5:1 (KJV)

[32] Ephesians 1:2-3 (KJV)

[33] 2 Peter 1:3 (Taken from Norlie, Olaf M., Norlie's Simplified New Testament c. 1961)

[34] John 10:10 (TCNT Part 1)

[35] Genesis 50:20 (KJV)

good to them that love God, to them who are the called according to his purpose."[36]

Living by faith can only be accomplished by means of grace. The doing of good works which God desires is not the result of determination and willpower, but the faith in our hearts. That faith is yours by God's gift. You just need to agree and say, "Yes, it's mine" even though your thoughts, or someone at a pulpit, tell you otherwise. The preaching of God's grace is not a license to sin, but a call to allow the life and character of Christ to reign in your life. It is the only way to please God. Grace enables us to fulfill the righteousness of the Law by believing God's *truth*, which God says is better to Him than if we could perfectly obey all His Law."That the righteousness of the law might be fulfilled in us, who walk not according to flesh, but according to spirit."[37] It is the source of the type of good works that please God.

Paul confirms that righteousness is dependent upon believing the *truth* rather than obeying the Law: "But now the righteousness of God without the law is manifested, being witnessed by the law and the prophets; even the righteousness of God which is by [the] faith of Jesus unto all and upon *all them that believe*." [38] Paul goes on to say, "Do we then make void the law through faith? God forbid: yea, we establish the law."[39] How? Hearing and believing the *truth* fulfills the requirements of the Law in two ways: (1) when we are born-again, we are made one with Christ's obedience and righteousness and (2) since we live what we believe, as we increasingly believe the *truth*, we increasingly live like Jesus.

According to Paul, grace makes it possible to be saved by simply believing God's *truth* apart from works. "For by grace you have been saved by means of believing the *truth*."[40] Paul told the Romans that they had access and stood, immovable and immersed, in grace by believing the *truth* (Chapter Thirteen Endnotes #5). He said, "We have

---

[36] Roman 8:28 (KJV)
[37] Romans 8:4 (JEC)
[38] Romans 3:21-22 (KJV)
[39] Romans 3:31 (KJV)
[40] Ephesians 2:8 (JEC)

access by faith into this grace wherein we stand."[41] In other words, grace makes believing the *truth* the means to salvation and continued believing makes it possible to access more of God's abundant grace, thus giving us a sure expectation (hope) that the glory of God (Christ in us) is ours. Jesus is the source of our obedience, and this is how God makes His obedience our obedience.

Obedience through Grace

God's grace means that no matter what, God's love for us cannot diminish. "I'm absolutely convinced that nothing—nothing living or dead, angelic or demonic, today or tomorrow, high or low, thinkable or unthinkable—absolutely nothing can get between us and God's love because of the way that Jesus our Master has embraced us."[42] The natural mind cannot absorb it. How can a righteous and just God unconditionally love someone who commits evil and continue to view that *sinner* with unlimited favor? The same way that God the Father could give God the Son to die for a world in total rebellion against God. He is Love.

God was and is the sole hope of humankind. He has never considered people, before or after the Cross, to be capable of raising themselves to God's standards. Rather, God was waiting for the opportunity to do it for us. He did it in Christ. It's kind of like you don't expect your children to grow up and teach themselves how to behave, you must teach them. And God is doing just that through this book. The life of Christ in the believer is how we are destined to experience the glory of God—God living His life, His righteousness, and His holiness in us. "Christ is the end of the law for righteousness to all who believe."[43] This does not mean the Law is no longer relevant, but that one person, Christ, has fulfilled it. Rather than remain subject to the conditions of

---

[41] Romans 5:2 (KJV)
[42] Romans 8:38-39 (msg)
[43] Romans 10:4 (JEC)

the Law, a believer has simply entered Christ's complete obedience by union with Him. Christ truly is our life.[44]

Maybe this explanation will help. Under the Jew's twisted concept of God's Law, people cursed themselves with an impossible curse. Because they refused to hear God and decided they could attain righteousness by doing everything right, they had to keep doing everything perfectly, with no mistakes, until they died. At that time, they would be declared righteous because they had done it completely—or at least, that was the idea—but no one could do it. Christ never tried to follow the Law as the Jews had conceived it. Rather, He obeyed it as the Father had instructed. Once He had attained the fruit that was a result of submitting to hearing with the intent of believing, His ministry began. After those three and a half years, He became our sin with us, and then died. When He died, we died too. Since we were united to Him when He died, our obligation to fulfill the Law until death was completed because we were members of His body. God isn't just pretending we are righteous when He declares us so, He says we are, because we are one with Christ! This is the mystery of godliness. God says we were in Jesus when He fulfilled the Law, died, went into the grave, rose again, and ascended. I don't understand how God did that, but He did. His life, death, burial, resurrection, and ascension went backward and forward through all time. God doesn't have to explain; it just *is*.

We were incapable of obeying the Law, so Jesus did it in our place, but as us. In His life on Earth, He was not acting independently from the rest of humanity as though we were going to be given credit for what He did. Jesus became us; so, when He died, every human being to ever live did too. Then when He rose from dead, we did too. As John said in his first epistle, "As He is, so are we in this world."[45] He was talking about the fact that whatever you can say about Jesus in Heaven, you can say about His body on Earth. It cannot be otherwise! How could that be? Whatever is true of Him is true of us in this world right now, because we are one with Him. God united all of humankind with Jesus

---

[44] Colossians 3:4
[45] 1 John 4:17 (KJV)

Unseen

so that like Paul, we can say, "I was crucified with Christ."[46] You can't explain it. Faith agrees.

We are united to, and one with, His obedience, but that does not mean God now expects us to struggle to obey the Law. Flesh is still flesh and is not capable of the strength and determination necessary to keep all the Law. However, since a believer is united to Christ in an inseparable and indivisible oneness, he can allow Jesus to bear the yoke.

> Come to me, all you who are toiling and burdened, and I will give you rest! Take my yoke upon you, and learn from me, because I am gentle and lowly-minded, *and you will find rest for your souls;* for my yoke is easy, and my burden is light.[47]

Jesus now lives in us and with us throughout our lives. As we learn to believe what He believes, we automatically act as He acts. No longer is it necessary to follow in His footsteps as though we are still somehow separate from Him. Since He lives in us, the only faith we have is His faith. That is what being in Christ does to us. His faith is now our faith because we are one with Him, even when we don't feel it.

History is filled with Satan's attempts to counterfeit a similar union with man by use of deception. He knew Adam and Eve were created to live what they believed, so the rulers of the darkness of this world have fed us a continual stream of lies from the time we were born. Believing Satan's lies causes us to do them; hence, we become his servants. "Know ye not, that to whom ye yield yourselves servants to obey, his servants ye are to whom ye obey; whether of sin unto death, or of obedience unto righteousness?"[48] Satan can seize control and reign as lord over anyone who believes enough of his lies. But, we now believe the *truth* because Christ's faith is our faith through our union with Him. We are not seeking to know our purpose so we can live it because we know our purpose is to *be* loved. God lives our purpose within us.

---

[46] Galatians 2:20
[47] Matthew 11:28-30 (TCNT Part 1)
[48] Romans 6:16 (KJV)

God didn't create mankind to serve Him, but so He could love us and show us His kindness throughout all the coming ages. "That in the ages to come he might shew the exceeding riches of his grace in his kindness toward us through Christ Jesus."[49] Out of our *being* comes our obedience. We love to hear God, so we can believe His *truth* and do it. What happened to the struggle? It was based on the *lie*, so when that darkness was exposed to light, the struggle ceased to exist. Those that believe enter His rest. "For we which have believed do enter into rest."[50] We have believed. Finally, we are beginning to see the rest, which was already ours. We don't "try" to see it; it eventually just appears, and you see it from inside of you to the outside.

This is why Satan wants us to be performance and results oriented. Because if that is our natural mindset, then it is the filter through which we will see everything. Satan is not opposed to anyone reading the Bible, if they interpret it from the standpoint of what they should *do;* because they believe the *lie*, people do this automatically. If we think a primary focus of God's Word is our performance, we will never appreciate the effectiveness of His grace. If we believe that God is primarily concerned about what we do and how much we do it, then Satan has little about which to be concerned. If the Bible does nothing but establish standards of performance, grace remains nothing more than an icon to worship. If His Word is a description of correct performance, the penalty for failure is condemnation.

The lie says that our results are more important than how they are achieved. To *the lie*, performance motivated by flesh is acceptable if the results are good. God's grace expects something else. Since we live what we believe, our performance is always a consequence of what we believe; thus, the fruit of our lives is also. God's grace says that the outcome is *not* more important than the means. "And anything not done as the result of faith (believing God's *truth*) is sin (error)."[51] There is only one means that is acceptable to God—believing His *truth*. Paul said that works performed by this means are called spirit. "But if you

---

[49] Ephesians 2:7 (KJV)

[50] Hebrews 4:3 (KJV)

[51] Romans 14:23 (JEC)

put to death (kill) the deeds of the body, *by spirit* you will live. For as many as by God's Spirit are led [to put away the deeds of the flesh by believing the *truth*] shall live."[52] If we reach a goal by believing a lie, God does not find it pleasing. "Without believing the *truth*, it is impossible to please God."[53] This is not to say He is angry with us. It just means that works that are not the response of faith do not please God, even though they may seem proper in our eyes. "There is a way which seems right to a man, But its end is the way of death."[54]

When we achieve objectives by believing His *truth*, He is always pleased. Obtaining a particular result is never our responsibility. Our job is to believe. That is the way we can do things as God would do them. God gives the increase; He is responsible for the results.[55] The power of God's life energizes those who believe His *truth*. We enjoy His life by believing the *truth*, and our minds experience renewal the same way. It is always a free choice. God never attempts to trick us into believing His *truth*. He is never devious and, unlike Satan, His promises are never lies.

God has no desire to control our lives. He longs for fellowship in which we willingly cooperate with His Spirit and He, in turn, gifts (graces) us with His active presence inside us. Paul described this experience thus: "I laboured more abundantly than they all: yet not I, but the grace of God which was with me."[56] The grace of God makes the power of His life *freely* available inside us. It is only by means of His grace that we can obey. Any other type of *obedience*, regardless of the results, is disobedience.

Use Your Symptoms to Learn God's Solution

Grace makes it possible to use the symptoms of our error to help correct our error. The grace of God means that instead of being afraid of

---

[52] Romans 8:13-14 (JEC)
[53] Hebrews 11:6 (KJV)
[54] Proverbs 14:12 (NASB)
[55] 1 Corinthians 3:7
[56] 1 Corinthians 15:10 (KJV)

mistakes, we can learn from them.[57] When I become aware of a sinful behavior (action or feeling), instead of feeling condemned, I thank God that my heart is not hardened. If it were, I would not have been aware of or concerned about doing wrong. I also thank God for the Holy Spirit because He is the one who makes me aware of the behavior which needs to change.

If you are willing to acknowledge you were wrong, you have just experienced fellowship with the Holy Spirit. He spoke, and you responded. Now let's take another step. The source of the behavior was an error in your belief system, and only the Holy Spirit knows what that is. This gives you an opportunity to develop intimacy with Him. Jesus promised that the Holy Spirit would teach us the *truth*.[58] So I cooperate by agreeing there is error (unbelief) in my heart (the container of my belief system) and if I don't know what it is, I say to the Holy Spirit, "Lord, my wrong behavior is evidence that I believe something wrong, but I don't know what it is. Search my heart and expose that error and show me the *truth* that should replace it." You may see it immediately or it may take a while. There are lots of reasons why it can go either way.

Use these experiences as opportunities to discover the kindness of the Holy Spirit. Talk to Him freely about His *truth* and your beliefs. There are no rules. You can't make a mistake. You're getting to know Him, and He welcomes you. As the writer of Hebrews says, we can "come boldly unto the throne of grace," which means without fear or anxiety of doing or saying something wrong. When you are talking to God honestly, you can't do anything to upset Him.[59] Intentionally lying to Him hurts His heart, but He still loves you and will always

---

[57] As discussed previously, a better translation of the Greek verb for sin (ἁμαρτάνω) is err, because sin has come to mean doing something wrong, whereas err covers the meaning of sin plus what causes the wrongdoing. This rendering emphasizes the reason for the sinful behavior rather than just the action. Eliminating a behavior may be pleasing to society, but is not pleasing to God unless we first remove the source—that is, the error in our believing and thinking.

[58] John 16:13: "But when he—the Spirit of Truth—comes, he will guide you into the whole Truth." (TCNT Part 2)

[59] Hebrews 4:16 (KJV)

be working to cause you to want to be honest with Him. God's grace is unconditional. It is never dependent upon what you do or don't do. Nothing you do can make God more or less gracious. People can reject His grace but the moment they are ready to take it, it is there in all its abundance. God never holds a grudge. His forgiveness is complete.

Isn't this simple? When the Holy Spirit makes you aware of something wrong in your life, acknowledge it. Then remember that the wrong thing points to an error in your beliefs, of which you are probably unaware. Ask the Holy Spirit to search your heart, expose your wrong beliefs, and show you the *truths* that should replace them. When you choose to believe His *truth* is right, the light of *truth* in your heart automatically destroys the power of darkness.

One last suggestion: when you read any New Testament passage that contains the word *faith*, substitute the definition "believing the *truth*" in its place. Also, in place of "sin" substitute the word *error*. The New Testament will begin to make sense like never before. For example, Ephesians 2:8 reads: "For by grace are ye saved through *faith*; and that not of yourselves: it is the gift of God."[60] Substitute *believing the truth* for *faith* and it reads thus: "For by grace are ye saved through *believing the truth*; and that not of yourselves: it is the gift of God."[61] Doesn't that make a whole lot more sense? Try this one from the King James Version: "Knowing this, that our old man is crucified with him, that the body of *sin* might be destroyed, that henceforth we should not serve *sin*."[62] But, let's make this verse very personal. Since the Greek word for *is* is in the aorist (past) tense, change it to *was*. Also, by replacing the word *sin* with *error and* using some of your other new insights from Unseen, read it like this: "Knowing this, that my old self *was* crucified with him, so that the body of *error* can no longer rule me, because I no longer believe it, thus I no longer have to serve *error*. Now Holy Spirit, begin showing me any error I believe and the truth you want to replace it with."[63]

---

[60] Ephesians 2:8 (KJV)

[61] Ephesians 2:8 (JEC)

[62] Romans 6:6 (KJV)

[63] When Paul spoke of the body of sin, he was referring to the body of error, which is a body of knowledge that includes all error. This erroneous body of knowledge

1 John 1:8-10 is another passage that causes much confusion simply because of a misunderstanding of *hamartia* (ἁμαρτία) (error). "If we say that we have no *sin*, we deceive ourselves and the truth is not in us. If we confess our *sins*, he is faithful and just to forgive us our *sins* and cleanse us from all unrighteousness. If we say that we have not *sinned*, we make him a liar, and his word is not in us." Now let's use *error* in the place of *sin*. "If we say that we have no *error*, we deceive ourselves and the *truth* is not in us. If we confess our *errors*, he is faithful and just to forgive us our *errors* and cleanse us from all unrighteousness. If we say that we have not *erred*, we make him a liar, and his word is not in us."

Without the help of the Holy Spirit, it is not possible to understand this. So before or after reading anything in the Bible, thank the Holy Spirit for giving you an attitude of believing the wisdom and revelation that pours out of what God knows and is constantly sharing. When you gain understanding of a passage, the Holy Spirit has caused it. Whether you use *sin* or *error*, it is the Holy Spirit that causes this to make sense; by using *error* as the true meaning of *sin*, the whole of scripture takes on a new aura. God no longer appears to be demanding perfect behavior, but honesty and *truth*. From there, the behavior takes care of itself. No more condemnation; just fellowship.

Let's try something else that will forever change your perspective of the scripture. When you read the Bible and see any promise from God to someone else, believe it applies to you too. The Bible is a book of covenant, and what God promises to one he promises to all. Here's an example using The Message Bible paraphrase:

> This is how much God loved the world: He gave his Son, his one and only Son. And this is why: so that no one need be destroyed; by believing in him, anyone can have a whole and lasting life. God didn't go to all the trouble of sending his Son merely to point an accusing finger, telling the world how bad it was. He came to help, to put the world right again.[64]

---

is the offspring of the lie.

[64] John 3:16-17 (msg)

Now, you can say it like this:

> This is how much God loves *me*: He gave his Son, his one and only Son. And this is why: so that *I* would not need to be destroyed; by believing in him, *I* have a whole and lasting life. God didn't go to all the trouble of sending his Son merely to point an accusing finger, telling *me* how bad *I* am. He came to help, to put *me* right again.

You can do the same with any promise. "For by grace are ye saved through faith; and that not of yourselves: it is the gift of God: Not of works, lest any man should boast."[65] Now say it this way: "For by grace I have been saved *by means of believing God's truth*; and that not of *myself*: it is the gift of God: Not of works, lest *I* should boast." You can do that with every one of God's promises. They all apply to you as much as anyone else.

* * *

Chapter Thirteen Endnotes

Note 1

Many translations render "ἐν πίστει ζῶ τῇ τοῦ υἱοῦ τοῦ Θεοῦ" in Galatians 2:20: "I live by faith in the Son of God." "So it is no longer I that live, but it is Christ that lives in me; and as for my present earthly life, I am living it by faith in the Son of God, who loved me and gave himself for me."[66] However, the Greek is in the genitive case and is more accurately translated as "the faith of the Son of God"—that is, the faith belonging to the Son of God, Christ's faith, or what Jesus believes, which is always the *truth* since He is *truth* itself.

---

[65] Ephesians 2:8-9 (KJV)
[66] Galatians 2:20 (TCNT Part 2)

Note 2

The Greek word for *saved* is σώσω. (σεσωσμένοι in Ephesians 2:8, which is the perfect passive participle). The perfect tense means something that has been completed and the results are still with us. Passive means it happened because of what someone else did. The only way to construe a participle, in this case, is that in Himself, Jesus achieved our complete and full salvation and is still working it within us. In other words, He is living His life in us. Now we simply agree with God regarding this *truth* and He enables us to see the unseen.

If you read a scripture and want to know what the Holy Spirit meant, then it is best to ask Him. (You don't have to know anything about Greek to do that.) God had no intention of believers making stiff theological doctrines out of His Word. He is simply revealing Himself to us and wants us to believe Him. Would you like to thrill the heart and mind of God? Then tell Him you would like to know Who He is. He is thrilled to tell you.

People can argue about Ephesians 2:8 and other salvation scriptures until they die and still never comprehend God's love for them, never know the love of Christ that passes knowledge. God isn't so concerned what you know *about* Him and His work. Rather, He is working to cause His body of knowledge to be the only one you believe.

Note 3

Paul compared *living by believing God's truth* with *living by law*. He mostly spoke of the Law because he was so often confronted with Judaizers. However, it is entirely appropriate to use substitute words like law (lower case), rules, regulations, commandments, etc. Regardless of what type of work someone is doing "for God" or how good the result, if it is motivated by flesh, especially to prove oneself worthy to God, it is error. Jesus didn't die to make us worthy. Rather, God considers each of us so worthy that He sent His Son to die for us. He doesn't need any additional convincing from us.

The following is just a cursory review of scriptures that collectively make Paul's point about following a set of rules to gain God's approval:

1. Romans 14:23 (KJV): "For whatsoever is not of faith (believing God's *truth*) is sin (error)."

2. Romans 4:5 (TCNT Part 2): "While as for those who do not depend upon what they do, but have faith in him (but believe the *truth* of Him) who can make the godless stand right with him, their faith (belief of God's *truth*) is regarded by God as righteousness."

3. Romans 4:15 (TCNT Part 2): "Law, indeed, brings punishment; but where no law exists, no breach is possible."

4. Galatians 2:21 (Knox translation, 1935): "I do not spurn the grace of God. If we can be justified through the law, then Christ's death was needless."

5. Galatians 3:10 (TCNT Part 2): "All who are depending on actions done in obedience to Law are under a curse, for Scripture says—'Cursed is everyone who does not abide by all that is written in the Book of the Law, and do it.'"

6. Galatians 3:11 (TCNT Part 2): "Again, it is evident that no one stands right with God by means of Law, for we read—'Those who stand right with God will find Life as the result of faith (believing God's *truth*).'"

7. Galatians 4:23-24 (TCNT Part 2): "Before the coming of faith (*the law of faith*), we were kept under the charge of the Law, under restraints, in preparation for the Faith (belief of God's *truth*) about to be revealed. So that the Law has proved a guide to lead us to Christ, in order that as the result of faith (believing God's *truth*) we may stand right with God."

8. Galatians 4:5 (TCNT Part 2): Christ came "to ransom those who were subject to Law, so that we might receive the privileges of sons."

9. Galatians 5:4 (KJV): "Christ is become of no effect unto you, whosoever of you are justified by the law; ye are fallen from grace."

10. Galatians 5:18 (JEC): "But if by spirit (an attitude of believing God's *truth*) you are led, you are not under law."

Note 4

Grace is an awesome subject and, because of *the lie*, beyond our ability to comprehend without the help of the Holy Spirit. The following is a repeat of a portion of Chapter Two, so you don't have to go back and look for it.

The King James Version renders Romans 5:2 as follows: "By whom also we have access by faith into this grace wherein we stand, and rejoice in hope of the glory of God." Can you sink your teeth into that? I can't. The King James Version just makes this sound like wishful thinking, whereas a literal rendering gives us reason to shout for joy! I see the original language saying something very different from the KJV. Paul didn't just mean that we are happy about something we wish in the future. He meant that we are so confident of the manifestation of God's life in us right now that we literally boast about our expectations.

Note 5

You may wonder how I am able to say that Romans 5:2 means we stand immersed in grace (See Chapter Two Endnotes #2). Here is my understanding of my translation of the verse:

> By means of Whom (Jesus) also we had, by the [same] (i.e., His) belief, the bringing [up] to [and then into] (as if He gently nudged us into) this favor within which we

stand [immersed], and boast upon [our] expectation of the splendor [that is the character, nature, and prosperity] of God [in our lives].

The access about which Paul was writing is by *the belief* (τῇ πίστει). This is unquestionably the belief (faith) of the Lord Jesus, hence I inserted [same] for emphasis—"the [same] belief." Though many translations render *have* in the present tense, the Greek is in the perfect tense. Thus, it has been done once and for all. We had access to grace in the past and still have it now. However, the word *prosagoghn* (προσαγωγήν), which is often translated as "access," can also mean "a bringing to or toward." I believe the latter meaning is what the writer meant.

So, after being brought to this grace, Paul goes on to say that we are standing (also in perfect tense) in it. The picture in my mind is that of baptism in which we walk up to the water, and without doing anything, we are then immersed by the water, as if the water did the work. I think this passage could easily be understood as: "We are brought to grace and then nudged into it." After being nudged into it, Paul finishes by saying "we are standing in it." I added the word *up* to smooth out my mental picture of being brought toward something (the bringing [up] to). Then I added *and then into* to fill in the gap between *being brought up to* and *standing in grace*.

How did we get from being brought to the grace to standing in it? A little nudge from the Holy Spirit works for me. Since Jesus said I can do nothing by my own strength, then it must have been by the Holy Spirit who got me from standing there looking at the grace to standing in it.

Immersion in His grace is by default. If we are in Christ and He *is* grace, then if we are standing in it we must be immersed in it. In fact, I believe it is the air we breathe. We breathe His grace. I think you get the point.

14
Only Believe

The message of God's grace applies to every area of life—mind, body, emotions, and anything that pertains to living today and tomorrow. Believing God's *truth* applies to every facet of life. Are you bound by sin? Let the Holy Spirit lead you into God's *truth*. Do you have family problems? Let the Holy Spirit lead you into God's *truth*. Are you sick? Let the Holy Spirit lead you into God's *truth*. Having problems on the job? Let the Holy Spirit lead you into God's *truth*. Do you have money problems? Let the Holy Spirit lead you into God's *truth*. The idea that God, the Father of glory, would wish any evil upon His children is preposterous. Satan is working destruction upon mankind with all his ability, and humankind is cooperating. God has no interest in helping darkness or confirming wrong knowledge as being the truth. He longs for us to know who we are but will not force what He knows upon us. He is just waiting for us to say, "Yes, I want to know what You know about me, because that is the only *truth*." In the meantime, the words of King Solomon resonate with us:

> Wisdom cries aloud in the streets,
> She lifts up her voice in the squares;
> At the head of noisy thoroughfares she calls,
> At the openings of the city gates she utters her words:
> How long, you simple ones, will you
> love simplicity, And scoffers delight in scoffing, And fools hate knowledge?

> If you but turn and pay heed to my admonition,
> Lo! I will open my mind to you,
> I will acquaint you with my thoughts:[1]

Now is your opportunity. Decide to believe His *truth* is right even though your experience may say otherwise. When we suffer something that contradicts God's *truth*, it is wrong to deny it happened, because it did happen. Nevertheless, because it is not consistent with *God's reality*, and its source is *the lie*, it is a lie. Be humbled before God and treasure the *truth* instead of your understanding. God's *truth* is a type of leaven; it will grow and grow inside you and produce marvelous fruit, including the victory of Jesus Christ.

Agreeing that God's *truth* is true will bring you to a place where you will be able to recognize the works of Satan as lies. God is Love and is always right even though we may not understand how or why He does or doesn't do something. When something bad happens, it does not mean that God caused it. Rather, when something is not consistent with God's truth, it is a lie. As you face truth and lies from God's perspective you will begin to experience another dimension of living, one that finds its source in Heaven where all of us in Christ are currently seated. Of course, you may not yet see that you are seated in Heaven with Jesus but, if you are willing to be trained by the Holy Spirit, that will change. The first place you will see it is inside you. The wonder of seeing it first on the inside is that it will forever after govern your life, which will no longer be tossed to and fro by what happens to you. You will begin to experience a real confidence in God and not a fake one. Others will come to marvel your life. This is what Jesus was referring to in the fourteenth Chapter of the Gospel of John. In Chapter ten, Jesus had said that He is the truth and in Chapter fourteen He declared that anyone believing into Him would do the same types of works that He did.[2] He went on to say that the Holy Spirit will cause us to *learn* all

---

[1] Proverbs 1:20-23 (Scripture is taken from *The Complete Bible: An American Translation*.)

[2] John 14:12

things.[3] Notice that He said ALL things. Jesus said whatever you want to learn the Holy Spirit will make it happen. Of course, you must be willing to learn *everything* He wants to teach you, because to learn what you want to know will likely require learning many other things first. But, if you want to learn how to do something, He delights to teach you. But, you must cooperate, which means you have to agree with Him even when flesh convincingly tells you that what God has said can't be true or that it is only for some day in the future. Being caused to learn is quite different from being taught. I have been taught many things during my life but only what I have learned has stayed with me. To learn what God knows requires personal training by the Holy Spirit. You may not have yet realized it, but that is what He has begun doing in you by means of this book. We pray you will embrace His words like never before and learn what He so greatly desires for you.

The unseen is real. In fact, it is more real than the seen because it has absolute dominion over it. The unseen is the Kingdom of God. Not only do we live in that Kingdom, but it lives inside us (Chapter Fourteen Endnotes #1). As you learn His *truth* and keep looking at it, the reality of God's Kingdom will become more and more real to you. You will see the unseen.

So, what sorts of things are you reading? To whom are you listening? Are they telling you the *truth*? Why don't you ask God if they are?

I used to struggle with trying to remember the amazing things God teaches me. Then my youngest son told me that he had realized the Holy Spirit is not only his teacher but his "rememberer." That changed my life. God doesn't teach us something and then take it away. He's our *rememberer*; He's our *reminderer*. When the Holy Spirit gives you something, it is yours forever. At the appropriate time, He will bring it back into your thoughts. He is the one working His *truth* inside us. It is just our job to say *amen* and *thank you*. I ponder His *truth* every day and tell Him I agree with Him. I want to know who He says He made me and not forget it. The rest is up to God.

Whenever you know that you are failing to follow the *truth*, approach it from this perspective: admit that your failure is proof of an

---

[3] John 14:26

error in your believing and ask the Holy Spirit to fix it. That's all. By doing that you agreed with the *truth*. Now the Holy Spirit will work that agreement into you. Remember that He is the Vine and we are the branches. The sap in vines gives life to the branches and enables them to perform according to their genetic design. You are a new creature inside Christ. You now have divine genetics. The life that is inside Jesus and now flowing in you will cause you to perform according to your new genetics. If you are unhappy with something in your life over which you seem to have no control, Paul said to do the best your understanding allows you to do and God, in His time, will fix it if needed. Until then, He does not condemn you. He loves and understands you.

> The one thing I am doing is to press on to the winning-post, to gain the prize of that heavenward Call which God gave me through Christ Jesus. All of us, then, whose faith is matured, should take this view of life. Then, if in any respect you take a mistaken view, God will make that also plain to you.[4]

In today's world, the word *judge* or *judgment* represents harshness. We often see God in a black robe banging his gavel as he hands out punishments for sins. But, the verb translated *"to judge"* has a simple meaning which is "to make wrong things right." His judgment (making things right) can range from a simple conversation to a miracle (did you ever think of miracles as God's judgment?). Judgment is *never* condemnation. Every believer should be excited for Judgment Day. Don't judge yourself, because you're bad at it and you're judgments are wrong. Let God do that in His time and His way—it'll work better.

The Power of God

We want to end this chapter of UNSEEN by dipping our toes into the power of God and fruit of the spirit, as described by Paul in Galatians.

---

[4] Philippians 3:14-15 (TCNT Part 2)

Many people think, "If God is love and all powerful, then why doesn't He help us?" Precisely because He is Love. After creating the *cosmos*, God made Adam and Eve and instructed them to be lords over it. His plan was to train them in its care and management. You may wonder why I say God created the *cosmos* when the Bible always talks in terms of the world. In the New Testament, we learn the writers' understandings of the Old Testament. Regardless what God may have called the world in the Old Testament, in the New Testament He used the term *cosmos*. We see this type of expansion of understanding from the Old to the New Testaments often, for instance, in references to the Messiah. We only learn the Messiah is Jesus after we get to the New Testament. We only learn about the Trinity from the New Testament. Likewise, the subject of mankind's power is only fully revealed in the New Testament.

The scope of our dominion is so massive many people have trouble believing it. Thus, many who translate assume the word *cosmos* can't mean the entire universe. To many, it just doesn't make sense. But, in John 3:16, God says He "so loved the *cosmos* that He gave His Only Begotten Son." God loves His whole creation up to and beyond the stars. Just because it became subject to corruption due to Adam's rebellion didn't mean He stopped loving it. It was His joy to create it for the man and woman He was going to fashion by hand. And, He was excited to re-make His beloved mankind within Christ (called the New Creation). He feels the same about the remake of the *cosmos* to come.[5]

The whole creation was God's gift to His humans. The fall of mankind in the Garden of Eden affected the entire universe, not just the Earth. Humankind was to rule all of it but instead chose to obey (submit to hearing) the serpent. Once slaves to Satan, because they *wanted* to believe *the lie* was *truth*, the power which had belonged to humans fell under the dominion of darkness. Though Satan has no power, he doesn't need any because he can deceive human beings and cause them to use their power on his behalf. How? By using the same tactics which caused one-third of the angels to believe him rather than God. The same tactics he used to persuade Adam and Eve that his darkness was light

---

[5] Revelation 21

and would enable them to see what God didn't want them to know. And, because mankind is convinced that *the lie* is *truth*, people are convinced they can figure out what God means, because the devil told them they would know the difference between good and evil. They think, "I'm not stupid." The thing is, they aren't. But, they aren't wise, either.

    I hear many believers say they need power. If they just had power, they could do wonderful things for God. They could heal the sick and win the world for Christ. But, how can we win something that God has already won? God hasn't asked us to win anything. Rather, He has offered us His rest, into which, if we enter, we will find that God has done everything He said He would do. The Kingdom of God has been here all along, but many don't believe it. Since they don't believe it, they can't see it. Thus, they keep working to make it happen. They have been fooled by *the lie* and are living what they believe, which is not what God believes. God said, "It is finished."[6] Now He is seeking beachheads among men where His leaven of *truth* can begin to leaven the whole lump. Remember, that is how Jesus described the Kingdom of God.[7] Unfortunately, many believers think that doing the right thing is more important than having hearts full of God's *truth*. God has restored humankind to our rightful place in the Kingdom of God and the power we need is already ours. Our Father wants to make it real to us.

    The biblical concept of heirship is different from the Western perspective. My parents were very generous but what they owned wouldn't belong to their kids until after they were gone. They spent the last couple decades of their lives in a very exclusive Colorado resort. Though I was welcome to visit anytime and use the property when they weren't there, my parents didn't consider it a family home. It was their home.

    In Jesus's day, Israel was a different culture. As Jesus illustrated in the story of the Prodigal Son, a son could demand his share of an inheritance and take it.[8] That was the law of their society. And, that is the law of the Kingdom of God, too. What God has can't be ours after He dies, because He can't die. It is ours right now, and God wants us

---

[6] John 19:30
[7] Luke 13:21
[8] Luke 15

to take all we want of what is His.⁹ Do you need power, healing, food, shelter, money? God says that everything He has is yours. Take what you need. But, this type of thinking is so far from anything our minds can conceive that many refuse to believe it. Also, some of us have seen many abuses of the teaching of faith. Some proclaimed that if you say something until you believe it, whatever you have said will be yours. I spent years learning these types of doctrines, but I wanted more. I wanted God. I wanted what Paul sought, "That I may know him, and the power of his resurrection, and the fellowship of his sufferings, being made conformable unto his death; If by any means I might attain unto the resurrection of the dead."¹⁰ As far as I am concerned, all the money in the world isn't enough if I can't rest peacefully in the confidence that God's love will take care of my family and me no matter what is happening and no matter how badly I might screw up. I refuse to accept money, success, or fame as a substitute for knowing God as Jesus does. The day will come when money isn't enough. Then what do you do?

According to Titus 2:12 (KJV), the grace of God has appeared, "Teaching us that, denying ungodliness and worldly lusts, we should live soberly, righteously, and godly, in this present world." To live godly means like-God. And, what is God like? Not only is He Love, He is joy itself, and He is shalom, which means far more than just peace of mind. It also includes wholeness, healing, health, completeness, and salvation. I think *shalom* is the biggest word in the Bible. It must be because Jesus is our *shalom*.¹¹ "Then Gideon built an altar there unto the LORD, and called it Jehovah-shalom."¹² You can understand more of Who God is and what He is like from Galatians 5:22 and 23.

---

[9] Matthew 7:7, John 15:7, Hebrews 12:28, Luke 15:31

[10] Philippians 3:10, 11 (KJV)

[11] The word *shalom* grew out of the prosperity and peace of Israel during King Solomon's reign. It means harmony, wholeness, completeness, health, prosperity, peace, and tranquility. It is also a commonly used blessing which commands a person's life to be whole and complete with health, peace of mind, and prosperity. It can be used in the place of "Hello" and "Good bye."

[12] Judges 6:24 (KJV)

Who God *IS* is an especially important subject because God originally made us in His image, and then restored that image in our union with Christ. That restoration is not a future expectation but a present reality. Since we are in Christ, we can't be His image in the future unless we are His image now. As we continue to look at Jesus, the Bible says we see ourselves. James writes of a person who forgets who they are. He then writes about looking into the Word and continuing to look. The Early Church understood that continuing to look at God's *truth* with the *intent* to believe it would result in doing the work. "But whoso looketh into the perfect law of liberty, and continueth (to look) *therein*, he being not a forgetful hearer, but a doer of the work, this man shall be blessed in his deed."[13] The issue for writers of the New Testament was not to hear so they could *do* but so they could believe and thus do. Do you see the difference? The first is not doing out of faith but flesh, will power. The second is doing because you so believe who God says you are that you see yourself as that person. When you see yourself to be who God says you are, you'll just be who you are. This is what Jesus meant when He said, "My Yoke is easy." It is very easy to be who you know and believe you are.

Man was created to live like who he believes he is. That's why God considers it critical that we believe about ourselves what He knows to be true and what He sees. And what does He see? Jesus. Since we are members of Christ's body, of which He is the head, we look like Him, and not some sinful image that the world and other "believers" paint us. God does not see us through a lens of Jesus but inside Jesus. The difference between these two perspectives is gulfed by an infinitely wide chasm. The reason so many teach that God sees us through Christ is because they believe they are only new creatures in theory. They don't believe they will be truly new creations until they see Jesus at His second coming. But that is an erroneous interpretation of Scriptures to satisfy their unwillingness to take God literally at His Word. They can't understand how it would be possible to be new creatures and still want to sin, so they have determined that God must mean something other than what He says. My view is literal. The Scriptures say that we

---

[13] James 1:15 (KJV)

are inside Christ. We are not separate beings from Him but united with Him in God right now. There is no degree of separation. God is the one Who has declared that is the *truth*. Though God loves to give us understanding and, in fact, declares its importance in Proverbs, He never says that we must have understanding before we believe Him. Rather, He says, "Trust in the Lord with the totality of your heart with no room for doubting what He says, and don't lean to any understanding; in all your manner of living know Him, know who He is, trust Who He is, and He will direct your every step, even if it doesn't seem like it."[14]

When we look into the Word, God wants us to see ourselves, who we are. "But we all, with open face beholding as in a glass the glory of the Lord, are changed into the same image." When you look into a mirror you do not expect to see what you will look like later but what you look like at that moment.[15] As we continue to look, the miracle of God's Word is that it washes our minds from who we thought we were to realize who we really are. This process takes time. Your current image of yourself, whether good or bad, didn't happen overnight. It has taken time to learn to see yourself as you do. Many see themselves as sinners. If you believe you are a sinner, that is who you will act like. But, now God wants you to see yourself as He sees you, which is as righteous as Jesus is, since you are one with Jesus and a member of His Body. You may think you are different than Jesus, but God says that isn't possible. Of course, if you believe you are different then you will act like it. But, as you continue to see yourself in the mirror of His Word, it will wash away wrong self-images and replace them with God's image of you. As that happens, we find ourselves increasingly acting like who God says we really are (Chapter Fourteen Endnote #2). It's so simple.

Sometime ago I realized that modern translations of Galatians 5:22 and 23 were missing something. Why was the last facet of the fruit of the spirit called self-control, especially since the other facets of the fruit of the spirit were components of self-control? Finally, I decided it was time to study the Greek text.

---

[14] Proverbs 3:5,6 (JEC paraphrase)
[15] 2 Corinthians 3:18

Before we can present you with an out-of-this-world shock, we need to explain some of what Paul wrote as he approached his comments about the fruit of the spirit. The Apostle is big on hearing. In Romans 1:5, Paul says God commanded him to teach the *submission to hearing* belonging to faith. This is usually translated *obedience to the faith*. In Matthew 28:30, Jesus told the disciples, "teaching them to *observe* all that I commanded you." Today the word *observe* means to do, but not back then. To early believers it meant, "to look at, to watch closely, to guard." In other words, "Fix your attention on God's *truth* and don't take your eyes off it. If you are looking at any knowledge that appears to contradict God's Word, STOP looking at it and look at God's *truth*. As you continue to look at God's *truth*, what is real to Him will become real to you." In Galatians 1:6, the Apostle begins pleading with them to stop listening to "another" gospel that isn't Christ's. And, He explains that even Apostles can be fooled into believing error.[16]

In 3:2 and 3:5, Paul asks if they took the Spirit and saw the Spirit's miracles by doing the right things (law's works) or the kind of *hearing* that belongs to believing the *truth* (faith's hearing) (Chapter Fourteen Endnote #3). Over and over Paul returns to the subject of what the Galatians were hearing and what they were being persuaded to believe. He re-explains what God knows to get them to return to it. But, the satanic compulsion to believe *the lie* is strong. It is like a drug, only stronger. Paul is using all his reasoning ability to *persuade* them to once again embrace God's grace. They must decide to embrace it because he knows God will not *force* anyone to believe the *truth*. All the New Testament writers' quantum use of the Greek language makes it very clear that God wants us to intentionally hear and believe (Chapter Fourteen Endnotes #4 and #5).

Paul knew that Satan seeks to convince people that we don't live inside the faith of Christ, but Galatians 2:20 says we do (Chapter Fourteen Endnote #6). He also knew that God looks at our desire and intention to believe and is moved by it. "But the LORD said to Samuel, "Do not look at his appearance or at the height of his stature, because I have rejected him; for God sees not as man sees, for man looks at the

---

[16] Galatians 2:14

outward appearance, but the LORD looks at the heart."[17] Paul understood the power of honest, determined intention, and how God works inside it. He also knew that within our intention to believe we discover the gift of faith.

My literal translation of Galatians 5:22 and 23 takes into consideration Paul's understanding of the different uses of the word spirit, as we have previously described: "Now, the fruit of *the* attitude that will not let go of God's *truth* is love, joy, shalom, enduring passion, usefulness, goodness, fullness of believing the *truth*, gentle force, and outward dominion" (Chapter Fourteen Endnote #7).[18]

So where is the power of God? It isn't magic. We start with Jesus's attitude, Who treasured God's *truth*. The fruit that His attitude in us produces will begin to appear. The order in which the facets of the fruit appear in our lives will vary. But, before we know it, we are seeing and living the love of God. That is, we are living the love of Christ because He is our life.[19] As we continue to grow in believing the *truth*, we see *joy* and *shalom* have become ours. At some point, we notice *enduring passion*. It was there long before we noticed it. We also find ourselves being more *useful*, in so many ways. The *goodness* in our lives is affecting others, yet we may not have even noticed. But, others have. At another point, we realize that we really do trust God and feel safe. We have grown fuller *of faith*. All of this is producing a new type of ability in our lives. Some would call it spirit controlled behavior. We realize we are living without cares or fear. We know God because we are filled with His *truth* and living it. But, something else is happening, of which we are not yet fully aware. The power of God's love in our hearts is causing everything we do and say to have a curious effect on people. Some feel a stir inside of them. They notice we are different than others. When they are with us they feel different. Some feel better; they may even say they feel cleaner, as though something washed them. They

---

[17] Samuel 16:7 (ESV)

[18] Since the New Testament was written in Greek, the writers used the Greek word for peace (*eirēnē*). However, the corresponding Hebrew word is *shalom*, which is the meaning they would have been thinking.

[19] Colossians 3:4

can't exactly put their fingers on it, but something is drawing them. Regardless how we think people are perceiving us, something about us is changing the world around us like light effects darkness. Then we remember *gentleness*. Yes, gentle force. We aren't being pushy. We aren't demanding anything of anyone. We are just being love. We are accepting and loving people like Jesus did, including the reviled "tax collectors and sinners." We are befriending them. People are having all sorts of reactions to us, good and bad. It doesn't matter, we know the power of God's Word is working inside us and through us, without preaching to anyone. His love is powerful, and gently forceful, not because we are trying to make it so but because Love treats people like Jesus did. And then the day comes when we are faced with a need that requires more than just gentle force. We need power. But, we don't even really think about it, because we are simply being who we are, heirs of God in union with Christ Jesus. We know what Jesus would do in this situation, because we already think like He does. We have the mind of Christ.[20] We know who we are… Christ in us. Whatever miracle is needed, we know we have both the authority and power, because we are one with Him Who is the authority and power. It's no big deal to us. We're just being who we are. We have outward dominion. We think what Jesus is thinking and speak. As we do so, God commands with us and as us, "Be it so!" To some, we look like Jesus, "Even the wind and waves obey Him."[21] (Chapter Fourteen Endnote #8).

God's power comes from Who He is, because it is Who He is that causes Him to do what He does. Mankind was created in that same image, to be just like Him.

* * *

---

[20] 2 Corinthians 2:16
[21] Mark 4:41

Chapter Fourteen Endnotes

Note 1

Many wonder where the Kingdom of God is. My answer is wherever Jesus is. The question is, are you going to see and enjoy it or be one of those that refuses God's gift and chooses to separate yourself from the only source of unconditional, unearned love?

The scriptures view the Kingdom from several perspectives. Our focus at present is seeing and enjoying it in this life. "'Believe me,' Jesus replied, 'unless a man is born over again, he cannot see the Kingdom of God.'"[22] He didn't say, "If a man goes to heaven, he shall see the Kingdom of God," though from a flesh perspective that would seem logical. The clear implication is we will see the Kingdom of God in this life, while in this body of flesh.

Paul said it is available to us right now. "For God has rescued us from the tyranny of Darkness, and has removed us into the Kingdom of his Son, who is the embodiment of his love."[23] The writer of Hebrews says we have been given the Kingdom of God. "Wherefore we receiving a kingdom which cannot be moved."[24] As "heirs of God and joint-heirs with Jesus Christ," doesn't it make sense that God has given you more than you have yet to see or realize? You don't have to wait until Heaven to see what God has given you, unless that is what you want to do.

The verb for receiving (taking) in the text is the present active participle which means it is ongoing. In other words, we can keep taking it. If you think you have already gotten everything that God is going to give you, stop thinking that now. God says He has an entire Kingdom that is yours for the taking—now! So, keep taking it. How? By believing His *truth*—Jesus, The Way, The *Truth*, and The Life.

---

[22] John 3:3 (JEC)
[23] Colossians 1:13 (TCNT Part 2)
[24] Hebrews 12:28 (KJV)

Note 2

The conjugation of the Greek verb often translated "being changed" is present indicative middle/passive. It means, "are changed," which is difficult for our Western logic to grasp. It means we *are* what we see in that glass, not "we are being changed to look like what is in that glass."

Note 3

Nestled between verses 2 and 5 of Chapter Three Paul asks a profound question, "Having begun in the Spirit, are ye now made perfect by the flesh?" Unfortunately, though the verse is commonly written this way, it is not what the Greek text says. I will leave an explanation of Greek grammar and analysis of vocabulary for another time, but I want to focus once again on the words *spirit* and *flesh*. Remember that we have written previously that *spirit* and *flesh* have several meanings. In this case, by *spirit*, Paul meant "an attitude set on believing God's *truth*." By *flesh*, he meant "an attitude set on believing that what we see, hear, and feel is the *truth*." In the original text, neither word is preceded by the article "the." Thus, to add an article potentially changes the meaning from *spirit* to *the Spirit*, which is what many translators do. It also changes *flesh* to *the flesh*, which strongly suggests Paul was referring to the body. Because of this slight change, the meaning of the rest of the passage through to "the fruit of the Spirit" in Chapter Five is changed. Whereas Paul is explaining how to live a life of ability, that understanding is wiped out and we are left trying to figure out how to get the fruit of the Spirit. Many interpret the passage as meaning that we are waiting for the Holy Spirit to do something. But, no. Paul is asking, "Having begun with an attitude that treasures God's *truth* are you now going to be made whole by an attitude determined to believe what your eyes, ears, and feelings are telling you?" Read through this passage yourself. You don't have to understand Greek to recognize that Paul is seeking to reason with the readers. He pleads with them to actively believe that God's *truth* is the only *truth*, and cease believing what flesh was telling them. He didn't want them to again embrace *the lie* just because it felt more *comfortable*. In so many ways, he was telling the Galatians to reject any logic that said they must follow the rules of religion. Religion may feel comfortable, because it is familiar, but it is still a lie. Paul was seeking to once again get them out of their comfort zone back into the *truth*, which would eventually feel comfortable, if they would keep looking at it.

The comfortable feel of religion was *flesh* beckoning them to believe their feelings were the *truth*. When you have lived a lifetime believing and thus feeling a lie, it may not initially feel comfortable when you use God's *truth* to reason through to a new conclusion. Believing the *truth* is not the result of some magic with which God zaps people. Sometimes we are persuaded to believe the *truth* yet don't realize what we did until afterwards. But, God never zapped us. Behind the scenes He had been reasoning with us using gentle power and, when we finally believed, the decision may have been sudden but never forced on us.

In Chapter Four, Paul writes about how Abraham had two sons. One was born because he stopped trusting God and impregnated his servant girl. The other son was born after Abraham had come to the end of his efforts. He and Sarah had finally become so old and so much time had passed that Abraham was convinced it was impossible for them to have a child. And, by then He knew having a baby with his servant girl was not God's plan. Finally, he had no choice but to trust the God Whom he had believed those many years earlier. When the time was right, God blessed Abraham's wife with the ability to become pregnant.

In verse 29, Paul writes, "But just as then, the son born to Abraham [while he had an attitude set on believing what his eyes, ears, and feelings told him] persecuted the son born while Abraham had an attitude of believing God's Word, so it is still the same." Paul is telling them that they can have one of two attitudes: (1) The attitude represented by the word *flesh* causes a person to seek justification by following rules, which causes them to fall out of grace. The grace is still there, but they won't take it because they are determined to earn it first. God will never reward someone who is working for what He wants to freely give them. He'll just wait until we quit working so there is no doubt that when we finally get it, it was His gift. God says, "NO!" to that type of "faith." "You can only have grace if you take it as a gift. If you want to work for it, then you are still believing *the lie*. Do you think you are wiser than Me? (Says God.) You can believe *the lie* until you decide you don't want to believe it anymore. The gift of My grace will be waiting here anytime you want to say, 'Thank you.' and let me do it." (2) The other attitude they can have is, "I will set my attention on your *truth* and learn to believe what you believe. I know that at some point, what I am looking at will be so real to me that I will know it is my reality. My faith will result in the actual substance of what I have been expecting."[25]

In Chapter Five verse 5, Paul writes that, "For we, through an attitude set on treasuring God's *truth* wait for the hope of righteousness by faith." This is difficult for someone who prefers to trust in themselves to earn salvation. When we seek to trust that God will do what He promised simply because He promised even when we aren't doing anything right, amazingly, God does it. Just like the first son of Abraham, everyone trying to earn their way into God's favor hates those who believe they don't have to do anything to earn God's blessing and favor except believe. It was the same with the older brother of the Prodigal Son in Luke 15. He was angry at his father for the love and grace freely bestowed on his wayward brother.

In 5:16, Paul says what we have been trying to tell you. "This I say then, live with an attitude of believing God's *truth* and you will not have an attitude that fulfills the desires of what your senses are telling you."[26] Whoa! If you didn't get that, read it again, and again, and again until you get it. This is freedom. This is grace working in your life.

Now in 5:17, Paul uses the article and writes *the flesh* and *the spirit* instead of *flesh* and *spirit*. What's going on? In this case, the article "the" means the terms flesh and spirit refer to specific instances of them, not our bodies and the Holy Spirit. Paul is using the article "the" to sum up both attitudes into one of two categories. "*The* attitude of believing what eyes, ears, and feelings tell us" and "*the* attitude of believing God's *truth* is the only *truth*." This latter *the* attitude is speaking of Jesus's attitude. But notice, according to many translations of this verse the flesh is opposed to the Spirit of God while *the* Spirit of God

---

[25] Hebrews 11:1

[26] Galatians 5:16 (JEC paraphrase)

is obviously warring in opposition to *the* flesh. Does that cause you to wonder? It appears the Spirit of God is opposed to our flesh. Some believe this means He hates our bodies and everything they desire. Yet, He created them. So, now He hates them? Really? He is God. Is our flesh such a problem that He is admitting He made a mistake? Is it possible that in His planning of the creation, He failed to consider the future weakness of flesh and after the mutiny realized He had created an uncontrollable monster that just needs to be ultimately destroyed? Is God saying that He must fight against the thing He created because it is so powerful that it is able to subvert His will? Boy, based on what many people obviously believe, our God has a real problem and has really screwed up.

In verse 18, Paul goes back to "an" attitude of believing that God's *truth* is the only *truth*. "But, if you are led by spirit (an attitude of believing God's *truth*) you are no longer under law (of any kind)." Okay, but if we aren't required to keep any law, what does that mean? Does God not care if we sin? Oh, He cares greatly and that is why He has given us His Word. He doesn't want us to err. He loves righteousness and is determined we will freely live like Him, but without threatening us if we don't. Because He created us to live what we *really* believe, He knows that once He gets us to keep considering that "perfect law of liberty," as we realize we are the reflection we see, we will automatically live it.

And now Paul approaches the subject of power. First, he lists the "works of the flesh." These really are a lot of work; they are laborious and never satisfy. They are accomplishments that produce no peace. As we have uncovered in UNSEEN, they are a result of believing other than God's *truth*.

Then Paul comes to "the fruit of the Spirit." However, he is not writing about the Spirit of God. He is referring to "THE" attitude of believing the *truth*. What attitude could that be? Paul wasn't referring to a "what" but a "Who," that is, Jesus' attitude, which Paul recognized was THE only attitude ever set on believing the *truth*. The only reason we can have an attitude of believing God's *truth* is because Jesus does, and we are one with Him. Of course, if we reject this reality and refuse to believe that God has made us one with Christ then, since we live what we believe, even though God says we are in Christ and live in heavenly places, something else will seem more real to us.[27]

Note 4

The subjunctive mood in the Greek language is problematic for many who have studied Ancient Greek. There is no brief English equivalent, so it requires a description that still doesn't make sense to Western minds. It is typically defined as the mood of probability yet more commonly translated as no more than a possibility (might, may, should, etc.). But, God has never been the God of might or may. He has always been the God of will, of absolute intention. Thus, I have learned that the subjunctive mood, in New Testament usage, should be understood as the mood of intention or will. Sometimes it is untranslatable, yet a teacher with understanding is well able to help learners understand how it affects the meaning of the writers.

Note 5

By James Q. Campbell - No book on religion would be complete without a short talk on the topic of quantum physics (I figured this opening would get your attention). There's a famous quantum physics experiment called the Double Slit Experiment. You can go look up videos on YouTube if you want to experience a real head-scratcher, but we'll summarize it here.

You may remember from high school physics class that light can be either a wave or a particle. It's a wave like what happens when you drop a rock into water and a particle like if you could throw a baseball perfectly straight. Maybe it would help if you think of a baseball passing through the air with waves coming out of it. Researchers wanted to know more about how this worked so they shot particles at a metal plate with a slit in it and watched what happened on the other side. As they watched the light pass through the slit in the plate it became a particle.

---

[27] Ephesians 2:6

But they discovered that if they didn't watch and just measured the results later, it acted like a wave. So, they learned that when the human mind tried to measure what was happening rather than just accepting that it happened, it changed the physical reality of the world.

Then things got weird.

They tried to trick the experiment. When they didn't watch the light pass through the slit, it acted as a wave. So, what would happen if they started watching *right after* the light passed through the slit? It turns out that watching what happened as it went through the slot caused the past to change. Yes, you read that right. Only observing the light *after* it had passed through the slit caused past events to change and the light to display as a particle when it should have been a wave.

You should really go search for the Double Slit Experiment on YouTube.

The Koine Greek language allows for the same. God's Covenant with mankind was made in the past, but he doesn't force anyone to see the benefits, so if someone doesn't accept it, they will continue to see what they have been seeing. But the moment our reasoning starts agreeing with His Covenant, we begin to realize it affects our present because it has changed what we knew about our past. So, what happened in the past only becomes real to us and changes our present experience once we accept that it literally changed our past when it happened, even though we didn't realize it until the present. What was past then becomes present and our present realization in turn effects what we now know of our past. As Paul said, "The old is gone and the new has appeared" (2 Corinthians 5:17). But, since the old included our past, how could both our past and present be new? How can we be new when we still look like we did when we were old? The Apostle Paul said it another way in Galatians 2:20 many years after Christ's crucifixion even though he nor anyone else could have seen him there. He wrote, "I was crucified with Christ and the effects are as present with me now as when it happened." English translations may not say this but the original Greek sure does. So, since things like this are conveyed by the original Greek Text, we call koine Greek a quantum language. We don't know how else to describe it. Maybe calling it a covenant language would work since Ancient Greek not only enables the linguistic expression of God's Covenant reality but gives us a new way to understand how covenants work in the world beyond time. But, we like the word quantum.

Note 6

The Greek text in Galatians 2:20 is, "ἐν πίστει ζῶ τῇ τοῦ υἱοῦ τοῦ θεοῦ." Reading it literally word by word, "within (inside) faith I live, that of the Son of the God."

Note 7

"But the fruit of the Spirit is love, joy, peace, patience, kindness, goodness, faithfulness, gentleness, self-control; against such things there is no law." (I have chosen the NASB version because it is closer to the original Greek.)

The first three facets of the fruit of an attitude set on believing God's *truth* are, "love, joy, shalom…" God is Love, so the first facet of the fruit of the spirit is God Himself.[28] When you see someone who is set on believing only God's *truth*, you are seeing an image of the God Who knows and believes only His *truth* is true. The first facet of the fruit is followed by joy. God's joy is the result of His love for His human creatures. As we realize His joy because of what He has accomplished in us, it strengthens us regardless of what flesh tells us about our weaknesses.[29] This is much like the confidence of leaders which gets transmitted to their followers. Then comes shalom. The New Testament was written in Greek from writers who grew up in the Hebrew culture. The Hebrew word *shalom* is much richer than the Greek word for peace so the writers would have had *shalom* in mind as they wrote the Greek word for peace. It is a wonderful word that means wholeness, health, healing, salvation, abundance, peace of mind, completeness. When we have an attitude that treasures God's

---

[28] This Greek word for fruit is singular, so the nine fruit of the spirit are facets of a singular fruit. All nine facets will appear in the lives of believers who have an attitude that is set on believing that what God says is always the *truth* even when it doesn't make sense.

[29] Nehemiah 8:10

truth alone, we discover the reality of His *shalom* becoming more and more real in our lives.

The next three facets of the fruit of an attitude set on believing God's *truth* are, "...patience, kindness, goodness..." The Greek word translated *patience* was a surprise to me. *Makrothumia* (μακροθυμία) is compounded from *makrós,* meaning *long* and *thymós,* meaning *passion* or *anger.* I believe it has been traditionally understood to mean patience because of the belief that God is angry and, thus, only tolerates us. But, the word actually means "enduring passion." It paints the picture of a God who doesn't quit. His passionate love and desire for His beloved children is so great that it does not diminish as He works to instruct and train us in "the way we should go."[30] The fifth facet of the fruit of an attitude set on believing God's *truth* is *kindness (chréstotés).* The word *kindness* is nice. It makes me feel good, but believing God's *truth* makes us more than kind, it makes us useful. The literal meaning of the word is "usefulness, profitableness." An attitude set on believing God's *truth* makes one useful to God and others. Then comes *goodness.* The word rendered *good* can best be understood by verses like, Jesus "went about doing good and healing all who were oppressed by the devil."[31] Jesus was passionate about benefiting and profiting people. He put other's needs ahead of His. Those whose attitudes are set on believing God's *truth* are good like Jesus. And, now we're creeping up on power. I like being useful, because I grew up feeling worthless. As I continue to fix my attention on believing God's *truth*, I am increasingly bearing the fruit of usefulness, both to God and mankind.

The last three of the nine facets of the fruit of the spirit are "... faithfulness, gentleness, and self-control." For many years, I have wondered why the last one was self-control. What aspect of this ability is not already included in the first eight? I wish I had checked long ago. The answer is so obvious. It remained hidden in plain sight. But first, *faithfulness.* The Greek word is a noun and can be translated *faith* or *faithfulness.* Either one works. So, I got to thinking about the English word faithfulness because logic told me the King James translators

---

[30] Proverbs 22:6
[31] Act 10:38

chose it for a reason. Because of my understanding of how words have changed, I wondered if the English scholars of the 1600s knew something that has been lost to us. So, I began playing with the word. I began to think about the adjective faithful. ("Ness" added to an adjective just turns it into a noun.) Today it means loyal, dependable, but, back then it obviously meant full of faith. Then I considered that Paul said it is the fruit of an attitude of believing the *truth*. Of course! When you have an attitude that treasures God's *truth above all else*, you will end up full of believing the *truth*. God's own attitude is to believe the *truth*. He is *truth* and He believes Himself. His reality is *truth*. So, it makes sense. When you have an attitude that treasures God's *truth* and refuse to believe anything else, you will end up full of His *truth*.

That led me to *gentleness*. What does it mean? One of my favorite sources for help understanding the original meanings of Ancient Greek words is Helps Ministries, Inc.[32] They define *prautés* to be "gentle strength," and "gentle force." You could say, "gentle power." I like "gentle force." Love is the greatest power in the cosmos but always gentle, never pushy, never rough. I like "gentle force" because enduring passion, like water over granite, applies a gentle pressure for the benefit of the beloved.

Finally, we come to self-control, which is a common meaning for *Egkráteia*. However, that can't be correct. *Egkráteia* is a compound word formed from *eg* and *kráteia*. According to Liddell & Scott, and simple observations of many Greek words, *eg* (ἐγ) is a variation of the preposition *ek*, which means "out of." Unfortunately, when a word begins with *eg*, if the translation doesn't make sense, it seems many people assume it meant something else. Remember, the meaning of the preposition *ev* is *inside* or *within* and is frequently used to replace *ek* "out of." The problem scholars face becomes apparent when you know that *kráteia* means *dominion* or *mastery*. So, they apparently feel they have a choice. To them, *Egkráteia* must mean either "inside dominion" or "out of dominion." *Inside dominion* is obviously self-control. Since *out of dominion* makes no sense, it is easy to see why *self-control* is

---

[32] HELPS Word-studies at TheDiscoveryBible.com. I don't always agree with them, but I often find their analyses very helpful.

chosen. However, this doesn't make sense. Given that all the other facets of the fruit of the spirit amount to perfect control of oneself, there is no necessity for it to have this meaning. In addition, when *prautés* (gentleness) is translated "gentle force," suddenly, we see *egkráteia* pointing to a meaning we can put as "Out of dominion" or "outward dominion," as in "Even the wind and waves obey Him."[33] Outward power is what we see in the miracles Jesus performed. It is not referring to Jesus's control of Himself but His dominion over the creation. It is dominion which proceeds out of a believer to affect the creation. As we come to know who God has made us within Christ, we realize that what John said is true, "As He is, so are we, in this world" (1 John 4:17).

Note 8

The word meta is a wonderful preposition. Though the ancient meaning is no longer with us, Liddell & Scott captured it in their 1875 Greek-English Lexicon (page 913). When used with the genitive case it can mean, "being with them, and…doing as they do." When we say what God says, "So be it!", He is saying it with us as we say it, with the same intention that we have.

---

[33] Mark 4:41

15
God's Power is Safely Hidden, in Plain Sight

In this third edition of UNSEEN, we have added another chapter. The historical record reveals the First Century Church enjoyed a type of life and power never seen before or since. Chapter Fifteen is for believers who are curious about where it went and how to get it back. What follows includes excerpts from an email to a friend with whom I communicate regularly. It is a look into the wonder which God has revealed and which He is passionately seeking to persuade His children to believe.

My Friend,

> I have been explaining to my wife some of the details of my understanding of God's paradigm. It is hidden in plain sight and, though Satan has done everything he can to eliminate it, it is still here. The serpent has only succeeded in causing mental confusion to distract us from realizing what we are seeing.
>
> This morning as I was delving into some of the details of this subject, Sandra suddenly said, "Okay, you've lost me. Now what you're saying is just words." Just words. Hmmm. Is there any such thing? What was my wife saying? Just words. When we consider that God sent His Son as the expression of Who He is, and named Him the Word, is it even possible for there to be words that are "just words." In calling Jesus The Word, God has exalted the importance of all words.

I began pondering *words* afresh. I thought about what has happened in my life. It's been words. A long time ago I began to see a sort of logic in certain combinations of words but didn't understand what I was seeing. It was curious. Something told me there were bugs hidden in the grass, so I kept looking. I stuck my nose in there and just kept looking. I could see something but was not at all sure what, but I wanted to know. I would think, "Yes, there is something here. I'm not giving up till I know what it is!" Gradually, the words made more and more sense, yet I still wasn't comprehending what I was seeing. And then, pop. And then another pop. And then, another. I began to understand. My intention grew. And, I had to know more. What I had been taught about having a relationship with God hadn't worked for me. "Please God, I want to believe you. I want to understand." I *craved to* know what I was looking at, though only now realize what was happening to me.

The words I had been pondering were changing my logic. My ability to reason using God's words and concepts was growing simply because I had set myself to believe everything God said. It was a paradigm shift, frankly, of epic proportions for me. And, the greatest door to my understanding has been what you have taught me about covenants.

Many years ago, I began wondering about the word paradigm. It fascinated me, yet I had no idea what it meant. I had heard it used many times, yet it made no sense. But, now I know a paradigm is the picture in my mind which is formed by my logic and a paradigm shift is a logic shift. They can come in little increments or big ones. This continues to be the target of Satan's attacks. To accomplish his objectives, he had to change Adam's and Eve's paradigm. Because all paradigms are founded on words, logic, and reason, he had to change all three. His strategy against people does just that.

Many years ago, I was struck by a statement I heard on the radio. "Words mean something." It haunted me. The greatest meaning in existence is The Word. Satan had to change the meaning of that Word. How? The weak link in the chain of God's creation is humans who He made in His image and likeness. Yes, humankind was created to be just like God, but we must be trained. However much time Adam and God spent together before Eve came on the scene (decades, centuries, millennia?), God had lots of time to begin his education and training him. And, a moment came when it was time to let Adam go practice what he had learned so far. So, God made Eve and told Adam to train her. Think about it. An excellent way to learn what you know is to teach someone else, right?

Satan's attack seems to have begun with questions about God when the objective was to cause Adam to question himself. This was the real vulnerability in God's plan. The Serpent said to Adam and Eve: "Did God really say that? Are you sure? Do you really believe what you heard with your own ears? I think you misunderstood. God wouldn't have said that. Think about it. He says He made you to look like Him and act like Him. Really? Just look at you. You don't look like Him. Forget about that guarding the Garden stuff. That is just a distraction to keep you from learning what is important. What's important here is you. Could He be fooling you? Did He really make you? It looks to me like something else is going on here. Whatever it is, it's clear the key to all of it is that fruit. There is something about that fruit that God doesn't want you to know. Oh, I realize He told you eating it would cause you to be separated from Him, but do you think He is really worried about that? Could it be that He is afraid you would become like Him? That you would become His equal? Hmmm, Adam. You need to rethink this." I could go on, but I'm sure you get my point. Satan was seeking to change Adam's paradigm, his logic. He couldn't just introduce a new form of logic because there isn't one. He could only confuse the logic Adam had been learning and which he was supposed to teach Eve.

The only way to accomplish that was to entice Adam and Eve into listening and pondering, because even all of Heaven knew how that would affect creatures. They had already seen it when Satan enticed angels to listen to him and was able to persuade one third of them to reject God. Thus, by letting down their guard, Adam and Eve transformed their own reasoning. Satan couldn't force it. He could only promote it... albeit, through deception. It was a paradigm shift of massive proportions. It did not happen rapidly; it was incrementalism, but it worked. Only God knew how amazing He had created Adam and Eve to be. If they had not rejected what God told them, they would have eventually learned.

Fast forward to the centuries just prior to the First. It was a period during which Greece was coming out of its dark age into an enlightenment. Something amazing was happening. It was a time during which the focus of Greek philosophy was reason and inquiry. I think it was the time in which the Greek language reached its zenith. Those scientists I mentioned previously said that Jesus, as well as others, taught Quantum Physics but not as a science; rather it was their reality; it was the way people were taught to live. How well the Greek speakers understood their own language is up for grabs. But, that language was created by God for the Jews first, and then for the world. When Jesus appeared and started using it as God intended, it made sense to them, though they had never heard anyone talk like Jesus. The Jews and gentiles could readily identify with the quantum aspect of the language, because they had been hearing it all their lives. It was just part of their logic, without really understanding it. Probably, they never questioned it. It was just one of those things that *was* because it had always been.

So, Jesus appeared and began using the language as God intended. It was not difficult to shift paradigms because the building blocks were already there. When confirmed by the display of God's power, it would not have been a hard transition. It would have been exciting. The people had been waiting for something. They knew it was coming. They just weren't sure what.

Today as well as then, the paradigm is visible in written form. It is codified in the complex and very specific language of Koine Greek. So, what was Satan to do? The same thing he did before. Attack reason and change meanings. Before God's paradigm had an opportunity to become firmly established, Satan issued an all-out attack from every conceivable angle, as I have explained to you previously.

The early believers' new paradigm had been a gift. They didn't have to labor to enter it. God had used wonderful events to bring the knowledge of God to humankind in a totally new form… the Word, His Son. They didn't initially have to be trained in this new way of reasoning. It probably required no conscious effort, because everything that happened was so marvelous and shocking, in a good way. Paul sought to change that. He was commissioned to teach (instruct, train) the *submission to hearing* which would enable believers to keep learning to believe and thus do. It's simple. It's what every good parent does with their children.

So, Paul began the training. At least, he sought to. But, I wonder how many ever realized what was happening. I'm sure many were just enjoying their new way of thinking, without appreciating the need to guard it. It was truly a gift. But, a gift must be handled properly, or it can be lost. So, it was lost, as I have discussed previously. But, what was lost? The paradigms so clearly embedded in the ancient Greek language.

This time in human history believers are going to know and learn what the Early Church failed to properly guard. (The first believers are not to be criticized for the failure. When we understand God's plans and the nature of the assault suffered by early believers, we can learn how to avoid the same outcome. In Christ, we are wiser than the darkness and learn from our mistakes, with no condemnation from God.) We will not be fooled into waiting for a Second Coming or some type of gospel magic that suddenly causes us to act like super human beings but will learn to cooperate with God as He trains us to *be* who we are, the image and likeness of the God Who so loved all of humankind that He gave His Only Begotten Son to take us from death into His life.

The tools the early believers needed were there, but they missed something and gave the devil opportunity to lead humankind back into the dark ages from which Greece had only emerged just hundreds of years before. But, this time we are going to gladly take God's gifts instead of trying to do something for Him in the weakness of flesh. God is not forcing the training on us. He is giving us the opportunity to embrace it and willingly and joyfully submit to hearing it. But, this training consumes our lives. It occupies our entire beings. So, to get it we must decide we want it, because it involves death. Dying daily. Of course, God makes it easy. What I have found over the years is that it is difficult precisely because it is so easy. We have not been trained to think like children of God but adults, who always make things more complicated. We know the Early Church had something wonderful and amazing, but they lost it. I not only want it back, I want everything that was to come with it, of which we can't conceive except as the Holy Spirit reveals it to us. We may not yet know what it is, but we surely know that it is.

And so, to me, words are no longer just words. They contain God who is the source of all words. And, I will keep looking at them until my paradigm is once again completely His paradigm. But it already is because I have the mind of Christ. As I told Sandra this morning, God is hardening me, as in battle hardened, but totally unlike the world's battle hardening. I am being hardened in the sense of being a child. I am learning to not be distracted, to not be pulled apart, because I am so caught up in being a child of God.

So, where in the New Testament can we find God's paradigm? It's hidden in plain sight in the Greek verb tenses and moods. They cannot be fully appreciated without a firm grasp on why God swore to a covenant instead of a contract. Your book about that is invaluable.

I am beginning to comprehend what Paul meant, "We are more than conquerors." The logic has been hard to grasp. What in the world could it mean? It's just a function of union with Christ. Yea, just. ☺

James

Dear readers,

This edition of UNSEEN contains some of the most fundamental teaching tools of the Early Church. Keep looking at them until they look and feel normal.

The Campbells

Now you know what to look for.
Without Him there is nothing.
Inside Him is everything.

God's Symphony

Picture this: The London Philharmonic.

Now, savor this, even the screeches:

You are a vessel of clay created to be filled with God, through whom He is going to live His life unique to you. No one else will look like you. So too with all His other vessels.

God is music Himself, and He is planning something special, never seen or heard, even in the heavens. A glory beyond anyone's ability to describe. God can't even yet explain it to us. He can only show us.

He begins with raw materials and forms each vessel in its time throughout all of history. Each vessel is a very special music instrument. All the vessels, throughout all time, form a great symphony each a member of the whole.

Once created and fashioned the real work begins. These musical instruments are unlike any He will ever create. They are all kind of like player pianos that can write and program into themselves their own scores. However, they can't do anything without someone supplying the power for them to play. God will do that.

As the real work begins, His plan is to teach each one of His grand instruments to both write the music they will play, program it into themselves, and play it. And so, He begins. What a challenge. How is He going to do it?

It's unimaginable.

But, we get little pictures. A small child who picks up a violin not having any idea what it is. He finds a bow and eventually ends up scraping it across the strings. It screeches. Ugh. But, the child is delighted. He has made a sound he never heard. Of course, others listening shiver. The sound goes straight up their spine, like fingernails on a chalkboard.

The child keeps screeching on that violin, but then a teacher arrives and begins instructing. Some children take to the instruction, and simple melodies start to form. Many just like the screeching and ignore the instructor. But, the teacher is unfazed and uses every means to get the children to listen and realize there is so much more to enjoy than screeching sounds. But, some kids just like the fact that they have control of something that makes sounds and they don't want anything else, yet.

But, other children like the music and press on for more. They begin to make something that sounds like music. The sons of screech may even become jealous as the children of music begin to make beautiful sounds. The way some kids of screech deal with their brethren is to try to stop the music because it sounds so much better than the screeching. The children of screech would like to make melodies like music, but they don't want to be taught. They want to do it themselves. Their screeching should be melodious, but it isn't, and they refuse to acknowledge the beauty they are beginning to hear in others. In fact, they try to stop those tunes because they are determined to keep doing what they are doing until it becomes music.

The children of music are only just beginning to learn how to play and have yet to discover the types of sounds of which they are capable, especially together. Some tinker on their pianos, others join the teacher in sound rooms for individual instruction in their instruments. Some of the screechers join little groups and try to play their screeches together. These latter groups don't care that their sound is bad. Since they don't yet know what a real tune is they have no way to realize what they are missing. They are just having fun being together and making noise together.

Unseen

But, once in a while, the instructor can get the attention of one or the other and let them hear a bit of real harmony. These get hooked. But like all the children, there is stiff opposition to them learning such things. Wherever they go, there is a disturbing noise that is not loud, yet so distracting that the more serious students have trouble focusing on what the Instructor is saying. But regardless of what music any of them are trying to play, it is better than that annoying background noise, so they all keep playing.

Eventually, a few of the teachable students learn how to make a real harmony, whether they continue to play by themselves or with a small group. Regardless, the sounds are beautiful, yet, not even close to what is coming. They can't even imagine it. In fact, they don't yet know enough to even consider there may be more. They are just happy with their improving sounds.

But, as the Instructor continues training each one, eventually a sound begins to develop that sounds heavenly compared with anything they have ever heard. These begin to realize what the Instructor is up to. If they listen and pay attention, fixing their attention on His instruction, they are going to hear something not heard since the beginning of time. But, this is going to require allowing the Instructor to teach them all how to be fit into His composition rather than their own, however good their music has been. And so, the Instructor begins to find a new cooperation from some of His students and begins to create a new sound through them. This new sound isn't just the students doing what the Instructor has told them but allowing the Instructor to fully express His music through them by literally writing it with them and playing it inside their vessels.

The Instructor continues the training. He wants His students to enjoy the ease with which He can play their instruments, an ease that makes the students think they are playing it themselves when in fact it is He doing it in them. But amazingly, He can't play it in them without their cooperation. So, really, is it Him playing in them, or is it them playing? They don't know or care because each stands in awe of his own transformation. Each discovers they are unique, and the glorious sound they are hearing is coming from themselves. They love what they hear in themselves as well as what they hear in the other students.

Yet none still realizes what is coming.

As more and more students understand what they have been hearing in their fellow students, even more and more students hear, also. Gradually, they begin coming together as small ensembles, then bands, then orchestras followed by little symphonies. When the Instructor has finally trained each student, even the ones who preferred to screech, billions and billions of vessels created throughout time, each a unique instrument with a sound distinct from the others yet capable of perfect harmony with them, they begin to discover a wonder. As they start to hear their own different sounds which they had been created to produce separately, yet together, they suddenly hear it. A sound never before uttered in all of time or eternity. (I say uttered because there is no word capable of summing up what they hear or from where it is coming. It fills up everything.) And all know, this is what they were created for, and throughout all ages to come it will continue to grow. They are a symphony unlike anything that any instrument could have ever imagined. They have found the life for which they were created.

Unseen

My Song

(To the tune from Zephaniah 3:17)

My Lord, my God
Who is my life
You're mighty, you're mighty

You have saved
You rejoice in me
With joy, with joy

You rest in Your love,
You joy in me with singing

My Lord, my God
Who is my life
You're mighty, you're mighty

My Lord, my God
Who is My Life
You're mighty, you're mighty, you're mighty

APPENDIX
– for students of Koine Greek

When beginning the study of Ancient Greek, it is especially helpful to know three things:

(1) Koine Greek is a quantum language meaning it enabled the ancients to experience paradigms far outside of normal human conversation.

(2) There is a distinct difference in perspectives between the Old and New Covenants, usually referred to as the Old and New Testaments. The Old Covenant points forward to the Messiah while, to most people, the New Testament points forward to the second coming of Christ. This view of the New Testament makes it impossible for them to comprehend the Greek text. In fact, as the Old Testament points forward to Christ, the New Testament points backwards to Him, in real time. As the Old Testament pointed to the mysterious work of a coming Savior, the New Testament points back to and explains the complete work of Christ from His birth to His death followed by His resurrection and ascension, AND the indwelling of the Holy Spirit, all to make each believers' joint reality with Christ real to them.

(3) The Scriptural meaning of *remember* and *forget*. In Western language, *remember* means to recall information. *Forget* means the opposite: the failure to recall information. Neither definition has any relationship to how they affect anything. But, the writers of the Old Testament had a different understanding. To *remember* meant to recall information from the past and apply it to the present as though whatever happened is as present now as it was back then. Likewise, to *forget* meant to consider information as if its present effectiveness is nullified by something in the past, or that something in the past that should

control the present doesn't. An example of remembering would be to take the promise of Proverbs 3:5 & 6 and apply it to your life today. "Trust in the LORD with all your heart, and do not lean on your own understanding. In all your ways acknowledge him, and he will make straight your paths."[1] Using the Hebrew concept of *remembering*, we would say, "Yes, LORD, I trust in You with all my heart and do not lean on my own understanding. In addition, I acknowledge you in all my ways, so I *know* you are now directing my paths." We are simply taking God's covenant promise to someone else as His personal promise to ourselves, also. To *forget* would be to believe that promise does not apply to you. When God says to remember or don't forget, He is referring to treasuring, or not failing to treasure, that His love for you is as real as it is for every one of His children.

My adventure of knowing God began as a freshman at the University of Florida in 1970. As I became more familiar with the Bible, I began to wonder about something I heard people say often, "God said it, I believe it, and that settles it." I saw a problem with that, because it only seemed to apply sometimes. When questioned about passages that seemed to contradict their primary body of doctrine, people had different explanations. Ultimately, we weren't allowed to take the whole Bible literally but had to pass its meaning through people who "knew" more than we.

After I began studying Ancient Greek, I discovered something shocking. The word "repent" was bandied about by believers everywhere, and was generally defined as, "to stop doing wrong and, instead, do right." Some said it was "to change your mind about what you are doing, feel sorry for your sins, and start obeying God." But, one day I happened upon the definition in a Greek-English lexicon. It said, "to change your mind upon reflection." That was a far cry from anything I had ever heard in church. That change in the meaning of repent, to me, meant God was interested in changing my mind before changing my behavior. I became curious. It seemed I had found something that many modern scholars had missed. Modern theologians were apparently so absorbed in dissecting trees that they forgot the trees were part of a vast

---

[1] Proverbs 3:5,6 (ESV)

forest and could only be appreciated and understood considering the forest itself. Of course, those slicing and dicing the trees would argue vehemently that the forest could only be known by first completely understanding everything about the trees in it. But, I began to have a different perspective. I wanted to learn to enjoy looking at the whole forest and later understand its parts.

Jesus once told the Pharisees, "You study the scriptures looking to find life in them when that life is standing right in front of you."[2] Jesus was saying, "If you want to understand the scriptures, get to know Me." That makes sense. How can I be sure I understand what someone has written if I don't know them. At the least, knowing them may enable me to recognize nuances not apparent in their written words. I have found that God is a wonderful Father/Teacher who wants His children to understand Him. There is nothing dark about Him, nothing hidden. He is light, "and in Him is no darkness at all."[3] And so, I began a search to know and understand Him, so that I could understand His words. But, how could I do that if I don't first understand what He says? That is why Jesus told us He was sending the Holy Spirit "to cause us to learn" all things. The Greek word usually translated "teach" means "cause to learn." There is an enormous difference between being taught and learning what you are taught. The Holy Spirit didn't come to give us a bunch of knowledge but to cause us to learn the knowledge God promised would be written in our hearts and minds. As He causes us to know Who God is, we realize we are increasingly understanding what He has written. Until then, we are just guessing, or trusting someone else to know for us. But, this is not the way a Father like God works. The purpose of the five-fold ministry is to lead believers into living the knowledge which God has already written inside them. This is something only He can cause us to know. And, as I have come to know Him in ways that I had been taught were reserved only for Heaven, He has worked to enable me to understand His Word like I could have never anticipated. I love the understanding God has given me. It has set me free to enjoy Him and be at rest regardless of what is happen-

---

[2] John 5:39 (JEC)
[3] 1 John 1:5

ing anyplace in the Earth. I now wake every morning with a wonderful expectancy that I can summarize in the question, "What are you up to today, Lord? I'm so glad you are my Shepherd and I am safe."

Several years ago, the Holy Spirit began rapidly expanding my understanding of Greek grammar including noun and verb forms. What I learned was often in direct opposition to modern rules of Ancient Greek. But, amazingly, seeming inconsistencies and contradictions in the Bible began to disappear. Things not understood by any of my professors, teachers, and pastors began to make perfect sense. All sorts of passages began fitting together as never before. God became alive to me in ways I had been taught died with the Apostles. Following are a few of the more obvious and prominent rules I now use in translating. Since God is a good Teacher, He is simple. If you find any of the following difficult, it's just because you have yet to learn how to allow God to teach you how He thinks, which He is intent on doing. God is passionate about teaching us what He knows. Of course, that is not going to happen while someone believes it isn't possible. As you increasingly understand how God thinks and the logic under-girding His reasoning, you will find the Greek text so phenomenally understandable that, like me, you may marvel that others didn't comprehend it long ago. Actually, they were on their way. Without what many others have discovered as they have sought God, I have wondered where my understanding would be today.

Please remember, I use the following rules as my starting point in translating and I keep to the basics. When I am tempted to start slicing and dicing, I don't. I tell God that I know He is simple and, since I am a child, He needs to make this simple for me, which I know is His intention without me having to ask. I realize many in the more advanced realms of theology would reject my approach as simplistic. To them I say, "It is your loss, because I now have wonderful, comprehensive, and very satisfying answers with which many great theologians are still struggling."

Prepositions: English prepositions generally have one meaning. *In* means *in*, *to* means *to*, *toward* means *toward*, etc. But, based on how many render Greek prepositions, apparently, they think this ancient language was different. Many think Greek prepositions can have multiple meanings. For instance, πρὸς may mean *against, toward, to, with,* or a number of other things, or it may be ignored entirely. ἐν may be translated *in, by, within, into, during, with, at.* You may find εἰς rendered *to, unto, toward, for, as to, as, etc.* How is one supposed to decide which definition to use? My first Greek professor told me to watch out for the authorities' translations of prepositions. He was concerned that they are often used to change the original meanings of passages to interpretations which theologians after the First Century prefer. So, my advice to you is to ask the Holy Spirit what He meant when He inspired the writer.

Nouns: have four basic cases: nominative, genitive, dative, and accusative, which I have learned to define as the cases of *is, possession, relationship,* and *direction,* respectively. Any Greek grammar book will likely subdivide those into 8 or more cases, and possibly more subdivisions after that. Ignore the complicated minutia frequently discussed in the grammars; God is not difficult to understand. The difficulty is on our side. I stick with the basics. For instance, the nominative case is the case of *is,* as in *"something is."* In this phrase, the noun *"something"* will be in the nominative case. When you see a noun or participle in the nominative case, understand it means that what is described by the substantive should be considered as simply existing.

Prepositions preceding nouns often determine the noun's case. Most prepositions can be associated with more than one case. Lexicons and grammar books will explain that to you. In these instances, the meaning of the preposition depends on the case of the substantive, however, prepositions tend to have a root meaning out of which the other meanings come. Again, grammars and lexicons can help you with that.[4]

The genitive case refers to possession and can generally be translated as "of or belonging to" a substantive. In genitive case words not proceeded by a preposition, the meaning implies some sort of possession like in: "…καὶ Πατὴρ τοῦ Κυρίου ἡμῶν Ἰησοῦ Χριστοῦ." I always start with the most basic translation, which is often incomprehensible

---

[4] For simplicity with prepositions, I prefer Dana and Mantey's *A Manual Grammar of the Greek New Testament*, (1957) though it, too, gets too complicated.

even to me, though this sentence was easy, "...and Father, the Lord of us, belonging to Jesus Christ," often rendered "and Father of our Lord Jesus Christ.").

Since the dative case refers to relationship, substantives following the preposition ἐν are always in the dative form. Ἐν means within or inside, which clearly refers to the relationship of being *inside* something. This case is used to indicate how a verb or noun relates to another substantive. Because the dative case signifies relationship, it can reflect emotion, and great emotion at that. Whenever I see this case, I become alert for potential emotional implications. This understanding has enabled me to discover how emotional God is about things. It often is used to indicate someone's passion about something, including God's passion, which may include anger, but not as though it comes from the hatred of someone.

The accusative case is used to infer direction. Εἰς (*into*) is a preposition which implies direction from the outside to the inside, thus, it is only followed by accusative case nouns. It clearly denotes direction.

Verbs: New Testament Greek verb forms offer a clear perspective of God's paradigm; that is, what He sees based on His understanding. They show us how God thinks about what He has accomplished inside us, inside Christ, in relation to time. They show us how God thinks. Another way to put it – God's understanding is based on His logic and reasoning. As well, humans understand based on our logic and reasoning, too.

This is why two people can view the same thing yet walk away with totally different perspectives, sometimes irreconcilably different.

When observing the same thing, why does one person come away with one impression while someone else sees something different? Though we can write a book explaining this, in just a few words, it is because each lives inside a different paradigm, a different picture of their world. Paradigms can change because of new knowledge or because of training. God uses both to change our paradigms.

Greek verbs are far more descriptive than English verbs. In some cases, to accurately explain a Greek verb would require paragraphs or pages of explanation. Yet, Greek speakers in the First Century were capable of conveying in just one word what would possibly require pages written in English. Most Greek verb forms include tense, mood, and voice. The most difficult tense and moods with which many people seem to have trouble are the aorist when combined with the subjunctive or imperative moods.

I have long been bothered by the idea of a God Who is Unconditional Love being described as Someone who *may* or *might* do something, which is obviously dependent on someone meeting His requirements. The subjunctive mood is usually translated so that it leaves the reader wondering, "What will it take to get God to move on my behalf?" Based on the way the subjunctive mood is so often conceived, or just ignored, the reader can never be sure what to expect from God. But, one day, God showed me that He is not the God of *I may,* or *I might*, but *I WILL*. Oh, did what I see in His Word begin to change. Modern grammarians define the subjunctive mood as the mood of probability, yet usually translate it as only a possibility. But, if it is the mood of probability, that means the probability of performing His will and intention. It is probable that He will do what He says, meaning He already has or will. God is not wishy washy, because love isn't. Love knows what it wants and intends to do for the beloved, and since God was willing to send His Only Begotten Son, He has made a definitive statement of His will and intention. He didn't send Jesus in hopes of success. He sent Him knowing that He would never give up on anything worth the life of His Son.

Greek verb tenses usually include a mood. When the aorist tense is combined with the subjunctive mood, a literal translation of the verb involves a logic not easily comprehended by someone who thinks like Westerners do, yet God is very comfortable with it, or He wouldn't have used that form. Of course, to understand the aorist with the subjunctive we must know what it means that He is the God of covenant and that every moment of time has been and still is right-now to Him. Remember, He said, "I am the God of Abraham, Isaac, and Jacob."[5] As far as God is concerned, when those people lived it was in God's *now*, just like our time on Earth is also God's *now*. Since God is always now, then every *now* moment is still right-now to God. Human beings solely

---

[5] Matthew 22:32

dependent on time have a lot of trouble comprehending how this can be. Once you understand God's perspective on time, His paradigms begin to make sense. As I have continued to ponder it, I have begun to think with new paradigms. Now, His paradigms often make perfect sense to me, though I may have trouble putting them in simple words for someone else. When I am speaking with someone who understands God's paradigms, to a listener we are probably speaking a different language even though we are using English words and grammar. Paul referred to this when he wrote of speaking spiritual to spiritual.[6]

God wants His children to think like He thinks, which means reasoning with His logic. The writers of the New Testament made abundant use of the aorist tense, yet modern scholarship seem uncertain how to interpret it, so if is often ignored. In some contexts, it can seem impossible that God was referring to the past, so they assume He wasn't. To aid in your adventure understanding Koine Greek, consider this: The writers of the Old Testament looked forward to the coming of the Messiah and, likewise, most Christians seem to think the New Testament looks forward to the Second Coming of Christ. This is where many of us have missed it. The Apostle Paul didn't say, "For I determined to know nothing among you except Jesus Christ, *and Him coming again,*" but "… to know nothing but Jesus Christ *and Him crucified.*"[7] While the Old Testament looks forward, the New Testament looks backwards, to the Cross and our participation in it in Christ. Hence, the writers use the aorist tense to take us back to where our new lives in Christ began… at the Cross. This is the whole emphasis of Paul's teaching about the body and blood of Jesus Christ in the communion. This understanding is central to taking up our Cross and dying daily, as well as living the victory of Christ on this Earth. The Cross of Christ was our Cross, too. The modern Church needs to remember this. Anytime you encounter the aorist tense with other than the indicative mood, keep in mind that God looks back to what He accomplished for all humanity by the Cross as the starting point for our lives today.

---

[6] 1 Corinthians 2:13

[7] 1 Corinthians 2:2

Since the aorist tense combined with the subjunctive mood means past-tense intention and will, God *intended* something to *exist* in the past, which means, even if we can't yet see it, it still does. The aorist subjunctive speaks of something done in the past that can be real to us now. Unlike the perfect tense, the aorist focuses on what happened. You can get a sense of how the aorist subjunctive works by the KJV translators' rendering of the perfect tense in Galatians 2:20. Since the perfect tense looks at the effects of something that happened in the past as still in full force, they translated "I was Crucified" as "I am crucified," as though Paul was saying he was still hanging on the cross with Jesus. To them, the most important thing was not to express that Paul was crucified with Jesus but that the effects of that crucifixion were still very present in Paul's life. So, with reference to the aorist subjunctive, the rendering may seem very different from what we consider to be likely. In fact, it will probably feel weird because it is past tense, and it is impossible to replace one past tense event with another one, since they have both already happened. But, even though a literal rendering of the aorist subjunctive may contradict what we know happened, we choose to agree with the God with Whom all things are possible. Then we live expecting the same things God expects as He works to cause us to see the reality of His expectations.

We see another example of God's aorist/subjunctive paradigm in 1 Peter 5:6. The King James Version reads, "Humble yourselves therefore under the mighty hand of God, that he may exalt you in due time:" I translate it, "Be humbled under the mighty hand of God['s love] so that [all of] you He exalted inside of time."[8,9] The form of the word usually translated *exalted* is aorist active subjunctive which, as you can see, if expressed literally, makes very little sense to our Western mindsets ("Be humbled in the past so that He will have exalted you in the past."). But, God is saying that when we "be humbled" it is because we agree with His intention regarding the work of Christ for us, in us, and as

---

[8] (JEC)

[9] As an aside, because I know God is love, as I read this passage I always insert the word *love* between mighty and hand, "the mighty love hand of God." I also understand it as "the mighty hand of God's love."

us, and thus have already accepted Christ's humbling as our own. This happened by His initiative not ours. As a result, Peter said that God exalted us when He exalted Christ, which was inside of time. God is not waiting to exalt us at some point in the future; He has already done it and is just waiting for our agreement so that we can begin to experience what He already sees. The common translation of "in due time" is incorrect because the Greek simply says, "in time." Many translators just feel it necessary to insert the word *due* between *in* and *time,* but that is an interpretation due to their lack of understanding how Peter could be referring to doing something today that occurred in the past.

You may wonder, "So what? It is obviously only theoretical until Jesus returns." This type of response displays a lack of understanding how the Kingdom of God works. As we agree with God's Word, the Holy Spirit works to make our reality in Christ real to us. Our reality is exactly as stated in God's Word so when we agree with God's command to *be humbled,* His command is sufficient to cause it to be, and thus it is. We not only are humbled, but have been humbled inside Christ's humbling of Himself 2000 years ago. A prideful attitude says, "No way. I have to humble myself," and rejects God's gifts. But, the Greek text makes it clear it is not a future but past tense reality, which we can begin enjoying now.

The other combination I am addressing is when the aorist tense is combined with the imperative mood. In this case, it creates the picture of a *past-tense command.* It appears God is commanding something to be done in the past. How could that be? You say, that is impossible. Sure, with man it is, but not God. Because God lives outside of time, when He issues a backward command, it can only be fulfilled by Him. He is able to go back and cause the command to have been fulfilled in the past. Actually, He is not causing it to become fulfilled. Rather, because of our agreement with Him, He causes us to begin seeing what was already fulfilled in Christ.

We see another example of God's paradigms, once again, in 1 Peter 5:6. As noted above, the King James Version reads, "Humble yourselves therefore under the mighty hand of God, that he may exalt you in due time:" I translate it, "Be humbled under the dominant hand of

God['s love] so that [all of] you He exalted inside of time." The form of the Greek word often translated "humble yourselves" is aorist imperative. Thus, it cannot be a present tense command. Actually, it is a command which takes you back to the Cross where Jesus humbled Himself. Because you were in Him, by your agreement, you are taking His humbling as your own. Interestingly, some translators render it correctly, "Be humbled." I wonder if they understand it as accurately as they translate it. Notice that "be humbled" is past tense English. For clarity in English, you could say, "Be already humbled." How can you do that? Only by realizing that God did it for you in Christ. God united you with Christ in His death and resurrection. "For the love of Christ controls us, having concluded this, that one died for all, therefore all died." So, in agreement with with the Hebrew concept of *remember*, you can say, "I am one of the 'all who died' people." Or, you can believe, "That doesn't apply to me." Whichever one you expect is what will sooner or later become real to you.

Satan does not want God's children to understand this because it is filled with tremendous power. This is why the Devil has sought to change the meanings of God's original words and rules of grammar. If we are using the wrong meanings for God's inspired words, how can we ever understand what He means? Some people say that God protected His word so that we can trust it.[10] If that is so, then why are there so many translations? If God decreed there is only one correct translation, then which one is it? And, would God do that? Or, would He plan on giving the Holy Spirit to each one of us so that He can have an intimate, personal relationship with each of His children so that He can teach them personally. (This statement in no way negates the need for those called to ministry. In fact, it makes them even more important). Since all modern translations are dependent on dictionaries written long after the Apostles died, and shortly before the Church was taken over by the government of Rome, how can we be sure definitions hadn't already been changed? In fact, we know that Satan was working furiously to change meanings. This is the reason the Church lost its foundation and could not prevent itself and the world from plunging into the Dark Ages.

---

[10] 2 Corinthians 5:14 - NASB

So, if Satan was working to change meanings, why didn't God stop it? Because, He gave the whole cosmos to mankind and mankind still has all the dominion. We were and still are supposed to protect what God has given us. God even warned Adam, but the First Couple rejected what God knew. Regardless, humans are still amazing wonders, now recreated in Christ so that the Holy Spirit can train us to *be* sons and daughters of God. It is time to learn to cooperate with Him. God knows the type of creature we are. God knows we are marvels of His work, created to look and act just like Him. And, through all that mankind has suffered, God has remained confident that we will ultimately respond as He wants and will take the dominion belonging to love that is ours in Christ. When we learn how to hear Him, (hint, hint, something you teachers should be teaching) God will be able to easily restore the foundations. I believe that time is now.

Through the plain logic presented in UNSEEN, you can reclaim understanding enjoyed by believers in the First Century. Ask God to show you His truth. He delights to do it.

References

Backus, M. C. 1980. *Telling Yourself the Truth.* Bethany House Publishers.

Bible, T. R. 1989. *New Revised Standard Version Bible.* Division of Christian Education of the National Council of the Churches of Christ in the USA.

Biblical Studies Press LLC. 1996-2006. *net Bible.* Biblical Studies Press LLC.

Cambridge University Press. 1949. *The Bible in Basic English.* Cambridge University Press.

Crossway, a publishing ministry of Good News Publishers. *The Holy Bible, English Standard Version®* (ESV® Bible), copyright © 2001

Harper Collins Publishers. 2012. *Collins English Dictionary.* HarperCollins Publishers.

Merriam-Webster. 2012. *Merriam-Webster's Collegiate® Dictionary* (Eleventh Edition ed.). Springfield, Massachusets: Merriam-Webster, Incorporated. Retrieved from www.Merriam-Webster.com

NavPress Publishing Group. 1993, 1994, 1995, 1996, 2000, 2001, 2002. *The Message.* NavPress Publishing Group. Retrieved from www.navpress.com

Norlie, O. M. 1961. *Olaf M. Norlie.* Grand Rapids, Michigan: Zondervan Publishing House. Retrieved from www.zondervan.com

Phillips, J. 1958. *The New Testament in Modern English Translated.* The MacMillan Company.

Scott, L. A. 1875. *Greek-English Lexicon by Liddell and Scott 1875.* New York: Harper and Brothers.

Smith, M. (n.d.). *The Search for Self-Worth work book, Chapter Five., www.MalcolmSmith.org.* San Antonio: Unconditional Love Fellowship.

Spurrell, H. (n.d.). *A Translation of the Old Testament Scriptures from the Original Hebrew.*

The University of Chicago. *The Complete Bible: An American Translation.* 1923, 1927, 1948.

The Lockman Foundation. *New American Standard Bible*® (NASB), Copyright © 1960, 1962, 1963, 1968, 1971, 1972, 1973, 1975, 1977, 1995.

Francois du Toit. *THE MIRROR.* Copyright © 2012.

The Twentieth Century New Testament Part 2. (n.d.).

Tyndale House Foundation. *Holy Bible, New Living Translation*, (NLT) copyright ©1996, 2004, 2007, 2013, 2015

CPSIA information can be obtained
at www.ICGtesting.com
Printed in the USA
BVHW050751060522
635996BV00082B/3770